COMPANIONSHIP AND VIRTUE IN CLASSICAL SUFISM

COMPANIONSHIP AND VIRTUE IN CLASSICAL SUFISM

The Contribution of al-Sulamī

Jason Welle

I.B.TAURIS
LONDON • NEW YORK • OXFORD • NEW DELHI • SYDNEY

I.B. TAURIS
Bloomsbury Publishing Plc, 50 Bedford Square, London, WC1B 3DP, UK
Bloomsbury Publishing Inc, 1385 Broadway, New York, NY 10018, USA
Bloomsbury Publishing Ireland, 29 Earlsfort Terrace, Dublin 2, D02 AY28, Ireland

First published in Great Britain 2024
This paperback edition published 2025

Cover design: Adriana Brioso
Cover image: Sufi s by a Mountain Spring, Harvard Art Museums/Arthur M. Sackler
Museum, Sarah C. Sears Collection. © President and Fellows of Harvard College, 1936.28

A catalogue record for this book is available from the British Library.

Library of Congress Cataloging-in-Publication Data
Names: Welle, Jason, author.
Title: Companionship and virtue in classical Sufism : the contribution
of al-Sulami / Jason Welle.
Description: London ; New York : I.B. Tauris, 2024. | Includes
bibliographical references and index.
Identifiers: LCCN 2024006374 (print) | LCCN 2024006375 (ebook) |
ISBN 9780755652273 (hb) | ISBN 9780755652310 (paperback) |
ISBN 9780755652297 (ebook) | ISBN 9780755652280 (epdf)
Subjects: LCSH: Sufism. | Fellowship–Religious aspects–Islam.
Classification: LCC BP188.7 .W43 2024 (print) | LCC BP188.7 (ebook) |
DDC 297.4–dc23/eng/20240904
LC record available at https://lccn.loc.gov/2024006374
LC ebook record available at https://lccn.loc.gov/2024006375

ISBN: HB: 978-0-7556-5227-3
PB: 978-0-7556-5231-0
ePDF: 978-0-7556-5228-0
eBook: 978-0-7556-5229-7

Typeset by Newgen KnowledgeWorks Pvt. Ltd., Chennai, India

For product safety related questions contact productsafety@bloomsbury.com.

To find out more about our authors and books visit www.bloomsbury.com
and sign up for our newsletters.

حسبي ربّي وبه توفيقي

CONTENTS

Acknowledgements ix
Transliteration, Dating, Primary Sources and Abbreviations xi

INTRODUCTION: WHAT DOES VIRTUE ETHICS HAVE TO DO WITH SUFISM? 1
Companionship and community 2
Virtue and character 3
Biography of al-Sulamī 5
Recent scholarship on al-Sulamī 7
Companionship and virtue 9

Chapter 1
THE EMERGENCE OF *ĀDĀB* IN AL-SULAMĪ'S SPIRITUAL METHOD 13
'*Adab* literature' 14
Works of Ṣūfī *adab* and *adab* literature 15
Ādāb, akhlāq and *aḥwāl* 17
Adab as MacIntyrean practice 20
Adab among al-Sulamī's Ṣūfī predecessors 24
Al-Sulamī's approach to *adab* 30
Dhikr ādāb al-ṣūfiyya 31
Mā'iyyat al-faqr wa-ādābihi 32
Ādāb al-faqr wa-sharā'iṭuhu 33
Adab mujālasat al-mashāyikh 35
Jawāmiʿ ādāb al-ṣūfiyya 36
Kitāb bayān al-sharīʿa wa-l-ḥaqīqa 37
Kitāb ādāb al-ṣuḥba 39
Conclusion 42

Chapter 2
VIRTUE AND CHARACTER IN AL-SULAMĪ'S THOUGHT 45
What does Athens have to do with Nishapur? 46
The treatment of traits 47
MacIntyre on tradition and virtue 48
Ṣūfī psychology 52
The stations (*maqāmāt*) 52
Spiritual centres 54
The ego-self (*nafs*) 55

The heart (*qalb*) 56
The [inner] secret (*sirr*) and the spirit (*rūḥ*) 58
Al-Sulamī's notion of *akhlāq* 59
Emotional *akhlāq* 64
Growth in virtue: Outside-in or inside-out? 67
Conclusion 69

Chapter 3
AL-SULAMĪ'S VISION OF FELLOWSHIP AND SPIRITUAL COMPANIONSHIP 71
Ṣuḥba and *'ishra*: A difference in degree or in kind? 72
The dangers of *ṣuḥba* 75
The many faces of *ṣuḥba* and *'ishra* 78
Acknowledged dependence, with a little help from my friends 81
O brother, who art thou? 82
Ṣuḥba in the relationship between master and disciple 85
Does *ṣuḥba* suffer fools? 90
Relations with women 93
The etiquette of the marketplace 96
Conclusion 98

Chapter 4
ṢUḤBA IN COMPARISON: AL-SULAMĪ'S NEAR CONTEMPORARIES 101
Philosophical approaches to friendship 102
Al-Tawḥīdī: The loyal friend of selfless care 104
The elevation of shaykhs and the bond of brothers 113
Al-Sarrāj: Companions to disturb and to serve 116
Al-Qushayrī: Stability and exclusivity on the path 120
Conclusion 125

CONCLUSION 127
MacIntyre, al-Sulamī and avenues for future research 128

Notes 133
Bibliography 189
Index of Proper Names and Places 215
Index of Qur'ān Citations 217
Index of Themes and Terminology 219

ACKNOWLEDGEMENTS

I give thanks first to God, from whom all good things descend as from the Father of lights (Jas 1:17). I undertook this study with a sense of vocation, and the process of this research has left me convinced that something transcending me desired its eventual completion.

Of course, in our pilgrimage on earth, God's blessings usually manifest themselves through the acts of good people. This project depended upon the support of many family members, friends and companions over a long period of time. My greatest debt is to my parents John and Sandy, who lived to see me complete the doctoral dissertation that provided the foundation for this monograph but did not survive to see its publication. May they rest in peace and rise in glory.

Paul L. Heck showed patient confidence as my work took shape, and I am even more grateful for his continued companionship afterwards. If an aspiring student were to ask me, '*man aṣḥab?*' – with whom should I keep company? – he is the sort of guide I would describe. I count myself blessed to have him as the chief link in my *silsila*. I terribly miss Gerard Mannion, who left this earth far too quickly. Someday we shall lift a glass again. I am grateful for many other colleagues at Georgetown University. Among the faculty, Daniel A. Madigan, Peter Phan, Leo Lefebure, John Borelli, Felicitas Opwis, John L. Esposito, Jonathan Ray and John Voll were each a boon in different ways, as were scholars from other schools in the Washington area, including Sidney H. Griffith, Pim Valkenberg and Ahmet T. Karamustafa. I dare not list my student colleagues from that period, many of whom have now become first-rate scholars in their own right, but they know how much small acts of mutual support kept each of us going.

My reflections on al-Sulamī's legacy continued to develop while teaching at the Pontifical Institute for Arabic and Islamic Studies in Rome. I hold my colleagues there in the highest esteem, including Martin Wullobayi, Valentino Cottini, Celeste Intartaglia, Christopher Clohessy, Wasim Salman, Hanan Ablahad, Alma Salem, Francesco Baronchelli, Bartolomeo Pirone and others. Chief among them is Diego Sarrió Cucarella, a formidable administrator, a fine scholar and, most importantly, a dear dear friend.

In preparation for events commemorating the millennial anniversary of al-Sulamī's death, I was blessed to work with Jean-Jacques Thibon, Safaruk Z. Chowdhury, Lutz Berger, Francesco Chiabotti, Demetrio Giordani, Paolo Urizzi, Yahya Pallavicini, Giuseppe Cecere, Abd al-Wadoud Gouraud and others. Their insights enhanced this study.

I am grateful for my new colleagues in the Theology Department at Boston College, where the final revisions to this monograph took place. I had long hoped to someday teach here, and the welcome and kindness I have been shown demonstrate that this desire was not misplaced. Special gratitude belongs to Megan Hopkins for her assistance with the index and other tasks in the final stages of publication.

I cannot thank enough the many Franciscan friars who supported me in various ways through the years, as a man and as a scholar. Leslie Hoppe, John Puodziunas and James Gannon held ministries of leadership in the brotherhood when this research took place. I resided primarily at the Franciscan Monastery of the Holy Land in Washington and at San Francesco a Ripa in Rome during my research but sojourned with many other communities for various lengths of time, including Holy Name Friary in Chicago, Santi Quaranta Martiri in Rome, St. Thomas Aquinas in Waterford, Assumption Friary in Pulaski and Holy Angels Cathedral in Gary. May God reward them for their hospitality and for their witness.

Finally, I thank my (blood) brother and best friend Scott. With God's help, in the years to come, I may write something you find less opaque, but for the time being I can say this: I have learned much about companionship from Abū ʿAbd al-Raḥmān al-Sulamī. I have learned more about it from you. I pray that God grant us many years for that learning to continue, *in shāʾ Allāh*.

TRANSLITERATION, DATING, PRIMARY SOURCES AND ABBREVIATIONS

This text follows the transliteration system of the third edition of the *Encyclopaedia of Islam*. Dates are given according to both the Islamic calendar and the Common Era. All translations from languages other than English are mine unless otherwise indicated in citations.

Arabic sources that have been published in multiple editions, including *ḥadīth* collections, will often be cited by *kitāb* or *bāb* rather than a page number, to assist a specialist who may not have the same edition at hand. Where the number of a *ḥadīth* or a paragraph permits further precision, these will also be given. References to translations of these sources will be given by page number when appropriate. Commentaries on the Qur'ān will be cited according to the *sūra* and *āya* under comment in addition to page number.

The writings of Abū 'Abd al-Raḥmān al-Sulamī have been edited and published by a variety of presses around the world over the course of decades and no standardized system exists for the citation of these texts. This monograph utilizes a system of abbreviations for primary texts attributed to al-Sulamī. When notes employ abbreviations (e.g. *KAṢ, JAṢ, UNM*), these refer to the Arabic text; notes indicating a full title of a work attributed to al-Sulamī (e.g. *Kitāb ādāb al-ṣuḥba wa-ḥusn al-'ishra, Jawāmi' ādāb al-ṣūfiyya* and *'Uyūb al-nafs wa-mudāwātuhā*) refer to introductory material composed by the modern editor or to footnotes or other parts of the scholarly apparatus accompanying the text in question. Citations normally follow paragraph numbers where editors have added these, permitting increased precision; elsewhere, citations refer to page numbers.

Several volumes contain collections of al-Sulamī's writings, some of which offer facsimiles of earlier editions published independently.

SII — *Sufi Inquiries and Interpretations of Abū 'Abd al-Raḥmān al-Sulamī and A Treatise of Traditions by Ismā'īl b. Nujayd al-Naysābūrī* (*Masā'il wa-ta'wīlāt ṣūfiyya li-Abī 'Abd al-Raḥmān al-Sulamī wa-yalīhi Juz' min aḥādīth Ismā'īl b. Nujayd al-Naysābūrī*), Gerhard Böwering and Bilal Orfali, eds (Beirut: Dār al-Mashriq, 2010).

STS — *Sufi Treatises of Abū 'Abd al-Raḥmān al-Sulamī* (*Rasā'il ṣūfiyya li-Abī 'Abd al-Raḥmān al-Sulamī*), Gerhard Böwering and Bilal Orfali, eds (Beirut: Dār al-Mashriq, 2009).

MAS	*Majmūʿa-i āthār Abū ʿAbd al-Raḥmān al-Sulamī* (*Collected Works on Early Sufism*), 3 vols., Nasrollah Pourjavady and Muḥammad Soori [Sūrī], eds (Tehran: Markaz-i Nashr-i Dānishgāhī, 2009–10).
TKS	*Tisʿat kutub li-Abī ʿAbd al-Raḥmān Muḥammad b. al-Ḥusayn b. Mūsā l-Sulamī,* Süleyman Ateş, ed. (Beirut: al-Nāshir, 1993).

If a text in the scheme of abbreviations that follows appears in one of the aforementioned collections, it has been so indicated; see the bibliography for the publication information of the other texts, published independently, including their translations where available.

Abbreviations Used in Citations of al-Sulamī

AIA	*Kitāb al-amthāl wa-l-istishhādāt fī l-ashʿār* (in *STS*, 87–116)
AMM	*Adab mujālasat al-mashāyikh wa-ḥifẓ ḥurumātihim* (in *MAS*, 1:89–120)
AṢ	*Kitāb alfāẓ al-ṣūfiyya* (*Tafsīr alfāẓ al-ṣūfiyya*) (in *STS*, 31–6)
AT	*Kitāb al-arbaʿīn fī l-taṣawwuf* (in *MAS*, 2:533–51; ed. Soori in *MAS*, 3:275–316)
BAṢ	*Bayān aḥwāl al-ṣūfiyya* (in *TKS*, 363–76)
BTF	*Bayān tadhallul* (*zalal*) *al-fuqarā'* (ed. Ateş in *TKS*, 429–63; ed. Honerkamp in *MAS*, 3:17–62)
DAṢ	*Dhikr ādāb al-ṣūfiyya fī ityānihim al-rukhaṣ* (in *MAS*, 3:533–56)
DḤK	*Kitāb dhikr al-ḥabīb wa-l-khalīl*
DḤṬ	*Kitāb dhikr al-ḥayāt al-ṭayyiba*
DM	*Darajāt al-muʿāmalāt* (ed. Ateş in *TKS*, 165–82; ed. ʿIrāqī in *MAS*, 1:465–502)
DMṢ	*Dhikr miḥan al-ṣūfiyya* (*Dhikr miḥan al-mashāyikh al-ṣūfiyya*) (in *SII*, 55–60)
DN	*Dhikr al-niswa al-mutaʿabbidāt al-ṣūfiyyāt* (in *MAS*, 3:483–532)
DṢT	*Darajāt al-ṣādiqīn fī l-taṣawwuf* (ed. Ateş in *TKS*, 377–90; ed. Honerkamp in *MAS*, 3:63–88)
DṬḤ	*Dhawq ṭaʿm al-ḥayāt al-aṣliyya* (in *SII*, 79–82)
DTU	*Dhamm takabbur al-ʿulamā'* (in *SII*, 27–48)
FNU	*Fuṣūl fī naṣīḥat al-umarā' wa-l-wuzarā'* (in *SII*, 49–54)
FT	*Fuṣūl fī l-taṣawwuf* (in *MAS*, 3:167–222)
GṢ	*Ghalaṭāt al-ṣūfiyya* (*Kitāb aghālīṭ al-ṣūfiyya*) (in *MAS*, 3:461–82)
ḤK	*Mas'alat al-ḥabīb wa-l-khalīl* (in *SII*, 75–8)
ḤMA	*Ḥikam muntakhaba min aqwāl al-ʿulamā'* (in *MAS*, 3:147–66)
ḤT	*Ḥaqā'iq al-tafsīr*
ḤW	*al-Ḥayā' wa-wujūhuhu* (*Mas'alat al-ḥayā'*) (in *SII*, 17–24)
JAṢ	*Jawāmiʿ ādāb al-ṣūfiyya* (ed. Ateş in *TKS*, 183–290; ed. Kohlberg in *MAS*, 1:311–408)
KAṢ	*Kitāb ādāb al-ṣuḥba wa-ḥusn al-ʿishra* (in *MAS*, 2:31–132)
KF	*Kitāb al-futuwwa* (in *MAS*, 2:207–334)
KMT	*Kitāb maḥāsin al-taṣawwuf* (in *MAS*, 3:121–46)
KS	*Kitāb al-samāʿ* (in *MAS*, 2:1–30)
KST	*Kalām al-Shāfiʿī fī l-taṣawwuf* (ed. ʿIrāqī in *MAS*, 2:171–206; ed. Soori in *MAS*, 3:407–40)

LM	*Bayān (Kitāb) laṭā'if al-mi'rāj* (in *STS*, 21–30; citations include Colby's numbering but rely on the Arabic text in *STS*)
MA	*Manāhij al-'ārifīn* (ed. Ateş in *TKS*, 141–64; ed. Kohlberg in *MAS*, 2:133–58)
MF	*Mas'alat (Kitāb) al-firāsa* (in *SII*, 25–36)
MFA	*Mā'iyyat al-faqr wa-ādābihi* (in *SII*, 11–16)
MḤQ	*Mustakhraj min ḥikāyāt Abī Ṣāliḥ Ḥamdūn b. Aḥmad al-Qaṣṣār* (in *MAS*, 3:331–46)
MḤṢ	*al-Muntakhab min ḥikāyāt al-ṣūfiyya* (in *STS*, 37–86)
MQ	*Fī ma'nā qawlihi: al-ṣawm lī wa-anā ujzī bi-hi* (*Qawl al-nabī yaqūl Allāh: al-ṣawm…*) (in *SII*, 69–71)
MT	*Mā l-taṣawwuf wa-man al-ṣūfī?* (in *MAS*, 3:317–30)
MTḤ	*al-Muqaddima fī l-taṣawwuf wa-ḥaqīqatihi* (ed. Ateş in *TKS*, 291–362; ed. Amīn in *MAS*, 2:457–532)
MWM	*Masā'il waradat min Makka* (in *MAS*, 3:441–60)
NA	*(Kitāb) Nasīm al-arwāḥ* (ed. Ateş in *TKS*, 411–28; ed. 'Irāqī in *MAS*, 2:159–70)
QF	*Fī qawl subḥānahu wa-ta'ālā: fa-la-nuḥyiyannahu* (in *SII*, 61–4)
QN	*Qawl al-nabī: Hadhāni sayyidā* (*Kitāb fī ma'nā mā ruwiya 'an rasūl Allāh*) (in *SII*, 72–4)
QTM	*(Mas'ala) Fī qawā'id al-taṣawwuf wa-mabānīhā* (in *SII*, 1–10)
RAK	*al-Radd 'alā ahl al-kalām*
RM	*Risālat al-Malāmatiyya* (in *MAS*, 2:335–440)
RMA	*Risāla fī ma'rifat Allāh* (in *MAS*, 3:347–62)
RRM	*Risālat rawḍat al-murīdīn* (*Waṣiyya*) (in *MAS*, 3:363–82)
SA	*(Kitāb) Sulūk al-'ārifīn* (in *TKS*, 391–410; in *MAS*, 3:557–80)
SD	*Su'ālāt Abī 'Abd al-Raḥmān al-Sulamī lil-Dāraquṭnī [fī l-jarḥ wa-l-ta'dīl wa-'ilal al-ḥadīth]*
ṢDM	*(Mas'alat) Ṣifāt al-dhākirīn wa-l-mutafakkirīn* (in *MAS*, 2:441–56)
SḤ	*al-Farq bayn 'ilm al-sharī'a wa-l-ḥaqīqa* (*Kitāb bayān al-sharī'a wa-l-ḥaqīqa*) (in *MAS*, 3:383–406)
SMḤ	*Sharḥ ma'ānī al-ḥurūf* (in *MAS*, 3:247–74; in *STS*, 1–20; citations follow the numbering of Böwering and Orfali)
TQ	*Fī ta'wīl qawl Allāh ta'ālā: li-yahlika man halaka* (in *SII*, 65–8)
ṬṢ	*Ṭabaqāt al-ṣūfiyya* (ed. Shurayba unless otherwise indicated)
UNM	*'Uyūb al-nafs wa-mudāwātuhā* (in *MAS*, 1:409–64)
ZḤT	*Ziyādāt ḥaqā'iq al-tafsīr*

Other Abbreviations

BEO	*Bulletin d'études orientales*
BJMES	*British Journal of Middle Eastern Studies*
BSOAS	*Bulletin of the School of Oriental and African Studies*
EI^2	*Encyclopaedia of Islam* (2nd edition)
EI^3	*Encyclopaedia of Islam* (3rd edition)
EI^r	*Encyclopaedia Iranica*
EI^s	*Encyclopaedia Islamica*

EQ	*Encyclopaedia of the Qur'ān*
GAL	Brockelmann, *Geschichte der arabischen Litteratur*
GAS	Sezgin, *Geschichte des arabischen Schrifttums*
ICMR	*Islam and Christian-Muslim Relations*
IJMES	*International Journal of Middle East Studies*
ILS	*Islamic Law and Society*
IOS	*Israel Oriental Studies*
IS	*Islamic Studies*
IrS	*Iranian Studies*
ISCH	*Islamochristiana*
JA	*Journal asiatique*
JAAR	*Journal of the American Academy of Religion*
JAOS	*Journal of the American Oriental Society*
JIE	*Journal of Islamic Ethics*
JIS	*Journal of Islamic Studies*
JNES	*Journal of Near Eastern Studies*
JPE	*Journal of Philosophy of Education*
JQS	*Journal of Qur'anic Studies*
JRAS	*Journal of the Royal Asiatic Society*
JRE	*Journal of Religious Ethics*
JSAI	*Jerusalem Studies in Arabic and Islam*
JSS	*Journal of Sufi Studies*
MIDEO	*Mélanges de l'Institut dominicain d'études orientales*
MW	*The Muslim World*
PAPS	*Proceedings of the American Philosophical Society*
Q	Qur'ān
RC	*Religion Compass*
REI	*Revue des études islamiques*
SI	*Studia Islamica*
ZDMG	*Zeitschrift der deutschen morgenländischen Gesellschaft*

INTRODUCTION: WHAT DOES VIRTUE ETHICS HAVE TO DO WITH SUFISM?

In recent years, the concept of character development has found a new prominence in both academic and popular discourse.[1] Major research projects continue to draw upon psychological, philosophical and theological perspectives in their exploration of whether character traits exist, how one can refine and shape them if they do and what place they should hold in ethical reflection.[2] This resurgence of interest in the modern West parallels an objective central to the thought of some major medieval intellectuals writing in Arabic. Some described this process as the refinement of character (*tahdhīb al-akhlāq*),[3] some as disciplining the soul (*riyāḍat al-nafs*),[4] and some in other ways, but one distinctive marker of the Ṣūfī path to spiritual growth was the indispensability of certain interpersonal relationships in that process of growth. For believers influenced by *taṣawwuf* (Sufism),[5] character development could never be construed solely as self-discipline or self-cultivation, but only as a dynamic engagement with fellow believers who play a constitutive role in the acquisition of virtue. The bond of companionship (*ṣuḥba*) enables a believer to attain saving knowledge, cultivate the virtues and, in sum, become a better person.

The present study focuses on the Nishapurian shaykh Abū ʿAbd al-Raḥmān al-Sulamī (d. 412/1021), a towering figure in the formative period of Sufism. Al-Sulamī's many writings have not received the scholarly attention accorded to his student Abū l-Qāsim al-Qushayrī (d. 465/1072) or Abū Ḥāmid al-Ghazālī (d. 505/1111) one generation later. As indicated by the book's title, the first central node of this study is al-Sulamī's notion of companionship (*ṣuḥba*). I argue that al-Sulamī provides a helpful corrective and counterweight to scholarly discussion of Ṣūfī companionship in the formative period for two primary reasons. First, several of al-Sulamī's treatises address believers at an early stage of spiritual progress, revealing a spiritual pedagogy more suited to ordinary believers than to the mystical elite. Second, al-Sulamī deals with companionship in a broader sense than the relationship between master and disciple, particularly in his long treatise *Kitāb ādāb al-ṣuḥba wa-ḥusn al-ʿishra* (*The Ways of Companionship and Good Fellowship*). In that text and beyond, al-Sulamī offers an account of how sincere believers can learn from their friends and how their friends can help them grow.

This study revisits current historical reconstructions of Ṣūfī companionship in the formative period, highlighting distinctive features of al-Sulamī's contribution.

Companionship and community

Alexandre Papas is but one scholar to note a 'divorce' in Ṣūfī studies over the course of the last century-plus.[6] One trend oriented itself towards the doctrines of Sufism, often focusing on esoteric texts and the heights of ecstatic mysticism. A second trend focused on the sociopolitical manifestations of Sufism. These two trends eventually diverged into the subfields of *taṣawwuf* studies and *ṭarīqa* studies, with different questions and methods governing each. Ṣūfī studies in the past generation have done much to transcend this division, and the present study also intends to transcend it, while acknowledging that concerns about interpersonal relationships and the developing institutions of the formative period of Sufism drive the present inquiry into medieval texts. Whether or not one accepts Émile Durkheim's famous maxim that 'religion is an eminently social thing',[7] one can certainly say with regard to al-Sulamī and his near contemporaries that 'Sufism is an eminently social thing'.[8] This latter claim does not reduce Sufism to its function of promoting social order and cohesion, the very reductionism that Durkheim's critics emphatically reject. Rather, the claim acknowledges that Ṣūfīs sought *ṣuḥba* not simply because they saw it, whether consciously or unconsciously, as an instrument to hold society together, but because their evolving collective history taught them to see companionship as a crucial instrument to achieve spiritual progress. The composition of books of etiquette for Ṣūfī lodges and the organization of brotherhoods into 'orders' (*ṭuruq*, sg. *ṭarīqa*) postdate al-Sulamī's generation,[9] but Ṣūfīs throughout the third/ninth and fourth/tenth centuries nonetheless saw companionship as a sine qua non for the development of an individual's awareness of the universal presence of God.[10] Companionship enabled Ṣūfīs to participate in the bond that joined the Prophet to his companions, the *ṣaḥāba*.[11] Through companionship, a believer makes possible his own spiritual progress and contributes to the progress of another.[12]

Many medieval Ṣūfī writers made strong claims about the absolute necessity of the guidance of a spiritual master to achieve the advanced stages of the spiritual life. An oft-cited maxim captures the assumption: 'If someone does not have a shaykh, then Satan is his shaykh.'[13] During the formative period of Sufism, the role of the shaykh became increasingly prominent in Ṣūfī literature, and modern scholarship of Sufism has tended to mirror that prominence in its currents of interest.[14] Perhaps in the future the currents will shift, but scholars often still treat companionship as functionally synonymous with guidance at the hand of a shaykh.[15] Subtler discussions of Ṣūfī companionship tend to acknowledge two realities: that the term *ṣuḥba* always signified something more than the master-disciple relationship, and that *ṣuḥba par excellence* consists in the master-disciple relationship.[16] The opening line of Mark Sedgwick's contribution to the first volume of Brill's *Handbook of Sufi Studies* follows this dual approach: 'Mysticism in Islam is organised through the relationship between *murshid* (guide) and *murīd* (seeker), and through collective institutions such as the *ṭarīqa*.'[17] Scholarly attention has centred overwhelmingly on the master-disciple relationship,[18] in accord with the (im)balance seen in Robert Moore's entry on *ṣuḥba* for the third edition of the *Encyclopaedia of Islam*. While Moore acknowledges that 'companionship is more basically a close and caring relationship' and that the practice of companionship has undergone numerous transformations, he accepts 'discipleship' as a valid translation of *ṣuḥba* and the entry deals almost exclusively with companionship as a hierarchical bond for the transmission of knowledge.[19] The great scholarly interest in companionship with Ṣūfī shaykhs has threatened to eclipse al-Sulamī's appreciation for the pedagogical value of 'ordinary' friendships and the spiritual fruits that can result from a believer entering and living these bonds with intention, consciousness, and commitment. A growth in companionship, properly understood, facilitates the subtle 'sufization' of society, the broader diffusion of the distinctive virtues that mark the Ṣūfī way.[20] Historians associate al-Sulamī with the synthesis of a variety of spiritual currents under the mantle of *taṣawwuf*, but his attention to the ways of companionship shows his instinct to propose, diffuse and spread more than to gather and include. He expects that by living with greater intention and piety the social bonds they already share, believers will transform their society according to the pattern of the Prophet's relationships with his companions.

Virtue and character

Al-Sulamī intends his writings, according to the argumentation proper to each, to function as pedagogical tools for believers. Whether through a long 'bullet-pointed' list of Ṣūfī ways bolstered by Qur'ānic citations, Prophetic traditions and wise maxims – as seen in *Kitāb ādāb al-ṣuḥba*, *Jawāmiʿ ādāb al-ṣūfiyya* (*A Collection of Sufi Rules of Conduct*), *al-Waṣiyya* (*The Spiritual Advice*) and several other similar treatises – or whether through treatises like *Adab mujālasat al-mashāyikh wa-ḥifẓ ḥurumātihim* (*Proper Comportment in the Presence of Shaykhs and Maintaining Reverence for Them*) and *Mas'alat mā'iyyat al-faqr wa-ādābihi* (*The Essence of Poverty and its Ways*), in which his own authorial voice predominates,[21] al-Sulamī presents his writings as instruments to educate and train the soul.[22] These texts, however, are not teaching tools in themselves *sensu stricto*. They guide and orient believers' thoughts and actions in the arena where the real growth happens, as believers struggle to integrate and emulate the practices described in the shaykh's writings.

I argue in this study that a renewed appreciation of al-Sulamī's moral and spiritual pedagogy benefits from a re-examination of several key terms in al-Sulamī's lexicon and how these terms interact with each other and herein lies the second node of this study. He builds his reflections upon evocative terms like *adab* (pl. *ādāb*, 'way[s]', 'custom', 'comportment', 'behaviour'), *akhlāq* (sg. *khuluq*, 'virtues', 'morals', 'character [traits]') and *ṣuḥba* ('companionship'), notions that build upon each other but are pregnant, elusive and ambiguous in themselves. Each of these terms had significant value for the literati in Khurasan, and each underwent shifts in meaning and emphasis when employed in evolving Ṣūfī discourse. The study that follows will examine these terms in light of recent developments in the renewal of virtue ethics. I argue that while al-Sulamī's texts show few direct marks of engagement with Greek-influenced *falsafa*, scholars of Sufism should attend to the numerous resonances between virtue theory and the Ṣūfī path. Philosophers today have sharpened the language at their disposal to speak about virtue and character and this stands to benefit Ṣūfī studies, a field that frequently functions with little consciousness of these developments in another discipline.

In recent years, more and more scholars of classical Islam have shown an interest in virtue ethics.[23] This trend manifests less interest in meta-ethics and more in applied ethics. By that I mean that they have attended more to particular virtues and their cultivation than to a general theory of virtue.[24] Ida Zilio-Grandi's recent monograph is a case in point. In the introduction, she writes:

> The good qualities that God and the Prophet love in a believer harken back to that branch of moral philosophy that, from Aristotle onward, has been called 'virtue ethics'. This branch insists on examining a person's way of being, antecedent to action and distinct from it.[25]

She then insists that one must not overestimate the contribution of the Greek tradition to Islamic ethics and must instead account well for pre-Islamic Persian foundations and for the fundamental contribution of the Qur'ān itself, as well as the complex background of Arab values that the Qur'ān itself presupposes, authenticates and reforms. Regardless of any Persian or Greek influences that historians may justifiably trace, Muḥammad played an irreducible role. According to a famous Prophetic tradition transmitted by al-Ṭabarānī (d. 360/971), 'God sent me to perfect noble virtues (*makārim al-akhlāq*) and to bring good actions to fulfilment.'[26]

Zilio-Grandi's impressive study coincides with the major trends of the field, both in the relative emphasis she places on various dynamics of influence on Islamic ethics and in her attention to applied ethics rather than meta-ethics. While each chapter of her monograph provides a finely researched sketch of a particular virtue, most of which emerge from the divine names (*al-asmā' al-ḥusnā*), the author never deals with the question of what a virtue is. If patience, gratitude and modesty are species of a genus that one calls 'virtue', how does one define and discuss that genus? Sophia Vasalou deals with the question at length with regard to greatness of soul and greatness of spirit, a line of inquiry born of her interest in Arabs' reception of Aristotle's *megalōpsychia*, but she enters little into mystical literature.[27] Scholars focused on the Ṣūfī tradition have followed a pattern closer to Zilio-Grandi's, focusing on specific virtues like humility (*tawāḍu'/khushū'*)[28] or on gratitude (*shukr*).[29] With the exception of extensive research on al-Ghazālī (d. 505/1111)[30] – whose ethics manifest thoroughgoing influence from the Greek tradition – scholars have not examined what a virtue is per se for classical Ṣūfī figures. For figures like al-Ghazālī and al-Rāghib al-Iṣfahānī (d. 502/1108), the question is not whether scholars should speak about virtue ethics but what kind of virtue ethics.[31] I maintain that the same was true two generations earlier, in the literary corpus of al-Sulamī.

This study utilizes the contemporary philosopher Alasdair MacIntyre (b. 1929) as a primary dialogue partner to explore al-Sulamī's spiritual method, concluding that MacIntyre's notions of tradition, practice and virtue broadly cohere with al-Sulamī's key insights. Moral philosophers have been speaking about the 'resurgence in virtue ethics' since the early 1980s if not before, but MacIntyre's contributions – especially his 1981 classic *After Virtue*[32] – are most frequently cited both as a stimulus of that resurgence and as symbolic of it. This study therefore generally takes MacIntyre as a representative of current debates surrounding the virtues, although additional studies of character and moral psychology will form part of the discussion. This approach attempts to establish points of contact between the discourse of scholars of classical Islamic theology and ethics and the debates of moral philosophers today. The relevance of MacIntyre for the study of Islam has been indicated by several scholars, even though the possibility has not yet been explored in depth.[33] The present study does not attempt a 'MacIntyrean reading' of al-Sulamī or other medieval mystics or to impose a foreign framework upon them. Instead, the study uses advances in virtue ethics as a tool to understand companionship and virtue in the formative period of Sufism with greater precision and conceptual clarity. Modern debates about questions of virtue and character provide an instrument to achieve this, despite the different vocabulary and conceptual framework of the classical Arabic texts in question.[34] The call to express the insights of the classical Islamic tradition in a modern idiom is not new; this monograph takes one more step towards comprehending a giant of medieval Islamic mysticism in a language that conforms to today's intellectual horizon, for believers and non-believers alike.[35]

Biography of al-Sulamī

The present study does not attempt to furnish the 'life and times' of al-Sulamī, as this has already been admirably accomplished by other scholars. Instead, a distinctive set of questions will come to the fore and readers will look elsewhere for a comprehensive synthesis of his contribution. A brief biography of the shaykh and survey of the major studies of him must, however, precede the questions of spiritual pedagogy at the core of this book to provide context for them.

Biographical information for al-Sulamī's life is far from complete and certain periods are difficult to reconstruct chronologically,[36] but the principal elements are not under dispute.[37] Abū ʿAbd al-Raḥmān Muḥammad b. al-Ḥusayn b. Muḥammad b. Mūsā b. Khālid b. Sālim al-Azdī l-Sulamī l-Naysābūrī was born in Nishapur, probably in 325/937.[38] The *nisba* by which he is most commonly known, 'al-Sulamī', derives from the tribe of Sulaym, from which he descended on the maternal side of his family.[39] Pride in his Arab heritage silently marks his literary œuvre, as al-Sulamī wrote exclusively in Arabic despite residing in a Persian-speaking city, and the infrequency of Persian loan words in his texts suggests a deliberate attempt to avoid them. He was raised in a family with a rich scholarly tradition and inherited from it an impressive library that also facilitated his own development. Al-Sulamī's father fostered his inclination towards *taṣawwuf* but moved from Nishapur to Mecca during al-Sulamī's adolescence. His maternal grandfather Ibn Nujayd (d. 366/976–7) then took primary responsibility for al-Sulamī's education and formed him more meaningfully in the Ṣūfī path.[40] A Shāfiʿī scholar and reputed traditionist, Ibn Nujayd was known for his excellence in *taṣawwuf* and his great learning. His discipleship under the ascetic Abū ʿUthmān al-Ḥīrī (d. 298/910) accounts for the strong influence of al-Ḥīrī in al-Sulamī's thought. For a period, Ibn Nujayd hid from his master al-Ḥīrī and ceased attending his sessions, a fault for which Ibn Nujayd later repented.[41] Al-Sulamī also struggled to practice patience with his teacher Abū Sahl al-Ṣuʿlūkī (d. 369/980), who commanded al-Sulamī to obey his master without question.[42] Al-Sulamī would later commend such behaviour as part of good Ṣūfī *adab*.[43] The nature and extent of al-Sulamī's work with other teachers is not clear from the sources.[44] He probably studied various disciplines, including aspects of the Ṣūfī path, under al-Ṣuʿlūkī, a foundational intellectual leader for what would become the Shāfiʿī-Ashʿarī faction in Nishapur.[45] Scholars often mention al-Sulamī's guidance in the Sufi path under the Shāfiʿī scholar Abū l-Qāsim al-Naṣrābādhī (d. 367/977–8) and reception of a *khirqa*, or Ṣūfī cloak, from him, but al-Sulamī himself does not refer to al-Naṣrābādhī as one of his teachers.[46]

Ibn Nujayd died while al-Sulamī was away on pilgrimage, bequeathing to al-Sulamī a splendid library that enriched the lives of those in al-Sulamī's circle. His scholarly peers, including al-Qushayrī's father-in-law Abū ʿAlī l-Daqqāq (d. 405/1015), visited al-Sulamī there for intellectual discussion and to use his library. In one famous vignette, al-Daqqāq identifies from a distance the precise location of a work in al-Sulamī's library.[47] So interested was al-Daqqāq in a small, red-covered volume containing some poems of the condemned mystic al-Ḥallāj (d. 309/922) that he knew where to find a book amongst the many on a shelf. Al-Sulamī resided in Nishapur for the remainder of his long life, although he likely continued to travel on occasion. He enjoyed the assistance of his personal secretary Abū Saʿīd Muḥammad al-Khashshāb (d. 456/1064) and some of al-Sulamī's students became prominent in their own right, none more so than al-Qushayrī, author of the famous *Risāla*. Others who studied with al-Sulamī to varying degrees include Abū Bakr al-Bayhaqī (d. 458/1066), the great traditionist who frequently narrates through al-Sulamī; Abū Nuʿaym al-Iṣfahānī, the Sufi, traditionist and author of *Ḥilyat al-awliyāʾ* (*The Ornament of the Saints*);[48] and Abū Saʿīd b. Abī l-Khayr (d. 440/1049), the famous mystic celebrated by the Persian hagiographical masterpiece *Asrār al-tawḥīd* (*The Secrets of God's Mystical Oneness*).[49]

The early sources report neither whether al-Sulamī married nor whether he fathered any children that reached adulthood. He died on Sunday, 3 Shaʿbān 412/12 November 1021 and was buried at the site of his lodge (*duwayra*) in Nishapur. For decades after his death, believers continued to visit his tomb seeking blessings, but nothing remains of al-Sulamī's lodge or tomb today.

Recent scholarship on al-Sulamī

The modern scholarly literature dealing with al-Sulamī and the Nishapur of his day is both daunting and limited. Scholars have attended carefully to the social, political and economic realities of Khurasan in the period, but research on al-Sulamī himself suffers from some imbalance. The last three decades have seen scholarship on al-Sulamī advance by leaps and bounds, primarily due to the availability of previously unpublished texts in good editions. Al-Sulamī's output was prolific, and even if one takes al-Khashshāb's statement that al-Sulamī composed seven hundred texts on Ṣūfī topics as a grand exaggeration, one can never know how many of his writings are lost or lie undiscovered in manuscripts.[50] Al-Sulamī's literary output can be divided by genre into three areas: his Qur'ān commentaries, his biographical dictionaries and his treatises.[51] The last of these three admits a great variety of stylistic and structural variance; one might instead choose to speak about his works of *tafsīr*, his works of *ṭabaqāt* and his 'everything else'. In the past thirty years, new discoveries and publications in all three of these areas have improved our knowledge of al-Sulamī's thinking.

Al-Sulamī's most famous work, the biographical dictionary *Ṭabaqāt al-ṣūfiyya* (*The Generations of the Ṣūfīs*), was published in two independent editions in the 1960s and subsequently was widely cited.[52] Beyond this, the few other texts available for most of the twentieth century were individual shorter treatises edited by various scholars.[53] The Turkish scholar Süleyman Ateş provided a great resource when he edited a collection of nine treatises in 1981,[54] but the 1991 discovery of MS Ibn Saʿūd 2118, a manuscript known as the *Sulamiyyāt*, provided a major leap forward.[55] The manuscript, copied only sixty years after al-Sulamī's death, contains twenty-six minor treatises ascribed to him. The short treatises extant in this source that are found nowhere else fill two volumes, edited by Gerhard Böwering and Bilal Orfali.[56] The manuscript also contains al-Sulamī's biographical dictionary of Ṣūfī women, *Dhikr al-niswa al-mutaʿabbidāt al-ṣūfiyyāt* (*Early Ṣūfī Women*).[57] At the same time that Böwering and Orfali were editing these texts, Nasrollah Pourjavady and Muḥammad Soori were preparing to publish a multi-volume set of al-Sulamī's collected writings. Some of the texts they collected were facsimiles of earlier editions, but others were new texts edited by Soori, Kenneth L. Honerkamp and others. Three volumes of this set have appeared, and a fourth is in preparation.[58] Especially when one factors in the publication of al-Sulamī's Qur'ān commentaries,[59] the state of the study of al-Sulamī today – in terms of the texts available to scholars – far surpasses where we were a generation ago. Translators have been likewise eager to render his works into European languages; the bibliography of this study gives full details of the translations currently available known to the author.

Regarding secondary scholarship and critical studies, al-Sulamī has been the specific subject of several important articles, by Böwering, Honerkamp, Frederick S. Colby and others.[60] Three monographs have been written on al-Sulamī, one in German, one in French and one in English. Each is a revised version of a doctoral dissertation and aspires to provide a one-volume synthetic introduction to this medieval master, including a full biographical sketch and a systematic overview of his thought and literary contribution. The first of these, Lutz Berger's 1998 volume, bears the limitations of the resources available to the author but nonetheless has stood the test of time.[61] Most notably, Berger lacked access to the texts in the *Sulamiyyāt* manuscript, but his portrait of al-Sulamī's thought nevertheless remains fundamentally accurate. The second, Jean-Jacques Thibon's monograph on al-Sulamī, is the longest, most ambitious and most comprehensive of the three.[62] Thibon's magisterial volume approaches al-Sulamī according to the different dimensions of his personality: the *muḥaddith* (traditionist), the *murabbī* (spiritual guide) and the *malāmī* (adherent of the Path of Blame). Thibon's monograph will serve as a handbook for scholars of al-Sulamī for years, particularly due to the third part of the book: Thibon selects twenty-five key texts of al-Sulamī for detailed discussion, preparing scholars not simply to understand the figure of al-Sulamī but to enter deeply into the study of his literary corpus. Of the three monographs, Thibon's thus has the strongest claim to be the indispensable resource for the study of al-Sulamī, and Thibon has subsequently published a wonderfully annotated French translation of *Ṭabaqāt al-ṣūfiyya* and has authored or edited a number of other fine articles on al-Sulamī and key figures from his milieu.[63] The third and most recent book on al-Sulamī, Safaruk Z. Chowdhury's *A Ṣūfī Apologist of Nīshāpūr*, falls somewhere between the prior two in terms of its ambition and scope.[64] Like the preceding two monographs, Chowdhury engages the most important scholarly literature about the formative period of Sufism and sketches well both al-Sulamī's biography and the relevant sociocultural features of the region. A distinctive feature of Chowdhury's study is the increased attention to al-Sulamī's work as a traditionist. Whereas Thibon concentrates more on figures that could be properly considered mystics, Chowdhury charts a large number of scholars active in the intellectual hothouse of Nishapur in the period, including *ḥadīth* transmitters and budding scholars of the Ashʿarī theological climate emerging there. He also dedicates one long chapter to surveying technical terms used by al-Sulamī in a key treatise, thus providing not a glossary of the Ṣūfī lexicon in the period but a glossary of al-Sulamī's usage of terms from that lexicon.

A fuller engagement with these three studies is not necessary at this point, as the three volumes will recur again and again in due course. But another recent book on early Sufism merits a detailed summary due to the author's methodological concerns in comparison with the present study. Arin Shawkat Salamah-Qudsi's 2019 monograph reacts against a tendency the author sees in Ṣūfī studies to emphasize a personal, ascetic and often quietist form of piety in the early period, in contrast to a more social and communal expression of piety in the fourth/tenth century and after.[65] She posits that 'the fabric of early Sufism, prior to the fourth/tenth century, included many more community-based elements than previously thought'.[66] Salamah-Qudsi does not attempt here to postulate earlier dates for the development of Ṣūfī institutions. The novelty of her approach lies in her focus on family relationships, on marriage and on other practical, concrete aspects of community ties that mark and shape emerging *taṣawwuf*. I find myself in fundamental agreement with her reading of most of the relevant texts and with her principal conclusions and therefore will not rehash most of the arguments in the monograph.

One should notice, however, that Salamah-Qudsi's primary quarrel is with the binary between individual and communal piety, insisting that scholars must redefine what individuality means in reference to early Sufism. But her discussion of *ṣuḥba* illustrates that perhaps prior scholarship had not been as focused on individuality as she assumes. The relationship between the master and disciple, for example, has long been a focal point of Ṣūfī studies, including discipleship in the early period. The attempt to trace the evolution of the formation that a shaykh provides for his *murīd* has occupied several great scholars, and even in the cases where this formation occurs in a one-on-one context akin to spiritual direction, no serious scholar of Sufism would call this an individualistic piety. The dynamism between two (or more) believers shapes the doctrine and practice of the aspirant who attempts to make progress on the path, and one may justifiably question whether – even in the earliest period – an aspirant who lacks such guidance from a master can be accurately labeled a 'Ṣūfī' at all. Put differently, her point that prior scholars place unbalanced emphasis on withdrawal, retreat, itinerancy and other forms of self-marginalization in the early period is well-taken but risks being exaggerated into a straw man. Scholars have always known that the Ṣūfī aspirants sought guidance from masters of spiritual wisdom and this formation is necessarily 'communal'.

One strength of her study, then, is putting flesh on these early Ṣūfī communities and sketching what companionship looked like. For even if prior scholars knew that early Ṣūfī piety was always communal, an error lay in the heavy focus on the master-disciple relationship to the exclusion of any other forms of companionship. Hypotheses about when shaykhs began giving personalized spiritual advice to their disciples instead of offering instruction to groups – the transition from the *shaykh al-ta'līm* to the *shaykh al-tarbiya* – are prominent in the literature, but the effects that other forms of fellowship and social mixing had on developing Ṣūfī piety have not received sufficient attention. The present study continues, then, along a similar trajectory to Salamah-Qudsi's, albeit concentrating less on a historical reconstruction of this social fabric and more on the way religio-moral growth is conceived in Ṣūfī writings in the light of this social fabric. In the minds of the Ṣūfīs, did these relationships affect and alter their spiritual progress? And how so?

Companionship and virtue

The first chapter of this monograph analyses the concept of *ādāb* for al-Sulamī in comparison with his near contemporaries. The chapter begins by identifying the prominent structural characteristics of key medieval texts by eminent literati like al-Jāḥiẓ (d. 255/868–9), texts commonly described as *adab*. The chapter also analyses the use of the term by early Ṣūfī masters like Dhū l-Nūn al-Miṣrī (d. 245/859 or 248/862), Sahl al-Tustarī (d. 283/896) and al-Ḥakīm al-Tirmidhī (d. 295–300/905–10). Their approach to *adab* frames the extraordinary gravitas al-Sulamī gives to the concept, which for him evokes proper comportment and never a literary genre. Indeed, the whole of the spiritual journey for him begins with and is constituted by *adab*. His regular use of this pregnant term in its plural form, *ādāb*, shows his understanding of it as an indicator of discrete and concrete practices. These practices are not merely behaviours like observable customs and ritual acts but habits of the mind and heart; al-Sulamī speaks frequently about interior *ādāb*. He follows here on the example of some luminaries of early Sufism, who used the term *adab* primarily in an attitudinal, interior sense, signifying an inner cultivation. Al-Sulamī tirelessly insists on the integration of interior orientation and exterior comportment. He neither simply assumes that one's inner life directly causes the external manifestations of holiness nor simply assumes that voluntary attempts to reform one's daily habits could chisel a new face onto the inner self. Rather, al-Sulamī searches for practice that unites the *ẓāhir* (external/visible) and the *bāṭin* (internal/invisible) throughout. To understand this dynamic, MacIntyre's notion of practice provides a helpful point of comparison. I argue that key elements of MacIntyre's definition of what a 'practice' is broadly conform to the dynamics at play in al-Sulamī's treatment of *adab/ādāb*.

Al-Sulamī's vision of Sufism involves a distinction between ways (*ādāb*), virtues (*akhlāq*) and states (*aḥwāl*) as fundamental elements of the Ṣūfī path. The second chapter focuses on second of these, analysing al-Sulamī's notion of virtue and character. Here too, MacIntyre provides a conversation partner, this time through his concept of tradition and tradition-based rationality. I argue that in the context of al-Sulamī's spiritual pedagogy *taṣawwuf* functions much like a 'tradition' in MacIntyre's scheme: Sufism is a larger reality composed of sets of practices which shape what practitioners can know. Bringing modern reflections on virtue ethics into dialogue with al-Sulamī involves serious, though surmountable, conceptual challenges. Al-Sulamī does posit the existence of acquired human qualities which enable a believer to achieve the goods of *adab*; he calls these *akhlāq* and emphasizes God's role in their acquisition. Two major problems hinder understanding these *akhlāq* as 'virtues' in the philosophical sense of that term. The first is psychological: al-Sulamī relies on a Ṣūfī psychology of spiritual centres foreign to thinkers more heavily influenced by the Greek philosophical tradition. The second hearkens back to the relationship between observable actions and character: while many Aristotelians insist that virtues must find outward expression, al-Sulamī encourages habits for interpersonal relations while discouraging any ostentation or recognition. The influence of the Path of Blame shows through here. Al-Sulamī urges believers to cultivate disposition through meritorious, repeated actions but whenever possible to reduce the visibility of those actions. After considering various modern conceptions of virtue, character and character traits, I argue that in the context of al-Sulamī's œuvre, one should speak about *akhlāq* as 'virtues'. While al-Sulamī does not intend precisely what Aristotelians denote with this term, it is the least inadequate translation of al-Sulamī's key insights, particularly as these find expression in his thought about companionship. The virtues al-Sulamī prizes support the practices that facilitate a believer's awareness of the presence of God at all times but especially in the encounter with fellow believers.

The third chapter focuses on spiritual companionship (*ṣuḥba*) and fellowship (*ʿishra*) in the writings of al-Sulamī, primarily in *Kitāb ādāb al-ṣuḥba*. I argue that he uses *ṣuḥba* and *ʿishra* to denote two different types of relationships and that in both cases al-Sulamī uses the terms in a broader sense than most scholarly discussions of Ṣūfī *ṣuḥba* presuppose. The *ṣuḥba* and *ʿishra* al-Sulamī describes do not relate primarily to relationships among a tightly knit community of Ṣūfī brothers. Rather, they refer respectively to the companionship believers voluntarily seek based on a mutual desire for moral growth and to the fellowship a believer shares with all persons that the believer meets, including the Islamic obligation to give testimony by one's manner of dealing with them. These are Ṣūfī concerns, to be sure, but al-Sulamī's counsels are not solely intended for those who have reached elite ranks of spiritual growth or close to it. He also shows his concern for a general audience at an earlier stage of spiritual development: he crafts practical guidelines for healthy and thoroughly Islamic relationships informed by the distinctive insights of the developing Ṣūfī tradition. Like many other spiritual masters, al-Sulamī recommends that believers keep company with persons of virtue, persons sincerely dedicated to the spiritual life. Several of his writings – most especially *Kitāb ādāb al-ṣuḥba* – manifest al-Sulamī's resignation that believers live their lives in this world amid persons either less able or less willing to cultivate a life of virtue. Al-Sulamī's habits of the mind in dealing with these people demonstrate his conviction that growth in character can occur through contact with them. Al-Sulamī's counsels here are more than mere coping strategies for dealing with the lamentable shortcomings of others; he sees more clearly than some of his contemporaries the benefit in *ṣuḥba* and *ʿishra* with less virtuous persons.

Chapter 4 examines the consequences of *ṣuḥba*, by means of a comparison with some of al-Sulamī's near contemporaries in philosophy and in *taṣawwuf*. I argue that the most significant fault line running between Ṣūfī reflections on companionship and philosophical reflections on love (*maḥabba*) and friendship (*ṣadāqa*) lies in the political consequences one expects to result from that bond. Abū Ḥayyān al-Tawḥīdī (d. 414/1023), even more robustly than his fellow philosophers, sees friendship as an instrument to promote social cohesion in the larger polity. Al-Tawḥīdī imagines these beneficial effects passing first through viziers and their courts; when these persons are transformed by friendship, the fruits of that bond will travel throughout the realm. By contrast, al-Sulamī's Ṣūfī contemporaries showed strikingly little interest in either courtly intrigue or reform. They also appreciated the public benefit which results from companionship but focused increasingly on a different class of elites, the shaykhs. Al-Sarrāj and al-Sulamī's student al-Qushayrī provide the primary points of comparison here. Each has a multifaceted approach to companionship, recognizing forms of the relationship depending on the spiritual ranks of the believers involved. Al-Qushayrī shares an insistence on respect and reverence for shaykhs that he inherited from his master, but demands – more so than did his own master – a solitary and unquestioning bond of obedience to a shaykh. Al-Qushayrī thus manifests not only a transformation in the relationship between shaykh and disciple but also the increasing restriction of the notion of *ṣuḥba*. Spiritual companionship became localized in the bond between master and disciple, reducing a believer's dependence on other companions in the spiritual journey and transforming the union of shaykh and *murīd* into the main portal by which God spreads blessings throughout the realm.

The conclusion to this study revisits MacIntyre's haunting invocation of St. Benedict of Nursia (d. 547) at the end of *After Virtue*. There, MacIntyre argued that the current dark age of moral discourse demands the formation of new, local forms of community in which the virtues can be sustained until the prevalent confusion passes away.[67] A close examination of al-Sulamī's moral pedagogy and the role companionship plays in it reveals a more optimistic vision. Al-Sulamī anticipates that Ṣūfī practice will not increase factionalism in the city he loved but rather contribute to social cohesion. By gently and quietly infusing the companionship and fellowship of ordinary believers with the virtues and practices of the Ṣūfī tradition, the unity of believers as one body will become increasingly manifest. They come to know God because this practice facilitates their consciousness of God's presence in their interaction with each other. This practice thus knits together believers' companionship with each other and their companionship with God, keeping them oriented towards the life to come.

Chapter 1

THE EMERGENCE OF *ĀDĀB* IN AL-SULAMĪ'S SPIRITUAL METHOD

As Ṣūfīs in Khurasan developed a recognizable identity as a social group, no consensus immediately emerged about which aspects of Ṣūfī life and practice functioned as the primary drivers of Ṣūfī identity. Some considered the Ṣūfīs primarily as believers marked by certain visible and virtuous behaviours; some considered them believers marked by a particular inner orientation; some considered them believers to whom God had granted the gift of mystical states or ecstatic experiences; some considered them problematic because they grasped at legal concessions not permitted to Muslims generally. Al-Sulamī laboured to frame a response to this question, both in his selection of traditions to hand down to his fellow Ṣūfīs and in his apologetic treatises defending Ṣūfī practice against their detractors, but his literary corpus offers additional examples of texts that promote Ṣūfī spiritual insights without explicitly covering those insights with the mantle of *taṣawwuf*. Al-Sulamī often does so through the concept of *ādāb*, the comportment that marks a believer pleasing to God. This chapter begins by introducing the prominent characteristics of Arabic texts commonly described as *adab*, because several of al-Sulamī's treatises could be and have been classified in this way. For al-Sulamī, *adab* first evokes proper comportment, not a literary genre, and the same is generally true for the Muslim mystics who preceded him. This background facilitates an analysis of *ādāb* and *akhlāq* as conceptual categories in al-Sulamī's articulation of the Ṣūfī path. I then sketch the understanding of *adab/ādāb* in the writings of several prominent Ṣūfīs who preceded al-Sulamī, focusing on al-Muḥāsibī, Sahl al-Tustarī (d. 283/896) and al-Sarrāj (d. 378/988). The most distinctive feature of al-Sulamī's teaching lies in the gravitas he gives to *adab/ādāb*: while preserving reverence for terms like *zuhd* (asceticism), *'ilm* (knowledge), *ma'rifa* (gnosis) and other central elements of the Ṣūfī lexicon, al-Sulamī transforms *adab/ādāb* into a governing concept that evokes the gestalt of all beliefs and behaviours that constitute spiritual progress. Finally, I draw in Alasdair MacIntyre's notion of practice, arguing that MacIntyre's development of this term can help scholars of Sufism understand the nature and function of *adab*.

'Adab *literature*'

Adab, in its etymological origin, denoted authoritative custom. The term served as a functional synonym for *sunna*, signifying the desirable habits of life in a given community.[1] From there, usage of the term evolved and it came to encompass both moral behaviour and social refinement, including the education and culture necessary to put these into practice. Al-Jāḥiẓ, the quintessential example of *adab*, expressed this by distinguishing between *'ilm*, the religious science which is the root of education, and *adab*, which is the branch.[2] Calling *adab* the branch in no way restricted or diminished it, for *adab* functioned as a totalizing concept for al-Jāḥiẓ, synonymous with the complete edifice of knowledge, both ethical and non-ethical.[3] By the fourth/tenth century, *adab* had three significations: first, good and correct behaviour; second, writings of the type that many modern scholars call '*adab* literature'; and third, the body of literary and linguistic knowledge presented by '*adab* disciplines'.[4] Focusing briefly on the second of these will clarify al-Sulamī's intentions, as they relate primarily to the first signification.

The classification of certain Arabic texts as '*adab* literature' or 'works of *adab*' has become ubiquitous in scholarly writing. Given the fact that modern Arabs use the word *adab* to translate the word 'literature', speaking of '*adab* literature' seems redundant at best and a nonsensical tautology at worst. With good cause, Antonella Ghersetti dedicates a section of her book on *adab* literature to the question of whether '*adab* literature' exists.[5] Ghersetti locates the use of '*adab* literature' as a type of text in the lectures of Carlo Alfonso Nallino published in 1948, noting that earlier orientalists tended not to employ this category. The term describes texts written to entertain and to cultivate, texts that aspire to be formative. But subsequent scholarship has noted that given the malleability of the term *adab* itself, the invention of the compound '*adab* literature' only compounds the ambiguity. 'Definitions of *adab* literature easily become circular, and there never has been a universally accepted definition of *adab*'.[6] Charles Pellat suggests that *adab* literature exists on three distinct levels: moral, social and intellectual.

> *Adab* literature, in the beginning, essentially comprised roles of behaviour going back to virtuous and able ancestors, whether Arabs, Persians, Indians, or even Greeks, and its actual purpose was the training of Muslims in the field of ethics, culture, and crafts. Essentially a prose genre, it was originally characterized by some common features: (1) use of Arabic simple prose without excessive ornaments, but generally supple and well articulated in an artistic and literary fashion; (2) derivation of substance mainly from Persia, either ethical or formative in intent yet restricted to general rules of behaviour or principles of activity; (3) lack of emphasis on Islamic elements; the Arab patrimony was confined to the Arabic language.[7]

Early *adab* authors drank deeply from the Iranian cultural heritage and themes of Persian courtly literature more than Greek thought, and in certain cases, more than Islam as a religion.[8] For this reason, al-Jāḥiẓ saw the Islam of the scribes of his day as superficial: these scribes learned only as much about Islam and about Arabic grammar and philology as they needed in order to sound educated and impress people. Al-Jāḥiẓ recognized that their minds were fundamentally Persian, and he saw in the *kuttāb* a transparent desire to re-impose Persian cultural elements and administration.[9]

'*Adab* literature' never indicated a specific literary genre;[10] variations in modern scholars' lists of which works count as *adab* demonstrate that the intention of the texts under consideration matters more than their literary form. These works had a pedagogical function and the primary characteristic uniting them is that their authors intended them to form their audience into a certain kind of person, depending on the author's particular goals. One cannot think about these works apart from this performative aspect. These texts were useful; their utility was a principle of their composition.[11] *Adab* literature attempted to impart a command of cultural capital, preparing a person for public, courtly life.[12] Despite the predominance of the Persian cultural frame, images of that courtly life were not exclusively restricted to a particular system of administration or government, as *adab* evoked the divine banquet and the abundance of the heavenly court.[13] Because scholars often see these texts as instruments to form someone for courtly service, they sometimes frame *adab* as a basically secular term, especially as the term *sunna*, with the passage of time, became more and more 'religious', increasingly restricted to indicate the customs of the Prophet Muḥammad rather than the customs of virtuous Arabs generally.[14] 'Secular' in this case should never be understood as anti-religious, but that works of *adab* may have a different horizon than Islamic literature generally. Even texts that seem to focus on eloquence in speech often still have a noticeably religious character, as they attempt to inculcate the religious, moral and social norms that are pleasing to God. One must collect virtuous qualities, acting with proper comportment towards God in public and in private.[15] Therefore, a purported contrast between 'religious' literature and 'secular' works of *adab* adheres more to works of *adab* that treat the specifics of professional behaviour. Texts on the *adab* of scribes, the *adab* of judges or other professions focus on the attitudes and skills necessary for exemplary performance of those professions. In this regard, one might see works of Ṣūfī *adab* as the heirs of a disciplinary approach to *adab*, guidebooks describing the *adab* of scribes, the *adab* of judges or the like. This would seem to be even more true in the case of later Ṣūfī works describing the behaviour proper in a Ṣūfī lodge.[16]

Works of Ṣūfī adab *and* adab *literature*

Al-Sulamī's literary corpus provides an abundance of texts that speak about *adab*, but whether these should be considered '*adab* literature' is an open question. By comparison with later books of etiquette in a Ṣūfī lodge, few of al-Sulamī's treatises unambiguously present themselves as professional guidebooks like the earlier *adab* of scribes.[17] Some of al-Sulamī's texts track in this direction, including *Risālat al-Malāmatiyya* (*Treatise on the Path of Blame*), documenting the customs of a particular spiritual trend, and *Dhamm takabbur al-ʿulamāʾ* (*Censure of the Arrogance of the Scholars*), sketching the meaning of being truly learned by means of a *via negativa*, condemning scholarly pride. But another treatise of a different character has also been classified by its editor as an *adab* work: *Kitāb ādāb al-ṣuḥba.*[18] Unlike texts penned for specific professions, the treatise does not provide a detailed account of the manners and customs common to a recognizably bounded Ṣūfī brotherhood. Its status as an '*adab* work' rests on its more general interest: it is an open-ended compilation, written in formal Arabic, that is didactic in interest. The treatise thus forms a link between ʿAbbāsid era *adab* literature and the Ṣūfī literature of successive generations because the treatise deliberately under-emphasizes Ṣūfī themes, at least in terms of explicit citation of Ṣūfī masters and explicit references to *taṣawwuf.*[19] Al-Sulamī's treatise stands out for its drive to anthologize, a common characteristic of *adab* literature; the treatise manifests *adab*'s 'many-sidedness and selectivity'.[20] Long lists of sayings function not simply as repositories of information that protect authoritative teachings from being lost. Rather, they show the importance of *muḥāḍara*, the ability to have the proper quotation at one's fingertips.[21]

The rhetorical style of this treatise parallels several of al-Sulamī's other shorter treatises: each paragraph consists of a point of *adab*, immediately followed by a Prophetic tradition, by a Qurʾānic verse, by verses of poetry or by a wise saying of a Ṣūfī master in support of that point. The precise date of the treatise's composition is not known, although it likely hails to the earlier part of al-Sulamī's literary activity and may have served in some sense as a prototype for other treatises he prepared with similar patterns.[22] The author attempts to show that for each custom of companionship, he knows the nuggets of wisdom from the tradition perfectly suited to illustrate it. Al-Sulamī and his contemporaries sought to demonstrate their cultivation by means of such citations: knowing the right maxim expresses more than a person's status among the literati. This ability expresses that person's spiritual advancement. He shows that he has integrated a given principle in his life because when asked about it, his mind reflexively turns to the maxim that best illustrates and clarifies it. This Ṣūfī *muḥādara* does not depend upon the strength of one's intellect or the breadth of one's study but upon the full synthesis of the outer, praxis dimension and the inner, attitudinal dimension that constitute authentic *adab*. Ṣūfīs believed that they had privileged capacities to achieve this synthesis.[23] Texts demonstrating reflexive command of the proper, insightful maxim show that this synthesis has been achieved and help less-advanced believers hone their instincts. Al-Sulamī shows his attempt to demonstrate this capacity not solely in *Kitāb ādāb al-ṣuḥba*; other treatises exhibit his favour for the trait as the fruit of Ṣūfī wayfaring (*sulūk*). In *Kitāb al-amthāl wa-l-istishhādāt fī l-ashʿār* (*The Book of Parables and Quotations in Poetry*), he documents other Ṣūfī masters enriched with the same ability; the collection consists of a long series of vignettes in which different Ṣūfī masters were put on the spot with a question and they always respond with the perfect verses for the moment.

While I have tentatively categorized al-Sulamī's writings as *adab* works, one may yet wonder whether the category is helpful. Debates about the scope of *adab* literature tend to err in favour of breadth; modern scholars have been reluctant to restrict this body of texts by defining what the category does not include.[24] In any case, the term is a modern construct; the most prominent examples of *adab* literature, including al-Jāḥiẓ, do not refer to their writings in this way. Likewise, al-Sulamī, his fellow Ṣūfīs and their successors cared little whether their writings 'count' as *adab* or not, but cared solely to promote the spiritual practices, the mental attitudes and the habits of behaviour that these texts attempted to instil. In that regard, examples of Ṣūfī *adab* literature rub against one of the purposes modern scholars often attribute to *adab* works. If these texts were supposedly intended to entertain and to cultivate, the interest of al-Sulamī and his fellow mystics falls almost exclusively on the latter. The most famous Ṣūfīs fascinated those around them but not because they sought to entertain, and this distinction holds for the works they penned. Absent is the playfulness of a text like al-Jāḥiẓ's *al-Bukhalā'* (*The Book of Misers*); instead, only rarely do moments of humour punctuate the seriousness that adheres to the Ṣūfī path. And insofar as modern scholars assume that *adab* literature prepares someone for a courtly life, al-Sulamī's texts do not fit the category. He did prepare one short treatise of advice for princes, *Fuṣūl fī naṣīḥat al-umarā' wa-l-wuzarā'* (*Passages of Counsel for Princes and Viziers*), but more widely read texts like *Kitāb ādāb al-ṣuḥba* and *Kitāb al-futuwwa* (*The Book of Ṣūfī Chivalry*) have nothing to do with service to the court. Kister's introduction to *Kitāb ādāb al-ṣuḥba* aptly describes the treatise as 'ideally suited to the man in the street', an attempt to raise the level of moral standards among Ṣūfīs and in society in general.[25] While the 'man in the street' for whom al-Sulamī writes was likely not an illiterate mendicant, he was also not an independently wealthy courtier. Works like this lie somewhere between *adab* literature and Ṣūfī literature, at a moment when – if one can say that these categories of literature separated – they yet remained fundamentally linked.[26]

Ādāb, akhlāq *and* aḥwāl

As mentioned earlier, Ṣūfīs in Khurasan did not share a consensus about which aspects of Ṣūfī life and practice functioned as the primary drivers of Ṣūfī identity. Al-Sulamī lived amid a war of words with regard to Sufism, devoting several treatises to the defence of *taṣawwuf* against its detractors.[27] The title of Chowdhury's monograph on al-Sulamī indicates 'apologist' as a central feature of his identity, and al-Sulamī's tireless efforts to preserve and transmit mystical practices and teachings suggests that the propriety of these practices and teachings was not universally accepted. Al-Sulamī uses other writings, however, to promote Ṣūfī spiritual insights without explicitly covering these insights with the mantle of *taṣawwuf*. *Kitāb ādāb al-ṣuḥba* manifests this latter approach, drawing on spiritual masters that al-Sulamī elsewhere associates with Sufism but not naming them as such. He focuses instead on *ādāb*, on the ways that mark authentic companionship and fellowship. By comparing al-Sulamī's writings with some of his near contemporaries, one sees that developments in Ṣūfī discourse about *adab* did not occur in a simple linear diachronic progression, but that different shades of meaning in this pregnant term waxed and waned, receiving different levels of emphasis in the teaching of various spiritual masters. The most distinctive feature of al-Sulamī's teaching lies in the gravitas of *adab/ādāb*. While preserving reverence for terms like *zuhd*, *'ilm*, *ma'rifa* and other elements of the Ṣūfī lexicon that had been dear to prior masters, al-Sulamī transforms *adab/ādāb* into a governing concept that evokes the gestalt of all beliefs and behaviours that constitute spiritual progress.

Even a brief glance at al-Sulamī's literary corpus reveals the centrality of *ādāb* in his discourse. The clearest expression comes in the famous maxim al-Sulamī attributes to Abū Ḥafṣ al-Ḥaddād al-Naysābūrī (d. *c.* 270/883), 'The whole of Sufism is proper ways' (*al-taṣawwuf kulluhu ādāb*).[28] The commitment of Abū Ḥafṣ to the Path of Blame excludes the possibility that one could understand *ādāb* in this maxim either as noteworthy eloquence or as rituals that set Ṣūfīs apart from ordinary believers. The Malāmatiyya cultivated a piety that was hidden in plain sight. In stark contrast to the public religiosity and ostentatiousness of Karrāmī renunciants, adherents of the Path of Blame hid their pious acts from onlookers' eyes, choosing a subtle and quietist way of self-deprecation. Al-Sulamī's citation of the maxim of Abū Ḥafṣ likewise indicates that true Sufism does not lie in the legal licenses or distinctive rituals that led the critics of *taṣawwuf* to disparage it, but that certain habits of mind and heart were important and indispensable. The maxim does not restrict Sufism to these norms and manners but gives rhetorical emphasis to them.[29]

Al-Sulamī explores *ādāb* as but one of the constitutive categories without which one cannot apprehend the fullness of the Ṣūfī path, categories that include virtues (*akhlāq*) and states (*aḥwāl*). He summarizes: 'Sufism has three spheres (*maqāmāt*): ways, virtues, and states. Ways are acquired, virtues involve a model for imitation, and states are a gift (*mawhiba*).'[30] Elsewhere, he speaks of Sufism existing in four modalities (*madārij*): ways, virtues, states and licenses (*rukhaṣ*).[31] These two examples were succinct citations, but elsewhere he frequently clusters these concepts together when discussing the Ṣūfī path, as one sees in *Bayān aḥwāl al-ṣūfiyya* (*Explanation of the States of the Ṣūfīs*). 'Among the ways of poverty (*ādāb al-faqr*) and its duties (*mawājib*) are training (*ta'addub*) with a leader of the group; actualizing his virtues (*takhalluq bi-akhlāqihi*); following the Sunna in deed, in word, and in the spiritual states (*aḥwāl*); and avoiding innovation and companionship with innovators.'[32] Later in the same treatise, he includes a passage that closely parallels the citation that led this paragraph: 'The duties (*mawājib*) of Sufism are four: ways (*ādāb*), virtues (*akhlāq*), exercises (*mujāhadāt*), and spiritual states (*aḥwāl*). Ways are acquired; virtues and exercises are the following of the Sunna; spiritual states are a gift (*mawhiba*) from God.'[33] In his treatise on the reverence due to shaykhs, he writes, 'What distinguishes the Ṣūfīs in their mystical states (*aḥwāl*), their ways (*ādāb*), and their virtues (*akhlāq*) is detachment and complete freedom from the concerns [of this world].'[34] Later in the same treatise, he adds, 'Service of the shaykhs is obligatory for the aspirant until he no longer wavers in will, in mystical states (*aḥwāl*), in the path of discipline (*ta'addub*), in the virtues (*akhlāq*), in spiritual exercises, and in striving.'[35] Similar examples are strewn throughout al-Sulamī's literary corpus; regardless of which other elements al-Sulamī occasionally chooses to associate with *ādāb*, *akhlāq* and *aḥwāl*, he clearly sees these three as constitutive of the Ṣūfī path.

In various texts, al-Sulamī sets the categories *ādāb*, *akhlāq* and *aḥwāl* in an ascending hierarchy, based on the agent involved.[36] A Ṣūfī's progress begins with attention to ways, then progresses to virtues and states.[37] These categories interpenetrate each other to some degree, but al-Sulamī sees the Ṣūfī path as progress through this hierarchy, which involves a gradual shift in agency from the believer to God. The spiritual labour that a believer performs generally falls into the categories of *ādāb* and *akhlāq*, while God alone grants *aḥwāl*.[38] In all cases, growth in Sufism involves a collaboration between a believer and God: a believer freely submits to the religious law, carries out that law and puts into practice the norms of the Ṣūfī brotherhood. That process culminates in God's gift of spiritual states.

In al-Sulamī's writings across his corpus, *ādāb* refer to rules of conduct, particular practices that characterize the community. Whether al-Sulamī discusses these *ādāb* in terms of external, visible behaviours, or in terms of internal attitudes, they involve the believer's volition. God never carries out *ādāb* in the life of the believer; such actions are the believer's obligation and responsibility. God has revealed these *ādāb* in the life of the Prophet and the lives of the saints (*awliyā'*) who keep these ways alive; the individual believer must choose to act in accordance with these ways. One should not transpose the intricacies of Ash'arī debates about the creation of human actions onto al-Sulamī's rhetoric here. Nishapur was the most important incubator in Islamdom for Ash'arī theology, and al-Sulamī's teacher al-Ṣu'lūkī was a key figure in cementing its dominance there.[39] Like most members of the Shāfi'ī *madhhab* in Nishapur, al-Sulamī's commitment to Ash'arī theology was clear, although he demonstrates a disinterest in the debates of speculative theology. His general distaste for *kalām* appears both in a treatise dedicated to criticising the discipline[40] and in his near-total lack of attention to it elsewhere. Occasionally he does use distinctively Ash'arī terminology, like his description of *ādāb* as *iktisāb*,[41] but even here the term has a greater sense of active performance rather than the 'acquisition' or 'appropriation' common in scholarly discussions about Ash'arism.[42] Much research remains to be done regarding the Ash'arī element of al-Sulamī's intellectual contribution, but for now it suffices to note that the shift in agency from the believer to God occurs at the level of rhetoric rather than dialectic theology.[43] Al-Sulamī saw believers themselves as the agents, as performers, of *ādāb*.

By comparison with *ādāb*, which refers to particular customs or habits of the mind, *akhlāq* for al-Sulamī function at a higher level of generality, collecting all aspects of the religious law. The moral behaviour signified by *akhlāq* does not exclude acts of worship, the *'ibādāt* of jurisprudence. Al-Sulamī clearly considers regulations regarding purity, prayer, fasting, almsgiving and the pilgrimage to Mecca as part of *akhlāq*.[44] However, al-Sulamī uses the term to refer to one's behaviour or character in a more collective sense and does not attempt to theorize *akhlāq*.[45] Someone who makes this behaviour real (*takhallaqa bi-hādhihi l-akhlāq*) experiences the transformation of his blameworthy character traits into praiseworthy ones, an overall refinement of character.[46] Here al-Sulamī's emphasis vacillates. At times, he emphasizes the believer's agency in this transformation and at times God's gift of virtues like modesty, generosity, courage and the like. When he focuses on God's action, al-Sulamī speaks of God bestowing (*awratha*) these traits or adorning (*zayyana*) a believer with them.[47] In the case of mystical states, the initiative and the agency belong to God alone. No one can earn or merit a mystical state. These states descend upon a Ṣūfī and open a Ṣūfī's heart,[48] and God imparts these states in accord with God's mercy.[49] After successful discipline of the ego-self by means of *ādāb* and *akhlāq*, one has good cause to hope that God will grant the blessing of mystical states.

Adab *as MacIntyrean practice*

The remainder of this chapter will treat the theme of *adab/ādāb* in greater detail, postponing further discussion of *akhlāq* until the following chapter. But to augment the analysis of al-Sulamī's thought regarding *adab*, I introduce MacIntyre's notion of 'practice'. I argue that Ṣūfī *adab* provides a viable analogue for what MacIntyre means by practice and that MacIntyre's notion of practice can help scholars of Sufism understand the nature and function of *adab*. This parallel functions particularly well for al-Sulamī but can apply to Ṣūfī *adab* more generally during the formative period.

Practice plays a key role in the argument of MacIntyre's groundbreaking monograph *After Virtue*. In MacIntyre's diagnosis, the present social order in the West involves an incoherent mélange of fragments of moral concepts drawn from incompatible social orders. Moral philosophy stands in an unproductive impasse because philosophers do not recognize this situation fully; they fail to apprehend the nature of the present confusion.[50] The problem is not merely academic. Also at the level of popular discourse, people continue to make moral arguments with confidence in the persuasive power of those arguments despite the fact that the very language of those arguments betrays them because discourse about morals has become disconnected from reality. MacIntyre argues that whether they acknowledge it or not, most people talk, think and act as if no rational justification for an objective morality exists.[51] Emotivism reigns and moral utterances have become nothing but the expression of personal preferences, attitudes or feelings.[52] MacIntyre's project, therefore, attempts to describe this moral disarray more clearly and proposes tradition-based rationality rooted in the virtues as the most adequate path forward to reduce or resolve the confusion.[53]

MacIntyre insists that one can only understand moral or scientific beliefs as a commentary on or a response to what preceded them. The social and historical context in which a person matures and lives governs how that person learns and what that person can know. He faults the Enlightenment for blinding us to the fact that rational inquiry occurs in the context of a 'tradition',[54] a central concept in his approach not just to moral philosophy but to human rationality as such. Traditions are arguments extended through time, 'in which certain fundamental agreements are defined and redefined'.[55] Traditions by their nature are dynamic and in flux, evolving as they face new questions and challenges. This development is a genuinely rational process that 'if it goes well, moves in the direction of an ever-fuller grasp of reality'.[56] Traditions thus have a strong epistemic function. A tradition limits an individual's acquisition of knowledge because the discourses of a tradition affect the questions an individual considers relevant and the style of the individual's response to those questions. Further, an individual will not achieve excellence without a robust and vigorous personal investment in engaging the discourses of that tradition. If one does not commit to the goods that constitute a tradition and strive to develop a tradition's virtues, one cannot develop the capacities of insight and judgment necessary to grasp the central texts and commitments of that tradition. This process finds concreteness in what MacIntyre calls 'practices', a distinctive feature of his account of virtue ethics. Traditions are constituted by sets of practices.[57] For MacIntyre, a 'practice' is:

> any coherent and complex form of socially established co-operative human activity through which goods internal to that form of activity are realized in the course of trying to achieve those standards of excellence which are appropriate to, and partially definitive of, that form of activity, with the result that human powers to achieve excellence, and human conceptions of the ends and goods involved, are systematically extended.[58]

On this account, while in any age one will likely be able to identify exemplars of outstanding achievement in a practice, there is no one person who set the standard, born to be the exemplar for all ages. Practices generate their own standards of excellence organically, and these standards evolve according to and are reconstituted by the prudential judgments of practitioners striving for excellence.[59] In MacIntyre's schema, a practice's standards of excellence involve not only skilfulness and artfulness but also morality, the realm of virtue. Pursuing the goods internal to practices entails the development of certain moral qualities, whence the deep connection to virtue.

> The virtues therefore are to be understood as those dispositions which will not only sustain practices and enable us to achieve the goods internal to practices, but which will also sustain us in the relevant kind of quest for the good, by enabling us to overcome the harms, dangers, temptations and distractions which we encounter, and which will furnish us with increasing self-knowledge and increasing knowledge of the good.[60]

MacIntyre maintains in this account his consistent position that virtue pertains to the individual, but in the context of practices, one can see the robust and constitutive role an individual's community plays in that individual's growth in virtue. To be clear, while communities (and more specifically, institutions) are the social bearers of practices, MacIntyre does not value community as such.[61] He simply observes that 'the best type of human life, that in which the tradition of the virtues is most adequately embodied, is lived by those engaged in constructing and sustaining forms of community directed towards the shared achievement of those common goods without which the ultimate human good cannot be achieved'.[62] Such lived narratives have a teleological character: we live our relationships in light of certain conceptions of a possible shared future.[63]

MacIntyre might seem a strange dialogue partner for al-Sulamī as he is neither a theologian nor a mystic nor a Muslim. MacIntyre's escape route from our modern moral quagmire involves a robust recovery of virtue ethics along Aristotelian-Thomistic lines, a philosophical framework al-Sulamī does not share. He and al-Sulamī share one assumption undergirding MacIntyre's notion of practice: that the human person has a *telos*, that life lived well drives towards something. MacIntyre conceives ethics as a concrete, practical science dealing with how one moves from one-as-one-happens-to-be to one-as-one-could-be-if-one-realized-one's-essential-nature.[64] MacIntyre insists that without a sense of what the human person's function and proper end is, one cannot speak about a 'good' person.[65] While al-Sulamī would not describe that end in Aristotelian terminology, he nonetheless clearly sees human life well lived driving towards something. Al-Sulamī's invocations of the Prophet as a man whose *adab* God has perfected suggest that reaching that end is possible,[66] and the lives of saints and shaykhs likewise show that progress into what God desires for the human person is a real, and not merely theoretical, possibility.

Several aspects of MacIntyre's definition of practice merit discussion in the context of *adab*: a practice is 'coherent and complex', it is a 'socially established cooperative human activity', it involves 'goods internal to that form of activity' and employs evolving standards of excellence. First, MacIntyre defines a 'practice' as a 'coherent and complex form'. The scope of what is complex enough to be considered a practice has been a bone of contention among philosophers engaged with MacIntyre's work.[67] Scholars of Sufism frequently speak about Ṣūfī practices like litanies, *dhikr*, audition sessions (*samāʿ*) or the like, but none of these are sufficiently complex to qualify. I avoid calling such rituals 'practices', with the intent of retaining 'practice' as a technical term. *Dhikr* and *samāʿ* function as repeatable actions that mark and sustain the community's identity and enable advancement towards the ends towards which the community strives, but they do so in a derivative and instrumental sense.[68] Calling them 'customs' is therefore more suitable, retaining 'practice' for the gestalt of Ṣūfī behaviours united to mental attitudes that, when integrated, facilitate growth in virtue. *Adab* functions as an analogue for practice because al-Sulamī never uses the singular noun *adab* to denote one particular custom among the larger constellation of customs, as in *adab min al-ādāb*. When he uses the word in its singular form, he uses it in a holistic and comprehensive sense. Al-Sulamī's penchant for using this term in the plural – speaking of *ādāb* more frequently than of *adab* – does not impede comparison with MacIntyre's notion of practice here. Ṣūfī practice does not consist of an exhaustible list of narrowly defined customs, but a complex mélange of behaviours and attitudes that mark a believer's engagement with the world.[69] Notionally, all of these ways hold together somehow, and al-Sulamī retains *adab* as an umbrella concept, as a collective term capturing the total comportment of adherents and the larger constellation of goods they hope to achieve. *Adab* embraces both social behaviour and one's internal orientation; it includes both specific instructions about greetings and posture as well as more general principles that demand interpretation for their application.

Turning to a second element of MacIntyre's definition, one cannot doubt that *adab* is socially established and cooperative. One must learn *adab* from someone else, and one must perform it with someone else. Al-Sulamī claims, of course, that proper *adab* has a divine origin, but except for the Messenger of God, whose *adab* God perfected directly,[70] *adab* is taught to people by people. *Adab* cannot be actualized in the life of a believer without the education and training of another believer; in this sense, *adab* is socially established and cooperative by definition.

Third, a practice seeks goods internal to that form of activity. Here, one must add a terminological caveat, because the study of Sufism so frequently relies upon the contrast between outer and inner, external and internal, *ẓāhir* and *bāṭin*. MacIntyre's distinction between external goods and internal goods obviously has nothing to do with the *ẓāhir/bāṭin* dichotomy. External goods, for MacIntyre, are truly good – they might be useful and beneficial rewards for one's success – but their achievement demands different virtues than the goods internal to a practice. For example, an architect who grows in excellence stands to make more money and receive more prestigious commissions. The goods internal to the practice of architecture do not consist of these. Internal goods might be increased capacity for imagination about space, excellence in the expression of an interior vision for designs and sketches, the ability to integrate the concerns of a diverse group of patrons or the like. These internal goods are not meaningful rewards in a utilitarian sense, but they are meaningful and fulfilling for a sincere practitioner.[71] 'Internal goods are indeed the outcome of the competition to excel, but it is characteristic of them that their achievement is a good for the whole community who participate in the practice'.[72] With regard to Ṣūfī *adab*, the influence of the Path of Blame on al-Sulamī strengthens the correlation with MacIntyre's notion here. The obsessive attempt of the Malāmatiyya to expunge any hint of ostentation shows their narrow focus on the goods internal to the practice they embrace. Adherents of the Path of Blame had little doubt that excelling in their practice would benefit their religious community and the broader society even though this would not occur through worldly recognition. The first masters of the Path of Blame were not concerned with establishing a school or systems to hand down and perpetuate their teachings; their methods were excessively interiorized.[73] However, given their belief that all human actions are stained by imperfection, the Malāmatiyya certainly assumed that the cultivation of sincerity among believers would positively affect a society tarnished by hypocrisy and corruption.

Finally, the norms of *adab* involve evolving standards of excellence. MacIntyre's favour for practices does not derive merely from a conviction that a practitioner should love her practice for its own sake and derive satisfaction from it. Rather,

MacIntyre relishes the fact that the goals of practices are not immutable. The goals themselves evolve throughout the history of the activity and the pursuit of excellence by practitioners.[74] This element of MacIntyre's definition also coheres with Ṣūfī texts in the formative period. It might seem odd to imagine *ma'rifa* evolving, if one imagines that the experiential knowledge given to spiritual elites as a gift by the eternal unchanging Creator of the universe must necessarily remain unchanged itself. However, Ṣūfī manuals show that the hierarchy of stations and states were described differently; the goods that the most excellent members of the Ṣūfī tradition considered that tradition's highest goods were not regarded its highest goods by subsequent generations. Generations of practice changed the way that practitioners understood these realities; the greatest masters found new names for the goods internal to their practice or re-evaluated the relative worth of the goods internal to the practice.

Adab *among al-Sulamī's Ṣūfī predecessors*

With these elements of practice in mind, I will now survey the approach to *adab* in the writings of several of al-Sulamī's most important predecessors in Sufism,[75] before outlining and analysing his own approach. Ṣūfī authors in the formative period give varying shades of meaning to the term *adab/ādāb*,[76] and if one attempts a representative rather than exhaustive survey of their approaches, one could classify the fundamental differences between them along two major axes. First, does an author primarily think about the term in the singular (*adab*) or in the plural (*ādāb*)? Second, does the term denote one's outward conduct, one's inner attitude or both? These two axes not only run through Ṣūfī literature in the formative period but also continue to colour discourse in later Ṣūfī texts.[77] To be sure, many masters operated with the firm conviction of an inextricable link between theory and practice,[78] but whether *adab* evokes first one's outward conduct or first one's inner orientation depends upon the author in question. Texts produced during al-Sulamī's lifetime – including al-Sulamī's own *Ṭabaqāt al-ṣūfiyya* – provided the sources for the competing emphases regarding *adab/ādāb* that continued to flourish in later periods.

During the lifetime of al-Ḥārith al-Muḥāsibī, a mystic famous for the intensity of his introspection, most scholarly discourse about *adab* used the term in the singular and with a restricted scope. The practice of learning and transmitting Prophetic traditions was growing exponentially and the major *ḥadīth* collections attest the use of *adab* for the Prophet's social etiquette and mode of conduct with people, nearly always using the term in the singular as a collective descriptor.[79] Other texts from the period take a similar approach: *adab* denoted courtly etiquette, the conduct of judges, the habits of scribes or other social groups, usually to reflect the behavioural norms proper to certain persons at appropriate times.

Al-Muḥāsibī, born in Basra but spending many years in Baghdad before his death there, left a corpus of writings that manifests a twofold shift. First, he employs the term in the plural rather than as a singular collective. Second, and more significantly, al-Muḥāsibī saw *adab* primarily as a way to train the ego-self,[80] using it at times as a functional synonym for *ta'dīb*.[81] He did not, of course, abandon the connotation that proper *ādāb* conform to the Prophet's behaviour, but saw *adab* as a spiritual exercise or discipline, including ascetic practices by which a believer strives and trains the soul.[82] Al-Muḥāsibī sought moral, ethical and behavioural perfection[83] by means of incisive examination of conscience with the utmost scrupulosity.[84] For this reason, al-Muḥāsibī has been called the 'most psychological' of the Ṣūfīs of his day.[85] His understanding of the close relationships between well-formed behaviour and spiritual realization sets the course for later Ṣūfīs and their fundamental assumption that cultivating proper comportment serves a productive purpose.[86]

> The ideal religious subject is not simply subject to rules of outward conduct. For Muhasibi, the primary mode of fulfilling God's rights is the performance of certain inner duties. Crucially, these inner duties are to be performed by the subject while avowing that his *nafs* is naturally averse to their performance. The subject must understand that great, constant and painstaking effort would be needed to produce acquiescence in the psyche about obeying God internally.[87]

Al-Muḥāsibī's approach paves the way for the adherents of the Path of Blame who so influenced al-Sulamī: like the Malāmatiyya, al-Muḥāsibī considered any display of piety or religious behaviour as dangerous ostentation.[88]

Al-Muḥāsibī's treatise *Ādāb al-nufūs* (*Etiquettes of the Soul*) offers a variety of counsels one can employ to overcome the blameworthy characteristics and sinful tendencies of the ego-self.[89] Until the *nafs* has been reformed, supererogatory actions have no worth or potential. The treatise, however, never offers a constructive definition of *ādāb* and mentions the term rarely.[90] Al-Muḥāsibī focuses more on the soul itself; an early section on the governance of the soul (*siyāsat al-nafs*) sets the stage for him to describe the techniques that can reform and purify the soul, techniques he usually describes as *a'māl*.[91] One could frame these counsels and techniques as instances of *ādāb*, but in both *Ādāb al-nufūs* and the much celebrated *al-Ri'āya li-ḥuqūq Allāh* (*The Observance of the Rights of God*) al-Muḥāsibī does so only infrequently.[92] He does speak about discipline often in *Ri'āya*, but in the context of training another person – the discipline of a novice (*ta'dīb al-murīd*) – rather than self-discipline.[93] In terms of rhetoric, al-Muḥāsibī's *Bad' man anāba ilā Allāh* (*The Beginning for the One who Returns to God*) charts a middle course between *Ri'āya* and *Ādāb al-nufūs*.[94] He uses the term *ta'dīb* to describe self-discipline, but the rhetoric of that treatise depends upon regarding the *nafs* as an entity separate from oneself, an entity with an evil nature.[95] For this reason, one can better describe the training in question as '*nafs*-discipline' than as 'self-discipline'. While scholars rightly laud al-Muḥāsibī for his contributions to Ṣūfī practices of the purification of the soul, his writings do not greatly advance Ṣūfī discourse about *adab* as a concept. The novelty of al-Muḥāsibī lies in his use of the term in the plural in the few occasions when he does invoke it,[96] but al-Sulamī's failure to attribute any sayings about *adab/ādāb* to him does not surprise given the infrequency with which the term appears in al-Muḥāsibī's writings.[97]

Al-Muḥāsibī's literary corpus reflects the fact that the term *adab* never carried the cachet for Baghdad mystics that it would later enjoy in Khurasan.[98] The concept recurs more frequently in one master of lower Iraq: Sahl al-Tustarī. Al-Tustarī never devotes a treatise to *adab* but shifts the usage of the term to make it a matter between the believer and God, not a matter between the believer and others. Texts from this period classified as '*adab* works' or '*adab* literature' often attempt to train persons in courtly behaviour, but al-Tustarī shows no interest in elite social etiquette.[99] For him, proper *adab* involves making the Qur'ān real in one's own life, a believer's response to the voice of the Qur'ān.[100] *Adab* thus stands alongside knowledge (*'ilm*) and initiative (*mubādara*) as one of the backbones of religion.[101] Al-Tustarī sees both *adab* and knowledge not as the customs or learning of the cultured elite but as a life of poverty and simplicity.[102] This practice involves ascetic disciplines that lead to the attainment of correct attitudes internally once one becomes more spiritually adept.[103] Al-Tustarī discerns two fundamental and antagonistic psychic forces within a person: the negative force of the *nafs*, which inclines one towards one's own ego, and the positive force of the *qalb*, which turns one towards God.[104] Fasting, prayer and *adab* provide assistance against the vile whispers of the ego-self.[105] Keeler notes that in several places, al-Tustarī places *adab* alongside obedience to divine commands and prohibitions, functionally equating *adab* with *sharī'a*. *Adab* appears as an attitude or state of mind that assists a person in having the fortitude to obey the law[106] and to live with meritorious scrupulosity, refraining from actions about which there is doubt.[107] Keeler's translation of al-Tustarī's *Tafsīr* often renders *adab* as 'propriety', indicating the fitting manner with which one's internal movements should be ordered.[108] The Way (*adab*) does not refer to a collection of particular rules or codes of conduct. Rather, it signifies 'an inner cultivation that is *manifested* in comely and seemly attitudes, states and conduct'.[109]

Al-Tustarī's definition of *adab*, which Keeler calls the most detailed in early Ṣūfī literature, cements the connection between propriety and happiness.[110] Maintaining this propriety is exacting and restrictive, but far from a dour asceticism.

> [*Adab* is that you should] let your food be barley, your sweetmeat dates, your condiment salt, and your fat yogurt. You should let your clothes be of wool, your houses be mosques, your source of light the sun, your lamp the moon, your perfume water, your splendour cleanliness, and your adornment wariness. Moreover, you should let your work consist in being content (*irtiḍā'*) – or he said: contentment (*riḍā*) – your journey's provision be mindfulness of God (*taqwā*), your eating be at night, your sleep in the day, your speech be remembrance (*dhikr*), your resolve and your aspiration be for contemplation (*tafakkur*), your reflective thought (*naẓar*) be to take example, and your refuge and the one who helps you be your Lord. Persevere in this until you die.[111]

Al-Tustarī offers a vision of a daily religious life that is every bit as regimented and intentional as the manners that characterize courtly etiquette,[112] but that in this case focus on simplicity in lifestyle and sincerity in prayer. The fullness of *adab* lies in repentance, in weaning the soul from carnal desires (*shahawāt*), in silence and in spiritual retreat. If one does not discipline oneself (*ta'dīb*) in this way, one invites punishment in the next life.[113] If a believer undertakes this discipline, the door lies open to intimacy with God. The *ādāb* of this intimacy are nobler (*a'azz*) than harmony (*muwāfaqa*), witnessing (*mushāhada*), sincerity (*ikhlāṣ*) and deed (*'amal*).[114]

Active at the same time as al-Tustarī, al-Ḥakīm al-Tirmidhī's treatment of *adab* focuses even more intensely on the notions of training and discipline. A native of Transoxania, al-Ḥakīm al-Tirmidhī was somewhat detached from developments in Iraqi Sufism and did not call himself a Ṣūfī but considered al-Muḥāsibī – a Baghdādī who also did not call himself a Ṣūfī – his most important intellectual predecessor.[115] Modern scholars often contrast al-Ḥakīm al-Tirmidhī with both Baghdadī Sufism and the Path of Blame in Khurasan, but his contemporaries in Transoxania considered him a sage (*ḥakīm*), a distinct cultural role that did not exist per se in the Baghdadī milieu.[116] Al-Muḥāsibī's use of the plural *ādāb* did not influence al-Ḥakīm al-Tirmidhī, however, who consistently speaks about *adab* in a more restricted scope than did al-Muḥāsibī, limiting his usage to the singular.[117] Like al-Muḥāsibī, al-Ḥakīm al-Tirmidhī authored a text with *adab* in the title but never fixates on *adab* as a technical term: al-Ḥakīm al-Tirmidhī uses *adab*, *ta'dīb and riyāḍa* as functional synonyms, the last being by far the most common. Al-Ḥakīm al-Tirmidhī's concern for training and discipline is omnipresent in his famous treatises *Riyāḍat al-nafs* and *Adab al-nafs*,[118] but his assessment of the ego-self and the purpose of discipline vacillates. His differences with the Malāmatiyya emerge from a differing assessment of the ego-self.[119] Al-Ḥakīm al-Tirmidhī did not share the complete disparagement for the *nafs* that the Path of Blame did, at least insofar as believers who focus excessive concern on their ego-self (by means of blaming it) fail to transcend the ego-self and live with incomplete trust in God.[120] When al-Ḥakīm al-Tirmidhī discusses the ego-self, he does not exclusively concentrate on its inclinations towards what is evil. Discipline has a value beyond the mere avoidance of violations of the law; training the soul yields benefits of its own. The effort involved in this moulding and shaping of the soul, in this self-restraint, bears good fruit. Discipline for the sake of discipline does not suggest the prohibition of actions that God considers permissible. Al-Ḥakīm al-Tirmidhī rejects this notion and insists that he has added no new proscriptions to the divine law.[121] His positive valuation of discipline for discipline's sake aspires to take a believer's permissible actions – in particular, a believer's habits – and set them in a sensible order. A benign image for *adab* as discipline captures this approach well: the homeowner. When one visits a home and sees everything in it properly arranged, one knows that its owner is an *adīb*, an adept of *adab*.[122] This proper arrangement does not occur by accident but requires care, intention and ongoing attention to ensure that things stay in the proper place God has designated for them.[123]

More often, though, al-Ḥakīm al-Tirmidhī does presume the evil inclination of the ego-self: the ego-self is the centre of negative qualities like lust, desire, fear and anger, and any such desire (*shahwa*) must be transformed (*tabdīl*).[124] Self-restraint (*adab al-nafs*) provides the means to this reform.[125] A believer must strive from his heart to rectify his *nafs* and wean it from its negative qualities; doing so, one can trust that God will provide the necessary assistance.[126] A different image captures this instinct to see the believer and the *nafs* in a state of antagonism: the image of a riding animal. Bridling and saddling a beast function as an analogy for the believer's attempt to heel the *nafs* and restrain its perverse habits and inclinations.[127] Unlike the image of the homeowner, this image inclines towards the approach of the Path of Blame.

Ṣūfīs in Khurasan relied on a number of concepts and metaphors to express the importance they placed on training and discipline. Al-Ḥakīm al-Tirmidhī's decision not to rely upon *adab* as the central concept for this therefore was not uncommon. If Abū Bakr al-Kalābādhī (d. 385/995) is a fair representative of Ṣūfī thought in Bukhārā, an indifference to the term *adab* was closer to the norm during the period of al-Sulamī's youth.[128] Based on al-Kalābādhī's *al-Taʿarruf li-madhhab ahl al-taṣawwuf* (*The Doctrine of the Ṣūfis*), one may safely conclude that the notion held no great import for his circle.[129] He aspires in that text to describe the essentials of the Ṣūfī lexicon, and al-Kalābādhī neither defines *adab/ādāb* nor uses the term with any frequency, preferring instead *muʿāmalāt* for the modes of conduct of the Ṣūfīs. The few times that al-Kalābādhī does speak about *adab*, the term signifies for him external behaviour that conforms to the divine law and perhaps is coextensive with the divine law. Such an approach illustrates the apologetic intent of *Taʿarruf*; al-Kalābādhī deems *adab/ādāb* neither a necessary nor particularly useful notion to demonstrate the accord between the doctrine of the Ṣūfīs and both Ashʿarī theology and the major legal schools.

The strongest influence and closest parallel to al-Sulamī's approach to *adab* certainly lies in al-Sarrāj (d. 378/988). Al-Sulamī knew al-Sarrāj's *Kitāb al-lumaʿ* (*The Book of Flashes*) well, and al-Sulamī's writings contain more than one example of al-Sulamī abridging, without acknowledgement, his predecessor's work.[130] Both al-Sulamī and al-Sarrāj show an increased interest in *adab* as a theme, a more frequent predilection to use the term in the plural and a shift towards *adab/ādāb* as a means of designating the modes of conduct and attitudes proper to and adopted by Ṣūfīs.[131] Al-Sarrāj composed *Kitāb al-lumaʿ* to capture the authentic teaching and practice of the Ṣūfī path, devoting a long section to *ādāb* in which he compiles the distinctive ways Ṣūfīs approach a wide range of activities.[132] Al-Sarrāj considers these *ādāb* in three basic categories: worldly practices like eloquence and literature, practices of the people of religion like training the soul and body and practices of the elite like purification of the heart and living in the present moment.[133] Ṣūfīs have their own ways, lived out in the different circumstances of their daily responsibilities. Al-Sarrāj's writings do not display any conceptual distinction between *adab* and *ādāb,* but his fluid movement between singular and plural could reflect the retention of prior masters' usage of the term; *Kitāb al-lumaʿ* compiles the teachings of many of al-Sarrāj's predecessors. The most novel citation comes in Kulthūm al-Ghassānī's use of the term in the dual, claiming that there are two *adab*s, one of speech and one of action.[134] Al-Sarrāj also elides any conceptual distinction between *ādāb, akhlāq* and *aḥwāl*, a distinction on which al-Sulamī consistently depends. Ṣūfis have *ādāb* in their moments (*awqāt*), in their virtues (*akhlāq*) and in their movements (*ḥarakāt*) that are distinct from others' ways, enabling others to know the Ṣūfis by their appearances.[135] Al-Sarrāj gives many details about these *ādāb*, including Ṣūfī practices for washing, ritual purity, circumstances that render the canonical prayer valid or invalid, fasting and the major pilgrimage. He occasionally regards these Ṣūfī ways as instruments of discipline to train the ego-self,[136] but more generally he presents them as pious customs that mark the behaviour of a certain group of believers, that remain inextricably bound to the norms of the divine law and that also foster the integration of the internal and external aspects of those legal precepts. Fritz Meier claims that al-Sarrāj restricts *ādāb* to these sorts of rules, but this assessment might reduce their scope too much; the term also connotes more for al-Sarrāj than a code of etiquette for particular situations.[137]

Al-Sarrāj devotes a chapter of this manual to the ways of companionship (*ādāb al-ṣuḥba*), but unlike the chapters that precede and succeed it, the chapter does not rely heavily on *adab* or *ādāb* as concepts.[138] The term *ādāb* appears only in the chapter header and the material is of a different character. Rather than instructions about the type of clothing to wear, the number of days to fast, the proper mosques to visit on pilgrimage and the like, al-Sarrāj's advice about companionship provides broad principles one can apply. Al-Sarrāj gives concreteness to these broad principles in the colourful vignettes about masters like Abū Ḥafṣ al-Naysābūrī, al-Junayd (d. 298/910) and Abū Yazīd al-Bisṭāmī (d. 261/874–5). These anecdotes stand as exempla from which sincere believers can infer beneficial wisdom.[139] Ideals include the preservation of harmony with one's companions and the blessings of companionship over a long period of time, but the section on companionship deals more with matters of character than of custom. For example, elsewhere in his manual, al-Sarrāj offers detailed instructions about whether, when and how Ṣūfis can enter the *ḥammām*. His treatment of companionship hovers above these kinds of precise prescriptions, which elsewhere fall under the mantle of *ādāb*.[140] When al-Sarrāj transmits the teaching to avoid companionship with someone who says 'my sandals' – rather than 'our' – he points to the self-centred mindset and character of a potential companion, not to a violation of a rule of etiquette.[141] Statements of this kind indicate immaturity on the path, a continued instinct to regard one's possessions as one's own. A comment attributed to al-Junayd captures this approach, 'A transgressor of good character (*rajul fāsiq ḥusn al-khuluq*) who keeps company with me is more beloved than a Qur'ān reciter of poor character.'[142]

Al-Sarrāj preserves a close connection between *sharīʿa* and *adab*, without simply equating the two. Recalling al-Jalājilī l-Baṣrī (d. 287/900), he reports:

> The declaration of the unity of God (*tawḥīd*) is an obligation that requires faith; therefore a person without faith cannot declare God's unity. Faith is an obligation that requires [the observance of the] Divine Law (*sharīʿa*); therefore

> a person without the Divine Law can have neither faith nor the declaration of the unity of God. The Divine Law is an obligation that requires good manners (*adab*); therefore a person who has no manners can have neither the Divine Law, nor faith, nor the declaration of the unity of God.[143]

Al-Sarrāj's stress on the unity between *adab* and the divine law appears also in his consistent reference to the example of the Prophet as the foundation for Ṣūfī ways. He uses *ādāb* as a functional synonym for *sunan* on occasion,[144] showing that the shifts in al-Sarrāj's rhetoric between the custom (*sunna*) of the Prophet and the customs (*sunan*) of the Prophet act in parallel with his alternating references to the practice (*adab*) of the Ṣūfīs and the ways (*ādāb*) of the Ṣūfīs.

The final distinguishing mark of al-Sarrāj's approach to *ādāb* is the dual aspect, inner and outer, that al-Sarrāj often sees at work.[145] One's visible ways manifest one's internal ways, and al-Sarrāj considers this true in all the various aspects of *ādāb:* one's conduct with and before God; one's conduct with one's master, one's companions, and others; and one's conduct with oneself. In certain cases, like 'my sandals', the link between a point of custom and the interior attitude manifested is more immediately evident, but in general, the duality of *ẓāhir* and *bāṭin* functions for al-Sarrāj, an assumption he shares with al-Sulamī.

Al-Sulamī's approach to adab

The centrality of *ādāb* stands out as a distinctive feature of al-Sulamī's literary corpus. Ṣūfī ways do not merely occupy one chapter in a larger work, but several independent works in which al-Sulamī grants the theme prominence. Thibon thus wonders aloud whether al-Sulamī's interest in the topic reflects the spiritual discourse in Nishapur in his day or merely al-Sulamī's personal preoccupation. Al-Sulamī aspires to inscribe Ṣūfī *adab* into the heart of daily life in his native city, to suffuse the spirituality of Nishapur with ways (*ādāb*) that he considered not exclusively Ṣūfī but inclusively Islamic.[146] In this, al-Sulamī prepares the way for later masters whose works can be described accurately as an '*adab* theology'.[147] A comprehensive survey of al-Sulamī's corpus is not necessary to show the malleability and flexibility of this polyvalent term under his pen. Seven treatises provide an adequate picture of the shades of meaning al-Sulamī expresses with *adab/ādāb: Dhikr ādāb al-ṣūfiyya fī ityānihim al-rukhaṣ* (*A Recollection of Ṣūfī Ways for Carrying Out Legal Dispensations*), *Mā'iyyat al-faqr wa-ādābihi* (*The Essence of Poverty and Its Ways*), *Ādāb al-faqr wa-sharā'iṭuhu* (*The Ways of Poverty and Its Conditions*), *Adab mujālasat al-mashāyikh wa-ḥifẓ ḥurumātihim* (*Proper Comportment in the Presence of Shaykhs and Maintaining Reverence for Them*), *Jawāmi' ādāb al-ṣūfiyya* (*A Collection of Ṣūfī Rules of Conduct*), *Kitāb bayān al-sharī'a wa-l-ḥaqīqa* (*The Clarification of the Difference between the Divine Law and Reality*) and *Kitāb ādāb al-ṣuḥba wa-ḥusn al-'ishra* (*The Ways of Companionship and Good Fellowship*). In each case, *ādāb* stands as a constitutive element of the Ṣūfī path, but considered together, these texts posit to *ādāb* a centrality in al-Sulamī's spiritual method it did not hold for his contemporaries.[148]

Dhikr ādāb al-ṣūfiyya fī ityānihim al-rukhaṣ (A recollection of Ṣūfī ways for carrying out legal dispensations)

The treatise *Dhikr ādāb al-ṣūfiyya* contains diverse and jumbled approaches to Ṣūfī ways (*ādāb*) because the treatise combines three different types of subject matter of unequal length: legal concessions, companionship and mystical stations. While the text has likely undergone heavy redaction since al-Sulamī's original work, it nonetheless represents his thought on the matter.[149] The treatise is short – only seventeen printed pages in Pourjavady's edition – and the matter of legal dispensations (*rukhaṣ*) occupies the bulk of the text. Such dispensations occupy al-Sulamī in other treatises as well, as he desires to rebut the polemical charge that Sufism consists primarily in *rukhaṣ*, in a supposedly lax or incomplete fulfilment of the precepts of *sharīʿa*.[150] The introduction to the treatise shows al-Sulamī's general discouragement regarding *rukhaṣ*. 'Utilizing legal concessions, according to Ṣūfī doctrine, is a reversion from the reality of praxis (*ḥaqīqat al-ʿamal*) to external knowledge (*ẓāhir al-ʿilm*). This shows a deficiency in their state.'[151] Al-Sulamī considers the question of legal concessions in light of the stages of an individual's journey – the legal concessions appropriate for a believer do not depend simply on whether that believer is a Ṣūfī or not but on where that believer is on the path. Disputes about specific items of clothing that someone may or may not wear stimulate jurists and traditionists concerned with the Prophet's precedent, but al-Sulamī will not broach any discussion of *rukhaṣ* unless a believer sincerely embraces the behavioural norms and the virtues of the Ṣūfī path. This intense and personal embrace makes a discussion of *rukhaṣ* relevant and not merely theoretical. Here, al-Sulamī employs the notion of *ādāb*.

> Thus, for [the Ṣūfīs], in their legal concessions there are proper ways of behaviour (*ādāb*) and virtues (*akhlāq*). Utilizing legal concessions requires knowledge (*maʿrifa*) of these [ways and virtues] and adherence to them, so that a person can follow according to their [the Ṣūfīs] pattern (*mutarassim bi-rasmihim*) and be adorned with their ornaments until he reaches the stations of those who are being granted access to reality (*maqāmāt al-muḥaqqaqīn*).[152]

Al-Sulamī begrudgingly accepts the validity of legal concessions and pairs each concession with a discussion of specific *ādāb* that relate to it. Whether the concession governs the performance of canonical prayers, attendance at audition sessions, visiting someone while on a journey or other matters, the Ṣūfīs have particular behavioural norms distinct from the concession itself, and these norms validate the concession.[153] The most detailed example is the *adab* of *samāʿ*. Al-Sulamī insists that appropriate behaviour for *samāʿ* had remained consistent since the time of al-Junayd: an audition session should only occur with a suitable number of sincere brothers, only in a suitable place and only at a suitable time. Al-Sulamī's legal defence of these audition sessions adheres only to sincere disciples who have cultivated the proper mindset and behaviour. Speaking about Ṣūfī *rukhaṣ* therefore is misleading in itself: these concessions are not general permissions or licenses for all believers who happen to be members of an organization or institution, whether Ṣūfī or otherwise. Ṣūfī initiation – whatever that meant in al-Sulamī's day – does not entitle a believer to *rukhaṣ*. Rather, al-Sulamī insists that these concessions are valid for the proper person, in the proper place, at the proper time, when carried out piously. In these proper places and times, they allow a flood of divine mystery to become transparent.[154]

The section of *Dhikr ādāb al-ṣūfiyya* devoted to companionship continues al-Sulamī's focus on an individual's progress in the spiritual path, discussing the ways of companionship in relation to this. Al-Sulamī posits three main stages on the journey, that of the aspirant (*murīd ṭālib*), the intermediate (*mutawassiṭ sā'ir*) and the one arriving (*muntahā wāṣil*). Growth in *adab* primarily relates to the intermediate stage of the journey, and al-Sulamī in this section seems to use *adab* interchangeably with *'amal*. The aspirant must strive constantly, but al-Sulamī expresses this striving in relation to knowledge (*'ilm*), not *adab*. Al-Sulamī's idea here continues a theme from the preceding section on legal concessions: reverting from the reality of praxis (*ḥaqīqat al-'amal*) to external knowledge (*ẓāhir al-'ilm*) amounts to a lamentable digression, a return from the intermediate stage to the beginning stage.[155]

Also in keeping with the preceding section on legal concessions, al-Sulamī's instructions on *ādāb* can become very specific, down to the greetings and salutations appropriate to authentic companionship. The moral behaviour of common people expresses their selfishness and their lack of commitment to each other and lack of trust in each other. Signs of this selfishness mark their conversation: 'This is mine', 'That is yours', 'Why did you do that?', 'Why didn't you do that?' and the like.[156] Companions do not speak like this. When a person says, 'Come with us', the true companion does not ask the destination. He simply goes. Such minute instructions are not common in al-Sulamī's other treatises, where his *ādāb* take the form of general guidelines like greeting one's brothers warmly. Al-Sulamī often supplements these guidelines with anecdotes from the lives of previous Ṣūfī masters or maxims attributed to them, but these anecdotes serve more as supporting evidence than the instruction in itself; in *Dhikr ādāb al-ṣūfiyya*, any such distinction between the teaching and the illustration evaporates.

Mā'iyyat al-faqr wa-ādābihi (The essence of poverty and its ways)

Mā'iyyat al-faqr wa-ādābihi focuses on the question of spiritual poverty (*faqr*), a central element of the spirituality of many Ṣūfīs throughout the centuries.[157] The theoretical nature of al-Sulamī's very brief treatise sets it apart from the author's discussion of *faqr* elsewhere. Al-Sulamī states his intention to present the *ādāb, akhlāq* and *siyar* of those who are spiritually poor.[158] His distinction between *ādāb* and *akhlāq* is familiar, but the addition of *siyar*, 'patterns of conduct', stands out as a conceptual category alongside ways and virtues. Al-Sulamī does not suggest here that he will compile stories that illustrate the virtues and behavioural norms of spiritual poverty,[159] but the difference between *ādāb* and *siyar* is not crucial for him because neither concept recurs as such in the body of the treatise. Whereas in other treatises, al-Sulamī proceeds by heading most paragraphs with a leading phrase like 'among their ways is…' (*wa-min ādābihim…*), al-Sulamī begins each paragraph in this treatise by stating simply what spiritual poverty is or by naming signs or identifying marks of the spiritually poor person (*wa-min ʿalāmāt al-faqr*). The sole mention of *ādāb* in the body of the treatise deals with the practices of servanthood. 'Poverty is a mystical state that obligates the servant to the ways of servanthood.'[160] His descriptions of *faqr* are highly spiritualized and attitudinal. He focuses on the mindset a believer should bring to a situation. *Māʾiyyat al-faqr* thus illustrates in its brevity the way al-Sulamī instinctively thinks about *ādāb*, precisely because the treatise focuses almost exclusively on the *faqīr*'s internal orientation. Here and elsewhere, al-Sulamī's default framework for discussing a believer's internal orientation is not *ādāb*, for that term denotes rules of conduct that necessarily have a visible, external component and involve the freedom to actualize those external actions. Other texts that discuss spiritual poverty classify it as a mystical state (*ḥāl*), suggesting both that a believer experiences *faqr* primarily as a phenomenon in the interior life and that God freely bestows the state apart from any action on the part of the believer. *Ādāb* nowhere enter the discussion.[161]

Al-Sulamī preserves in *Māʾiyyat al-faqr* the unity of the *ẓāhir* and the *bāṭin* yet also distinguishes between them. *Faqr* involves forsaking any self-aggrandizement in externals like food or clothing and in the internals by constantly returning to interior silence.[162] The treatise does, however, contain a powerful sense that the interior life has a temporal and logical priority and that the interior life initiates any transformation that occurs in the externals. Just as the title of a book indicates not only the book itself but also the content written within, the practices of servanthood indicate the status of the *bāṭin* of the individual servant.[163] Absent here is the idea, even implicitly, that certain customs or behavioural norms freely undertaken could work their way into one's interior and reshape one's *bāṭin*. Inward changes must precede any external manifestation. This assumption may not hold for all stages of spiritual progress; spiritual poverty signifies that a person has already journeyed a great distance on the Ṣūfī path. Once someone can be authentically called a *faqīr*, *ādāb* have little direct relevance to ongoing growth.

Ādāb al-faqr wa-sharāʾiṭuhu (The ways of spiritual poverty and its conditions)

By comparison with the more theoretical and esoteric *Māʾiyyat al-faqr wa-ādābihi*, the brief treatise *Ādāb al-faqr wa-sharāʾiṭuhu* deals more with concrete customs and invokes more frequently *adab*/*ādāb*. *Ādāb al-faqr wa-sharāʾiṭuhu* is appended to *Sulūk al-ʿārifīn* in printed editions but may be considered a separate work that should not be confused with *Māʾiyyat al-faqr*.[164] Nadia Zeidan's edition carries the title *Ādāb al-faqr wa-sharāʾiṭuhu*; the text as it appears in *Sulūk al-ʿārifīn* begins with *wa-min ādāb al-fuqarā' wa-mawājibihi*, to signal the transition into a different theme. The content could just as well be drawn from the Path of Blame, as the importance of keeping one's *faqr* hidden pervades al-Sulamī's counsels and the final paragraphs of *Sulūk al-'ārifīn* involve the juxtaposition of Iraqi Sufism with that of Khurasan. Maintaining integration between the *ẓāhir* and the *bāṭin* is another recurring theme in the treatise, and a concern likewise tied closely to the heritage of the Path of Blame. Sara Sviri cites a passage that illustrates the criticism the Malāmatiyya levied against the Karrāmiyya. Sālim b. al-Ḥasan al-Bārusī blasted the followers of Muḥammad b. Karrām (d. 255/868) by saying, 'If the longing of their interior were seen manifest in their exterior, and the asceticism of their exterior were concealed in their interior then they would have been "men".'[165] While al-Sulamī typically ignores the Karrāmiyya in his writings, his full adherence to the approach of the Path of Blame here is consistent, particularly when he explicitly invokes *ādāb*. Speaking about the true *faqīr*, al-Sulamī writes, 'His exterior is the standard for the ways of the aspirants (*ẓāhiruhu imām ādāb al-murīdīn*) and his interior is the mirror for the lights of the gnostics (*bāṭinuhu mirāt anwār al-'ārifīn*).'[166] This *faqīr* therefore lives the alignment of his inner and outer self,[167] but al-Sulamī associates *ādāb* both with the visible elements of Ṣūfī practice and with an earlier stage of spiritual progress. Al-Sulamī implicitly suggests here that based on what one sees from the outside, one would never know a person is a gnostic (*'ārif*). One can only know that the person follows the good comportment appropriate to an authentic seeker. But al-Sulamī does not posit the existence of *ādāb* of the gnostics; their nature is hidden to the eye.

This short treatise also draws upon the notion of *adab* as discipline, including the need both to give and to receive formation. The true *faqīr* must be formed by the shaykhs and must discipline his companions (*yata'addab bi-l-mashāyikh wa-yu'addib al-aṣḥāb*).[168] Even if these two actions perhaps occur at different points in the life of a *faqīr*, their combination in close proximity in a long list of the customs of spiritual poverty is a novelty in al-Sulamī's corpus. The need to receive formation from qualified masters recurs frequently in the text.

> He [the *faqīr*] is formed (*yata'addab*) by a master (*imām*), adheres to the Sunna, keeps company with those who follow it, avoids innovation and its people, does not dress in the patched frock unless compelled, does not marry unless he fears that he will violate what is sacred, does not take the place of honour in sessions and does not speak in front of the people.[169]

This list of counsels represents well the flavour of this brief treatise. Al-Sulamī occasionally uses the word *ādāb* and its derivatives, but even when he does not, he catalogues observable customs that characterize the *faqīr*, despite the fact that the truth of his *faqr* could never be observed. Honerkamp has described this approach as 'applied Sufism' when al-Sulamī discusses *faqr* in other contexts, like *Bayān tadhallul al-fuqarā'* (*The Humble Submission of Those Aspiring*),[170] to which the content of *Ādāb al-faqr wa-sharā'iṭuhu* largely conforms.

Adab mujālasat al-mashāyikh wa-ḥifẓ ḥurumātihim (Proper comportment in the presence of shaykhs and maintaining reverence for them)

This treatise, only slightly shorter than *Dhikr ādāb al-ṣūfiyya*, focuses on proper comportment in the presence of shaykhs.[171] *Adab mujālasat al-mashāyikh* proceeds in more of a spiral than a linear fashion, returning again and again to the importance of magnifying and venerating spiritual masters.[172] Thibon describes it as the completion of *Kitāb ādāb al-ṣuḥba* because it specifies the general notion of companionship given in *Kitāb ādāb al-ṣuḥba* by developing the relationship between master and disciple.[173] The theme of companionship itself will receive extended discussion in Chapter 4; here the treatise will be examined for its distinctive approach to the nature of *adab*. One cannot bypass, however, the central argumentative move in the treatise, which relates to both *adab* and to companionship: al-Sulamī takes the bond between the Prophet Muḥammad and Abū Bakr as the prototype for the relationship between master and disciple.[174] The quest to learn proper comportment and put it into practice does not merely involve imitation of the Prophet but also knowledge of the attitudes and customs of the Prophet's closest companions in the presence of the Prophet. Actualizing these behavioural norms – *ta'addub bi-ādābihim* – is the proper response to God's command to 'follow the way of those who turn back to me'.[175] Al-Sulamī reserves his strongest language about true *ṣuḥba* – including a passage in which al-Sulamī distinguishes between companionship and fellowship – for the sections in which he demands uncompromising adherence to the *ādāb* of one's shaykh, in the roots (*uṣūl*) and in the branches (*furūʿ*).[176]

While the title of the treatise uses *adab* in the singular and this usage occurs several times in the text, al-Sulamī continues his pattern of speaking about *ādāb*, the plural form. The noun signifies particular modes of conduct, and while he does not consistently equate these *ādāb* with the divine law, he insists that the true Ṣūfī both presumes and wilfully chooses a total obligation to *ādāb al-sharīʿa* and takes pains to avoid any possibility of their neglect.[177] Any failure in this belongs only to self-styled Ṣūfīs who wrongfully employ legal concessions though they fail to follow the *ādāb* of the Ṣūfī path. Al-Sulamī's rhetoric here in his criticism of *rukhaṣ* shows the apologetic intent seen in several of his other treatises, including an emphasis not only on respect and service for Ṣūfī masters but for authentic scholars.[178] These errors, among others, open the door to developing evil *adab*; in this treatise, the term *adab* does not have an unambiguously positive connotation.[179]

Al-Sulamī insists on the unity between good comportment in what is external and what is internal. He attributes to Abū Ḥafṣ al-Naysābūrī the saying, 'Good comportment with regard to the externals is a manifestation of good interior comportment.'[180] Al-Sulamī draws upon this teaching in other writings, but in this treatise he applies it to the disciple's behaviour in the presence of the shaykh, a matter that permits al-Sulamī a much great specificity of instruction than his discussion of *adab* elsewhere.[181] Attending a shaykh's session (*mujālasa*) demands silence, patience, vigilant attention and total adherence. Unsurprisingly, an emphasis on *adab* as training pervades this treatise due to its subject matter.[182]

God trained the Prophet and disciplined his ways,[183] so the *adab* of disciples demands constant refinement in their behaviour, conforming their virtues to the *adab* seen in the behaviour of the Prophet with his companions. Without this refinement in comportment one cannot hope to receive the blessings of the shaykhs' companionship and the benefits to one's soul.[184]

Jawāmiʿ ādāb al-ṣūfiyya (A collection of Ṣūfī rules of conduct)

The longest of al-Sulamī's treatises on *ādāb* treats the topic in a manner that is fundamentally consistent with the works already discussed. *Jawāmiʿ ādāb al-ṣūfiyya* was probably the first treatise that solely focused on Ṣūfī *ādāb*[185], and of the texts discussed thus far, *Jawāmiʿ* became the most influential model for later works on *ādāb*.[186] *Jawāmiʿ* has an apologetic edge: al-Sulamī states his goal of providing critics of Ṣūfīs with an accurate formulation of Ṣūfī ways and beliefs.[187] The treatise often feels, however, like an insider document directed towards aspirants, providing them answers with which they may respond to critics. The concluding section addresses the necessities of an aspirant directly, not with the intent of describing the aspirant's journey accurately for a third party but to express concern for a sincere *murīd* eager to learn these *ādāb* and anxious about finding a fitting master.[188]

> Nobody becomes sound in practice (*adab*) without following the example of a guide from among the leaders of the people who may show him his shortcomings, his errors, and his missteps. … He shall lead the novice on his path and clarify for him his right moments from his bad ones … And if such a guide (*sālik*) … leaves him, let the novice turn to a learned mentor (*ʿālim nāṣiḥ*) whose knowledge can benefit him and who shuns the things and concerns of this world. … And if the novice's willingness to learn is firm and sincere, God will send him a guide who is nearby or a learned mentor … In the absence of a learned mentor or a saintly guide, let the novice turn entirely to his Lord, so that [God] may take charge of his training (*taʾdīb*) and instruction (*taʿlīm*) if [God] sees in him a genuine willingness and determination.[189]

The combination of discipline and instruction in the conclusion to this treatise demonstrates that al-Sulamī understands *adab* as something larger than exercises in discipline or self-restraint. Ṣūfī conduct demands knowledge. *Adab* is concomitant with knowing, along with reverence and respect.[190] These ways must be learned, whether through the ordinary means of a shaykh's instruction[191] or through the less-travelled path of instruction directly at the hand of God.

Jawāmiʿ ādāb al-ṣūfiyya predominantly uses *ādāb* in the plural but does not abandon the evocative power of *adab* in the singular, particularly when citing earlier masters. The plural form al-Sulamī uses to head each paragraph in the body of the treatise shows that he understands these as discrete norms, individual examples of proper Ṣūfī ways, but he occasionally slips back into the singular *adab* and shows that the distinction between singular and plural is neither systematic nor consistent.[192] Al-Sulamī's usage of singular/plural does not correlate to whether a teaching pertains to interior attitudes or to behavioural norms.[193] The treatise mainly proposes correct spiritual attitudes, with certain spiritual masters recurring as illustrations for each type of advice; specific Ṣūfī rituals and customs are present but do not take centre stage.[194] Counsels attributed to Abū Ḥafṣ al-Naysābūrī tend towards the concrete,[195] while those attributed to Abū Muḥammad b. Khafīf solely involve interior orientation and intention.[196] While some of the *ādāb* compiled in *Jawāmiʿ* involve the details of ritual,[197] fasting[198] and ethical courtesies like paying for what one eats,[199] the majority are inward looking, involving mindsets and attitudes.[200] Al-Sulamī's material about spiritual poverty is an outlier in this regard. While the treatise *Māʾiyyat al-faqr* offers a more esoteric and theoretical discussion of the matter, the isolated instances in *Jawāmiʿ* dealing with *ādāb al-faqr* revolve around external signs like the clothing of the spiritually poor person,[201] as was the case in *Ādāb al-faqr wa-sharāʾiṭuhu.*

Al-Sulamī's identification of the ways of the Ṣūfīs with the ways of the Prophet includes the intimate connection he sees between proper *ādāb* and the divine law. Al-Sulamī never simply equates *adab* with the *sharīʿa*, but he does insist that the *maʿrifa* that Ṣūfīs attain leads a Ṣūfī to obey the divine law.

> Gnosis (*maʿrifa*) must never carry [the Ṣūfīs] into transgressing even a part of the divine law (*sharʿ*) and its ways (*ādāb*) or to neglect it. Rather, they must strive to magnify the divine law and the external manifestation of knowledge (*ẓāhir al-ʿilm*) in every moment that comes to them.[202]

His rhetoric here conforms to other passages that mention *ādāb al-sharʿ*[203], but does not indicate the difference between *ādāb* and the divine law.[204] The distinction cannot be the difference between theory and implementation, as if the *sharīʿa* provided principles and *ādāb* consisted of the resulting application of those principles in a particular situation. Al-Sulamī pre-empts such an erroneous interpretation when he acknowledges the possibility of transgressing a part of the law – independently of transgressing its *ādāb*. He retains here a distinction between the divine law and its *ādāb* but assumes that certain ways of conduct inescapably attend to the law. A believer obeying the law will also follow these ways. He does not frame these *ādāb* as matters of local etiquette or preference, a customary way of following the law in this region that might differ from other equally valid customary ways in other regions. His concern lies with *ādāb* that are properly universal and universalizable. A Ṣūfī will neglect none of these, for they have been faithfully transmitted from the Prophet.

Kitāb bayān al-sharīʿa wa-l-ḥaqīqa (The clarification of the difference between the divine law and reality)

I earlier indicated two primary axes along which Ṣūfī reflections on *adab* tend to travel: whether an author understands the term primarily in the singular or in the plural and whether an author understands the term primarily as a descriptor for external, observable behavioural norms or for internal, attitudinal orientations. By this point, the relationship between *adab* and the divine law has emerged as another complicating factor. The clearest articulation of this relationship for al-Sulamī lies in *Kitāb bayān al-sharīʿa wa-l-ḥaqīqa*. This short work locates *ādāb* at the level of the divine law, tying *ādāb* and *sharīʿa* closely together. Here, al-Sulamī associates *ādāb* solely with the externals of the divine law, accessible to all believers and obligatory upon them, and not with the interior realities of the *ḥaqīqa*, which God reveals only to the elite. Al-Sulamī continues to insist that *adab* involves an integration between what is external and what is internal, but notionally, he connects *ādāb* to the adherence to *sharīʿa* in one's visible behaviour.

Long before al-Sulamī, Ṣūfīs cemented *ḥaqīqa* as a prominent term in their lexicon, despite the difficulty in defining it.[205] Most modern scholarly discussion of the formative period glosses the term as 'reality', 'ultimate reality' or 'divine truth',[206] depending on the context. All of these serve provided that the element of concreteness in this reality is never obscured – *maʿrifa* signifies concrete experiential knowledge of this divine reality. Al-Sulamī locates *ḥaqīqa* in the believer's heart; this 'reality' consists in the heart ceasing its wandering and standing aright between the hands of God.[207] Al-Sulamī elsewhere often describes the greatest Ṣūfī masters as *ahl al-ḥaqīqa* or *ahl al-ḥaqāʾiq*,[208] and in this treatise he frames the difference between *sharīʿa* and *ḥaqīqa* as a distinction of two different kinds of knowledge (*ʿilm*). 'The knowledge of the divine law is the knowledge of the ways (*ādāb*) and the knowledge of reality is the knowledge of mystical states.'[209] One will never reach the states without soundness in the ways (*ādāb*). The divine law involves striving, human effort, service to others and the ways that relate to the externals of the law; the states are reserved for the elite of God's servants, for they involve the fullness of God's guidance and true contemplation of what lies within.[210] Believers must exert every effort in striving (*mujāhada*) if they hope to arrive at the reality of God's guidance. Still, striving and guidance are not the same: striving is a sign and indication of guidance, but it is not the same as guidance.[211] The divine law governs human effort to put God's commands into practice, while *ḥaqīqa* is a gift that comes from God for the believer.[212]

This close association of *ādāb* with the *sharīʿa* does not annul al-Sulamī's insistence that Ṣūfī ways have an outer and an inner element. In his binary of divine law and reality, *ādāb* appear on the side of the law, as a matter pertaining to the externals. However, knowledge of reality grants a believer a fuller – a more real – apprehension of how to actualize these *ādāb*. 'Knowledge of the divine law enables determinations about appearances (*yaqtaḍī l-rusūm*) and knowledge of reality enables determinations about carrying out the ways of these appearances (*yaqtaḍī l-qiyām bi-ādāb al-rusūm*) and the obligation that the heart be present in them.'[213] *Rusūm* does not here mean 'appearances' in a shallow or superficial sense. Al-Sulamī uses the term, as had al-Sarrāj, to unite speech and action. An individual's *rasm* connotes that person's total external comportment,[214] a complete adherence to the commands of the divine law.[215] The *ādāb* thus still belong to the realm of the law, but the people of reality appreciate *ādāb* on another level. The people of reality perceive that what occurs when someone actualizes these *ādāb* can be and should be a transformation in the believer that involves both what is seen and unseen. The involvement of the heart, the spiritual centre most aware of the divine spark, enables this perception.[216]

This distinction between *sharīʿa* and *ḥaqīqa* and the knowledge proper to each captures a dynamic already seen in *Jawāmiʿ*. Al-Sulamī locates his discussion of the divine law and of Ṣūfī ways of behaviour at the level of what is visible and external, but when he imagines the authentic Ṣūfī, he resists any practical attempt to separate these ways from their interior reality. 'Every internal thing that is not performed externally is false, and every external thing that is not performed internally is false.'[217] The *sharīʿa* involves external commands that ordinary believers can obey without achieving this level of awareness, but the Ṣūfī senses and makes real the connection between the *ādāb* and the heart's contemplation. These *ādāb* do not merely belong to the realm of custom or etiquette – even the etiquette of the Prophet! – but are signposts of the activity God stirs in the interior of the believer. Knowledge of the law involves the outer sense of the blessings of God, while knowledge of reality conveys the inner sense of these blessings.[218]

Kitāb ādāb al-ṣuḥba wa-ḥusn al-ʿishra (The ways of companionship and good fellowship)

Among the texts discussed here, the most interesting contrast regarding *ādāb* lies between *Kitāb ādāb al-ṣuḥba* and *Jawāmiʿ ādāb al-ṣūfiyya*. These two treatises bear a structural similarity that exceeds any other two treatises in al-Sulamī's corpus: a lengthy list of *ādāb*, each supported by one or more citations of Qurʾānic passages, Prophetic traditions or teachings of Ṣūfī masters. The major difference, however, is that *Kitāb ādāb al-ṣuḥba* barely uses the term *adab/ādāb* within the teachings themselves and the citations mustered in support of them. Paragraphs in *Jawāmiʿ* often begin, 'among [the Ṣūfīs'] ways (*ādāb*) is ...' and then explicitly probe what *adab/ādāb* could mean.[219] In *Kitāb ādāb al-ṣuḥba*, paragraphs begin, 'among [companionship's/fellowship's] ways (*ādāb*) is ...', and then al-Sulamī provides a teaching that almost never explicitly explores the meaning of *adab/ādāb*.[220] If the titles of treatises by al-Muḥāsibī and al-Junayd mislead readers by suggesting that *adab* will be an important governing concept for the author, *Kitāb ādāb al-ṣuḥba* vexes in a different fashion. The term is omnipresent, but al-Sulamī probes it by stacking on more examples of it rather than by anything resembling a conceptual discussion. One rare example in which the term appears in the body of a paragraph deals with forgiveness and follows on a citation of al-Fuḍayl b. ʿIyāḍ (d. 187/803), the proto-Sunnī renunciant to whom al-Sulamī dedicates the very first entry in *Ṭabaqāt al-ṣūfiyya*.

> [Al-Fuḍayl said:] 'Spiritual chivalry (*futuwwa*) is pardoning the mistakes of the brothers.'[221] For a servant, it is obligatory to journey in search of knowledge, learning by means of it how to improve his behaviour (*ādāb*) in service of his master (*sayyid*). Just so, it is obligatory upon him to journey in search of someone

> who will keep fellowship with him in order to support him in his obedience to his Lord (*mawlā*).[222]

The text continues to describe the bond of fellowship established here, one of affection based on the nature and disposition of one's friend. Deeds are transient, but true affection (*wudd*) is stable. In this case, the *ādāb* in service of the Lord can only mean habits of behaviour. Individual evil deeds wax and wane and must be forgiven, but the nature and disposition constituted by well-established patterns of good deeds possess a power to attract a fellow believer towards true friendship. This consistent concern for interpersonal relationships distinguishes the subject matter of *Kitāb ādāb al-ṣuḥba* from *Jawāmiʿ*; while *Jawāmiʿ* is very inward looking, *Kitāb ādāb al-ṣuḥba* is genuinely concerned about the world.[223] Al-Sulamī's discussion of the *ādāb* of the Prophet with his servants shares this vision of *ādāb* as external behavioural norms. Surely, each individual instance of the Prophet's behaviour offers a salutary example for believers, but al-Sulamī calls his brothers to practice the same ways that the Messenger of God practiced with his servants.[224]

With each paragraph offering a particular illustration of *ādāb*, *Kitāb ādāb al-ṣuḥba* compiles a widely varied catalogue of religious and social mores. Discipline stands out as a frequent theme, but not discipline as the training or exercises given to a believer by a spiritual director. The discipline is one of awareness, a vigilance regarding the rights of Muslims and the interconnected duties one holds towards the various people with whom one comes in contact. These are rules of conduct that one must learn and one must practice; al-Sulamī does not presume that a believer knows them intuitively. The elite among God's servants 'were trained in the ways (*muta'addabīn fī ādābihim*) of the seal of the prophets, who himself conformed to the way of God (*ta'addaba huwa bi-adab Allāh*) and held fast to [God's] subtle commands'.[225]

Al-Sulamī claims that God taught and disciplined the Prophet, but *Kitāb ādāb al-ṣuḥba* is less overt in its explanation of how believers gain access to this knowledge. Without doubt, the transmission of the Prophet's ways by means of *ḥadīths* is a key method of learning God's *adab*. The treatise shows al-Sulamī's clear commitment to *ḥadīth* science as it was practiced in his day. Many of the teachings in *Kitāb ādāb al-ṣuḥba* contain full chains of transmission, whereas al-Sulamī's other treatises, including *Jawāmiʿ*, often truncate these. Al-Sulamī's reputation as a *ḥadīth* transmitter was much maligned, and some critics dismissed the soundness of his traditions and accused him of forging traditions for the benefit of the Ṣūfīs.[226]

Subsequent analysis reveals that al-Sulamī's standards meet those of other scholars in the period.[227] Al-Sulamī's terminology for the mode of transmission – *akhbaranā*, *ḥaddathanā*, *samiʿtu*, *ʿan* and so on – certainly does not meet the exacting precision of some later scholars of *ʿilm al-ḥadīth*, but he shows throughout his œuvre his devotion to the discipline and demonstrates in this treatise his accomplishments in it according to the standards of his day.[228] *Taṣawwuf* grew and spread in the midst of an '*ahl al-ḥadīth* culture', a culture of authority grounded in perceived continuity with the Prophet's community.[229] The many marks of *ḥadīth* science in the treatise show not merely al-Sulamī's commitment to the Prophet's *sunna* but to preserving the Prophet's *sunna* in a particular way, through the transmission of traditions.

The question of 'how to learn *ādāb*' points to a vexing aspect of *Kitāb ādāb al-ṣuḥba*, as the treatise offers few concrete clues about what that learning process looks like. The text gives example after example of the customs of companionship, describing a status quo – albeit an idealized, aspirational status quo – that believers learn simply from their contact, in companionship and fellowship, with other believers. Similar souls draw near to each other and support each other.[230] Practically speaking, a believer supports another believer in good deeds and discourages hateful deeds.[231] *Kitāb ādāb al-ṣuḥba* quietly suggests that one does not first learn *ādāb* at the feet of a shaykh, nor in a session of *ḥadīth* transmitters (despite the prominence of Prophetic traditions in the treatise), nor in a *madrasa.* A believer lives into the *ādāb* alongside companions who encourage other believers and offer their sincere counsel.

Another obvious difference between *Jawāmiʿ* and *Kitāb ādāb al-ṣuḥba* lies in the sources for *ādāb.* Al-Sulamī states early in *Kitāb ādāb al-ṣuḥba* that in every people (*qawm*), different aspects (*wujūh*) of the *ādāb* of companionship and fellowship can be observed.[232] While this treatise discusses the distinctively Islamic version of companionship, companionship is not an exclusively Islamic phenomenon.[233] Non-Muslims experience *ṣuḥba* and *ʿishra*, as well as the *ādāb* appropriate to them. Both *Jawāmiʿ* and *Kitāb ādāb al-ṣuḥba* turn first to Prophetic traditions for support, but where *Jawāmiʿ* draws upon Ṣūfī masters as authorities to buttress its teaching, *Kitāb ādāb al-ṣuḥba* frequently invokes poetry and other forms of popular wisdom.[234] The ways of companionship that al-Sulamī describes in *Kitāb ādāb al-ṣuḥba* deal with external, observable behaviours but at a high level of generality. Instead of intricate instructions for ritual and custom, these counsels provide guidelines that shape and inform the specific choices a believer must make. Al-Sulamī's advice about speech and silence illustrates the point well. Elsewhere, his exhortations to silence are precise, categorical or both. *Risālat al-malāmatiyya* reports an anecdote about Abū Ḥafṣ al-Naysābūrī that contrasts the *adab* of the Path of Blame with the behaviour of Baghdad Ṣūfis. When pressed about why he chooses silence rather than speaking about his knowledge, Abū Ḥafṣ replies:

> Our shaykhs keep silence about their knowledge and only speak about what is truly necessary. If the time is right for them to speak, they do not do so until after turning their minds to God, and they become his faithful ones on this earth, for the faithful man desires only to protect his fidelity.[235]

The habit of silence demonstrated by the Malāmatiyya shaykhs appears also in *Jawāmiʿ*,[236] where the influences of the Path of Blame appear in an un-tempered form.[237] The habit of silence intensifies, of course, in the case of a disciple working with his master. In *Adab mujālasat al-mashāyikh*, al-Sulamī does not content himself with a broad exhortation to silence but makes explicit the conditions under which silence is required. In the presence of a shaykh, one must speak little and ask few questions. An aspirant must always begin his session with the shaykh in silence,[238] must not ask a question intended to demonstrate the aspirant's own knowledge,[239] must not ask the shaykh to add anything to what the shaykh had intended to teach and must be patient with the spiritual exercises that the shaykh chooses for the disciple.[240]

The approach to silence in *Kitāb ādāb al-ṣuḥba* is more elusive, although al-Sulamī still places high value on the restraint of one's tongue. The treatise deals with general social mores, so al-Sulamī takes the speech that accompanies life in public as a given.[241] Aside from occasional counsels of humility that urge believers to remain silent when possible[242] and to preserve their companions' right to speak,[243] al-Sulamī's etiquette for conversation underlines the importance of speaking truthfully, keeping promises[244] and speaking well of others instead of criticizing them.[245] Greeting brothers warmly serves a meaningful social function[246] – especially in the case of a dispute, proper comportment demands reaching out to the estranged brother to reconcile the relationship.[247] Such counsels are adaptable to a myriad of social situations, not merely the more closed set of encounters committed Ṣūfīs regularly experience among themselves.

Conclusion

In conclusion, this examination of several of al-Sulamī's treatises shows the centrality of *adab/ādāb* in al-Sulamī's understanding of spiritual growth. Al-Sulamī does not attempt to probe *adab* as a theoretical concept or craft a succinct definition for it, but his discourse revolves around it and he presupposes that sincere believers desire to learn good comportment and grow in it. *Ādāb* stand at the heart of al-Sulamī's spiritual method, as he utilizes a pregnant term dear to the non-Ṣūfī literati who surround him and infuses it with the wisdom of the developing Ṣūfī tradition in his attempt to advance the sufization of Khurasan. By comparison with his predecessors, three characteristics mark the use of *adab/ādāb* in al-Sulamī's literary corpus. First, his writings reveal a notable shift from the singular to the plural, from *adab* to *ādāb*. While he retains interest in a believer's behaviour in a collective, holistic sense, al-Sulamī's writings move towards a focus on particular norms of conduct as both instruments of that believer's refinement and markers of spiritual progress that has already been achieved. He does not, however, use *ādāb* primarily as a descriptor of the specifics of religious ritual or minute points of social etiquette. Especially in *Kitāb ādāb al-ṣuḥba*, the term refers to patterns of behaviour more general than the details of greetings, initiation and vesture.

Second, but related to the first, al-Sulamī's discussion of *ādāb* consciously straddles a line between external, observable conduct and an inner, attitudinal orientation. On balance, his treatises tend to frame *ādāb* as customs, etiquette or modes of conduct that others can see and learn. In *Kitāb ādāb al-ṣuḥba*, he continues to present *ādāb* first as behavioural norms that others can observe, but his exhortations locate these *ādāb* somewhere in the midst of the Ṣūfī binary of the *ẓāhir* and the *bāṭin*. His counsels about forgiveness, honesty, pride and other aspects of social relations could be considered discrete behavioural norms that characterize the comportment of believers, but they function more as habits of the heart. Their level of generality necessarily locates these *ādāb* in the middle space between the external and the internal, for they are patterns of observable interpersonal relations that could not endure without the accompanying attitudinal orientation.

Third, al-Sulamī develops a notion of Ṣūfī *ādāb* as a matter distinct from the divine law but perfectly in accord with it and operative mainly at the level of the *ẓāhir*. In one sense, these ways are neither greater than nor less than the *sunna* of the Prophet, but in another, they cannot merely be equated with the *sharīʿa*. When he discusses *ādāb* in conjunction with *sharīʿa*, he associates both with the *ẓāhir*, but his discourse elsewhere about *ādāb* as a matter of its own gives way to an understanding of proper comportment that integrates what is internal and what is external. Insofar as one connects Ṣūfī ways to the law in phrases like *ādāb al-sharīʿa*, these ways refer to externals. Insofar as one considers *ādāb* on their own accord, one must speak first about what can be seen but know that good comportment involves a reality far deeper.

Several of the major Ṣūfī figures I have discussed here give accounts that largely conform to MacIntyre's account of practice as I have presented it. Some fit less cleanly, especially those who identify *adab* with interior discipline to the partial or full exclusion of any visible element. The three distinctive elements of al-Sulamī's approach to *ādāb* each comports well with MacIntyre's definition of practice. Al-Sulamī's favour for speaking about *ādāb* in the plural does not impede the parallel with MacIntyre because al-Sulamī so rarely uses the term to describe the minutiae of ritual. Rather, al-Sulamī's *ādāb* act more like aspects or snapshots of the total comportment that a believer can find so difficult to express in words. Al-Sulamī's attempt to define and describe Ṣūfī practice does not 'define' anything in the sense of exhaustive, limiting description, but provides an endlessly snowballing list of moral principles and wise vignettes from the lives of past masters. I have thus favoured 'ways' as a translation for *ādāb* in no small part because this plural word can function well alongside its evocative singular form. Ṣūfīs have their ways, and they journey together along the Way. The same parallel would function if one spoke about Ṣūfī Practice and Ṣūfī practices, or Ṣūfī Custom and Ṣūfī customs, but these English words do not consistently connote the religious and moral seriousness that marked the Ṣūfī masters of the formative period. These masters cultivated intense discipline to excel in their practice. In a certain sense, the goods of that practice were arbitrary; the practice was socially established and constantly evolving as adepts lived into their practice. But, more importantly, their exercise of discipline involved the extension of human powers to achieve internal goods in a transcendent manner.[248]

In relation to *sharīʿa*, MacIntyre's discussion of the importance of rules comes to the fore. MacIntyre insists that persons entering into a practice subject themselves to that practice's standards and to its rules.[249] On its face, this poses no problem for the comparison; al-Sulamī and other apologists for Sufism tirelessly insist, against both their detractors and against pseudo-Ṣūfīs, on the obligations of the *sharīʿa*.

However, one must analyse the nature of the rules obeyed. Much of modern duty-based moral theory involves the centrality of rules, whereas one aspect of Aristotelian virtue theory that MacIntyre desires to retain is a vision of rules as a common set of loves or desires.[250] Ṣūfīs find different ways to express the nature of the *sharīʿa* norms to which they are bound, but if one contrasts an image of the *sharīʿa* as a canon of divine precepts with an image of the *sharīʿa* as a field of shared values, one sees both that the latter comports better with MacIntyre's account and that many Ṣūfīs instinctively find themselves more at home in the latter. Further, if one understands *adab* as Ṣūfī practice, then the standards for excellence in Ṣūfī *ādāb* evolve; the more strongly one asserts this evolution, the more carefully one must distinguish *ādāb* from *sharīʿa*.

Chapter 2

VIRTUE AND CHARACTER IN AL-SULAMĪ'S THOUGHT

This chapter examines the role of virtue and character in the thought of al-Sulamī, with a particular focus on how one develops good character. Having discussed al-Sulamī's understanding of Ṣūfī ways (*ādāb*) in the context of MacIntyre's notion of practice, this chapter explores the relationship between al-Sulamī's understanding of *akhlāq* and that of virtue ethics, past and present. I argue that in the context of al-Sulamī's spiritual pedagogy, *taṣawwuf* functions much like a 'tradition' in MacIntyre's scheme, both regarding the manner in which participation in a tradition affects one's acquisition of virtue and the manner in which rationality and debate evolve within a tradition. The chapter begins by examining philosophical reflections on virtue, both medieval and modern. A survey of how al-Sulamī's near contemporaries discussed this theme gives way to modern reflections on virtue ethics, sharpening the use of terminology and foreshadowing the connections I will draw with al-Sulamī's thought. I argue that, despite some difficulties that hinder the parallel, 'virtues' presents the best translation of *akhlāq* as al-Sulamī understands the term. Persons of noble *akhlāq* have acquired stable human dispositions that enable them to attain the goods of *adab*. I explore some philosophical currents that may have influenced al-Sulamī's understanding of the virtues, concluding that he shows little cognizance of any Greek influence and that a Ṣūfī psychology of spiritual centres informs his approach to *akhlāq* much more than any medieval precursor to virtue ethics as modern scholars usually conceive that approach. Beyond the issue of dependence on foreign influence, the influence of the Path of Blame on al-Sulamī hinders a simple identification of *akhlāq* with virtues. Many virtue theorists, especially Aristotelians, insist that virtues must find outward expression, while al-Sulamī encourages habits for interpersonal relations that outwardly conform to the religious law but do not attempt to garner recognition or renown for one's spiritual advancement. I argue that although al-Sulamī does not intend precisely what Aristotelians denote by 'virtues', that term is the most adequate expression of al-Sulamī's key insights. The virtues al-Sulamī prizes support the practices that enable a believer to perceive the presence of God, especially in the encounter with fellow believers.

What does Athens have to do with Nishapur?

Al-Sulamī lived and worked in a city with a rich philosophical heritage in addition to its outstanding exponents in other fields of knowledge. Assessing al-Sulamī's approach to *akhlāq* thus depends upon an appreciation of philosophical works on ethics and virtue that could have influenced him. In the decades before al-Sulamī was born, Persian-speaking philosophers like Muḥammad b. Zakariyyā' al-Rāzī (d. 313/925), al-Fārābī (d. 339/950) and others facilitated the transmission of ideas from Baghdad outward until Khurasan became a philosophical hotbed in its own right.[1] Abū l-Ḥasan al-ʿĀmirī (d. 381/992) held great prominence locally during al-Sulamī's lifetime and was regarded as 'the Philosopher of Nishapur' until he was eclipsed throughout the region by the genius of Ibn Sīnā (d. 438/1037). Residents of Nishapur had access to Arabic translations of a number of Greek writings, including the works of Aristotle. Al-ʿĀmirī himself authored commentaries on at least three Aristotelian texts. These philosophers assimilated and integrated the pre-Islamic Arabian tradition, Qur'ānic teaching and traditions about the Prophet, as well as elements of Persian and Greek origin. Treatises on Islamic ethics often drew on traditions that the Messenger of God was sent to perfect the traits of a noble character.[2] Scholars in the period therefore often struck a balance, combining the weighty influence of translated Greek texts like Galen's *Fī l-akhlāq* (*On Ethics*) with the norms of the Prophetic *sunna*. The former provided a theoretical framework to consider questions of virtues, vices and character, while the latter remained the recognized standard for living in a virtuous way. Al-ʿĀmirī's work displays this combination most clearly: while he esteems a philosopher like Aristotle for providing general criteria for veracity, he insists that Aristotle cannot furnish a fully developed set of guidelines for life well lived. Only religious knowledge accomplishes this.[3]

Many Muslim philosophers throughout the translation movement and in al-Sulamī's Nishapur shared the misgivings seen in al-ʿĀmirī about the sufficiency of Aristotle. However, certain patterns of reflection on virtue and character initiated by Aristotle, particularly in his *Nicomachean Ethics*, manifest themselves again and again in the most prominent philosophers writing in Arabic.[4] The Christian philosopher Yaḥyā b. ʿAdī (d. 363/974) used his treatise *Tahdhīb al-akhlāq (The Reformation of Morals)* to provide a novel synthesis of Aristotle, Galen and other Greek works.[5] Aḥmad b. Muḥammad Miskawayh's (d. 421/1030)[6] debt to Aristotle is also obvious, although neo-platonic influences led him to take a more intellectualist approach to human fulfilment.[7] Aristotle famously posits happiness (*saʿāda*) as the highest good (*khayr*) that human choices seek, describing happiness as 'a certain activity of the soul in accordance to perfect virtue' (*faḍīla kāmila*).[8] The virtues are neither accidents (*ʿawāriḍ*) nor faculties (*quwā*) but states (*ḥālāt*) that represent a person's behaviour in a general, stable way.[9] When a person actualizes a certain virtue by making decisions in accord with it, these practices become habitual and the person can be said to possess the virtue in question. Yaḥyā, Miskawayh, al-ʿĀmirī and others share this basic approach, with the primary tension being whether true happiness can be pursued in the bodily realm – a life of practical virtue – or whether it consists in a life of perfect contemplation.[10]

Yaḥyā b. ʿAdī and Miskawayh accepted Aristotle's fundamental assumption that no person possesses the virtues by nature. Virtues must be acquired through practice, and the task incumbent upon every rational being is to acquire virtuous traits and to avoid vicious traits.[11] Also like Aristotle, they were less interested in the nature of goodness than they were in becoming good: they inquire pragmatically how one acquires the virtues and grows in them. The virtues are not fully voluntary, in the sense that discrete actions are, but a person nonetheless has power over the virtues by choosing to induce the beginning of a virtue and striving to act in accord with it.[12] Both Yaḥyā and Miskawayh see virtue as a social action, resulting in the purification of the soul from evil.[13] Virtue involves a measure of self-concern but by definition must go beyond oneself to include others.

The treatment of traits

The preceding philosophical reflections emerge from a body of literature dedicated to *akhlāq*, broadly understood as 'ethics'. Modern scholars might differentiate between theological ethics in Islam and religious ethics in Islam, with the former using dialectical methods and rationalist themes and the latter concentrating on the spirit of Islamic morality,[14] but what about Ṣūfī ethics? Scholars assume that Ṣūfī ethics involve selfless behaviour that surpasses the actions required by the divine law, behaviour infused by awareness of the universal presence of God, but the place of Ṣūfī ethics in relation to other approaches to *akhlāq* remains elusive.[15] Increased clarity about the use of certain terms will assist, even though the debate about how to 'characterize' *akhlāq*, if one will pardon the play on words, surpasses simple questions of translation. But starting with those questions, the work of Christian B. Miller illustrates the difficulties at hand, as one considers whether 'character', 'character traits' or 'virtues' would represent *akhlāq* less inadequately. Miller's research bridges analytic philosophy and psychology, using data from the latter to refine the way in which he speaks of virtues and traits. Summarizing his rich body of research would take the present discussion too far afield, but suffice it to say that Miller argues, based on psychological studies, that most people possess neither virtues nor vices, which is to say that most people do not exhibit the types of behaviour and concurrent mental dispositions traditionally described as 'virtuous' or 'vicious' to a degree that would enable researchers to accurately say that those people possess virtues or vices. Rather, Miller argues for what he calls a 'mixed-trait' approach that captures better the complexity and degree of coherence in most people's behaviour. This argument depends upon a sketch of different *genera* of traits, as seen in the figure below (see Figure 2.1).[16]

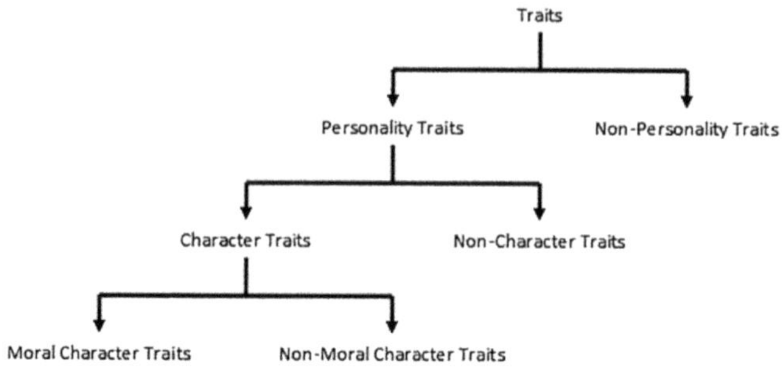

Figure 2.1 Two kinds of character traits

In Miller's schema, a trait is simply a feature or a property of a thing. Some traits are personality traits, meaning that they are concerned with the mental life of a person and express the tendencies or dispositions in that person's mental life; non-personality traits like height or weight are not concerned with mental life. Some personality traits are character traits, meaning that a person who has that trait is, in that respect, an appropriate object of normative assessment by the relevant norms. The relevant norms could be moral, legal, aesthetic or of other types, which drives a distinction between moral character traits and non-moral character traits. Some character traits – being artistic, clever, nervous, logical or witty are among Miller's possible examples – do not permit moral evaluation according to relevant norms in the way that traits like honesty or compassion would. Further, although the resurgence of virtue ethics most commonly involves discussion of virtue and vice in the context of morality, Miller posits the existence of non-moral virtues and vices: excellence in logic would be an epistemic virtue and excellence in art would be an aesthetic virtue. The virtues are good traits of character that dispose their possessor towards good actions done for appropriate reasons.[17] This framework for types of traits presses a question for Ṣūfī studies, as to whether Ṣūfī *akhlāq* are necessarily moral, or whether Ṣūfī literature might hold some examples of *akhlāq* in unambiguously non-moral contexts.

MacIntyre on tradition and virtue

With Miller's schema in mind, one can turn back to two key concepts from MacIntyre's writings – tradition and virtue – to analyse their functions vis-à-vis *taṣawwuf* and *akhlāq*. In Chapter 1, I argued that MacIntyre's notion of practice adequately expresses al-Sulamī's core insights regarding *adab*. Recall that for MacIntyre, tradition is a broader concept than practice: a tradition is a larger reality composed of sets of practices. The importance of tradition in MacIntyre's scheme comes from its epistemic function: a tradition shapes and bounds what practitioners can know. MacIntyre acknowledges that his notion of tradition involves a departure from Aristotle insofar as MacIntyre insists upon a historically grounded epistemology.[18] Against the Enlightenment confidence that human reason can function in a vacuum, MacIntyre argues that one can only understand a tradition's teachings as a commentary on or a reaction to the teachings that preceded them.[19] Such an approach comports well with al-Sulamī's understanding of the development of Ṣūfī history. One may justly accuse al-Sulamī of artificially tempering some very real differences between the various early Ṣūfī masters he chronicles in *Ṭabaqāt al-ṣūfiyya*, but he allows a significant measure of diversity to stand. He sees a consistent, constitutive core to the Ṣūfī tradition, a core that remains faithful to the Prophet's *sunna*, but he has no problem acknowledging the transformation and evolution of this tradition. Al-Sulamī's Sufism is dynamic, in flux and changing with the new questions and challenges that face it. His reverence for the *ahl al-ḥadīth* shows his assumption about the consistent, golden cord of knowledge that ties the tradition together, and the diversity of complementary spiritual currents does not annul the unity of this tradition.

A number of modern specialists in Islamic Studies turn to Talal Asad's understanding of tradition and discourse as a resource for their work.[20] I favour MacIntyre's account of tradition for several reasons, not the least of which being the high degree of commitment and investment from the practitioner that MacIntyre assumes. This assumption fits well with the medieval mystics at the centre of the present study, not because al-Sulamī, al-Qushayrī and similar masters were a full-time 'professional Ṣūfīs' but because of the intensity with which they strove for excellence in the practices that constitute *taṣawwuf*.[21] A tradition consists of sets of practices, so someone like al-Sulamī could strive for excellence in Ṣūfī *adab*, in jurisprudence, in mathematics and as a cobbler, each of these being practices in their own right. Al-Sulamī only strove for excellence in the first of these, but many Ṣūfīs were also jurists, *ḥadīth* transmitters or other devotees of practices present within the tradition. Speaking about *taṣawwuf* as a tradition in the MacIntyrean sense underscores both the variety of practices that could fall under the aegis of Sufism in the case of individual believers and the level of commitment presupposed on the part of the adherents. Here, following on the discussion of *adab* in Chapter 1, one might consider alternative schemes for how these practices fit together.

From the beginning of the Ṣūfī movement, its critics have asserted that its adherents embrace practices that are not sanctioned by the divine law. At the very least, Sufism involves a troublesome embrace of elements that are licit but outside the mainstream; more frequently, critics claim that Ṣūfīs take part in proscribed innovations and antinomian behaviour.[22] Figure 2.2 illustrates the reality of Sufism according to this criticism: much of Ṣūfī practice conforms to the divine law, but *taṣawwuf* contains many elements that are beyond the pale. A different schema – the schema that accords better with the self-understanding of al-Sulamī and many of his contemporaries – conceives the Ṣūfī tradition as a subset of Islamic practice, entirely subsumed within the divine law.

Figure 2.3 comes closer to the relationship between *taṣawwuf* and Islam in the mind of al-Sulamī. All Ṣūfī *ādāb* fall within the scope of the divine law, which does not imply that every single Muslim will adopt Ṣūfī *ādāb*. The dictates of the divine law are necessarily situational. Duties and prohibitions adhere when the relevant circumstances are present to trigger them, and likewise, not every Muslim

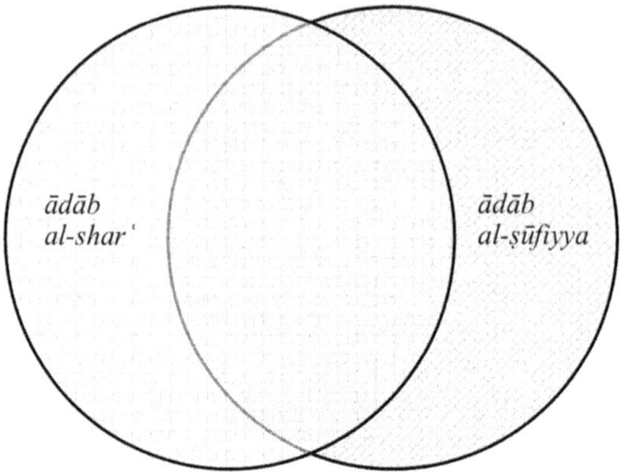

Figure 2.2 Overlap between the divine law and Sufism

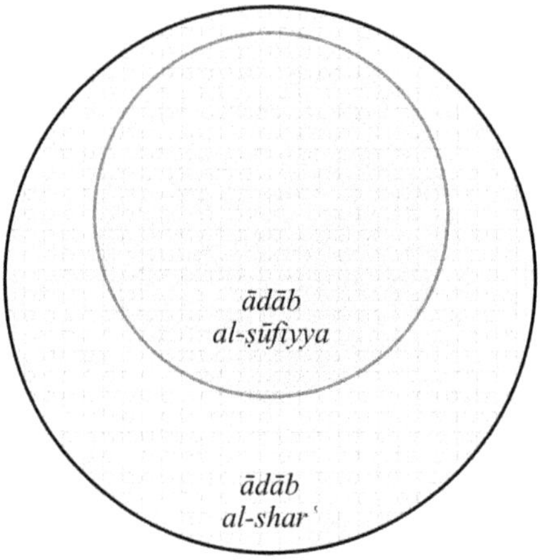

Figure 2.3 Sufism subsumed within the divine law

will encounter circumstances in which *ādāb al-ṣūfiyya* become relevant. Figure 2.3 thus expresses al-Sulamī's mind, but it could leave the mistaken impression that *taṣawwuf* functions as a practice in the MacIntyrean sense. Instead, al-Sulamī quietly understands Sufism as a larger reality that combines and integrates different sets of practices into itself; *taṣawwuf* serves as an umbrella concept, a mantle that gathers in spiritual currents of diverse origins. Whereas in Baghdad, Sufism began with a circle of believers clustered around a set of practices that – despite any disagreements or tensions within the circle[23] – they fundamentally shared, al-Sulamī's contribution lies in maintaining diverse streams of mystical spirituality in a creative tension with each other, under the mantle of *taṣawwuf*.

Several spiritual currents cross-pollenated in Khurasan to produce the Sufism that emerged there in the generation after al-Sulamī. Rehearsing the process

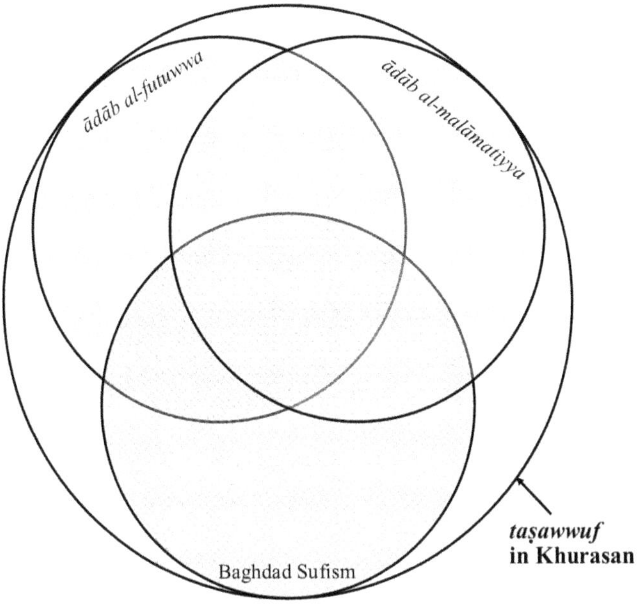

Figure 2.4 Spiritual currents constituting Sufism in Khurasan

of this integration is not necessary here, as other scholarly histories of Islamic mysticism have already done so effectively.[24] It suffices to note that the *adab* of each of these three currents functions as a fair analogue for a practice, each with its own internal goods and evolving standards of excellence. Their combination in Khurasan initially led to texts contrasting the approaches of Khurasan's Ṣūfīs and Iraq's Ṣūfīs, as one sees in certain passages of al-Sulamī,[25] but eventually it led to the total effacement of the Malāmatiyya as a spiritual trend distinct from Sufism and to the emergence of *taṣawwuf* as the unifying marker of identity that characterized the mystically inclined in that region. Sufism served as the larger tradition to which spiritual seekers adhered, and they strove to develop the virtues distinctive to that tradition.

MacIntyre knits his concepts of practice, tradition and virtue closely together. Traditions consist of sets of practices, and the virtues are those dispositions that sustain practices and enable persons to achieve the goods internal to practices.[26] Virtues are not merely skills that enable the efficient accomplishment of particular tasks; the goods internal to practices demand specific excellences that distinguish one set of practices from other different sets of practices.[27] Considered alongside al-Sulamī's conception of *ādāb* and *akhlāq*, MacIntyre's understanding of the relationship between virtues and practices is counter-intuitive. Virtues seem to serve practices, and one might instinctively resist the idea that al-Sulamī's *akhlāq* could serve *ādāb*, given that al-Sulamī frames *akhlāq* as a higher stage in the hierarchy of spiritual growth. But when one looks deeper, one sees that *akhlāq* do serve *ādāb*, because *akhlāq* are the stable dispositions that enable a believer to persevere in proper practice (*adab*). A believer takes the initial steps along the path by voluntarily learning proper *adab* and striving to actualize it, but the acquired human qualities – *akhlāq* – that facilitate ongoing achievement in *adab* result from a combination of human volition and divine volition. God responds to the good actions of God's servants by adorning them with noble *akhlāq*, and these dispositions themselves serve the servant because they keep the servant directed towards the proper goods for which an authentic servant should strive.

Ṣūfī psychology

One of the stark differences between al-Sulamī's approach to virtue and that of the philosophers stands in the disparity between their understandings of the constitution of and the organization of the soul. Yaḥyā b. ʿAdī and Miskawayh generally accept the platonic tripartite division of the appetitive, irascible and rational soul, and contemporary philosophers draw upon it with modifications as they see necessary.[28] This psychology yields a schema of the cardinal virtues that enable the three faculties of the soul to act in harmony with each other,[29] but absent a platonic psychology, such a schema of the cardinal virtues loses some of its persuasive force. However, abandoning platonic psychology does not mean one must jettison with it the notion of virtue. Scholars in other traditions, whether ancient, medieval or modern, can and do sustain robust accounts of the virtues built upon radically different psychologies.[30] Such is true for al-Sulamī. His understanding of *akhlāq* depends upon his Ṣūfī psychology, a schema involving mystical stations and spiritual centres of perception that neither acknowledge nor manifest a debt to the Greek tradition.

The stations (maqāmāt)

Ṣūfī manuals in the formative period nearly always describe progress on the spiritual path in terms of *maqāmāt*. Some stations, like *tawba*, are normally framed as initial stages on the path, while others are higher, but masters do not posit a fixed hierarchy of ascent up a ladder, with stations occurring in the same sequence for every wayfarer. Rather, the stations represent various periods in a believer's *sulūk* in which a certain emotion, or perhaps better, a certain mode of apprehending God and the world, predominates. The idea that a traveler passes through stations was not the exclusive purchase of Ṣūfī masters, as poets also described the stations of love,[31] but the image of the mystical stations was particularly ubiquitous in *taṣawwuf*. Dhū l-Nūn al-Miṣrī famously distinguished between the mystical stations (*maqāmāt*) and the mystical states (*aḥwāl*), and early Ṣūfīs generally assumed that the difference lay in the duration and constancy of the experience. States are transitory and might be only momentary; stations involve longer duration, and a believer generally remains in one station until passing over to another. Al-Sulamī generally concurs with reigning assumptions about the fleeting nature of the states, assumptions he inherited from al-Junayd and his followers,[32] but by comparison with some other Ṣūfīs in the formative period, al-Sulamī's use of the term *maqāmāt* is less central and less consistent. He does not always separate the states from the stations,[33] even speaking in one place of 'the states of the stations'.[34] Elsewhere, he speaks about traversing the stations by means of the states, further muddying the distinction between these terms.[35] In one text, he seems to use the terms *maḥall* and *maqām* synonymously.[36] Further, within one treatise, he defines the term *maqām* in two different ways. The beginning of *Manāhij al-ʿārifīn* (*The Pathways of the Gnostics*) includes the line, 'Ṣūfism has a beginning, an end and stations (*maqāmāt*).'[37] Al-Sulamī later claims that 'God disposed the means to arrive at the realities according to stations (*maqāmāt*) and stages (*darajāt*)', specifying that some of the stations are the station of health (*ṣalāḥ*), the station of the martyrs and the station of the truthful (*ṣiddīqūn*).[38] At the conclusion of the treatise, al-Sulamī adds that 'Sufism has three spheres (*maqāmāt*): ways (*ādāb*), virtues (*akhlāq*) and states (*aḥwāl*). Ways are acquired, virtues involve a model for imitation and states are a gift (*mawhiba*).'[39] Here we see the same threefold hierarchy already mentioned – *ādāb, akhlāq* and *aḥwāl* – but gathered under the heading of *maqām*. Al-Sulamī chooses not to wed himself to a technical definition of *maqām*. Thibon correctly analyses that in *Manāhij al-ʿārifīn* the first usage of *maqām* has a dynamic and progressive character; a believer advances through a series of stations.[40] The final usage involves enumerating constitutive elements, rendered more complicated by the fact that the constitutive elements named – *ādāb*, *akhlāq* and *aḥwāl* – can each be further subdivided into different stages or elements. One may summarize by noting that like his contemporaries, al-Sulamī provides lists of some of the virtues and spiritual states, but unlike some of his contemporaries, he neither relies on the term *maqām* nor consistently invests it with technical meaning. He remains committed to the Ṣūfī vision of religio-moral growth as a journey along a path, but the stations do not provide his default mode or his preferred image to express progress on the path.

I have dwelled on al-Sulamī's usage of *maqām* to highlight an element of Atif Khalil's monograph on *tawba* in early Sufism, a book that draws extensively on al-Sulamī.[41] One novel element of Khalil's study is the author's consistent description of the *maqāmāt* as 'virtues'. He writes: 'The *maqām* is supposed to be a virtue that becomes embedded within the soul, typically following a rigorous process of spiritual and ethical training. It is a virtue acquired through the effort and exertion of the *sālik*, the traveler.'[42] Al-Sulamī presents a challenge to Khalil's approach due to al-Sulamī's inconsistent use of the term, but the more significant prima facie challenge for other mystical writers in the period is the notion of progression from one station to another. The problem is not that advancing from one station to another involves the abandonment of the former station, discarding one's previous experiences. When an early Ṣūfī author claims that a traveler has surpassed a station and reached another, the reader must presume that the traveler has integrated the knowledge and the experience of the lower station into newly acquired and more profound knowledge and experience. In a sense, the traveler surpasses a station while still retaining it. Rather, the problem lies in the assumption that advancing from lower stations to higher stations involves the acquisition of novel experiences, and Ṣūfī authors did not tend to chart such a progression within the *akhlāq*. For his part, al-Sulamī certainly does not articulate such a progression within the *akhlāq*. He does claim that a believer grows in the virtues – *al-takhalluq bi-akhlāq al-mashāyikh* (or *bi-akhlāq Allāh*) does not happen overnight – but this growth does not seem to involve acquiring new virtues like generosity, humility or forbearance one by one in the way that a believer passes into a new *maqām*.

Spiritual centres

If al-Sulamī's approach to the *maqāmāt* was less consistent than some of his near contemporaries, he left a deeper mark on the Ṣūfī tradition with his seminal reflections on the subtle spiritual centres. Here, his work to map a recognizably Ṣūfī geography of the soul provided a foundation upon which later Ṣūfīs would build. He was not the first mystic to develop such thinking, and his own reflections are not absolutely uniform, but the key elements of later Ṣūfī psychology can be found in his œuvre.[43] While philosophers preferred to speak about the faculties (*quwā*) of the soul, al-Sulamī and later Ṣūfīs distinguished spiritual centres (*laṭāʾif*).[44] In al-Sulamī's schema, one moves through these centres, progressing from the ego-self (*nafs*) to the heart (*qalb*) to the secret (*sirr*) to the spirit (*rūḥ*), with ever-increasing levels of interiorization and growth.[45] Each of these four *laṭāʾif* has its own particular area of experience, from grosser to subtler. The higher spiritual centres are cognizant of the centres inferior to them, but when one rises to a higher centre, the lower centres do not sense this ascent. The lower centres do, however, perceive as ostentatious and inappropriate what becomes manifest in a higher centre. In this regard, these spiritual centres act as independent loci of perception, though they are not each capable of perceiving the same realities. The practical value of this fourfold psychology is clearest when al-Sulamī applies it to *dhikr*, as he uses *dhikr* to describe the different and ever-deepening levels by and in which one encounters God through this ritual practice. A believer moves from *dhikr* of the tongue to that of the heart, secret and spirit.[46] Each level of *dhikr* carries its own unique risk in relation to the other spiritual centres. While the secret may not be conscious of the spirit as spirit, the secret is aware that something else is occurring and can resist the remembrance of God. Access to multiple spiritual centres signifies noteworthy spiritual advancement, evidenced by the fact that in several passages, al-Sulamī speaks about multiple centres in discussion of *faqr*. The true *faqīr* is rare, but as al-Sulamī quotes Ruwaym, the *faqīr* guards his *sirr*, protects his *nafs* and observes all religious duties.[47] Authentic *faqr* 'is the emptiness of the ego-self, the heart, and the inner secret of any content, whether possessions, judgments, or pretences'.[48]

While the notion of progress from one centre to another suggests a parallel with the *maqāmāt* – and a mystic no less profound than al-Ḥakīm al-Tirmidhī uses the term *maqām* in this way[49] – al-Sulamī sees the spiritual centres as living organs of apprehension. They are loci that actively perceive God and the world and that are acted upon; al-Sulamī does not speak about the *maqāmāt* as having agency in themselves. Several major scholars of al-Sulamī therefore rely on this fourfold psychology of the *laṭāʾif* as a schema for his understanding of spiritual growth.[50]

Many texts in his corpus distinguish in different ways between the spirit, secret, heart and ego-self,[51] but he sets out the fourfold theory clearly in *Risālat al-malāmatiyya*, and occasional references elsewhere to these spiritual centres depend on that treatise to give them their full context. Dyads of the ego-self and heart or the heart and the secret often appear in a manner consistent with the full schema but lacking one or two key terms. Elsewhere, a different term might substitute for one of these spiritual centres. *Ṣadr* can stand in for *qalb* in one place[52] while functioning as a spiritual centre in its own right, alongside the heart and the secret, in another.[53] Each of these spiritual centres – or perhaps better, spiritual organs[54] – therefore merits brief discussion in turn to attain a full understanding of al-Sulamī's image of the human person and ground his understanding of the virtues.

The ego-self (nafs)

By comparison with philosophers who used *nafs* to translate the Greek *psychē*, al-Sulamī employs a more restricted, localized and disparaging understanding of *nafs*. Like many of his Ṣūfī predecessors, he relies heavily on the notion of the *nafs* as the ego-self. His student al-Qushayrī sums up Ṣūfī usage of the term: 'In [the Arabic] language, a thing's *nafs* is its being. However, when the Sufis utter the word *nafs*, they imply neither being nor a [physical] body. Rather, they imply the deficiencies of one's character traits (*awṣāf*) as well as one's reprehensible morals (*akhlāq*) and deeds (*af'āl*).'[55] For al-Sulamī, the *nafs* signifies mere physicality: at this level, one sees with only one's physical eyes. It represents the initial level of progress – or rather, one's place of departure, because at the level of the *nafs*, one has made no progress at all.

Al-Sulamī's fullest description of the *nafs* occurs in *'Uyūb al-nafs wa-mudāwātuhā (The Maladies of the Soul and Their Remedies)*, a treatise that both conforms to and resists the fourfold schema just described. In keeping with the sense of the *nafs* as the ego-self, *'Uyūb al-nafs* offers a dark and pessimistic psychology. The treatise also complicates a discussion of the spiritual centres because al-Sulamī subdivides the *nafs* into three parts (*aqsām*).[56] He cites Qur'ānic verses to support his distinction between the soul that incites to evil (*nafs ammāra bi-l-sū'*),[57] the blaming soul (*nafs lawwāma*)[58] and the soul at peace (*nafs muṭma'inna*).[59] While several modern scholars have examined the parallel between Ṣūfī notions of the lower self or carnal soul and platonic ideas about the appetitive soul, al-Sulamī does not seem influenced by the Greek tradition, and the three *aqsām* are doubtlessly not the Qur'ānic equivalents for the Greek rational (Ar. *nāṭiqa*; Gr. *logistikon*), spirited (Ar. *ghaḍabiyya*; Gr. *thymoeidēs*) and appetitive (Ar. *shahwāniyya*; Gr. *epithymētikon*) souls.[60] He frames his partition of the soul as a response to the Qur'ānic voice, and when one factors in the antecedent traditions of the Path of Blame, *futuwwa*, and early Sufism, one has no need to posit a Greek influence in order to account for al-Sulamī's thinking here. Curiously, this three-part framework does no real work for al-Sulamī in the remainder of *'Uyūb al-nafs*. One may assume that the maladies he discusses adhere to the soul that incites to evil, but the distinction between these souls does not play a role in the 'soul therapy' that occurs through the various remedies al-Sulamī proposes. Likewise, the three *aqsām* do not return in his other writings. This absence shows that the Path of Blame left a deep but uneven mark upon al-Sulamī's geography of the soul. The assumptions of the Malāmatiyya regarding the inclination of the *nafs* towards sin run through both *'Uyūb al-nafs* and *Risālat al-malāmatiyya*, which rely heavily on the Qur'ānic notion of the soul that incites to evil.[61] But *'Uyūb al-nafs* lacks the four spiritual centres so important to *Risālat al-malāmatiyya*, indicating that al-Sulamī has not attempted to integrate the discourse of the Path of Blame comprehensively. That he fails to smooth over differences and harmonize tensions regarding customs and etiquette does not surprise, as the Path of Blame was much more a spiritual trend than a 'school' with clearly defined rules.[62] But that he fails to do so regarding the infrastructure of the soul leaves open questions regarding al-Sulamī's thinking here. He doubtlessly assumes that the *nafs* inclines towards evil, that self-delusion constitutes a part of this inclination and that this self-delusion renders the *nafs* vulnerable to diabolic manipulation,[63] but al-Sulamī does not attempt to map the soul with the precision that will be seen in some of his successors in *taṣawwuf*.

Despite his pessimistic assessment of the *nafs*, al-Sulamī's denigration of the flesh is not absolute. He does not scorn the body as such but the tendency of our physical self towards self-absorption. A Ṣūfī must then doubt his ego-self at all times.[64] Until a person recognizes and understands this inclination of the ego-self towards fruitless desires, vanity and pride will dominate,[65] but if a person recognizes this inclination, the practical strategies al-Sulamī offers in *'Uyūb al-nafs* enable a believer to address and remedy the defects that exist. Without such self-awareness – or better, *nafs*-awareness – the ego-self naturally busies itself with the defects of others while remaining blind to its own defects.[66] The true objective of the Path of Blame emerges here: one does not blame oneself in order to focus on oneself. One blames oneself – in conjunction with silence about the faults of others – to overcome the tendency of the *nafs* towards self-reference and self-concern. Disdain for the ego-self lies behind all the duties of Sufism. Al-Sulamī's grandfather Ibn Nujayd taught him that 'he to whom his ego-self has been kind, his religion will become of little importance.'[67] Al-Sulamī thus shuns anything pleasurable to the ego-self and holds it in disdain,[68] leading also to hesitance about the *dhikr* of the tongue. This more physical *dhikr* can be pleasurable in a base way because it leaves one too conscious of oneself and one's own pleasure.[69] A Ṣūfī should aspire to a higher *dhikr*, because the purpose of *dhikr* is to pass out of oneself.[70] True progress on the path occurs and new avenues of contact with God open up when the submission of the *nafs* occurs in conjunction with the next discrete spiritual centre, the heart (*qalb*).[71]

*The heart (*qalb*)*

Ṣūfī masters refer frequently to the *qalb*, even calling at times the field of knowledge dedicated to interior growth the 'science of the heart' (*'ilm al-qalb*).[72] Al-Sulamī's usage shows all the flexibility that marks the prominent Ṣūfī masters who preceded him. Qur'ānic incidences of *qalb* connote at different points the heart as a centre of knowledge, of intellect, of belief, of emotion and of volition, but Ṣūfī reflection on the heart further expanded the range of this term.[73] Al-Ḥakīm al-Tirmidhī used *qalb* as the comprehensive term for all of a person's interior stations.[74] Al-Sulamī records a teaching of al-Tustarī along the same lines. Commenting on the verse, 'Your Lord knows best what is in your souls',[75] al-Tustarī interprets the Qur'ānic *anfusikum* (your selves/souls) as *qulūbikum* (your hearts), because the heart unites the intellect, the spirit, the soul and one's desires.[76] At the same time, al-Sulamī, al-Tustarī and others spoke about the heart as one specific component of this inner life, often taking care to express whether they used the term in an inclusive sense or in a more focused sense.

When he speaks for himself rather than transmitting the teachings of others, al-Sulamī often proceeds as though the ego-self and the heart made decisions independently about whether to yield to reformation; when the *nafs* and *qalb* respond in the same way, God protects them and raises them up to God.[77] Al-Sulamī's description of the heart retains the physicality that marks his description of the *nafs*,[78] but the heart possesses an increased level of perception for divine things: he speaks about the awareness (*murāqaba*) of the heart.[79] He transmits many Qur'ānic interpretations that use the non-Qur'ānic root *l-ḥ-ẓ* to describe the attentiveness of a believer's heart.[80] The heart acts as a meeting place, a reception hall, for the encounter with God through meditation and reflection.[81] The *qalb* thus occupies an intermediate realm, that is able to perceive both mundane and heavenly things,[82] and must be protected from the very real possibility that it fixate on the things of this world.[83] Al-Sulamī suggests in several places that reflection (*tafakkur*) is the Ṣūfī activity proper to the heart.[84] He does not directly associate the rational intellect with the heart, but neither does he limit the heart to an association with emotions, desires or feelings. The heart acts as a seat of knowledge in a more comprehensive and inclusive sense,[85] and his citation of a *ḥadīth qudsī* in which the heart is the subject of the verb *ya'qalu* should be understood in this broader sense.[86] The heart accepts and absorbs the divine spark, the light of faith,[87] both enabling and pulling the Ṣūfī onward. The heart's knowing can carry the ego-self into a transformation of the blameworthy aspects of the ego-self's nature.[88] For this reason, although al-Sulamī sees the ego-self and the heart as separate 'organs' that can stand in tension with each other,[89] he posits a strong correspondence in their orientation towards God or lack thereof. Al-Sulamī cites a *ḥadīth* to this effect: 'In the body, there is a piece of flesh (*muḍgha*); if it becomes sound (*idhā ṣalaḥat*), the rest of the body is sound.'[90]

Etymologically, *qalb* draws upon meanings of motion, transition and change.[91] Al-Sulamī utilizes this background to describe the heart at its worst. He cites al-Junayd's description of the difference between spiritual insight (*firāsa*) and speculation (*ẓann*). Speculation evokes the palpitations of the heart, the vicissitudes of a wandering, fickle mind unable to settle or find peace. Spiritual insight emerges when stillness settles upon the heart, granting a believer miraculous insight beyond normal sensory perception.[92] This insight occurs due to God's light, which illuminates the heart and enables it to see beyond what it could previously apprehend.[93] Sometimes this insight involves intuition about another's inner life, but al-Sulamī recounts many stories of the supernatural clairvoyance exhibited by the Prophet's companions, who could make accurate judgments about matters like an alleged act of adultery without having personally witnessed the events.[94] In addition to stillness, al-Sulamī draws heavily on the notion of purity when discussing the heart[95] and occasionally on the imagery of absence and emptiness.[96] In the absence of all aversion, opposition or grumbling, the heart rests in agreement with what the Lord has set forth for the believer.[97] Only freedom from the desires (*shahwāt*) that typically plague the ego-self can grant the heart satisfaction (*riḍā*) and peace.[98]

*The [inner] secret (*sirr*) and the spirit (*rūḥ*)*

Al-Sulamī never states his intention to focus his reflection on the ego-self and the heart at the expense of the loftier spiritual centres, but perhaps the manifest failure of most believers to recognize their *nafs* for what it is and overcome it leads him to do precisely this. He mentions the third and fourth spiritual centres, the [inner] secret (*sirr*) and spirit (*rūḥ*), far less frequently than the ego-self or heart, and with the exception of the capacity of the secret and spirit for the contemplation (*mushāhada*) of God,[99] the difference between the two is murky.[100] At times he even blurs the difference between the heart and the secret.[101] Both the heart and the secret act as the subject of *firāsa*.[102] When the light of God floods one's secret, one feels that the light has unveiled (*kashf*) the truth about good and evil and pulled the curtains down on realities that a person could otherwise not perceive.[103] Al-Sulamī's discussion of the secret also draws upon the same vocabulary of purity, emptiness and stillness with which he discusses the heart.[104] Muḥammad of course stands as the perfect example of a pure and empty secret. God preserved Muḥammad's *sirr* by cutting it off from all other things so that he could gaze upon his Lord with the eye of certainty.[105] He also connects the secret to the station of certainty (*yaqīn*). If the purity of a believer's secret is made certain, then many other things will be revealed: a believer will recognize and understand the defects in his knowledge, religious duties, strivings, moral behaviour, desires, customs and more.[106] The secret must not expect or desire anything in this world but come to gentle acceptance;[107] for this reason, the *sirr* acts as the organ of self-control.[108] Authentic *faqr* occurs when the secret is vacant, for this places a person in complete dependence on God who alone is sufficient (*al-Kāfī*).[109] At the level of spiritual practices like *dhikr*, al-Sulamī places the secret and the spirit in a manifest hierarchy above the ego-self and the heart.[110] Al-Sulamī mentions the spirit the least frequently of all the spiritual centres.[111] Al-Sulamī attributes to Abū l-Ḥusayn al-Nūrī (d. 295/907), the highly eccentric associate of al-Junayd, a comment on a Qur'ānic verse mentioning *rūḥ*. This enables al-Sulamī to connect the verse to spiritual insight and contemplation.[112] He draws on images of purity, as with other spiritual centres, and uses esoteric interpretation of letters to link the spirit to love (*ḥubb*),[113] but all in all, al-Sulamī's understanding of the spirit remains underdeveloped by comparison.[114]

One should not wrongly assume that al-Sulamī consistently relies on these four *laṭāʾif* as a schema that governs his discussion of the soul throughout his literary corpus. To the contrary, al-Sulamī occasionally inverts the hierarchy of these spiritual centres, makes inclusions or exclusions[115] or uses one of them to stand for the entire person rather than a specific organ.[116] He also draws upon other imagery, like *ʿayn*, *ṣadr*, *fuʾād*, *ʿaql*, *baṭn* and *badan*, albeit not with the frequency of the main four already discussed. One should not attempt to extract a system from al-Sulamī's scattered, diverse statements,[117] but if one accepts that such language to describe the believer's inner life may be elusive and slippery, the spiritual geography of the *laṭāʾif* clarify al-Sulamī's constant concern for integration between what is external and what is internal. When a believer's visible actions and attitudinal orientation move in unity, access to the loftier spiritual centres becomes possible. The journey to access the loftier centres is better conceived as a progressive journey inward than as a pitched struggle between autonomous faculties. He favours these names – the ego-self, the heart, the secret and the spirit – to identify the locations of this ongoing spiritual growth, to isolate a place where the ideals of purity, emptiness, poverty and obedience can reside. At the risk of stretching a metaphor too far, emptiness cannot occur in a vacuum. It needs a place. Emptiness demands a space that becomes empty. The *laṭāʾif* function effectively for al-Sulamī because they name the locations of these levels of spiritual growth for the believer who lives in integration.

Al-Sulamī's notion of akhlāq

This discussion of spiritual centres provides just one more example of a hierarchy active in al-Sulamī's understanding of the spiritual life. The hierarchy of *ādāb*, *akhlāq* and *aḥwāl* involves both inward and outward elements, as progress occurs when believers integrate their visible behaviours with the invisible orientations of their soul. The spiritual centres, by contrast, involve a hierarchy entirely contained within one's inner life, albeit one that still manifests al-Sulamī's concern with integration. For maximal spiritual growth, these different organs of perception must function well together, operating in tandem. When they do, a believer gains increasingly full perception of divine realities. To return now to the discussion of the virtues, one may note an important parallel to the way the spiritual centres function: the labour begins with the believer, in an effort to overcome the *nafs* and to practice proper ways. A believer must struggle and strive to subdue the ego-self. The higher spiritual organs respond to God's activity, whether one uses the imagery of the divine light, the divine breath or others. Here too, the perception of the *qalb*, *sirr* and *rūḥ* acts in parallel with al-Sulamī's understanding of *akhlāq*, because the transformation of one's *akhlāq* depends upon divine assistance. Indeed, the prominent role God plays in the acquisition of virtue contrasts al-Sulamī's usage of the term *akhlāq* with various philosophers. Al-Sulamī assumes that believers will not experience a transformation of their morals without making free choices to walk the necessary path: one must decide to make real the ethics that characterize the Ṣūfī brotherhood. However, he likewise asserts that God grants a believer virtues (*awrathahu Allāh tilka l-akhlāq*) like modesty, generosity or courage,[118] and that God adorns (*zayyana*) a believer with them.[119] Once a Ṣūfī grows in discipline by means of *ādāb*, God assists him along the path. This assistance differs from the matter of mystical states, in which the initiative and the agency clearly belong to God alone. Based on one's effort, one has good cause to hope that God will grant the blessing of mystical states, but this is far less certain than the transformation of *akhlāq* many believers experience. The mystical states are a pure gift of mercy that descend upon a Ṣūfī and open the Ṣūfī's heart.[120]

Apart from the question of direct divine assistance, al-Sulamī conceives the believer's volition in the transformation of *akhlāq* differently than do the philosophers. Yaḥyā b. ʿAdī, for example, defines moral qualities (*akhlāq*) as states in which one performs actions 'without deliberation or study'.[121] Miskawayh agrees, aspiring to enable people to acquire a noble character (*khuluq sharīf*).[122] In virtue theory, the fact that an agent need not think about an action before performing it does not annul the agent's volition. The agent had previously made free choices to begin the reformation of morals and persist in this, so the agent's current stable states of moral perception and behaviour do result from the agent's volition even if the agent does not seem to make deliberate, free, discrete decisions at the present moment. This conforms to al-Sulamī's understanding of *akhlāq*, with the caveat that he shows less confidence about the permanence of a believer's *akhlāq*. His preferred terms for stable characteristics are *awṣāf* and *ṣifāt*, and he often uses *akhlāq* in parallel with commands (*awāmir*) and actions (*afʿāl*), wilful deeds by which a believer kills the ego-self and what remains of its stirrings.[123] The accumulation of these deeds over time grants *akhlāq* stability – al-Sulamī's use of the phrase *takhallaqa bi-hādhihi l-akhlāq*[124] suggests that the change is lasting and not momentary – but the particular decisions that constitute and facilitate the desired moral and religious transformation never depart the picture for al-Sulamī. God completes and perfects the servant's efforts,[125] granting *akhlāq* as an adornment that distinguishes a sincere servant from others, but servants must choose to continue to behave in this pleasing way. He presumes that someone who has developed good character will remain in good character but more actively considers the possibility of regression than do medieval Arab philosophers.

Thus far, one sees that al-Sulamī's understanding of *akhlāq* is constant, not momentary, even though it is not as stable as the disposition described by some philosophers. One also sees the role of divine assistance in the acquisition of these dispositions. The question of the number and classification of these dispositions yet remains. Virtue ethicists often develop their reflections with a list in mind – even if that list is not comprehensive – of the major virtues that a human being might strive to acquire. The four cardinal virtues are merely the best-known instance of this approach. Al-Sulamī makes no such attempt to catalogue the virtues. He rarely uses the term *faḍīla* (pl. *faḍāʾil*), the term commonly translated as 'virtue' in philosophical texts, though his use of *khuluq* (pl. *akhlāq*) to refer to a stable disposition or state does cohere with texts by

Galen and Yaḥyā. They seem to use *akhlāq* and *faḍā'il* as a genus to a species; *akhlāq* are stable dispositions, regardless of their morality, and *faḍā'il* meritorious stable dispositions (virtues).[126] Al-Sulamī never lists the *akhlāq*, and some of the character traits reckoned as virtues (*faḍā'il*) by other medieval scholars writing in Arabic appear among al-Sulamī's stations (*maqāmāt*) and states (*aḥwāl*), not among al-Sulamī's *akhlāq*. Al-Sulamī does, however, occasionally provide illustrative examples of the *akhlāq*. 'Regarding the virtues, they are good character, generosity, humility, forbearance, accepting judgments with contentment, and minimizing disharmony with the brothers.'[127] He attributes sayings about the *akhlāq* of the substitutes (*abdāl*) to Sarī l-Saqaṭī (d. 251/865)[128] in at least two places. 'Among the virtues of the substitutes is blamelessness of heart and sincere counsel for the brothers.'[129] 'Five things belong to the virtues of the substitutes: scrupulous inquiry, making spiritual aspiration authentic, blamelessness of heart, compassion for people and sincere counsel for them.'[130] Although his emphasis shifts according to the objective of the text in question, if one attempted to construct a composite list of the Sulamaic virtues, pardon and forgiveness would probably top the list, with generosity, courage, compassion and blamelessness of heart not far behind. Late in the treatise *Kitāb ādāb al-ṣuḥba*, he specifies some examples of *maḥāsin al-akhlāq*.

> Among its ways is to develop excellent virtues (*yatakhallaq bi-maḥāsin al-akhlāq*) and to use discernment in companionship (*yatamayyaz fī l-ṣuḥba*). I heard … al-Jurayrī say, 'The fullness of a man consists in three things: voluntary exile, companionship, and cleverness. As for voluntary exile, it consists in overcoming the ego-self. As for companionship, it consists in developing the virtues of [excellent] men. As for cleverness, it consists in discernment.'[131]

This brief teaching demonstrates the breadth of companionship in al-Sulamī's imagination, which will be the focus of the next chapter. Any growth in virtue contributes to one's living as an authentic companion.

The absence in al-Sulamī's corpus of a clean-cut taxonomy of the virtues does not dilute the general coherence between his approach to character development and that of other virtue theorists. Yaḥyā and Miskawayh had clear catalogues of the virtues, but many other virtue theorists did not, and such lists are less common for virtue ethics today. MacIntyre, for all his effort to reinvigorate virtue ethics, never offers such a list. Although fully engaged with classical categorizations of the virtues, MacIntyre willingly departs from them when circumstances demand it. The standout example, predictable given MacIntyre's diagnosis of the ills of modern philosophy, is this: the virtue of having an adequate sense of the traditions to which one belongs. MacIntyre's description of this virtue fits al-Sulamī to a tee, a spiritual master who framed himself as a mere compiler of his tradition's wisdom.

> In practical reasoning the possession of this virtue is not manifested so much in the knowledge of a set of generalizations or maxims which may provide our practical inferences with major premises; its presence or absence rather appears

> in the kind of capacity for judgment which the agent possesses in knowing how to select among the relevant stack of maxims and how to apply them in particular situations.[132]

What MacIntyre describes here is closest to the Arabic notion *muḥāḍara*, the intuition of a great anthologist to select, from a myriad of possibilities, the apposite quotation that addresses properly the circumstances in question.[133] To my knowledge, al-Sulamī never counts *muḥāḍara* among the ways or virtues of Sufism, although his treatises doubtlessly demonstrate that he attempted to realize this virtue. The larger point here is that the absence of a comprehensive catalogue of the virtues does not threaten the attempt to locate al-Sulamī within the realm of virtue ethics; some of the most prominent exponents of that stream of thought today do not offer an exhaustive list of the virtues.

In MacIntyre's approach, one acquires virtues through participation in a tradition, and as already mentioned, *taṣawwuf* functions as a good analogue for MacIntyre's notion of tradition. While al-Sulamī certainly does deny the moniker 'Ṣūfī' to pseudo-Ṣūfīs who cause scandal to other believers, his general approach is a big-tent vision of *taṣawwuf*. Sufism is the larger reality constituted by sets of practices, and al-Sulamī integrates a number of different spiritual currents under the mantle of Sufism. One does not need to anticipate the advent of the *ṭuruq* in later Sufism to recognize that not all persons who self-identified as Ṣūfīs shared an identical *adab*. The basic distinction between 'drunken' Sufism and 'sober' Sufism provides one clear example, as this binary describes two different, complex and internally coherent styles of *adab* that were expressions of the same larger movement.[134] Al-Sulamī himself draws in *futuwwa*, *malāmatiyya* and other currents so long as they accord with *sharīʿa*. Unfortunately, especially in the case of the Path of Blame, historians suffer from a paucity of sources outside al-Sulamī's corpus and thus struggle to provide a full sketch of these spiritual currents, but al-Sulamī draws upon them for the purpose of integrating them into Sufism and demonstrating their fundamental consistency with Sufism.

Al-Sulamī's literary activity functions with both centripetal and centrifugal force. For all his labour to gather local spiritual currents under the mantle of *taṣawwuf*, he equally attempts to expand and diffuse the core insights of that tradition. The treatise *Kitāb ādāb al-ṣuḥba* places the latter instinct on full display, not through overt 'evangelism' but by attempting to expand the Ṣūfī tradition in a quiet and subtle manner. This approach also places an advocate of MacIntyre's approach to tradition in something of a bind. MacIntyre's notion of tradition functions best for persons with deep commitments to the tradition of which they are a part. Tradition plays a strong epistemic function, shaping what adherents could come to know, due to the questions, data and virtues adherents have been encouraged to find relevant. For many texts in al-Sulamī's literary corpus, this presents no challenge: a reader of *Manāhij al-ʿārifīn* would never expect someone to arrive at *maʿrifa* without intentional and intense focus on excellence in the practice of this tradition and the acquisition of its virtues. In *Kitāb ādāb al-ṣuḥba*, however, al-Sulamī does not explicitly attempt to describe the virtues of a tightly knit community of Ṣūfī brothers. Rather, he chooses customs and mental attitudes distinctive to the Ṣūfī tradition and frames them as the values and virtues of society broadly speaking. This collection of wise counsels for believers at an earlier stage of spiritual growth – believers who have not necessarily entered into an intense adherence to Ṣūfī practice – amounts to a gradualist approach to the spread of *taṣawwuf.* Al-Sulamī attempts to gently inscribe the Ṣūfī tradition into the heart of the city,[135] a process I call his project of 'sufization'. In as much as al-Sulamī attempts to saturate the rhetoric of his city with Ṣūfī wisdom by popularizing these maxims, at the level of individual readers al-Sulamī attempts to 'set the hook' and coax them into a deeper engagement with this tradition. In other treatises, al-Sulamī identifies clearly the internal good he attempts to promote (*ḥayā'*, *faqr*, *ma'rifa* etc.). In *Kitāb ādāb al-ṣuḥba*, al-Sulamī identifies these goods only in a broad and sweeping way: he compiles material 'concerning respect for believers, the glorification of the rights of Muslims, and the virtues of the saints, the pious, the nobles, and the best of people'.[136] In one sense, this *adab* has a restricted scope: al-Sulamī describes a set of customs that will achieve goals which the *adab* of other peoples would not achieve. In MacIntyre's language, the practices of other peoples have different evolving sets of internal goods that would not bring about respect for believers, the glorification of the rights of Muslims and so on. But in another equally important sense, al-Sulamī leaves the scope of *adab* wide open. He incorporates some evocative Ṣūfī terms, like *akhlāq al-awliyā'*, but mixes them in with more innocuous language that appeals to Muslims in general. In the framework of tradition and practice, one should still refer to this treatise as a repository of Ṣūfī *adab*, but only in the sense that al-Sulamī highlights social behaviour that both Ṣūfīs and non-Ṣūfī Muslims esteem. The treatise promotes and advances the behavioural norms that Ṣūfīs share with all believers – omitting the distinctively Ṣūfī elements of ritual – and thus involves the 'systematic extension' of goods as MacIntyre describes. The treatise acts as a bridge document, a point of overlap, wherein al-Sulamī's inclusion of certain Ṣūfī points of emphasis advances the goods internal to the practice of Ṣūfī *adab.* Turning readers' attention to these customs and not to others invites readers along a path of practical wisdom that slowly shapes their character in accord with Ṣūfī tendencies. They integrate reverence for the *sunna*, blame for one's ego-self, an imperative to sound companionship, honour for spiritual masters and other aspects of al-Sulamī's spiritual method.

By speaking in MacIntyre's language of internal goods, I do not intend here to accidentally suggest that the growth in virtue al-Sulamī encourages here occurs strictly in the believer's interior life. Al-Sulamī sets *ādāb*, *akhlāq* and *aḥwāl* in a hierarchy, but not one that involves increasing degrees of interiorization. He insists upon the unity of interior and exterior in his discussion of Ṣūfī practice (*adab*), but his discussion of *akhlāq* tilts much towards the *ẓāhir* and his discussion of *aḥwāl* entirely towards the *bāṭin.* Simply put, al-Sulamī assumes that one can witness a fellow believer's *akhlāq* and can learn and implement them through imitation (*qudwa*).[137] While al-Sulamī might accept a distinction between character and action,[138] he could never separate the two. The possibility of someone having 'hidden *akhlāq*' presents a contradiction in terms. In both his discussions of spiritual chivalry (*futuwwa*) and of *taṣawwuf*, al-Sulamī emphasizes the importance of putting these noble virtues into practice in a visible, public way.[139]

Emotional akhlāq

Scholarly discussion of classical works in Islamic ethics, including those that frontload the virtues as an element of their approach, tend not to probe the question of the emotions in depth.[140] Normative, objective and often rationalist characteristics dominate ethical discussion, even while key medieval figures either covertly or overtly acknowledge emotional responses as a major driver for their own reflections. Ibn Ḥazm (d. 456/1054) perhaps stands as exhibit A, with his famous declaration that repelling anxiety (*ṭard al-hamm*) is the common objective that all human beings search for and approve in their decision making.[141] Ibn Ḥazm does not frame the desire to repel anxiety as something unfortunate, an instinct that a wise person sublimates and transcends. While this objective certainly could lead someone to immoral decision making in certain cases, in general, the suffering of *hamm* that a person seeks to avoid orients a person beneficially. Modern scholars can overlook the benefits of such emotional responses in their evaluation of medieval figures, implicitly equating emotion with selfish and sinful desire.[142] That is not the position of Ibn Ḥazm, who ultimately finds freedom from anxiety in working for salvation in the next world and thus pre-empts any suggestion that *ṭard al-hamm* could amount to egoistic hedonism.[143] But Ibn Ḥazm was far from the only medieval thinker who gave affect the prominent place in his writing that many believers likely gave it in their practical lives. Ṣūfī thinkers also – particularly in discussion of *maqāmāt* and *akhlāq* – account for the role emotions play in a believer's moral life, even if modern scholars tend to overlook their doing so.[144] By incorporating the emotions and the re-formation of a believer's emotional responses into their moral theory, they follow an element of Aristotle that philosophers had tended to ignore until recent decades: virtue entails the experience of emotional reactions.[145]

Philosophers and psychologists today often distinguish between 'emotion', 'feeling' and 'affect'.[146] Mapping these distinctions onto medieval Arabic texts presents difficulties, as they lack a perfect analog. Modern speakers of Arabic often use *'awāṭif* for 'emotions', but the root *'-ṭ-f* appears only once in the Qur'ān[147] and rarely in major collections of *ḥadīth*, carrying a meaning close to that intended here.[148] The concept thus did not prompt well-developed theories from the very medieval scholars we now seek to question and, perhaps predictably, leaves a relative vacancy in contemporary scholarship on the subject.[149] Taneli Kukkonen's analysis of al-Ghazālī highlights that al-Ghazālī's 'pleasure principle', a key element of his moral psychology, involves an act of cognition.[150] For this reason, I take 'emotion' as a more useful category than 'feeling' or 'affect', insofar as theorists today more often emphasize the physiological, pre-cognitive elements of feeling and affect, especially affect. Oliver Leaman notes a distinctive element of Ṣūfī emotional responses in his study of aesthetic reactions to art and poetry. The Ṣūfī affection for the tradition 'God is beautiful and loves beauty' is well known.[151] Leaman observes that Ṣūfī thinkers tend to regard aesthetic responses as objective. The assumption that art and poetry yield insight into a deeper level of reality leads Ṣūfīs to a 'dogmatism' insisting that a certain work of art or poetry should provoke a certain reaction and that only that reaction is appropriate.[152] While Leaman commends the peripatetic philosophers on this point for their flexibility in appreciating profound works capable of provoking various valid appreciative reactions, his analysis of Ṣūfī aesthetics applies well to Ṣūfī emotional responses in the moral life. *Sulūk* involves progress in one's feelings about God and the surrounding world, feelings that range from instinctive, possibly superficial, reactions to joys and aches that are deeply felt in one's core. A particular set of circumstances 'should' provoke a certain emotional response, and Ṣūfīs often assumed that an integral element of traveling their path was the cultivation of these appropriate responses. That this held true for al-Sulamī and his contemporaries can be illustrated with the example of one highly affective virtue: shame.

A comprehensive treatment of al-Sulamī's engagement with emotions lies far beyond the scope of this study, but his approach to *ḥayā'* (shame/modesty) offers representative indications of his thinking. *Ḥayā'* should be considered a virtue insofar as it represents a stable disposition to react in certain ways when confronted with certain stimuli but could also be considered an emotion insofar as *ḥayā'* primarily denotes the painful feelings evoked by those stimuli. It therefore is arguably the best example of a Ṣūfī virtue that carries a strong emotional reaction as a constitutive element and thus conforms to Leaman's assumption that certain sets of circumstances should cause a Ṣūfī to react in a certain way. Al-Sulamī also devoted more space to reflecting on this virtue than did his near contemporaries, authoring a short treatise dedicated to the topic and touching it at various degrees of depth in several other sources.[153] Lexically, *ḥayā'* refers to physical contraction or withdrawal, or emotional discomfort; broadly speaking, this contraction or discomfort occurs due to aversion at an inappropriate action. Because of the aversion involved in *ḥayā'*, an emotional response that involves an evaluative judgment of the object of one's thought, Marion Holmes Katz argues that '*ḥayā'* is a good candidate for the affective disposition that classical Muslim thinkers considered most fundamental to the formation of a Muslim moral self'. A maxim attributed to ʿĀʾisha (d. 58/678) captures this succinctly, 'Shame is the crown of noble virtues.'[154] Especially because authentic shame lies in the ache within one's heart more so than in observable behaviours or customs, the challenge lay in how to cultivate *ḥayā'*. Katz herself, despite asserting the centrality of the virtue, observes that jurists were implicitly 'pessimistic about the possibility of actively fostering [*ḥayā'*]'.[155]

Just as jurists do not impart *ḥayā'* with a special sense in *fiqh* apart from the ordinary use of the word, Ṣūfī masters do not attempt to define the term apart from its ordinary usage.[156] The glossaries of Ṣūfī terminology one finds in al-Sarrāj, al-Sulamī and al-Kharkūshī do not contain the term. Based on the widespread usage of the word in his society, al-Sulamī is not alone in pointing to the pain in one's heart – the *qalb* – as the principal manifestation of shame.

> Shame is the heartache from the knowledge of the sinful deeds one has carried out. Shame is the disdain for acts of obedience on account of one's knowledge of their inadequacy before what is [truly] necessary. Shame causes thoughts to fall away from the servant. Shame keeps a servant far away from any false claims and allows him to see his failures. Shame cleanses the spirit and the intellect from the vestures of satanic whisperings. Shame is the admonishment of the heart preventing a person from showing his states and the good in his actions.[157]

The important element of what Chowdhury frames as a 'spiritual modesty' is the affective response involved.[158] *Ḥayā'* chastens a believer by making the believer aware of the imperfections in his or her sincerity.[159] The sting of shame thus functions as a preventative mechanism that assists a believer's conscience at the moment a believer stands to disobey God, primarily due to the believer's awareness of past and present shortcomings and inadequacies.[160]

Al-Sulamī shows his commitment to the *ahl al-ḥadīth* culture of his intellectual milieu by constructing his treatise on *ḥayā'* around a Prophetic tradition.[161] This *ḥadīth* was cited, at least in excerpts, by several Ṣūfī masters discussing this virtue.[162]

> The Messenger of God said, 'Be properly ashamed before God (*istaḥyū min Allāh…ḥaqq al-ḥayā'*).' They said, 'Messenger of God, all of us are ashamed!' The Prophet said, 'That is not it. Let the one who is properly ashamed before God protect his head and what it contains, his belly and what it contains, and remember death and [the moment of trial]. One who desires the next world leaves behind the adornments of this world (*al-dunyā*).[163]

Al-Sulamī comments extensively on this tradition, using it as the framework to explain different types of shame. He shows his commitment to the discipline of *ḥadīth* transmission when he shores up each of these types of shame with additional shorter traditions that also recur in other Ṣūfī texts, including 'Shame is part of faith',[164] 'Shame is a branch of faith',[165] 'Shame is entirely good',[166] 'Shame brings nothing but good'[167] and others.

By comparison with his near contemporaries, al-Sulamī dedicates more attention to shame, both within and without the treatise focused on the topic. The importance of *ḥayā'* did not increase with each generation that passed; al-Qushayrī spent less energy on the topic than did his teacher, and al-Ghazālī's reflections on shame are muted and brief by comparison, even if they provide a concision and a precision that had been previously lacking. The most novel element of al-Ghazālī's contribution is his re-engagement with al-Muḥāsibī, whose seminal reflection had been largely overlooked in the intervening generations. The heavily psychological and introspective al-Muḥāsibī grants the sting of shame a significant place in the spiritual growth of believers, particularly because ideal *ḥayā'* is an internal voice and not something socially imposed. This emotion is 'God's mechanism for making people do good things they otherwise, because of natural self-interest, would avoid'.[168] Faraz Sheikh focuses here on the pedagogical discourse of al-Muḥāsibī more so than on a normative theory of shame; al-Muḥāsibī's counsels about the use of shame to scrutinize one's own *nafs* and grow in self-awareness reveal a moral subject that 'inhabits a complex and dynamic emotional space'.[169] The same could certainly be said for al-Sulamī, even though he does not seem to draw directly on the writings of al-Muḥāsibī on this topic. Al-Sulamī's insistence on the importance of shame and his detailed attempt to map it onto a believer's inner life – the meaning of shame in one's head and what it contains and in one's belly and what it contains – show his concern for the subtle differences in the effects of *ḥayā'* upon different parts of a believer and what the presence of this emotion indicates about a believer's spiritual life.

Growth in virtue: Outside-in or inside-out?

The case of *ḥayā'* illustrates a significant dilemma in understanding how one can cultivate the virtues. Al-Ghazālī considers the appearance of shame in a youth an important sign of religious maturation but does not indicate how to foster that maturation (regarding this virtue).[170] Ideally, this virtue is manifest precisely when it is not visible: authentic shame is felt as an internal voice or ache in the heart, and it seems that insofar as believers can actively cultivate this virtue, they do so through silent, inward self-scrutiny rather than through any observable customs or mores. Al-Sulamī inherits from the Path of Blame the intention to keep spiritual growth hidden, a quietist path of virtue. This comes into tension with most classical accounts of virtue ethics, which typically see virtue as an excellence developed in public and lived in public. The treatise *Kitāb ādāb al-ṣuḥba* illustrates the point. On one level, the word *ṣuḥba* presents established norms of proper social conduct that onlookers should recognize as virtuous, impressive and exemplary. Nothing in the treatise suggests that this conduct should generally be shielded from others' eyes.[171] On another level, the inner growth to which a believer should aspire as a more meaningful goal lies within and should remain obscure, unknown by others, because the Malāmatiyya considered the outward appearance of religiosity ostentatious – and the majority of the spiritual masters cited in the text are associated with the Path of Blame.[172] If proper conduct demands keeping the secrets of one's companions regarding mundane matters like loans and borrowing,[173] so much more must a believer protect knowledge about inner growth. The best windows into this process of character development come in a handful of references to the familiar Ṣūfī binary of *ẓāhir* and *bāṭin*, passages that tie together al-Sulamī's insights on *ādāb* and *akhlāq* as discussed thus far.

Near the conclusion of *Kitāb ādāb al-ṣuḥba*, al-Sulamī summarizes that 'External ways of comportment are the sign of the activities of one's inner mysteries'.[174] He draws upon Abū Ḥafṣ al-Naysābūrī for this, who told al-Junayd that good comportment in what is external is the sign of good activity internally.[175] The meaning of this passage hinges on the ambiguous term 'sign' (*'unwān*). Does the *ẓāhir* simply manifest what existed previously in the *bāṭin*? Can the *ẓāhir* effect change in the *bāṭin*? Can a believer voluntarily transform or improve the *bāṭin* independently of the *ẓāhir*? Al-Sulamī's citation of a Prophetic *ḥadīth* reveals his position on the matter. The Prophet saw a man touching his beard during prayer, then said, 'If his heart were humble, his limbs would be humble too.'[176]

Three important elements of al-Sulamī's spiritual method are present in this passage and the paragraph that follows it, elements consistent with scattered comments throughout the remainder of the treatise and his literary corpus. First, he asserts the temporal and the logical priority of the interior life. Al-Sulamī states clearly that a believer must take care of his interior life first, for this is the place that God alone sees.[177] Care for one's interior life is necessary to develop sincerity, trust, fear, hope, satisfaction and many other blessings familiar to Ṣūfī readers as the names of stations and/or states but not identified as such here. Second, al-Sulamī assumes that a believer can focus on this internal growth in isolation from external comportment. In keeping with the Path of Blame, he assumes not only that one's inner spiritual state cannot be known by looking at a person but also that someone who attains an advanced state should keep this a secret. One can and should hide one's mystical states but not one's *akhlāq*. The Malāmatiyya encouraged constant attention to external comportment in accord with *sharīʿa* norms[178] – by contrast with later Qalandars or other antinomian and socially deviant groups[179] – while at the same time engaging in a conscious struggle against the instinctive desire to seek the approval of others through the appearance of supererogatory piety or an abundance of blessings. Third, al-Sulamī assumes that one's external comportment – in particular, the behavioural norms with which a person habitually acts – can affect one's internal life. Masters of the Path of Blame were known for their intensely quietist self-examination, but *Risālat al-malāmatiyya* contains a number of spiritual exercises as instruments to discipline the ego-self: one can leverage these means of discipline against one's blameworthy ego-self. Examples of this approach to character building occur in *Kitāb ādāb al-ṣuḥba*, like the passage in which one must search for seventy reasons to excuse a brother's fault even though the hyper-critical ego-self refuses to accept these excuses.[180] The believer's greatest enemy lives within: the ego-self.[181]

A number of Muslim mystics in the period functioned with great pessimism about the state of the ego-self, especially al-Muḥāsibī, al-Tustarī and al-Ḥakīm al-Tirmidhī. Regarding a person's capacity for growth in virtue, these shaykhs may creep closer to aspects of Aristotle's thought than does MacIntyre despite MacIntyre's Aristotelian framework. Aristotle famously believed that only a slight few in the population had the potential to truly acquire the virtues and that those who were not born into noble families who trained them in the virtues could harbour little hope. Many texts in al-Sulamī's corpus share this disdain for the ego-self, but when he shifts away from discussion of the *nafs* to the discussion of the *ẓāhir* and the *bāṭin*, a new dynamic arises. He operates with a more benign understanding of the relationship between one's external comportment and one's inner life in *Kitāb ādāb al-ṣuḥba* than in his other writings, assuming that progress in one area will occur in tandem with progress in the other. The treatise, which is focused more on believers on the early stages of the journey than on spiritual elites, ends on such a note. 'If you train the inner according to these ways and train the outer according to what we have mentioned above, you may hope to be among those to whom God grants success.'[182] To import a modern image, one could imagine the *ẓāhir* and the *bāṭin* as two trains running on parallel tracks. Different fuel causes them to move forward – obedience to the norms of the *sunna* in the case of the former and to the rulings which pertain to the interior life in the case of the latter[183] – but for al-Sulamī, progress in one accompanies progress in the other. He certainly never pits them against each other, but promotes in this treatise a bi-levelled anthropology that good comportment keeps in integration.[184]

Conclusion

I have advanced here the sketch of al-Sulamī's spiritual method by fleshing out his understanding of *akhlāq* to complement the discussion of *ādāb* in Chapter 1. I have drawn upon MacIntyre's notions of practice, tradition and virtue to describe what the transformation of a believer's character looks like for al-Sulamī and suggest some new ways of understanding it. *Akhlāq* for al-Sulamī denote acquired human qualities that are fairly stable, depend upon constant volition by the agent and usually involve divine assistance. Despite al-Sulamī's failure to compile a tidy list of the *akhlāq*, we are right to call them 'virtues', as they are cultivated excellences that enable a believer to achieve the goods of Ṣūfī practice. While al-Sulamī understands the virtues primarily at the level of visible action – habitual action in a proper way – his approach to spiritual growth shows his constant concern for the integration of a believer's interior orientation and external comportment. Al-Sulamī's psychology of the four subtle spiritual centres also illustrates the importance of this integration, as believers strive to align their attitudes with their behaviour. Al-Sulamī's focus on this unity between *ẓāhir* and *bāṭin* manifests his assumption that many persons live with their *ẓāhir* and *bāṭin* disjointed, decoupled or, at the very least, imbalanced. The remedy for this disconnection varies across his corpus. The texts that are most sceptical and pessimistic about the *nafs* tend to emphasize the importance of external discipline, to heel the ego-self and realign its blameworthy desires. Elsewhere, al-Sulamī asserts the logical priority of the inner life and that a believer can focus on the inner life first, allowing this internal transformation to manifest itself in action. The consistent element across his corpus is the conviction that from the earliest stages of religio-moral growth, integration is both necessary and possible. If a believer puts into practice the wisdom handed down within the Ṣūfī tradition, a believer has good cause to trust that he will advance with the *ẓāhir* and *bāṭin* moving in tandem. This integration enables a believer to benefit self and others through the relationships of companionship and fellowship that mark his life in society.

Chapter 3

AL-SULAMĪ'S VISION OF FELLOWSHIP AND SPIRITUAL COMPANIONSHIP

Like many Ṣūfī masters, al-Sulamī highly esteems personal and solitary expressions of piety, including periods of spiritual retreat and the habits of ascetical women who lived largely as hermits. But overall, he assumes that Ṣūfī practices and virtues find expression in relationships of fellowship and spiritual companionship, the interpersonal relationships through which believers express their service to God and benefit their companions and associates. *Ṣuḥba* finds its fullest manifestation in the bond between a shaykh and his disciple, a matter that has received extensive attention in the scholarly literature about this period. I here treat this theme briefly, to shift the focus towards the other types of relationships in a believer's life. In many cases, the treatise *Kitāb ādāb al-ṣuḥba* being the most prominent example, al-Sulamī does not concentrate on the companionship of a tightly knit community of Ṣūfī brothers in a lodge but on the companionship a believer seeks based on a mutual desire for spiritual and moral growth and on the fellowship a believer shares with all persons a believer meets. These are Ṣūfī concerns, to be sure, but al-Sulamī speaks of companionship to a broader audience, offering guidelines for healthy and truly Islamic relationships subtly informed by aspects of the Ṣūfī tradition that al-Sulamī knows all believers can affirm. By noticing al-Sulamī's contribution regarding the more 'ordinary' instances of companionship and fellowship – not solely the bond between master and disciple – one sees different valences in the way God acts in a believer's life through the bond of companionship. Here too, modern articulations of virtue ethics can illuminate al-Sulamī's approach, particularly regarding the nature of dependence in human life. For al-Sulamī, progress on the Ṣūfī path depends not exclusively upon faithful adherence to the guidance of a shaykh but can also depend upon one's growth in the knowledge of God through the common-ness and weaknesses of one's ordinary associates and companions. Al-Sulamī primarily adheres to the simple and prudent Ṣūfī assumption that a believer should find only the most excellent persons and walk with them, but his œuvre offers fleeting glimpses that prompt a modern re-evaluation of Ṣūfī companionship through the lens of questions of dependence.

This shift in focus from shaykhs and more intimate companions in Sufism towards the more 'ordinary' instances of companionship and fellowship in a believer's life has immediate consequences for one's understanding of the way companionship affects a believer's relationship with God. If a believer assumes that *ṣuḥba* should only occur with a master who is a fount of wisdom and knowledge, a person exalted in virtue and advanced in the spiritual life, this restricts the number of candidates for companionship. But if companionship can occur with believers who are less virtuous, a believer's perception of the presence of God in the relationship changes. *Ṣuḥba* with a fool offers a different sort of access to God than does *ṣuḥba* with a shaykh. Here, I continue to draw upon the insights of MacIntyre, particularly his line of argument in *Dependent Rational Animals*. In that monograph, MacIntyre augments his prior accounts of human social life by developing an account of the virtue of acknowledged dependence and making a person's growth as an independent practical reasoner dependent upon the acquisition of this virtue. In sum, a person cannot grow into the fullness of the virtues without recognizing in all stages of life his or her dependence upon others. This argument illuminates al-Sulamī's expansive notion of companionship. It is one thing for a Ṣūfī to acknowledge that his spiritual growth depends upon companionship with a wise and learned shaykh; it is another to extend this dependence into a broader network of relationships in the world and locate his growth in the knowledge of God in relationships with persons who are not paragons of virtue. Here, al-Sulamī takes something of a middle ground, though leaning strongly towards the former claim. Throughout al-Sulamī's literary corpus, he consistently exhorts believers to choose only the best of persons as their friends and companions, expecting that the bond will yield mutual benefit. At the same time, one can see an implicit assertion of the positive value that lies in companionship with 'lesser' persons. Al-Sulamī's discussion of companionship with fools, fellowship with women, and fellowship in the marketplace shows that a believer's colleagues are not merely an arena in which a believer exercises the virtues, nor are they merely a potential obstacle a believer must avoid to persevere in obedience to the divine law. Al-Sulamī offers glimpses of a religious vision in which not just the normalcy but the weaknesses of one's ordinary associates and companions serve as a vehicle to grow in the knowledge of God. These are fleeting glimpses, however, as the lion's share of al-Sulamī's counsels on companionship encourage believers to keep company with persons of great knowledge and virtue who can spur them on to grow in their interior lives and to obey the precepts of the law more perfectly.

Ṣuḥba *and* ʿishra*: A difference in degree or in kind?*

From the time when the term *taṣawwuf* first came into use in the third/ninth century, figures associated with that path developed a distinctive vocabulary to describe their practices and their experience. The movement had an avant-garde, cutting-edge resonance to it, and while the rapidly developing Ṣūfī lexicon certainly confused many Muslims of the day, including on occasion their own colleagues, it likely also fuelled some of the fascination that surrounded the Ṣūfīs.[1] The preceding discussion of terms like *adab* and *akhlāq* offers a window on the breadth of reflection among the Ṣūfis who worked to craft a rich and varied lexicon of technical terms for their mystical experience. Spiritual masters like al-Sarrāj, al-Sulamī and al-Hujwīrī (d. *c.* 465–9/1073–7) developed glossaries for Ṣūfī terms that built on al-Ḥallāj's seminal attempt to write a lexicon,[2] but like al-Ḥallāj, their glossaries tended to focus on the interior life – the experiences of profound consciousness often classified as 'mysticism' – and not on relationships between believers. Esoteric terms like *fanā'*, *baqā'* and *'ishq* demanded definition because they aroused controversy, but figures like al-Sulamī and al-Sarrāj felt no such need to define terms for interpersonal relationships like *ṣuḥba* (companionship) and *'ishra* (fellowship). *Ṣuḥba* was pregnant with meaning, evoking images of the relationship of the Prophet with his Companions, but this did not create a felt demand to delineate precisely what it meant.

The absence of definitions for *ṣuḥba* and *'ishra* poses a challenge in the interpretation of al-Sulamī's writings, particularly for the treatise *Kitāb ādāb al-ṣuḥba*, in which al-Sulamī at times seems to use companionship and fellowship interchangeably but at times maintains a clear distinction between them. Their etymology provides some clues, although medieval dictionaries locate the distinction between *ṣuḥba* and *'ishra* differently than does al-Sulamī. The overall sense of lexicographers like Ibn Fāris (d. 395/1004) and al-Jawharī (d. 397/1007?) is that the mixing denoted by *'-sh-r* involves constancy; the shared existence of *'ishra* or *mu'āshara* often means life in the same tent.[3] Because nouns based on this root denote relationships of clan or tribe, *mu'āshara* can often be involuntary. While *mu'āshara* can also signify the mingling that results from voluntary bonds of marriage, it does not consistently involve the freedom that adheres to *ṣuḥba*. One does not choose one's tribe, but one does choose one's *ṣāḥib*.[4]

That al-Sulamī often does not structure his treatises in a systematic way has already been mentioned, but this problem does not solely relate to his inconsistent use of terminology.[5] At times, a reader cannot be certain which term al-Sulamī is talking about. *Kitāb ādāb al-ṣuḥba*, for example, carries a very fragmentary structure. The treatise primarily consists of a long series of isolated teachings, each beginning with the header phrase 'among its ways is…' (*wa-min ādābihā*) or a near variant. At a glance, the text seems to deal primarily with *ṣuḥba*, but the antecedent of *hā* (its) often remains grammatically ambiguous and could, in different places, refer to *ṣuḥba* or to *'ishra*. A close reading reveals that one cannot assume that al-Sulamī has always reconciled the pronouns with the proximate antecedent, and no scholar has identified a logic to the argument of the treatise that could resolve such quandaries.[6] At points, al-Sulamī groups sayings with similar themes in close proximity to each other, but this seems to occur more due to similarities in the *isnād* than to similarities in content. One could never claim, knowing the structure of treatises like *Fuṣūl fī l-taṣawwuf* (*Paragraphs on Sufism*) and *al-Muqaddima fī l-taṣawwuf wa-ḥaqīqatihi* (*Introduction to Sufism and its Reality*), that al-Sulamī preferred a *musnad* structure organized by transmitter to a *muṣannaf* structure organized by theme, but insofar as the difference applies, *Kitāb ādāb al-ṣuḥba* is closer to a *musnad*. No compelling evidence suggests a process of composition more complex than that the compiler continually tacked teachings about *ṣuḥba* and *'ishra* to the end of the collection and that the confusion about the antecedent of *hā* results from this 'disorganization'.

These ambiguities adhere most severely to one treatise, *Kitāb ādāb al-ṣuḥba*, but elsewhere al-Sulamī does maintain a distinction between *ṣuḥba* and *'ishra* and makes claims about *ṣuḥba* that he would not make about *'ishra*. The distinction runs on two different axes: on the duration of the relationship described and upon the level of voluntary closeness in the relationship described. Al-Sulamī's most straightforward articulation of this distinction, one focused on the first axis, appears in *Adab mujālasat al-mashāyikh*. 'It is obligatory for one to distinguish between *'ishra* and *ṣuḥba*, for *'ishra* is only temporary and *ṣuḥba* is enduring.'[7] This temporal distinction layers well onto *Kitāb ādāb al-ṣuḥba*, which implicitly relies on the second axis, that of voluntary closeness. Where al-Sulamī clearly distinguishes *ṣuḥba* from *'ishra*, both relationships have a spiritual component from the standpoint of the believer. In both cases, believers must pattern their social relations on that of the Messenger of God, but *ṣuḥba* denotes a relationship founded on mutual religious commitment. *Ṣuḥba* denotes spiritual companionship, the intentional decision to form and persist in a bond motivated by and sustained by religious commitment. By contrast, *ḥusn al-'ishra* primarily denotes life in society, the good social mores that mark the behaviour of believers in all their social dealings.[8] The 'mixing' suggested by *'ishra* is not the permanent, inseparable mixture of family members residing together; *'ishra* signifies the equally involuntary mixing that happens in the *sūq*, the normal goings-on of life. *Ḥusn al-'ishra* denotes a believer's response, inspired and guided by the Messenger, to the daily realities that confront believers, whether these realities involve an interlocutor who is pious, impious or somewhere in between. Both *ṣuḥba* and *'ishra* have their relevant guidelines for behaviour, but *ṣuḥba* unsurprisingly takes on more specific codification, as it refers to a bond of great intensity and intention.

Understanding *ṣuḥba* as spiritual companionship does not restrict *ṣuḥba* to Islamic companionship. Al-Sulamī clearly states that *ṣuḥba* and *'ishra* manifest themselves differently in the various peoples of the world.

> Know that the ways of companionship and good fellowship are varied, and that for every people (*qawm*), there are varying types of comportment in companionship and good fellowship. It is the believer's responsibility to safeguard the rights of brotherhood and good companionship and fellowship of every Muslim. Regarding this, I intend to present the matter clearly, so that a rational person will infer from it what lies behind the reverence owed to believers and the magnifying the rights of Muslims, and the virtues of the saints (*akhlāq al-awliyā'*), the pious (*abrār*), the elect (*nujabā'*), and the most worthy of people (*al-akhyār*).[9]

Al-Sulamī thus sets forth the distinctively Islamic notions of *ṣuḥba* and *'ishra* without assuming that these are exclusively Islamic realities.[10] Spiritual companionship exists among non-Muslims, but a Muslim should never enter into companionship with a non-Muslim, or, indeed, with a Muslim insufficiently committed to one's own path within Islam. Even social relations (*mu'āshara*) are discouraged with someone who differs in doctrine (*i'tiqād*).[11] Al-Sulamī cites several reports about the Messenger of God to emphasize the mutuality of empathy and service that must characterize the bond between Muslim believers. A *ḥadīth* likens the community of Muslims to one body in their mutual love and mercy; when one part of the body is in pain, the rest of the body suffers.[12] 'A believer for another believer is like a building whose parts support one another.'[13] 'The example of two believers when they meet is like that of two hands: one washes the other.'[14] Souls behave like soldiers, becoming friendly with those with whom they are familiar.[15] The most succinct summary comes in the well-known tradition, 'A man follows the religion of his friend (*khalīl*), so let each of you consider whom you treat as a friend.'[16]

Al-Sulamī shows his rhetorical ingenuity in the early paragraphs of *Kitāb ādāb al-ṣuḥba* by insisting on entering into spiritual companionship with true believers, not innovators or those ruled by their passions, but citing verses of poetry with no apparent religious content as support for his exhortation to choose companions carefully. He attributes two lines to 'one of the poets', lines that are now accepted as the work of the pre-Islamic poet Ṭarafa b. al-ʿAbd (d. *c.* 569):

> Ask not about a man, but of his friend inquire,
> For in his friend is seen the model he admires.[17]

While these lines rouse the listener to consider the content of a companion's character and the effect that character has upon the listener, the lines in no way demand the necessity of a spiritual aspect to the bond. A poem about befriending fools, attributed to Muḥammad's nephew and son-in-law, ʿAlī b. Abī Ṭālib (d. 40/661), also fails to emphasize religious considerations in the choice of a friend.[18] Al-Sulamī thus proceeds in *Kitāb ādāb al-ṣuḥba* in a rhetorically inviting and attractive way. His maxims about *ṣuḥba* consistently stress the religious element to the bond and the discernment this demands, but he draws upon prized sources from the culture around him that do not carry all the assumptions he holds about the nature and value of *ṣuḥba*. His argumentation contrasts sharply with a representative passage in *Adab mujālasat al-mashāyikh*. There, al-Sulamī uses an elegant and biting rhetorical flourish to forbid *ṣuḥba* with any shaykh who differs in *uṣūl* or *furūʿ*. Their difference in legal methodology would result in departure from the reality of *tawḥīd*, in neglect of the *sunna* and the *ādāb*, in darkness of heart and scatteredness in the secret (*sirr*) and in an evil comportment (*adab*) in both external behaviour and inner inclinations.[19] Such stern warnings do not mark *Kitāb ādāb al-ṣuḥba*, which urges spiritual companionship with fellow believers but does not wander into intra-Sunnī squabbles.[20]

The dangers of ṣuḥba

Al-Sulamī's caution about the selection of a shaykh extends into his larger rhetoric about companionship. He treats *ṣuḥba* as a matter of paramount importance for a believer's religious journey and thus at times strongly discourages believers from entering into this bond, knowing the severe damage it can cause if things go awry. The treatise *'Uyūb al-nafs wa-mudāwātuhā* presents this caution at its sharpest. Interestingly, that text never speaks about shaykhs. *'Uyūb al-nafs* reads much more like a self-help guide than an 'other-help' guide, if the latter were a document encouraging someone with a malady of the soul to seek assistance from others to remedy a defect. Al-Sulamī's hesitance here about *ṣuḥba* comes from his concern that believers act to win the esteem of others, as well as their forgetfulness of the next life.

> Among its [the *nafs*] maladies are the inclination towards fellowship with one's peers and companionship with the brothers. The remedy is knowing that any companion he has will be separated from him and any fellowship will be ultimately cut off. It was narrated on the authority of the Prophet that Gabriel said to him, 'Live as you will, for you will die. Love whom you love, for you will be separated from him. Do what you will, for you will be called to account for it. Know that the honour of the believer is in performing the night vigil and his esteem is that he has no need of others.'[21] Abū Qāsim al-Ḥakīm said, 'Friendship is enmity unless you act with purity, and accumulating wealth is an affliction unless you act with charity, and mingling [with people] causes confusion unless you act with good disposition.'[22]

As is the case for many maladies al-Sulamī addresses in *'Uyūb al-nafs*, attachment poses the primary risk for the believer. Nothing in this world will last, even companionship and fellowship, and a believer must remember the transient nature of these earthly bonds. Elsewhere in the treatise, the risk in social relations usually adheres to vanity or cognate vices, seeking the praise of others, the attention of others, positions of importance, and so on. To be clear, one could never suggest that *'Uyūb al-nafs* encourages a hermetic lifestyle or antisocial behaviour. This would run roughshod over al-Sulamī's thinking. Several of the remedies al-Sulamī describes in *'Uyūb al-nafs* involve associating with righteous people (*ṣāliḥūn*), and he presumes that companionship with pious people provides healing in a believer's life, despite the dangers of choosing the wrong companion.

Al-Sulamī's words of warning regarding companionship are strongest in *'Uyūb al-nafs* but not found solely there. In *Kitāb ādāb al-ṣuḥba*, a vignette about 'Alqama al-'Uṭāridī's counsel for his son strikes a similar note.

> When 'Alqama al-'Uṭāridī was about to die, he called for his son and he said, 'O my son, if you wish to take someone as your companion, keep company with a person who, if you serve him, will protect and preserve you; if you keep company with him, will adorn you; and if you are in need, will provide for you. Take as your companion a person who, if you extend your hand towards something good, will assist you in it; if he sees you do something good, will remember it; and if he sees you doing something bad, will prevent you from doing it. Take as your companion a person who, if you ask something, will give it to you; if you are silent, will take the initiative; and if something unfortunate befalls you, will

> support you. Take as your companion a person who, if you say something, will trust your word; if you attempt something, will give you counsel; and if the two of you dispute about something, will give you preference.[23]

Al-Sulamī's interpretation of the passage emerges in his decision to preserve a separate line of commentary on it. That commentary gives the justification for ʿAlqama's advice: ʿAlqama desired his son not to befriend anyone and thus described a disposition that no person possesses. Al-Sulamī preserves here – as valid commentary on the advice of a sage – a radical distrust in the benefits of deeply committed spiritual companionship.

Commentary like this typically appears on the lips of persons scarred by broken relationships, but al-Sulamī's personal context distinguishes his advice from other similar examples in the literature of the period. The profound sadness of Ibn Ḥazm at his friend's betrayal is well known; his heartbreak at his friend's inexplicable decision to sever their relationship fed Ibn Ḥazm's daily expectations of treachery and duplicity from those around him.[24] Abū Ḥayyān al-Tawḥīdī likewise opined about his struggles to find a patron amid courtiers who failed to appreciate his gifts and talents, leaving him isolated and unaccompanied.[25] Al-Sulamī, by contrast, elsewhere in his corpus does not reveal preoccupation with the possibility of such personal betrayal or rejection, despite social conditions that might well have sparked such concern. Al-Sulamī lived in a time of growing factionalism in Nishapur, an ever-increasing toxic *ʿaṣabiyya* that eventually contributed to the city's conquest by the Seljuq Turks in 429/1038.[26] He never experienced the direct persecution and imprisonment that his student al-Qushayrī did,[27] but during his lifetime, the 'social fabric was beginning to unravel'.[28] His writings – especially *Kitāb ādāb al-ṣuḥba* – show his concern to shore up the social bonds that knit the community together. That context renders his interpretation of the ʿAlqama vignette very curious. Nowhere else in *Kitāb ādāb al-ṣuḥba* – or in other texts, to my knowledge – does al-Sulamī suggest such a categorical discouragement of companionship. One wonders, then, why al-Sulamī preserved the commentary.[29] A hesitance about entering into spiritual companionship – and in this case, a hesitance lacking any reference to the religious component of such companionship – does not mark *Kitāb ādāb al-ṣuḥba* overall. To the contrary, the treatise presupposes that many believers do form such bonds, with persons from all social classes, for good reasons and with beneficial fruits. Al-Sulamī's exhortations to only take as a companion someone learned (*ʿālim*) or intelligent, gentle, and God-fearing (*ʿāqil ḥalīm taqī*) does not promote an intellectual or social elitism.[30] Rather, they promote an elitism of virtue and orientation: choose the best people – in the eyes of God – for your companions.[31] The more casual social relationships discussed as *ʿishra* carry a similar caution. A certain amount of social mixing is unavoidable and involuntary, but insofar as possible, a believer should avoid *ʿishra* with those who are seeking the things of this world (*ṭulāb al-dunyā*) because such people will direct a believer to seek these things. Social relations with the best people (*ahl al-khayr*) will direct a believer towards the next life and obedience to the Lord.[32] In sum, al-Sulamī urges serious discernment in choosing relationships that will facilitate spiritual progress. *Ṣuḥba* with wisely chosen companions who submit to the external demands of the law, who remind others of God and who conduct themselves with modesty, humility and shame for their shortcomings, will induce a believer towards the good.[33]

The many faces of ṣuḥba *and* ʿishra

This description of the distinction between *ṣuḥba* and *ʿishra* and the virtues that one should desire in a companion frames al-Sulamī's descriptions of what *ṣuḥba* looks like with different sorts of people. Sincere and virtuous believers are found in many walks of life, and al-Sulamī knows that companionship takes a different form according to the rank and station of one's companion. The treatise *Kitāb al-futuwwa*, a collection of teachings on spiritual chivalry that bears many similarities to *Kitāb ādāb al-ṣuḥba*,[34] contains this brief synthesis of what these relationships look like with different ranks of people. The behaviour that al-Sulamī elsewhere promotes as good *ṣuḥba* here appears in perfect symmetry with the values of the virtuous young man, a practitioner of *futuwwa*.

> Spiritual chivalry (*futuwwa*) means noble companionship and practicing good comportment (*ḥusn al-adab*) in it. This means keeping company with those who are superior by magnifying them, keeping company with those who are equal in status by showing agreement and love and keeping company with those of lower status by showing kindness, compassion and mercy. [Chivalry] means keeping company with one's parents by submissiveness and obedience, keeping company with one's children by mercy and good education and keeping company with wives by taking good care of them. [Chivalry] means keeping company with one's relatives by righteous deeds and visiting them, keeping company with one's brothers by authentic affection and eliminating anything that impedes love and keeping company with neighbours by good hearted smiles. [Chivalry] means keeping company with commonfolk by a cheerful appearance and kind generosity, keeping company with the poor (*fuqarāʾ*) by magnifying respect for them and knowing their value[35] and keeping company with the rich by showing that one needs nothing from them. [Chivalry] means keeping company with scholars by accepting what they indicate to others and keeping company with the saints (*awliyāʾ*) by humbly submitting to them, accepting their guidance and abandoning any criticism of them. [Chivalry] means avoiding at all times companionship with innovators, heretics and those who flaunt their asceticism in the desire for others to follow them and thus take what they have.[36]

This paragraph provides a thumbnail of the approach al-Sulamī uses at greater length elsewhere in his writings. One of his favourite rhetorical devices is to take a theme and sketch its various aspects (*wujūh*) as they appear in or with different sorts of people or at different stages in a believer's journey.[37]

Kitāb ādāb al-ṣuḥba utilizes this stylistic device, but uniquely in al-Sulamī's corpus, al-Sulamī expounds on the various aspects of *ṣuḥba* in three separate passages of the treatise. Twice he does so to articulate the *wujūh* of companionship[38] and once in a passage attributed to Abū 'Uthmān al-Ḥīrī.

> [Abū 'Uthmān was asked about companionship and said,] Companionship with God is through good comportment and abiding constantly in awe and awareness [of God]. Companionship with the Messenger of God ... is through adherence to knowledge (*'ilm*) and following the Sunna. Companionship with the saints (*awliyā'*) is through reverence for and service to them. Companionship with the brothers is through joy and gladness, abandoning any accusation against the brothers so long as they do not violate the religious law (*sharī'a*) or debase the reverence [that a brother should show a person deserving it]. God (Exalted is He) said to His Prophet, *Show pardon, command what is good, and turn away from ignorant people.*[39] Companionship with fools is by looking upon them with the eye of mercy, seeing that God has blessed you and did not make you like them, and by making supplication for them, that God heal them from the affliction of ignorance.[40]

The similarities between this paragraph and the passage from *Kitāb al-futuwwa* just cited show the consistency not just within al-Sulamī's thought but with that of a master of the Path of Blame he much admired. But at the structural level, the presence of three separate descriptions of the aspects of *ṣuḥba* in different parts of *Kitāb ādāb al-ṣuḥba* does strike a reader. In literature of this type, one should not expect juristic precision in al-Sulamī's taxonomy of *ṣuḥba*; treatises that attempt to 'define' pregnant concepts like *taṣawwuf* often do so by multiplying aphorisms rather than crafting a logically restrictive definition.[41] But these three schemas of *ṣuḥba* nonetheless stand in a curious tension with each other.

Two such passages deal with the proper expressions of *ṣuḥba* with persons in clearly defined religio-social roles. The first comes early in the treatise, saying that *ṣuḥba* and *mu'āshara* occur in different *wujūh*.

> Companionship and social relations (*mu'āshara*) have different aspects. Social relations with the venerable elders and the spiritual masters means showing reverence for them, serving them and acting on their concerns. Social relations with relatives and contemporaries means offering them sincere counsel (*naṣīḥa*) and sharing one's possessions with them in view of the precepts of the law, so long as it is not sinful to do so. Social relations with the young and with seekers (*murīdūn*) means offering guidance (*irshād*), discipline (*ta'dīb*) and prompting them to carry out what is obligatory in outer knowledge (*ẓāhir al-'ilm*), in the ways of the Sunna, in the rulings which pertain to the inner life (*aḥkām al-bawāṭin*) and in giving guidance about how to put these things into practice with good comportment.[42]

By comparison with the passage attributed to Abū 'Uthmān, here the social categories are defined more cleanly. *Juhhāl*, for example, does not delimit a particular group in the social hierarchy but persons lacking knowledge, some of whom certainly count themselves among the brothers. Here, the use of more distinctively Ṣūfī vocabulary – like *mashāyikh* and *murīdūn* – permits greater precision about the persons intended. But the third and final passage about the different aspects of companionship, which provides an imperfect combination of the prior two, demonstrates that al-Sulamī chose not to revise or remove prior material.

> Companionship has different aspects (*wujūh*), and each aspect has its own ways, obligations and requirements. Companionship with God means following God's commands, avoiding what God has prohibited, persevering in remembrance of God, studying God's Book, and being scrupulously mindful (*murāqaba*) of God's mysteries so that whatever does not please God never pervades them. It means contentment with God's decree, patience in times of trial, showing mercy and compassion for God's creatures, and doing what is in keeping with these noble virtues.[43]

Al-Sulamī then adds additional aspects of *ṣuḥba*, including *ṣuḥba* with the Prophet's companions and family (the *ṣaḥāba* and *ahl al-bayt*), with the authority (*sulṭān*), one's children, scholars (*'ulamā'*), one's parents and with a guest, offering in several places Prophetic traditions or verses of poetry in support of an aspect of *ṣuḥba*. Each of these is longer and better developed than prior iterations, offering similar explanations but not verbatim repetition. He allows the slight differences to stand. This third passage thus offers the greatest variety of aspects of *ṣuḥba* but also the fullest description of each. Al-Sulamī never mentions *mu'āshara* as he had in the first passage.

The presence of three different passages in the same treatise that address fundamentally the same question prompts some confusion. One could posit to al-Sulamī the intention to deepen his reflection subtly and gradually on the topic, moving from a simple truism that companionship looks differently with various classes of people to the consideration of companionship with God and the Messenger of God to, ultimately, an integration between these types of companionship.[44] Given the organization of the other material in the treatise, such an intention seems unlikely. The paragraphs surrounding these three passages do not suggest that al-Sulamī has crafted three taxonomies of *ṣuḥba* as lynchpins or turning points in the treatise's overall argument. The third passage, if it were to provide a summary synthesis of what came before, does not smoothly segue into the treatise's conclusion. Rather, the treatise winds down as it proceeded, with the inclusion of some material – arguably tangential – that does not seem immediately relevant to what preceded it and perhaps was added by the compiler simply as it became available to him. Julian Baldick has attacked al-Sulamī's rhetorical style, saying that al-Sulamī's literary corpus – and much of early Islamic literature – suffers from 'the atomistic and disorderly presentation of materials [that] hinders us from seeing the continuity of patterns from late antiquity'.[45] Whether Baldick extends this assessment too far is beyond the scope of the analysis here, but in the case of al-Sulamī's *Kitāb ādāb al-ṣuḥba*, a modern reader certainly does struggle to recognize the logic governing the overall structure of the text. Given the great advances that the study of Semitic rhetoric has yielded for Qur'ānic studies in recent years, one cannot exclude the possibility that future scholars will recognize a genius in al-Sulamī's organization of materials that eludes us today.[46] It suffices for now to say that for several important texts that organizational genius still eludes us.

Acknowledged dependence, with a little help from my friends

At this point, the main contours of al-Sulamī's approach to companionship are clear: *ṣuḥba* is a mutual, voluntary, stable commitment, and one should choose companions from among like-minded believers who excel in virtue and piety. Al-Sulamī rarely wavers from this approach, though cracks occasionally appear in the façade. A believer should choose persons of virtue as companions, but many people in this surrounding world simply are not persons of virtue, and al-Sulamī recognizes that companionship and fellowship do occur with them in different ways. To assist in understanding the differences between a believer's relationships with 'lesser' persons and a believer's relationships with persons of great virtue, I turn again to MacIntyre's work on acknowledged dependence.

MacIntyre styled *Dependent Rational Animals* in no small measure as a response to critics who wondered whether philosophers today could re-appropriate an Aristotelian approach to virtue ethics in the absence of Aristotelian biology.[47] MacIntyre uses human disabilities and the differences between humans and other animals to probe this problem, arguing that becoming an independent practical reasoner demands the acknowledgement of one's own vulnerability. One must see one's own dependence, rationality and animality in relationship to each other.[48] MacIntyre laments the general norm in philosophy in which scholars mistakenly take as the fundamental state of the human person the short window of adulthood in which one has well-formed social relationships, makes efficient economic contributions, and enjoys a developed mind and a good education.[49] In contrast, MacIntyre insists that there is no time in one's life when one ceases to be dependent upon others, and self-knowledge depends in large part upon what one learns about oneself from others.[50] Practical rationality involves the awareness of one's social embeddedness, particularly in coming to a positive valuation of the common good and recognising the goods of one's community as goods that one must make one's own.[51] MacIntyre seeks to augment an Aristotelian account of friendship, moving beyond elitism and fundamentally valuing the sharing of one's vulnerability and one's wounds.

MacIntyre's line of argument here probes the states of vulnerability and dependence in human life and thus does not demand a deep inquiry into disability as such, even though disability provides for MacIntyre helpful and illustrative test cases. One may note, however, an increasing interest among scholars of Islam in recent years in the question of disability. Pre-modern theology and jurisprudence do not share a unified terminology to address disability, the closest analogue being *ʿāhāt*, 'defects' or 'blights'.[52] Mohammed Ghaly notes that authors of *adab* literature addressed the question of 'people with blights' more frequently than jurists or theologians and named the issue more clearly.[53] Such discourse covers not only physical or mental disabilities but characteristics like baldness or bad breath that persons today would not classify as a disability; for classical writers, the issue had as much to do with otherness – a distinguishing characteristic – as with defect. *ʿĀhāt* were marks that spoiled the perceived wholeness of something.[54] For this reason, Kristina Richardson frames her pioneering study of blightedness through the lens of 'disability aesthetics', examining how such differences made Mamlūk and Ottoman authors feel and how they make us feel today.[55] She provides a micro-history of several works explicitly dedicated to individuals who were cognitively and physically different, searching out the ways in which personal relationships and literary topoi shaped the presentation of their stories and their histories.

The Ṣūfīs of al-Sulamī's day did not dedicate any works to the question of blightedness, although such markers of difference recur again and again as features of narratives in the lives of spiritual masters. They thus colour the approach to vulnerability and dependence that marks the literature of the period, often when God intervenes to overcome a perceived defect or when an externally blighted person exposes the inner blightedness of another believer. The fundamental frame, of course, is that the submission of oneself to God at the heart of the Islamic tradition is itself an acknowledgement of dependence. Al-Sulamī's reverence for transmitted knowledge – the *ḥadīth* culture of his day – further illustrates this sense of dependence because it demands an active recognition not just of a believer's dependence upon the Prophet but also upon the many other people who transmitted the Prophet's words and deeds in the intervening period. MacIntyre's virtue of acknowledged dependence requires more than this, however, as will be made clear in a discussion of some of the persons with whom al-Sulamī encourages believers to keep company.

O brother, who art thou?

When al-Sulamī discusses the ways of companionship, he almost always reverts to speaking about the brothers, *ikhwān*. This should not surprise, for Muḥammad used the concept of religious brotherhood as an important instrument to cement the bonds between Muslims. He 'promoted the principle of brotherhood in faith as the most practical way of bringing about fraternity and equality amongst all Muslims'.[56] Indeed, much of Islamic literature uses *ikhwān* as a functional synonym for *muslimūn*. Based on the introduction to *Kitāb ādāb al-ṣuḥba*, one could describe the audience of al-Sulamī's treatise as 'believers' or 'Muslims' and the purpose of the work as a description of their duties towards fellow Muslims regarding companionship and social relations. Ambiguity enters when one considers the specific groups towards which certain duties or demonstrations of respect and honour are owed. Apart from certain passages that identify companionship and fellowship with specific classes of persons, the text nearly always reverts to speaking about 'the brothers'. Who are these *ikhwān*? Does the term describe a broader group, a larger fraternity than the community of Muslims? Alternately, might *ikhwān* refer to a subgroup of Muslims, whether Ṣūfīs, Shāfiʿīs, *fityān*, *ʿayyār*s or someone else?

One finds little evidence in *Kitāb ādāb al-ṣuḥba* to suggest that al-Sulamī intends 'the brothers' to include non-Muslims. He shows little interest in Christ or Christians throughout his literary corpus, despite the presence – albeit a marginal one – of Christians in Nishapur.[57] Modern scholarship on al-Sulamī has thus mirrored the author's lack of concern for Christ or Christians[58] and one might say the same for the main historical studies of both Khurasan in general and Nishapur in particular.[59] Historians of the region often emphasize the diversity of the city and its cosmopolitan nature due to the constant flow of trade passing through it, thus suggesting that Muslims in Nishapur likely would have encountered Christians with some regularity, particularly visitors and travellers, but the number of Christians was certainly small and Islamic literature from the period generally passes them over in silence. This silence could also result from the fact that intra-Islamic and eventually intra-Sunnī *ʿaṣabiyya* constituted the more pressing social tensions.[60] Regardless of the reason that chroniclers gave their attention to intra-Islamic *ʿaṣabiyya*, some evidence suggests that Jews, Christians and Zoroastrians experienced less tumult and violence under the Seljuqs than in preceding periods.[61] But little evidence suggests that Jews, Christians and Zoroastrians might have become partners in any of these *ʿaṣabiyya* conflicts in a way that would render them part of the *ikhwān* as al-Sulamī discusses it. Jews, Christians and Zoroastrians have *ṣuḥba* proper to their own traditions, but al-Sulamī's concern is the responsibility of Muslim believers to maintain the duties of Islamic brotherhood towards their fellow Muslims, including the companionship and social mores proper to Islam.[62] Al-Sulamī's self-description as 'the clarifier (*mubayyin*) of this matter', almost certainly continues this scope: the norms of etiquette that mark how Muslims treat fellow Muslims.

If al-Sulamī restricts the scope of brotherhood to fellow Muslims, does he restrict it further than this? Passages in *Kitāb ādāb al-ṣuḥba* that discuss brotherhood (*ukhuwwa*) tend not to rely upon terminological distinctions and precision. For example, in the introduction al-Sulamī writes that 'the bond of intimacy (*ulfa*) makes brotherhood an obligation, and brotherhood makes good fellowship and noble companionship obligatory.'[63] In the logic of *fiqh*, this claim would suggest that establishing the bond of intimacy indicates that a believer thus is bound out of obligation – is required by the law – to maintain a bond of brotherhood with someone. That bond of brotherhood would thus generate legal obligations not just for social relations but for companionship – itself a bond more restricted and intentional than merely being a fellow Muslim. But the verb *awjaba* here certainly does not denote such a legal obligation, whether an obligation universally valid for believers or one dependent upon a particular case or circumstance (like entering into *ulfa*). Al-Sulamī writes here as an *adīb*, not a *faqīh*, to evoke the other characteristics that should mark the behaviour of one who claims to be a friend, a brother or a companion. His claim in the next paragraph that believers must maintain the duties of Islamic brotherhood for their fellow Muslims strikes the same note: al-Sulamī stirs believers' aspirations to practice these social mores with dignity more so than details for them *fiqh* mandates. The same can be said for *Kitāb al-futuwwa*; although spiritual chivalry could be said to consist in a 'body of rules by which to lead a virtuous life', al-Sulamī casts these more in terms of ideals of character, integrating them into a mystical outlook.[64]

Because many of al-Sulamī's writings compile wise maxims of previous masters, a reader struggles to find a consistent definition of who is 'a brother'. The fragmentary structure of *Kitāb ādāb al-ṣuḥba* renders the problem more severe in that treatise and forces one to consider passages on a case-by-case basis in their proper context. When he simply uses the word *ikhwān*, he most often means all fellow Muslims, urging believers to behave humbly around their brothers, to show joy and gladness in the presence of their brothers, to direct their brothers towards what is pious and the like.[65] When *ikhwān* arises in a sentence mentioning *ukhuwwa*, however, al-Sulamī often describes a closer and more intentional bond. For example, one point of etiquette entails that 'a believer, if he gains a brother or a friend, doesn't let the relationship slip away. He should know that brotherhood and friendship are precious (*'azīza*).'[66] In this case, 'brother' cannot simply mean a fellow Muslim. Nishapur was full of nominal Muslims. *Ukhuwwa* refers here to a bond of friendship, an intentional but fragile bond that one must work to protect. Such an understanding of *ukhuwwa* also comes through in passages claiming that a believer should be averse to a person who lacks brothers. If someone chooses not to enter into *ukhuwwa* with others – or if others refuse to enter into this bond with him! – this absence testifies to the state of that person's character. And yet, an unnamed philosopher states that 'it is easier to find red sulfur than to find an agreeable brother or a friend. I myself have been seeking one for fifty years, and I have found nothing more than half of a brother! And even he rebelled against me and escaped!'[67] Mystics often used red sulfur as an image for the rarest of treasures sought on the mystical path, and al-Sulamī thus follows this image with another claim about the rarity of *ukhuwwa*, casting this great intimacy as rarer than gnosis. 'Know that there are three types of people: acquaintances (*ma'ārif*), friends (*aṣdiqā'*) and brothers. Among people, acquaintances are many, friends are few while a brother is rarely found.'[68] None of this suggests that al-Sulamī uses *ikhwān* or *ukhuwwa* to denote a particular organization or social group within the *umma*. Some scholars have wondered this about *Kitāb al-futuwwa*, another text that speaks frequently about the *ikhwān*. There too, one must resist the temptation to retroject later notions of *futuwwa* as a corporate association onto an earlier period.[69] The rhetoric of *ukhuwwa* in that treatise constantly implores generosity and self-sacrifice for the brothers but says little about the organizational aspect of their bond. As is the case in *Kitāb ādāb al-ṣuḥba*, this language is hortatory, calling forth the highest standards of mutual respect and responsibility from believers. Very few believers behave as true brothers ought. One ought to aspire to such behaviour and seek out those who manifest it.

Even when *ukhuwwa* refers to a more intimate bond than the brotherhood that all Muslims share, the relationship between *ukhuwwa*, *ṣuḥba* and *'ishra* remains fluid. One section in the middle of *Kitāb ādāb al-ṣuḥba* contains several types of advice for one's dealing with the brothers, including counsels that believers should rejoice in their brothers' material prosperity, avoid envy and eschew any disharmony that results from the things of this world. But al-Sulamī then muddies the waters with the following paragraph:

> Among its ways is to avoid mutual hatred (*tabāghuḍ*) and mutual envy (*taḥāsud*). The Prophet ... forbade this, saying, 'Do not hate one another, do not envy one another, and do not turn away from one another. Servants of God: be as brothers!'[70] By saying this, he informed us ... that mutual hatred and mutual envy abolish any degree of brotherhood and that sound brotherhood (*ṣiḥḥat al-ukhuwwa*) and noble companionship are not immune from these reprehensible inclinations (*al-khiṣāl al-madhmūma*). Nothing makes for (*yaṣiḥḥ*) good fellowship (*'ishra*) other than sound brotherhood.[71]

At other points, one could imagine the key terms of *Kitāb ādāb al-ṣuḥba* as concentric circles of relationship with ever-growing intensity: *ṣuḥba* in the centre as the strongest and most intimate bond, *ukhuwwa* and/or *ṣadāqa* a wider circle that is less intimate but still deeply meaningful and *'ishra* the social relations that mark the entirety of a believer's public life with all persons a believer meets. The last line of this passage suggests an inversion, making good social relations conditional on one's soundness in more closely knit bonds. More likely, al-Sulamī merely intends here that someone who is a good brother with his intimate brothers will also behave admirably with persons who are not his intimate brothers. Good customs of brotherhood provide a sure indicator of one's good comportment generally; of this al-Sulamī is sure.

Ṣuḥba *in the relationship between master and disciple*

Many scholars of Sufism in the formative period continue to assume that *ṣuḥba* par excellence, *ṣuḥba* in its most complete form, exists in the bond between shaykh and *murīd*. In the case of al-Sulamī, this assumption is both true and misleading. Al-Sulamī does address at some length the comportment a disciple should have in the presence of a shaykh, but he does not always cast this in terms of *ṣuḥba*; instead, he uses a combination of different terms. As is the case for his discussion of *ṣuḥba* in other relationships, he never offers a single succinct definition of this bond, but instead gradually fleshes out the customs that mark the behaviour of a sincere disciple making progress on the path.

To start, al-Sulamī does not insist that a believer needs a shaykh. He describes the *adab* of the disciple who has sought a master but does not urge every believer to seek one. The treatise *'Uyūb al-nafs*, for example, does not encourage close personal guidance under a spiritual master.

Rather, al-Sulamī there seems to encourage fellowship and association with good people in a broader sense. *'Uyūb al-nafs* thus runs into a longstanding debate within the Ṣūfī tradition: when does a believer most need a shaykh?[72] Is the master most essential at the beginning, to guide a seeker's initial progress on the path, after which the *murīd* knows what is necessary to make continued progress alone? Or should a believer do the initial work without a shaykh, seeking out and relying on a master only for the higher levels of spiritual achievement? Al-Sulamī does not address this question explicitly, but in *'Uyūb al-nafs* he implicitly seems to favour the latter, at least insofar as the shaykh goes unmentioned for initial treatment of these maladies. *'Uyūb al-nafs* thus could silently support a vision of the shaykh as indispensable in the achievement of the higher levels of spiritual progress. In this schema, a mature disciple depends not only upon God but must come to realize as a fact his dependence on an earthly master.

Several of the sayings in *Kitāb ādāb al-ṣuḥba* bear on the *ṣuḥba* between shaykh and *murīd*, but al-Sulamī addresses the topic most directly in *Adab mujālasat al-mashāyikh wa-ḥifẓ ḥurumātihim*, a treatise that Thibon considers the completion of *Kitāb ādāb al-ṣuḥba* because it specifies and develops the notion of companionship in the earlier work, with a focus on the relationship between shaykh and *murīd*.[73] Al-Sulamī often speaks there of *mu'āshara*, connoting association with shaykhs, in addition to *ṣuḥba*. Thibon regularly translates this term *fréquenter*, driving home the point that this relationship is not a casual association but requires sustained commitment to meeting each other frequently.[74] Although Ṣūfīs in later centuries engage in discipleship by correspondence or in modes of companionship that do not require them to encounter their shaykh with regularity, al-Sulamī's notion of *ṣuḥba* seems to have no space for this. Pilgrimage or other obligations might separate a disciple from his master for a time, but regular direct contact remains the norm for true companionship.

Adab mujālasat al-mashāyikh reminds readers again and again of the importance of serving shaykhs. Service is a constitutive element of a disciple's encounters with the shaykh, and the form of this *khidma* does not necessarily mirror the service that characterizes relationships between other believers. The theme of service recurs frequently in al-Sulamī's writings. In *Kitāb ādāb al-ṣuḥba*, one section relies on a tradition about the Prophet to inculcate a notion of servant leadership, a notion that al-Sulamī then extends to believers generally. All believers must see themselves as servants of each other, for even the most important members of the community share this obligation to serve the others.[75] Here and elsewhere, selfless service provides an instrument to discipline the ego-self (*nafs*), which attempts to convince people that they should not serve and may comfortably continue in their indifference to the needs of their brothers. However, in *Adab mujālasat al-mashāyikh*, al-Sulamī transcends a general exhortation to service as a destruction of the ego-self and grounds the imperative to service of the shaykhs in a different way. One should serve them and respect them because of their relationship to the Prophet, the Prophetic heritage which they bear. If a servant venerates and serves the *awliyā'*, this will result in following the *sunna* of the Prophet in the *ẓāhir* and in the *bāṭin*.[76]

Al-Sulamī grounds service to shaykhs in a series of strong claims that became staple claims of Ṣūfī literature. If one neglects respecting the *awliyā'*, whom al-Sulamī considers the successors of the messengers and prophets, one abandons respect for the messengers.[77] Companionship with elders, nobles and wise people entails showing them respect, because they keep the *adab* of the Prophet alive in the community of believers. Q. 68:4, one of the verses al-Sulamī cites most frequently, stands as the central prooftext for the reverence believers should show to shaykhs who manifest the presence of the Prophet: 'Truly, you [Muḥammad] have magnificent character (*khuluq 'aẓīm*).'[78] Another Prophetic tradition commonly cited by Ṣūfīs supplements it: 'Truly, God trained me with the best way of conduct and perfected my conduct.'[79] The Prophet's character remains manifest in the community in the behaviour of the *mashāyikh*; believers see in their customs the result (*natīja*) of the Prophet's *adab*. However, this continued presence of the Prophet's character among the believers is more than simply an example to admire. Al-Sulamī assumes that one cannot grow in the acquisition of the Prophet's virtues without the living light of the shaykhs. Without them, a believer has no light to guide him. One must show the highest honour for this proximate light by serving and venerating it. Thus, Thibon rightly refers to al-Sulamī's approach as a 'spiritual caliphate'.[80]

Al-Sulamī offers here a precursor of the even stronger claims that would be made about shaykhs by Ṣūfīs in subsequent generations, claims that fuel many polemics against Ṣūfīs for their exaltation of the role of the shaykh.[81] While many of these criticisms of the Ṣūfī path condemn such reverence for shaykhs on the ground that it is an innovation to the *sunna* of the Messenger of God, others today might resist the claim on strictly philosophical grounds. MacIntyre, for one, would regard this spiritual caliphate with reluctance. The voluntary acknowledgement of dependence on a teacher or spiritual guide is certainly a virtuous act, but the intense concentration of all of a disciple's hopes, dreams and possibilities into the person of the shaykh threatens if not annuls a healthy and holistic acknowledgement of one's dependence on others as MacIntyre describes it. Many human beings are disproportionately dependent on one person and one person only: an infant on his or her mother, a severely disabled person on a caregiver or the like. But even these persons are indirectly dependent on a network of persons. An infant depends not only upon his or her mother but upon the mother's doctor, her grocer, her plumber and all the many other persons who enable the mother to flourish and care for her child. The intense reverence for shaykhs seen occasionally in the writings of al-Sulamī and with greater emphasis in later masters does involve awareness of such a network: a chain of believers that link the shaykh to the Prophet. Al-Sulamī's writings do not contain a developed notion of an explicit *silsila* in the way that one finds in the later *ṭuruq*, but any emphasis on the exalted role of the shaykh never neglects the other circles of relationships in which a *murīd* is enmeshed, even if the shaykh stands tall as the most important of these.

This concern about insularity arises again in al-Sulamī's insistence that a believer should avoid the company of shaykhs who differ from or oppose the spiritual path of that believer's own shaykh.[82] Al-Sulamī does not suggest here that a believer must restrict himself to one shaykh and one shaykh only; he assumes that individual disciples might choose to attend sessions led by several shaykhs independently of each other. This confirms data from *Ṭabaqāt al-ṣūfiyya*, in which having multiple masters stands as the clear norm.[83] But this pluralism of persons does not denote a pluralism of thought: al-Sulamī insists that keeping company with multiple persons who do not agree on doctrine (*iʿtiqād*) will result in one's departure from the reality of *tawḥīd*, in one's disdaining the *sunna* and the *ādāb*, in an unjust heart, in the frigidity of one's inmost core (*sirr*) and in an evil *adab* in both externals and internals.[84] Al-Sulamī's counsels in *Kitāb ādāb al-ṣuḥba* are not as exclusive in this regard, because that text deals little with the intimate relationship of instruction in a teaching circle. *Kitāb ādāb al-ṣuḥba* treats proper social mores regardless of whether one meets a Ḥanafī, a Shāfiʿī or someone else.[85]

Abū Bakr provides the perfect model of the attitude of a true companion, and when al-Sulamī discusses him and other pious companions, his terminology shifts from *muʿāshara* to *ṣuḥba*. Drawing on Abū Bakr, al-Sulamī distinguishes between three different aspects of one's relationship to a shaykh: *ṣuḥba*, *khidma* and *ḥurma*. *Ṣuḥba* involves learning the spiritual qualities incarnate in the master, much as Abū Bakr learned these qualities from the Prophet. Believers must strive to put into practice the customs of Abū Bakr, the pre-eminent example of authentic *ṣuḥba*.[86] These include not criticizing the master, showing gratitude after being admitted to his company, accepting directives from him, keeping his secrets, speaking little in his presence and other things. In sum, the disciple should focus his entire intention (*niyya*) on the shaykh.[87] These particular counsels about how to behave in companionship with, service to and respect for the master serve a real and practical function in the teaching and education that occurs in the company of the shaykh.[88] Al-Sulamī does not see these counsels as dispensable accidents of a particular culture or teaching circle. They constitute an essential element of spiritual progress, a sine qua non for movement along the path. God will bless a disciple who puts into practice service of the shaykhs and proper respect for them by replacing many of the disciple's shortcomings and faults with positive traits. Al-Sulamī lists twenty-one separate blemishes that become adornments, vices that become virtues, by the action of God in response to proper service to and respect for the shaykh.[89]

The customs that characterize proper comportment with shaykhs do, then, carry the same tension between *ẓāhir* and *bāṭin* present throughout al-Sulamī's corpus. He assumes that proper etiquette in the externals manifests a good inner orientation. Visible blessings come from interior blessings; interior lights reveal their effects on the outside.[90] Such statements suggest that in one's spiritual growth, the causality flows from one's inward being to one's outward habits, that the attitudes of the heart effect the transformation of one's visible behaviour. However, the basic rhetorical strategy of the treatise calls this assumption into question because exhorting believers to practice points of etiquette has no purpose if this behaviour lacks the effective power to shape one's internal disposition. Al-Sulamī assumes that meritorious customs can accomplish this, but he frames the treatise as a response to the phenomenon of self-styled Ṣūfīs, people who wear the proper clothing, follow the proper licenses (*rukhaṣ*) but fail to show proper respect for their elders.[91] Al-Sulamī does not see observable behaviour as an infallible indicator of one's spiritual progress. Proper comportment is necessary but not sufficient. By carrying oneself in a particular manner in the presence of a shaykh, one gradually comes to realize and incarnate the deeper values those *ādāb* express. This transformation includes a reassessment of what a believer should truly value.

> The foundation of Sufism consists in two things: contempt for the ego-self and magnifying reverence for Muslims. … Whoever neglects the intermediaries (*asbāb*) will never arrive at their Originator (*musabbib*),[92] and whoever belittles what God has magnified, the magnification of [reverence for] God and the glory of God will never enter into his heart. Whoever keeps company with the shaykhs and listens to their words in order to use them to profit from common people and to be prominent in gatherings, this will destroy him and drive him to defile respect [for them] and he will enter into heresy … Whoever does not delight in the companionship of the brothers does not put into practice the ways of the shaykhs; whoever does not put their ways into practice, the blessings of their companionship will never reach him; and whomever the blessings of their companionship do not reach will be cut off from their observance of the legal obligations (*ādāb al-farā'iḍ*), and the practices (*sunan*), and from the blessings of these. Whoever withdraws from their observance of the legal obligations and their manner of following the *Sunna* will be deprived from attaining the station of gnosis. He will remain in a place of deception, and neither the blessings of contemplation nor a life of reflection will be evident in him, nor growth in the states, nor loftiness of deeds … Whoever serves the shaykhs, he must not allow a desired blessing [in the world] or an unwelcome ordeal to halt him in his service to them; his occupation should be to serve them, without aspiring to anything else, so that the blessings of their companionship and service will lead him to arrive at the Truth. Whoever clings to the path through the guidance of a wise counsellor, he [the counsellor] will bring him to the furthest goal, because he will indicate to him which paths are nearest and easiest, he [the counsellor] will be vigilant over all his [the seeker's] inner movements and, if an obstacle causes him an impediment, he will direct him back towards the right goal and to the right path.[93]

This passage brings the entire treatise full circle, especially regarding the concern about insularity in one's focused dependence on a shaykh. While al-Sulamī primarily discusses the comportment of a true *murīd* in the presence of a shaykh, this passage reveals the broader context – the importance of respect for fellow Muslims generally – for the respect owed to shaykhs. One's comportment in the presence of a spiritual master serves the purpose of bringing one to delight in companionship with other Muslims, to recognize one's dependence on them, and to serve them as brothers. Proper consideration of intermediaries – created effects, the good that God has accomplished in the shaykhs God favours – emerges as a reliable, and perhaps the only, path to the worship of God and to proper respect for all one's brothers.

Does ṣuḥba *suffer fools?*

Several times over the course of *Kitāb ādāb al-ṣuḥba*, al-Sulamī addresses relationships with fools (*juhhāl*). The Arabic root *j-h-l* evokes an abundance of connotations relating to ignorance or foolishness. Even if the original Qurʾānic usage of the term *jāhiliyya* did not signify a period of ignorance in a broad cultural sense,[94] by al-Sulamī's day, the work of Arab Muslim historians had cemented in the minds of the populace this conception of pre-Islamic Arabia as an age of decadence and immorality. Ignorance stood in contrast to *ʿilm*, the sacred knowledge that characterized Muslim society and about which various groups in Nishapur contended for prominence. Al-Sulamī employs this usage of the binary between ignorance and knowledge, but generally uses the verbal root *j-h-l* in a manner less loaded, less fraught, than many of his contemporaries. At times it indicates persons wilfully and sinfully lacking knowledge that could benefit them, but just as often it denotes foolishness in a more innocent sense or a person lacking advanced mental capacity. Al-Sulamī's counsels thus swing between the admonition to shun and avoid foolish and ignorant people and the admonition to treat them with respect in accord with their capacity.

The opening paragraph of *Kitāb ādāb al-ṣuḥba* contains the oft-cited Qurʾānic passage exhorting believers to 'show pardon, command what is good, and turn away from ignorant people'.[95] Advice in the same vein continues early in the treatise, in the context of obedience to the *sunna*. 'A man follows the religion of his friend, so let each of you consider whom you treat as a friend.'[96] That teaching forms the backdrop for al-Sulamī's inclusion of several famous verses attributed to ʿAlī b. Abī Ṭālib, verses that condemn *ṣuḥba* with the ignorant. Tahera Qutbuddin translates:

> Do not befriend the fool
> Beware of him, beware!
> Many a fool has led into death
> the wise man who took him as brother.
> The measure of a man
> is the man he walks with.
> Each entity finds in another such,
> its true measure and like.
> When the two meet, one heart finds in the other
> the proof he seeks.[97]

Regardless of the original context for these verses, al-Sulamī musters them in support of choosing friends committed to the *sunna*, to sound religion and to stay away from the People of Whimsy and Innovation (*ahl al-hawā wa-l-bidaʿ*) and those who dispute with each other. Some other cautions and condemnations of companionship with those mired in *jahl* similarly arise in this context: al-Sulamī's consistent drive to root religious practice – among Ṣūfīs and more generally – in tradition-based Sunnī Islam. One cannot always tell whether *jahl* is a symptom and expression of one's innovation or whether *jahl* spurs a believer to innovation. That is, does the name 'fool' attach to the person who stubbornly relies on improper sources for religious knowledge or mis-prioritizes them? Or does 'fool' attach to someone unconsciously guided by the *nafs* running amuck? Al-Sulamī seems to favour the latter. The fool remains shackled to the ego-self, which leads to the lamentable consequence of transgressing the ways of the *sunna* and entering into innovation. The assumption that the *nafs* acts as the root cause for foolishness explains the many *ādāb* of the Path of Blame that al-Sulamī counsels as antidotes; one sees this in the latter part of *Kitāb ādāb al-ṣuḥba*[98] but throughout *'Uyūb al-nafs wa-mudāwātuhā* and *Risālat al-Malāmatiyya*. In any case, al-Sulamī normally uses *jahl* to express the strong correlation between ignorance, whimsy, innovation and the subtle yet pervasive power of the ego-self.

Foolishness is not, however, so simple. Al-Sulamī on occasion treats *juhhāl* in a sympathetic light, mindful of the general principle that authentic *ṣuḥba* considers the capacities of one's companion. One sees this principle at work when al-Sulamī discusses companionship with different types of believers: children, women, servants and with a *jāhil*. A believer accompanies a brother to the extent of the brother's capacity (*'alā qadr ṭāqatihi*).[99] In support of this principle, al-Sulamī recalls an aphorism of the great Basran *adīb* Shabīb b. Shayba (d. 162/778–9?), 'If you address an ignorant person (*jāhil*) with scholarly knowledge (*'ilm*), or a heedless person (*lāhī*) with legal reasoning (*fiqh*), or a stammerer with rhetorical clarity (*bayān*), you do injury to your companion.'[100] Al-Sulamī does not suggest here that a believer must categorically avoid the company of the ignorant but that prudence must guide behaviour during the encounter. The *'ilm* to be withheld here – mentioned in parallel construction with *fiqh* and *bayān*, words dear to elite literati – would be wasted upon an ignorant man. The Ṣūfī instinct to carefully guard one's speech regarding mystical experiences is well known, as the diffusion of certain statements – al-Ḥallāj and the *shaṭaḥāt* of Abū Yazīd al-Bisṭāmī being the best examples – can lead to widespread misunderstanding and confusion among other believers. Al-Sulamī extends this hesitance to different spheres of knowledge: certain types of learning and eloquence are not only wasted upon someone who lacks the capacity to understand them, but worse, can be actively harmful. Here and elsewhere, al-Sulamī uses *jahl* not to denote primarily someone wilfully ignorant or impious but someone with a simple mind. This approach to *juhhāl* more generally characterizes the treatise *Kitāb ādāb al-ṣuḥba*, as seen in another passage where al-Sulamī cites Q. 7:199, the verse mentioned above. The Qur'ānic mandate to 'turn away from ignorant people' does not foreswear companionship with *juhhāl*. This companionship occurs by 'looking upon them with the eye of mercy, seeing that God has blessed you and did not make you like them, and by making supplication for them, that God heal them from the affliction of ignorance'.[101]

Al-Sulamī's openness here to consider the possibility of companionship with ignorant people provides the best parallel to MacIntyre's notion of acknowledged dependence, because al-Sulamī regards ignorance in this context as an accidental misfortune much like a disability. While not a 'blight' in the explicit sense, *jahl* characterizes a person who is not entirely whole and not entirely capable. MacIntyre's closing words about disabled persons treat the matter in the context of common goods, and a community debating which goods it will prioritize, including responsibilities for and to dependent others. Independent practical reasoners must exercise the virtue of *misericordia* in caring for others, but this care transcends a simple act of service to a person in need.

> What kind of recognition is the recognition required to sustain respect both for [the disabled] and for those not disabled, as well as their self-respect? … [It will recognize] that each member of the community is someone from whom we may learn and may have to learn about our common good and our own good, and who always may have lessons to teach us about those goods that we will not be able to learn elsewhere … For even at those times when we are disabled so that we cannot engage in worthwhile projects we are still owed by others and we still owe to others that attentive care without which neither we nor they can learn what we have to teach each other.[102]

This passage stands as the high-water mark for what constitutes the virtue of acknowledged dependence for MacIntyre. Al-Sulamī does not explicitly recognize the value of disabled persons in this way. His counsel to look upon ignorant people with the eye of mercy amounts to service to them and counting one's blessings that one was not created in that unfortunate state. Again, however, the simple fact that al-Sulamī speaks about *ṣuḥba* with fools suggests some kind of mutual benefit in the relationship. Al-Sulamī's failure to tease out the implications of this leaves a question hanging over his work, a fundamental uncertainty about the benefits of befriending a fool. That such acts of kindness and generosity will be rewarded in the next world is obvious, but whether the relationship with a fool can teach a believer something he or she did not already know remains an open question.

In sum, al-Sulamī's varied maxims relating to *juhhāl* suggest that one's interaction with a foolish person demands an apprehension of the nature of his or her foolishness. Al-Sulamī certainly does not regard the *juhhāl* as completely simple or innocent; contact with an ignorant person has the power to corrupt a believer and a believer must be on guard against this.[103] Without explicitly stating it, however, al-Sulamī values the potential benefit to the ignorant person higher than the potential harm to the believer. The command to avoid acting with levity (*yujāhil*) around an ignorant person signifies not a categorical avoidance but providing a salutary example in accordance with the *jāhil*'s capacity to understand.[104] Beyond any benefit to the ignorant person, one sees in al-Sulamī's text an openness to the value of the fool. Al-Sulamī's willingness to speak about companionship with fools suggests a real mutuality to the relationship. *Ṣuḥba* is a relationship in which both partners benefit; even if the believer gives the fool more than he receives from the fool, the believer nonetheless is blessed by their bond.

Relations with women

Al-Sulamī's treatment of relations with women – and in particular, companionship with women – presents a point of tension in his literary corpus.[105] Scholars have hailed al-Sulamī for recognizing the spiritual capacities of women in ways that exceeded his contemporaries. His biographical dictionary of Ṣūfī women, *Dhikr al-niswa al-muta'abbidāt al-ṣūfiyyāt*, is the earliest collection focusing on women mystics, describing women who kept company with the male spiritual masters of their day and who rebuked those same men for their mistakes. But apart from this text, al-Sulamī's other writings manifest the presumptions of his male scholarly contemporaries: he describes women as deficient in intellect and religion and encourages pious men to avoid their company, which jeopardizes men's spiritual progress. The question of women's status for al-Sulamī thus cuts in both directions, as his recognition of the capacities of certain elite women who became spiritual masters does not fundamentally alter his assessment of women generally.

Rkia E. Cornell edited and translated al-Sulamī's *Dhikr al-niswa* in 1999, greatly augmenting the data available to scholars of women's Sufism. It immediately met with widespread interest, and, due to translations of *Dhikr al-niswa* into several languages, al-Sulamī's biographical dictionary of Ṣūfī women, considered lost only three decades ago, has become the most widely available work in his corpus. Al-Sulamī includes in this work entries for eighty-two different Ṣūfī women and attributes teachings to each of them, on their own authority. As is true for *Ṭabaqāt al-ṣūfiyya*, al-Sulamī intends in *Dhikr al-niswa* to legitimate the holiness of the persons he describes, to transmit their saving knowledge in a manner credible in the epistemological climate of his day, within the well-established genre of *ṭabaqāt*. While his works do preserve information of great use to modern historians, he labours in a discipline closer to that of hagiography: he intends to communicate saving truths, not to record historical 'facts'. Two stylistic and structural features differentiate *Dhikr al-niswa* from *Ṭabaqāt al-ṣūfiyya*. First, al-Sulamī uses far more narrative in his description of Ṣūfī women, transmitting brief anecdotes and vignettes that give context to the women's teachings, by comparison with the *dicta* of male Ṣūfī masters that often stand entirely on their own. These brief narratives often treat the women's interaction with, and occasionally their stinging rebukes of, Ṣūfī shaykhs known from *Ṭabaqāt al-ṣūfiyya*. *Dhikr al-niswa* provides comparatively more examples of colourful interpersonal exchanges that manifest the wisdom of female Ṣūfīs. Second, al-Sulamī's Ṣūfī women generally do not appear as *ḥadīth* transmitters. Al-Sulamī frames most Ṣūfī masters in *Ṭabaqāt al-ṣūfiyya* as *muḥaddithūn*, dedicated to the preservation of this source of knowledge through the audition and transmission of Prophetic traditions. With good cause, Thibon identifies *muḥaddith* as one of the three central dimensions of al-Sulamī's personality.[106] Unlike *Ṭabaqāt al-ṣūfiyya*, al-Sulamī does not attempt to validate these Ṣūfī women by framing them as *muḥaddithāt*; he only identifies one woman, Ziyāda bt. al-Khaṭṭāb al-Ṭazariyya (active early fourth/tenth century), as a *ḥadīth* transmitter.[107]

As already indicated, the basic dilemma that emerges from al-Sulamī's writings on women is that on the one hand, *Dhikr al-niswa* holds up many women as masters of the spiritual life, while on the other hand, his disparagement of women is consistent throughout all his other writings. Cornell's exuberant introduction to *Dhikr al-niswa* downplays this latter fact and nearly turns al-Sulamī into a proto-feminist. Cornell sees in this text al-Sulamī's witness that these women contributed more to the growth of their more famous male counterparts than is often acknowledged, as well as al-Sulamī's 'unique concern with disproving Muslim stereotypes about woman's supposed lack of religion and intellect'.[108] Whether al-Sulamī attempts to subvert these assumptions for women generally or only for female spiritual adepts,[109] Cornell considers it certain that the women remembered in *Dhikr al-niswa* are, in the eyes of al-Sulamī, 'fully the equals' of the men remembered in *Ṭabaqāt al-ṣūfiyya* and that al-Sulamī attempts 'to demonstrate that Sufi women possess levels of intellect (*ʿaql*) and wisdom (*ḥikma*) that are equivalent to those of Sufi men'.[110] If al-Sulamī considers these Ṣūfī women the equals of their male counterparts, his writings elsewhere demonstrate that he does not hold this assumption for women generally. To take the most glaring example, al-Sulamī states directly, in at least two places, that women are deficient in religion and intellect and he cites Prophetic traditions as support for this assumption.[111] He connects the Qur'ānic injunction to deal honourably with women, *wa ʿāshirūhunna bi-l-maʿrūf*, to this deficiency.[112] God created this deficiency in women, and therefore, what constitutes honourable treatment derives from acknowledgement of God's intent. One should not expect from women things for which God has not created them. This statement in *Kitāb ādāb al-ṣuḥba* appears directly beside a statement attributed to ʿAlī b. Abī Ṭālib, 'The intellect of a woman is her beauty and the beauty of a man is his intellect.'[113] Later in the same treatise, al-Sulamī transmits the Prophetic *ḥadīth*, 'A woman is like a rib. If you straighten her, you will break her. If you live with her, you live with her crookedness.'[114]

Occasional comments like this should not lead one to overemphasize al-Sulamī's derogation of women. Like many Ṣūfīs of the period, he generally ignores women and says little about them. For al-Sulamī, the prototypical Ṣūfī is male and references to women are infrequent. Salamah-Qudsi observes that in *zuhd* literature and early Ṣūfī writings,

> the general attitude of dislike for women … appears not to have been addressed to women because they are women, as the sociological definition of misogyny implies. It was, rather, a theoretical way to counter sexual activity, family ties and other social attachments that were all believed to distract men from a complete devotional life.[115]

This comment places al-Sulamī's negative comments about women in context, as they emerge in no small part from the genre and purpose of the texts he authors. Whereas *Dhikr al-niswa* serves to extol the elite status of certain Ṣūfī women, other writings designed to intensify men's commitment to their devotional lives – particularly texts with an apologetic agenda, defending Sufism against its detractors – simply have no place for women. Al-Sulamī knew that some believers were concerned about social mixing between Ṣūfī men and women and he desired to solidify the social palatability of *taṣawwuf* in Khurasan. The scandal of cross-sexual companionship recurs in other biographical dictionaries as well. These texts typically insist that men and women who met for prayer, study or spiritual direction did so for purely spiritual purposes, never for lustful or worldly motives.[116] The marginal role Ṣūfī women play in texts from the period probably does not indicate their actual level of participation in pious and mystical circles.[117] *Dhikr al-niswa* speaks explicitly about cross-sexual companionship; no fewer than twenty entries refer to a female Ṣūfī keeping company with a man.[118] This density of material certainly amounts to al-Sulamī's endorsement of cross-sexual companionship in that text, but outside of that biographical dictionary I count at least seven different writings in which al-Sulamī forbids such companionship – often coupled with a prohibition on accepting gifts (*arfāq*) from women – and none in which he acknowledges its permissibility.[119] With the exception of *Dhikr al-niswa*, nearly every comment al-Sulamī makes about women serves to disparage them or discourage companionship with them.

Turning back to themes of vulnerability and dependence, one can discern al-Sulamī's assessment of women's capacities in his choice of terminology. In *Kitāb ādāb al-ṣuḥba*, he never refers to *ṣuḥba* with women, but to fellowship (*ʿishra*) and social relations (*muʿāshara*) with them. This helps account for the sharpness of his rhetoric about women in that treatise; the women mentioned are not spiritual elites, but fellow believers whose weakness men must suffer as a fact of life, references to wives or women within one's family. His citation of the *ḥadīth* likening a woman to a crooked rib indicates the prudent guidance al-Sulamī desires men to provide. Women have the capacity to lead men astray; men must persevere in honourable behaviour towards their wives, teaching them proper *adab* and directing them towards obedience to the Prophet's *sunna*.

By contrast, when al-Sulamī approves of companionship with women in *Dhikr al-niswa*, he does so not for women as such, but for the spiritual heroines he lionizes in that biographical dictionary. The text does not, unfortunately, clarify the modes of *ṣuḥba* in question. In the case of certain outstanding women like Fāṭima of Nishapur (d. 223/838), we read that Dhū l-Nūn al-Miṣrī asked her opinion on doctrinal matters (*masāʾil*) and that he called her his teacher (*ustādh/ustādha*).[120] Does this mean that these two, or other cross-sexual companions, enjoyed a relationship like that of a *shaykh al-taʿlīm* and his student, or like a *shaykh al-tarbiya* and his *murīd*?[121] Did these women receive the equivalent of spiritual direction from a male shaykh – or give the equivalent of spiritual direction to men – or did *ṣuḥba* signify something else in a cross-sexual relationship? The evidence is not clear.

The data from Ṣūfī women adds one important element to the notion of *khidma* sketched earlier: giving economic support. Al-Sulamī insists that male aspirants should serve their shaykhs, but even if financial or material sustenance formed a part of this service, one struggles to find it unambiguously in the relevant texts of al-Sulamī, particularly *Adab mujālasat al-mashāyikh*. Although *khidma* was an ambiguous word in early Sufism, in Salamah-Qudsi's analysis its usage for women is clearer in certain texts. '*Khidma* involves the financial support granted by certain rich women to their fellow male Sufis as a means to practice *futuwwa*.'[122] The altruism and unquestioning loyalty connoted by *futuwwa* was highly attractive to many of these women and they dedicated themselves more to it than the study with a master often associated with formal *ṣuḥba*. Both the financial 'service' of these women and their personal service to male Ṣūfīs expressed their desire to live the generosity of *futuwwa*.[123] This rubs against Cornell's description of the piety of these Ṣūfī women. Cornell stresses that *ta'abbud* means selling oneself to God, serving God rather than persons, and she thus uses 'theology of servitude' as the chief descriptor for the devotional life of these women. The weakness in her account is that she casts the theology of servitude precisely as a means by which Ṣūfī women escaped some of the social constraints of their day. Her assessment is historically correct in many cases: a good number of these women lived alone and their habits of piety bear out Cornell's description of them as 'career women of the spirit'. But the *khidma* many of these women show for their men does not fit well with a vision of the theology of servitude that serves only God. Based on the sayings transmitted in *Dhikr al-niswa*, a significant number of the women described saw service to other people – whether their husbands, their families, shaykhs or others – as an integral component of their Ṣūfī practice. For other Ṣūfī women – another significant number – such service was not part of their practice or was resented by these women when their circumstances demanded it.[124] These vigorous worshippers included lifelong celibates who lived alone, embracing spiritual disciplines and exercises as a liberating alternative to the domestic life their society expected of them. These vigorous worshippers also included women who served their families and male spiritual companions in countless mundane and practical ways, understanding this service as an integral and indispensable part of their worship of God. If one searches for a summary description of the piety of al-Sulamī's Ṣūfī women, I concur with Cornell, that 'theology of servitude' is the least inadequate description.[125] I add the caveat that one English moniker, 'servitude', must embrace both *ta'abbud* and *khidma* as complementary expressions of service. Without this, the picture of these women's spirituality falls out of balance.

The etiquette of the marketplace

Al-Sulamī's concern for worldly, practical matters extends to 'the ways of fellowship with the people of the market and businesspeople'.[126] These detailed counsels for buyers and sellers fall under the scope of *'ishra* rather than *ṣuḥba*; the etiquette of the marketplace pertains to social relations in the general sense more so than to voluntary friendships involving mutual commitment. While al-Sulamī speaks about one's interlocutors in trade as *ikhwān*, he never states that the behaviour described depends upon whether one trades with coreligionists. He exhorts believers to honesty in their business dealings and fidelity to promises and commitments they have made in negotiations. Al-Sulamī never wades into *fiqh* here; matters about *ribā'* and the finer points of contract law lie outside his scope. He examines instead how the affairs of the *sūq* can affect the way believers look upon those they meet with the eyes of faith. The human tendency towards pride must prompt reflection on one's own status before God; in this, al-Sulamī's marketplace becomes a place charged with spiritual energy. When a believer sits in a shop, the believer should forgive the shopkeeper's faults and consider unknown circumstances that may have led the shopkeeper to behave in this way. Al-Sulamī tells someone who observes a sin while sitting in a shop to say to himself, 'Perhaps he is obliged to act in this way due to debt that he is striving to pay off, or he is striving to find food for his family or his feeble parents.'[127] One should withhold judgment and consider one's own sin, seeing in one's own sin a potential excuse for one's brother.

Across al-Sulamī's œuvre, his rhetoric about wealth changes in the light of his intended audience. Those who have made progress on the spiritual path receive deeper and more challenging admonitions. In al-Sulamī's treatises focused on the interior life, wealth and poverty serve as central symbols for the believer's relationship to God based on the Qur'ānic principle that God is rich and human beings are poor.[128] The person who is spiritually poor (*faqīr*) worries about neither worldly blessings nor worldly trials because he does not try to invert this natural order of things.[129] Material success or lack thereof does not stir hostility in the authentic *faqīr*; the *faqīr* finds richness by looking on God's signs in the world with a considering eye (*bi-'ayn al-i'tibār*).[130] The indifference to worldly success that characterizes spiritual adepts finds no expression in *Kitāb ādāb al-ṣuḥba*, a treatise devoted to social mores in daily necessities. Al-Sulamī looks positively on business and trade as occupations and encourages believers to recognize God's blessings in mundane matters of the marketplace. *Jawāmi' ādāb al-ṣūfiyya* offers a middle point in this regard, for al-Sulamī explicitly styles it as a Ṣūfī guidebook. There, al-Sulamī combines cultivation of interior poverty with proper behavioural norms when a Ṣūfī encounters persons who are economically poor. Put simply, Ṣūfīs should choose to live in poverty (*faqr*), frugality and lowliness,[131] but al-Sulamī does not signify by this that the norm for the Ṣūfī should be material destitution. To the contrary, he assumes – against the Karrāmī mendicants – that Ṣūfīs should work for their sustenance and thus will often have money. One sees this in his counsel about entering the house of a poor person. A Ṣūfī should not carry money into a poor house.[132] A Ṣūfī visiting a poor man should behave in keeping with the lifestyle of that household. If a Ṣūfī chooses to live in total isolation, trusting in God for everything, al-Sulamī upholds this as a valid and fruitful path. On balance, he shows greater concern with Ṣūfīs pretending to be poorer than they are, and he abhors this hypocrisy. He particularly disavows begging, in keeping with the heritage of the Path of Blame.[133] His prohibition of sitting with beggars if one has money suggests that some Ṣūfīs must have been doing this, but probably also provides an indirect indictment of the 'activist and ostensive asceticism' of Karrāmī mendicancy.[134]

The positive view of the marketplace that provides a backdrop for *Kitāb ādāb al-ṣuḥba* invites businesspeople to see their colleagues as emissaries from God. God provides their commerce for a businessperson as a means of sustenance. Consciousness of this divine gift enhances the obligation to honesty in the transaction. One should never tarnish God's sustenance through falsehood, deception, or manipulation in the transaction. Al-Sulamī, however, continually returns to his concern about envy in the marketplace. The greatest spiritual peril in the *sūq* lies in the scorn a trader holds for brothers who prosper. Al-Sulamī returns, again and again, to the basic principle that one should rejoice in a brother's success as one would rejoice in one's own, citing in one place the Prophetic tradition, 'A servant does not find sweetness of faith until he loves for his brother what he loves for himself.'[135] This includes a brother making a profit – difficult advice to accept if a brother has an adjacent shop in the *sūq* selling the same thing! Al-Sulamī insists that a believer should praise God for a brother's profit in a sale just as he would praise God for a profit in his own. Such idealistic counsels reflect not only his approach to the spirituality of the marketplace but his larger concern about forgiveness, reconciliation and overcoming tensions and conflicts within the Ṣūfī community.[136]

An inconsistency marks al-Sulamī's advice to traders. Most frequently, he exhorts equality: one should rejoice in a brother's prosperity as one rejoices in one's own. The Qur'ānic image of the scales (*mīzān*) reiterates this solemn warning. One should never exaggerate the value of one's own goods and criticize the value of a brother's goods – this is hypocrisy and one must recall the scales of justice and fate upon which one will be judged. However, al-Sulamī also uses the image of the scales to suggest that one should prefer a brother to oneself. Both in terms of personal virtue and goods in a business transaction, one should presume in favour of a brother; a believer should short-change himself and benefit a brother. Here, the Path of Blame meets the etiquette of the marketplace: one should criticize and lambast oneself, not others. The inconsistency between al-Sulamī's rhetoric about equality and his rhetoric about preferring others to oneself does not, however, manifest an internal contradiction in his thought. Al-Sulamī offers here practical advice for one's spiritual life, patterns of thinking that curb the powerful influence of the ego-self. The competition for profit provides a realm for the *nafs* to take over. For this reason, al-Sulamī places at the heart of the *adab* of the marketplace the tradition 'the intention of a believer is better than his deed'.[137] One of the sages clarifies that 'an intention without an accompanying deed is better than a deed without an accompanying intention.' Al-Sulamī's advice for buyers and sellers, in the end, amounts to a strategic attempt to purify their intentions.

Conclusion

This exposition has revealed that al-Sulamī does not use terms like *ṣuḥba*, *'ishra* and *mu'āshara* with absolute consistency but that a basic coherence ties together his understanding of these relationships. *Ṣuḥba* generally denotes a mutual, voluntary, stable bond of spiritual companionship. The purest example is the relationship between someone seeking to intensify and deepen religious observance and that person's teacher. However, al-Sulamī does not restrict *ṣuḥba* to the bond between a Ṣūfī master and a disciple – al-Sulamī uses the term *ṣuḥba* more freely to describe spiritual companionship both with brothers and with fools, suggesting a friendship with a leading spiritual edge. *ʿIshra* and *muʿāshara*, by contrast, tend to refer to involuntary relationships, either casual relationships like dealings in the marketplace or constant ones like bonds of kinship or marriage. The *sunna* of the Prophet guides believers in these matters and a believer must offer a good example that will guide others to proper living, but this fellowship lacks the intense and free decision to progress together on the spiritual path that al-Sulamī ordinarily describes with the term *ṣuḥba*. Companions learn from each other and grow in their relationship to God by means of their companionship, a fact that leads al-Sulamī to urge companionship with virtuous believers but occasionally to accept and reverence companionship with lesser persons. That fundamental question of whom one should choose as a companion – *man aṣḥab?* – will loom large in Chapter 4, which steps beyond concerns about terminology to place the bonds al-Sulamī describes in the context of friendship and companionship as these evolved among other Ṣūfīs and philosophers, illustrating the distinctive elements of al-Sulamī's contribution.

Chapter 4

ṢUḤBA IN COMPARISON: AL-SULAMĪ'S NEAR CONTEMPORARIES

Al-Sulamī's reverence for the bond of companionship encompasses both the natural and the Islamic aspects of this relationship. He sees *ṣuḥba* as a natural human activity, as all persons seek companions to support each other in spiritual and moral growth; he sees *ṣuḥba* as an especially Islamic activity, as believers conform their behaviour to the practice of the Prophet, a behaviour appearing in different modes (*wujūh*) depending on the identity of one's companion. Al-Sulamī counsels believers to keep company with the best of people but offers practical advice for believers' relationships with persons of limited capacity and for the fellowship that occurs during the daily social mixing of urban life. This chapter will clarify al-Sulamī's distinctive contribution to the meaning of companionship by comparing his thought to some of his near contemporaries, in the sphere of philosophy and in the sphere of Sufism. Abū Ḥayyān al-Tawḥīdī's celebrated writings on friendship concur in many areas with al-Sulamī's insights, but al-Tawḥīdī foresees social reform occurring through different avenues than does al-Sulamī. Al-Tawḥīdī assumes that a transformation of the larger polity can never occur without a fundamental transformation – indeed, the repentance – of courtly elites, while al-Sulamī's true interest lies in a different set of elites – persons of true knowledge. Their attitudes towards the corridors of worldly power manifest different visions of how social and religious change occur. The second part of the chapter deals with al-Sulamī's near contemporaries in Sufism, especially al-Sarrāj and al-Qushayrī, and attends primarily to the developing role of the shaykh in the Ṣūfī spiritual path. Al-Sulamī stands at a transition point, as many subsequent Ṣūfī texts cast the shaykh as the gateway both for individual growth and for broader social transformation. Al-Sulamī presents a vision of companionship that is available to, desirable for, and beneficial for ordinary believers, even though elites of great spiritual advancement – the shaykhs – are indispensable for individuals to achieve higher religio-moral growth and for society to enjoy the broader transformation it so desperately needed.

Philosophical approaches to friendship

Several of al-Sulamī's near contemporaries among the philosophers share al-Sulamī's fundamental assumption that one's friends or companions help or hinder one's refinement of character and that any person striving for virtue must attend to these relationships consciously and carefully. Certain cooperative interpersonal relationships facilitate people's attempts to control their natural irascibility, relationships that might be categorized as love (*maḥabba*), friendship (*ṣadāqa*) or affection (*wudd*) but only rarely as *ṣuḥba*.[1] A comprehensive survey of philosophical approaches to this question is not possible, as prominent thinkers like Yaḥyā b. ʿAdī, Miskawayh, al-ʿĀmirī and others each devote attention to it in various degrees. After noting some key issues around which philosophical discussions of friendship tended to revolve, al-Tawḥīdī will serve as an instructive figure for comparison with al-Sulamī.

Philosophers writing on friendship relied heavily on one notion at the heart of Aristotelian thought: the human person is a social being by nature.[2] Yaḥyā, Miskawayh, al-Tawḥīdī and others describe the process of the reformation of one's morals in the context of a profoundly social vision. Miskawayh, for example, foregrounds the fact that all persons are born with deficiencies and await completion in their friends; no individual can achieve the fullness of happiness alone. Each person needs others to achieve common goods, and through cooperative contact with each other, authentic happiness becomes more diffuse through society.[3] Nowhere is Miskawayh's emphasis on this point more visible than in his repeated attacks on Yaḥyā.[4] Like many Christians, Yaḥyā esteems hermits and ascetics, because they can credibly teach people – by their personal example – self-denial. Hermits and ascetics provide living proof that the irascible faculty of the soul can be subdued. For Miskawayh, the common good of their pedagogy does not suffice to justify monks' decisions to live in unnatural isolation; virtues, by their nature, find outward expression in relationships with others, so a hermit lacks virtue by the very definition of virtue itself. Miskawayh's recurring call to sociability serves as a reminder and a warning in a realm burdened by social and political strife that being human means needing others and that the diminishment of social tensions is an individual duty incumbent upon all.[5]

The question of hermits and ascetics illustrates why MacIntyre leans so heavily on the notion of the *polis* and the human person as the *zoon politikon* to press his account of human rationality. MacIntyre develops an elaborate account of what goods are in an attempt to surpass the foundational work of Aristotle and his medieval interpreters.[6] The *polis* provides a systematic ordering of goods, without which practical rationality cannot function.[7] That systematic ordering results from vigorous debates among the citizens of the *polis*,[8] debates that could swing in favour of either Yaḥyā or Miskawayh on this point. The citizens must decide which goods are most important to them, and MacIntyre's account of human nature suggests no easy resolution other than to say that a community composed of independent practical reasoners – persons with fully developed rationality and the requisite virtues to exercise it – will be committed to persisting in the public conversations that would move the debate towards resolution.

Al-Sulamī's greatest contribution to the question of hermitic life draws upon his heritage from the Path of Blame. He neither advocated an extreme asceticism in his personal lifestyle nor his literary exhortations, but he favourably recounts in his writings several examples of Ṣūfī masters making heroic and extreme sacrifices in the name of renunciation and self-discipline.[9] He speaks about limited periods of withdrawal and seclusion in several places.[10] While he never directly addresses the question of the solitary hermit, one may safely say that al-Sulamī falls somewhere between Yaḥyā and Miskawayh in his approach to such questions. Al-Sulamī encourages a style of personal renunciation that seems stricter than the moderation proposed by Miskawayh[11] but infuses that renunciation with Malāmatī efforts to avoid allowing others to see one's renunciation.[12] With the exception of spiritual retreats of temporary duration, al-Sulamī assumes that Ṣūfī ways will be lived in public – they will be lived sociably – but without any desire to impress, or the search for recognition or reverence that might help drive an ostentatious asceticism. Al-Sulamī's style of humility thus overvalues one side of a tension running through medieval Muslim philosophers: varied attempts to couple Aristotle's notion of pride as a virtue (Gk. *megalōpsychia*), in which one expects to receive the respect one is owed due to one's meritorious behaviour, with the rejection of pride, as the pernicious vice associated with Pharaoh.[13] Aristotle considered *megalōpsychia* the quality that belongs to 'the sort of person that thinks himself, and is, worthy of great things'.[14] *Megalōpsychia*, which Vasalou translates as 'greatness of soul', adheres to people who not only are great but justly evaluate their own greatness. Miskawayh retains *kibar al-nafs*, his interpretation of *megalōpsychia*, as the first sub-virtue of courage, though his treatment of it is perfunctory.[15] Al-Sulamī abandons this entirely in favour of a humility lived largely in silence. He often discusses the rights of fellow believers or the rights of companions but nearly always in the context of recognizing and respecting others' rights, rarely in the context of claiming one's own.[16]

Taking as a given the human person's natural sociability, al-Sulamī's near contemporaries in philosophy were deeply concerned with social stability. Yaḥyā, for example, discourages social elites from cultivating friendship with lower class people, because 'the best friendship is the one you weave between two looms of corresponding worth'.[17] These social boundaries were not absolutely impermeable – Yaḥyā recognizes the ability of monks and hermits, for example, to move outside their social class and call people to live chastely and cultivate abstinence.[18] However, in general, Yaḥyā's goal of shaping readers into the 'perfect man' (*al-insān al-tāmm*)[19] involves friendships that serve to maintain in stability the existing social order. While the perfect man is always friendly, philosophers reflecting on friendship express suspicion about the number of true friends a person can have.[20] Like Aristotle and Cicero before him, Miskawayh limits both the number of people capable of entering into authentic friendship and the number of friends those people might have.[21] Only the best of people possess the virtues that make true friendship possible, and Miskawayh assumes that the number of friends a virtuous person will have will not be large. He restricts the number most narrowly in the case of passionate love (*ʿishq*), which refers to an excess of love (*ifrāṭ al-maḥabba*) that can only be shared by two people.[22] Passionate love suffices neither to attain full happiness in an individual's life nor to contribute what one could to society. In general, Miskawayh exalts friendship as a social good and claims that love (*maḥabba*) can occur in groups, but he implies that the number of true friends an individual can have is small.

Perhaps predictably, philosophers reflecting on the refinement of morals tend to emphasize the importance of study, an emphasis that modern scholars rightly connect to the matter of friendship. The decisive impact of study on the acquisition of virtues[23] derives in no small part from the social nature of study in the period: studying books almost invariably occurred in close engagement with at least one other person deeply interested in the topic. This could take the form of study circles of intellectual elites with similar interests, but most often it occurred under the direction of a recognized expert and authority.[24] While a modern university student might greatly advance his or her learning in splendid isolation in a library, the medieval intellectuals in question here would have considered the notion not only uncommon but utterly strange. A famous comment by ʿAbd al-Laṭīf (d. 629/1231) is instructive here. He writes, 'I commend you not to learn your sciences from books unaided, even though you may trust your ability to understand. Resort to professors for each science you seek to acquire; and should your professor be limited in his knowledge take all that he can offer, until you find another more accomplished than he.'[25] The impetus to study demands attentive, engaged presence with learned people who facilitate one's growth in knowledge.

Al-Tawḥīdī: The loyal friend of selfless care

Both Miskawayh and al-Tawḥīdī engage profoundly with Aristotle's discussion of friendship in the *Nicomachean Ethics*.[26] Aristotle divides *philia* into friendship of disinterested care, friendship of utility and friendship of pleasure.[27] Miskawayh builds upon this framework by preferring to consider friendship according to its durability rather than according to its goals. He notices that certain types of friendship are established more rapidly than others, and certain types deteriorate more rapidly.[28] Al-Tawḥīdī takes a different approach towards Aristotle's division: he rejects the latter two types of *philia* outright. Al-Tawḥīdī insists that only a relationship of disinterested care constitutes true friendship, a position he painstakingly maintains throughout *al-Ṣadāqa wa-l-ṣadīq (Friendship and the Friend)*. Al-Tawḥīdī uses *ṣadāqa* to translate the Greek *philia* in this ideal form of selfless concern. Here, al-Tawḥīdī shifts the terminology of some of his colleagues among the philosophers. Miskawayh uses *maḥabba* to translate *philia* in its broadest and fullest sense, then relates *maḥabba* to *ṣadāqa* as genus to species.[29] Love (*maḥabba*) carries the affective aspects of sociability in all its various forms for Miskawayh, while friendship stands as a particular and more concentrated type of love. *Ṣadāqa* has an affective component, but especially by comparison with modern friendship, this affective aspect is understated. Friendship for al-Tawḥīdī, as for his predecessors in classical Greece and Rome, is much more an active and conscious bond than a subjective emotional warmth.[30] Friendship has more to do with objective reciprocal obligations than feelings of attachment; al-Tawḥīdī's *ṣadāqa* is rationally grounded and a higher stage of perfection for religious and social reform.[31] Miskawayh's understanding of friendship as affective thus contrasts with al-Tawḥīdī, who identifies the affective aspect of sociability primarily as *maḥabba*.[32] The two agree on the beneficial consequences of friendship for society. Their understanding of the nature and scope of *ṣadāqa* differs, but they both see the public good that results from stable, committed, reciprocal friendships. Just as they grounded their inclusive approaches to the search for knowledge in a desire to promote the goal of collective harmonious living, so they valued friendship as a means to promote one specific aspect of that knowledge to benefit the world in which they lived.[33]

Al-Tawḥīdī's narrow focus on the friendship of disinterested care opens him to criticism from MacIntyre and others. Many modern philosophers have either faulted or praised Aristotle for an egoistic account of friendship.[34] MacIntyre's vision of human flourishing transcends a simple binary in which actions are egoistic or altruistic.[35] He sees this as a false dilemma that troubles persons at a lower level of practical rationality. MacIntyre encourages an education programme that transforms any conflict between egoistic and altruistic goals into an inclination towards both the common good and individual goods. Put differently, the goal is not to be other-regarding rather than self-regarding. The goal is to become people whose passions and inclinations are directed both to their own good and to the good of others.[36]

Several modern scholars use humanism as a heuristic category to discuss certain developments in the Būyid era, and in particular the thought of al-Tawḥīdī.[37] If valid, this trend should doubtlessly be considered a religious humanism or theo-humanism, because by comparison with later secular humanism, the writings of key exponents in the Būyid era are shot through with a thoroughgoing religious sense.[38] Al-Tawḥīdī's esteem for friendship stands as a principle datum expressing a humanistic vision.[39] Al-Tawḥīdī's approach to *ṣadāqa* reveals him at his most synthetic and holistic: the act of *ṣadāqa* encompasses an individual's body and soul, an individual's religious and moral reform, and the unity between an individual's knowledge and action.[40] But despite these complementary levels of the reform of the individual, friendship is more a political question than a question of the personal improvement of one friend or of both friends in a pair. Philosophers in the fourth/tenth century consistently perceived the identity of the individual as secondary to the identity of the collective.[41] Al-Tawḥīdī thus sought to use *ṣadāqa* to reform the social order by shoring up the common moral ground throughout the realm.[42] The extreme pessimism one sees in many passages of al-Tawḥīdī creates some difficulty in interpreting him, as he constantly decries the moral decline in his society and the hypocrisy and corruption of the courts in Rayy and Baghdad. Regardless of whether one reads al-Tawḥīdī as a pessimistic crank mired in permanent complaint or as a more hopeful soul who believed that certain steps towards the betterment of society were yet possible,[43] al-Tawḥīdī lived in an intellectual milieu fraught with competing claims to knowledge and no stable consensus around which disciplines had greater value or merit. Proponents of each of the various *ʿulūm* insisted upon their field's superiority but could not demonstrate their claims convincingly, imperilling the common moral ground that united the populace throughout the realm.[44] Al-Tawḥīdī came to see theological debate as poison for the *umma*, augmenting doubt and scepticism in the culture rather than bringing clarity.[45] The little hope that he sees for his society lies in friendship. *Ṣadāqa* presents a means to encourage social cooperation and overcome the tensions and rivalries between rival scholarly factions and between different social groups. Friends enjoy a privileged window into each other's inner lives, granting the possibility of a mutual understanding that would otherwise be absent.[46] This mutual understanding enables the spread of knowledge coupled with action. Friendship thus has a pedagogical and social purpose that extends beyond the relationship between the friends themselves: it advances salvation and holiness throughout society, particularly when rulers and cultural elites participate in it.[47]

One sees the meaning of friendship and companionship for an author not merely in the theoretical exposition of these relationships but in the figures that an author chooses as the paradigmatic examples for the bond. In his treatise on the proper reverence for shaykhs, al-Sulamī frames Abū Bakr as the ideal model for companionship. Al-Tawḥīdī chooses instead a bond between two men from different intellectual fields as the paradigm for authentic friendship: in the preface to his book, al-Tawḥīdī discusses a dialogue between Ibn Sayyār, a *qāḍī*, and Abū Sulaymān al-Sijistānī (d. 375/985), a philosopher and former student of Yaḥyā b. ʿAdī. The two hailed from different places and occupied different social roles but experienced a unity of soul. Al-Tawḥīdī's description of friendship is, without doubt, idealistic, but his is not an abstract, ephemeral idealism. One does not find here a parable for the encounter of differences, a fable like Ramon Llull's (d. *c.* 716/1316) *Book of the Gentile and the Three Wise Men*. Al-Tawḥīdī's picture of an ideal friendship is a concrete portrait of real persons he knows, he esteems and whose friendship has affected those around them.[48] Thus, while some readers might be inclined to pigeonhole al-Tawḥīdī for his bitterness and grudges against those who rejected him, his discourse on friendship shows that he had tasted the exception to the general state of affairs in a decadent world.[49] He became a champion of friendship that could bring relief to the desperations and anxieties of this life.

The dominant stroke in al-Tawḥīdī's notion of true friendship is the overwhelming resemblance between the friends.[50] Difference in occupation, intellectual discipline or social class do not mitigate this resemblance, as the similarity is better understood as a resonance of soul. Like many other philosophers indebted to the Greek tradition, al-Tawḥīdī relies upon Aristotle's foundational notion of the friend as 'another self', but al-Tawḥīdī extends this seminal insight, attributing to al-Sijistānī a notion of union that Aristotle lacks.[51] 'Just as man is unified by all that makes him human, in a similar way once he has a real friend, the two merge into one through the bond of friendship.'[52] An excerpt of poetry synthesises this idea:

> His spirit is my spirit and my spirit is his spirit;
> If he wills something I will it and if I will it, he wills it.[53]

Al-Tawḥīdī extracts here the final line from a short poem of al-Ḥallāj, lines that most commentators interpret, in their original context, as a reference to friendship with God.[54] Al-Tawḥīdī presents them as a reference to union between two human beings, and his vision of the unity of friends here and elsewhere seems to surpass even that which he attributes to al-Sijistānī.[55] By comparison, al-Sulamī never comes close to collapsing the distinction between two individuals. But aside from the manner in which souls are united, some of the places in which al-Tawḥīdī extends Aristotelian insights provide agreement with al-Sulamī. For al-Tawḥīdī, friendship signifies something far more than basic social mores to live well together in close proximity. He sees *ṣadāqa* as a higher stage of perfection for religious and social reform.[56] One sees the implicit agreement of al-Sulamī in the way he infuses the divine presence into his counsels for social relationships. For al-Sulamī, the unavoidable social mixing characterized by *'ishra* is not simply a bond that must be managed and tolerated. Fellowship serves as a vessel for the divine because God wishes to bless God's servants in the marketplace by means of sending them customers. Al-Sulamī insists that God sustains God's servants in this way and thus enters into the midst of believers' haggling for prices, prompt payment and justice in weights and measures.[57] Following al-Sulamī's counsels for good fellowship in the marketplace thus allows tradesmen more than simply an opportunity to live well together; they can and ought to cultivate their awareness of the presence of God.

Al-Tawḥīdī's elegant language to describe the union of soul between friends reflects his anxiety about the factionalism and divisiveness in his society, the same anxiety that drives his emphasis that only disinterested care can be considered true friendship.[58] In this regard, a comparison of al-Sulamī and al-Tawḥīdī provides competing responses to the crisis of a fragile and crumbling society. Both men lived in the awareness that the social order they knew would likely pass away. Al-Sulamī lived in the growing tensions of toxic *'aṣabiyya* in Nishapur, whereas al-Tawḥīdī's writings show broader concern about the connective tissue of his society throughout the realm. Deeply ingrained formal methods of establishing individual commitments of loyalty knit Būyid society together,[59] but al-Tawḥīdī came to see the order maintained by these bonds as palpably fragile. He perceived them as agents of division rather than unity and thus attempted to subvert them.[60] Al-Sulamī's literary corpus provides no hint of such a response. He encourages *ṣuḥba* and *'ishra* in which believers maintain bonds of loyalty to each other, but these are bonds built on a more positive anthropology and upon greater confidence in God's action in history. For al-Sulamī, companionship and fellowship reflect both the nature with which God has created the human person and the vestiges of the revelation God sent through Muḥammad, the seal of the prophets.

A comparison with al-Tawḥīdī highlights the importance of al-Sulamī's claim that 'for every people, there are varying types of conduct in companionship and good fellowship'.[61] Al-Sulamī understands companionship as a natural phenomenon and a positive phenomenon and seeks to clarify the nature of Islamic companionship so that a natural relationship that is beneficial can become even more beneficial. To import the Thomistic notion that grace builds on nature would be anachronistic but an anachronism that makes a point. Al-Tawḥīdī assumes that the bonds holding his society together are, in fact, the very bonds that maintain it in the danger of coming apart. Al-Sulamī, by contrast, assumes that the bonds holding his society together can still function if someone can clarify for people the benefits and defects of these bonds so that they may serve their fullest purpose. Al-Sulamī paints himself as that clarifier (*mubayyin*), reminding believers of their obligations towards each other and the essence of the bonds that tie them together.

Al-Tawḥīdī suffers no illusions that his idealized image of friendship will become widespread;[62] only persons with higher moral qualities have the capacity to establish authentic *ṣadāqa.*[63] Among the many impediments to the development of true friendship, hierarchical forces have a special role. Hierarchy hinders friendship because it carries the element of self-interest and power. This concern diminishes the possibility for kings, aristocrats, landowners and even merchants to form bonds of friendship.[64] A populist streak emerges in al-Tawḥīdī's reflections here, albeit one with limitations. Unlike some other philosophers, al-Tawḥīdī insists that lower class persons are eligible for friendship and would benefit from it; he does not write them off as uncivilized rabble characterized by baseness of spirit. He does not also, however, idealize the *'awāmm* and invert the social hierarchy by proposing that common folk are more virtuous and thus better able to form bonds of friendship than the social elites. The pendulum does not swing that far. He simply insists that without being virtuous already, one cannot become a true friend. Selfish motivations and a power imbalance threaten the disinterested care at the core of true friendship and perhaps impede it entirely. Two categories of people are therefore best prepared for *ṣadāqa:* pious, religious people and people of knowledge.[65] They possess the virtues necessary to purify their souls, and when they embrace friendship, they share their love for the essence of knowledge. This sharing constitutes an act of obedience to God because this knowledge comes from God and enables the search for happiness and the avoidance of suffering.[66] It brings about the spiritual perfection of the individual but necessarily provides a larger social benefit.

Al-Tawḥīdī looks with suspicion on any forms of association that could threaten social harmony, but his failure in *al-Ṣadāqa wa-l-ṣadīq* to engage in depth with Ṣūfī notions of companionship is nonetheless striking. Although he was not well known for being a Ṣūfī himself, some of his writings suggest a highly philosophical mysticism, and he was known to visit Ṣūfī masters, as did other members of his philosophical circle.[67] Al-Tawḥīdī recalls several teachings of Ṣūfī masters in *al-Ṣadāqa wa-l-ṣadīq,*[68] though he reshapes their insights into a discourse on friendship rather than *ṣuḥba*. Occasional comments in the text like, 'Who is the true companion?'[69] are dwarfed by the massive number of sayings probing the nature of friendship by asking the nature of the true friend. In this, al-Tawḥīdī's terminology is usually precise. Instead of *ṣuḥba*, a concept etymologically linked to the relationship of the Prophet with his own companions, al-Tawḥīdī settled on *ṣadāqa*, a non-Qur'ānic term and a notion rarely found in *ḥadīth* literature, as the means for the religious and moral reform of the decadent society in which he lived.[70]

Taṣawwuf in al-Tawḥīdī's day involved a number of contributing spiritual currents above and beyond the well-known figures of al-Junayd's circle in Baghdad. If al-Tawḥīdī perceived a lack of consensus about the nature of companionship among these Ṣūfī masters, one can appreciate his attraction to an alternative notion, *ṣadāqa*, that lacks the complex web of connotations evoked by *ṣuḥba*. By focusing on *ṣadāqa*, al-Tawḥīdī could more effectively coin a term and gather others around his understanding of it. The interesting element in al-Tawḥīdī's relative neglect of the Ṣūfī tradition on this point does not relate to terminology but to the nature of the bond described. Al-Tawḥīdī remains silent about a bond, Ṣūfī *ṣuḥba*, that in several important respects promotes the social transformation al-Tawḥīdī desires. One could imagine al-Tawḥīdī's reverence for companionship taking one of two forms, but both are absent. First, any exaltation of the bond between teacher and student, master and disciple, does not enter into al-Tawḥīdī's notion of friendship. By comparison, Miskawayh, a philosopher with whom al-Tawḥīdī shares many Aristotelian presuppositions, holds the love of a student for his teacher in the highest esteem because God acts in the life of a diligent seeker through the teacher's assistance to that seeker in the search for happiness.[71] The resonance between MacIntyre's notion of acknowledged dependence, discussed in Chapter 3, and Miskawayh on this point does not surprise.[72] Neither Miskawayh nor al-Sulamī need to deal with MacIntyre's distinctively modern challenge of individuals falsely presupposing themselves to be radically autonomous and free from dependence on others,[73] but both do attempt to move beyond a shortcoming MacIntyre identifies in Aristotle: Aristotle's failure to admit the extent to which our human need for friendship is bound up with our vulnerability.[74] Miskawayh posits the connections between an individual's need for completion by others – a friend's role in contributing something an individual lacks – and the overall progress that results from this towards society's achievement of happiness. Given al-Tawḥīdī's constant emphasis on friendship as disinterested care, one might think that he would latch onto Ṣūfī *ṣuḥba*, shot through as it is with the rhetoric of service. Whether due to his aversion to hierarchy or for another reason, al-Tawḥīdī does not point to the Ṣūfī master-disciple relationship as a bond that could produce the fruit he hopes will emerge from *ṣadāqa*.

Second, any positive appreciation of the horizontal bonds between Ṣūfī brothers finds little expression in al-Tawḥīdī, and I account this absence primarily to al-Tawḥīdī's concern about divisiveness and factionalism. Al-Tawḥīdī's attempts to subvert traditional types of social loyalties point towards an alternative set of social bonds, new norms of behaviour and governance.[75] Perhaps al-Tawḥīdī fails to consider evolving Ṣūfī expressions of such norms precisely because they lack the universal aspirations fuelling al-Tawḥīdī's encouragement of *ṣadāqa*. In Christian history, egalitarian religious currents have often expressed themselves through alternative communities like monasteries or mendicant fraternities. While some of these certainly aspired to become what Arnold Toynbee called 'creative minorities' that stimulated broader social change, others either did not see themselves as agents of large-scale social transformation or were simply ineffective in bringing it about.[76] If al-Tawḥīdī perceived *taṣawwuf* as a movement restricted in its scope – as a self-limiting alternative community, whether by intention or de facto – this could partially explain his neglect of it. *Taṣawwuf* would be beneficial but insufficient for al-Tawḥīdī's more ambitious goals. Al-Tawḥīdī's reluctance may extend further and be more pessimistic than this, however. Instead of an alternative society that acts as a repository for virtue that then diffuses outward and promotes broader change, al-Tawḥīdī could fear an intra-Ṣūfī *taʿaṣṣub* doomed to exacerbate social problems. One sees this concern in al-Tawḥīdī's discussion of *futuwwa*. The high ideals of spiritual chivalry play a key role not only in al-Sulamī's rhetoric but in that of several near contemporaries.[77] At the same time, *futuwwa* connotes for some others the worst kinds of troublemaking and brigandage.[78] According to Sedgwick, it seems that *futuwwa* brotherhoods 'took multiple forms, some resembling military forces, some resembling trade guilds, and some resembling vagrant bands or youth gangs'.[79] Al-Sulamī is less concerned with the organizational aspect of *futuwwa* and more with its high ideals. *Futuwwa* 'stood for all the noble, moral and ethical qualities of a young man that were meant to be exemplary', incorporating pre-Islamic values and Qurʾānic values.[80] Al-Sulamī ignores any possible negative connotations for the term and gathers nearly all examples of honourable behaviour under the mantle of *futuwwa*, leveraging the term as an instrument for popular moral reform and the diffusion of the spiritual currents he found most valuable.[81] His œuvre includes texts like *Jawāmiʿ ādāb al-ṣūfiyya* and *Dhikr miḥan al-ṣūfiyya* (*Remembrance of the Trials of the Ṣūfīs*) that promote a strong sense of group identity among Ṣūfīs, as well as texts like *Kitāb ādāb al-ṣuḥba*, a treatise that promotes a highly spiritual code of etiquette for a believer's life in the world, including relationships that are more casual.[82] Al-Tawḥīdī struggles to appreciate the benefits of such group identity, seeing *futuwwa* as a gateway to a sectarian mentality. Al-Tawḥīdī maintains a firm distinction between *futuwwa* and religion (*dīn*) and insists that one can cultivate virtue without *futuwwa*.[83] Were he to address the specific social circumstances of Nishapur, al-Tawḥīdī would, without doubt, paint Ṣūfīs as partisan – perhaps irredeemably and destructively so – in the growing division between Ḥanafī patrician families and the Ashʿarī-Shāfiʿī patrician families of which nearly all Ṣūfīs were members. Al-Tawḥīdī cannot acknowledge that the ideals expressed in al-Sulamī's literary corpus illustrate the social benefits of companionship that al-Tawḥīdī otherwise urges. Al-Tawḥīdī's failure to explore *taṣawwuf* more robustly constitutes a lacuna not just in *al-Ṣadāqa wa-l-ṣadīq* but in the Tawḥīdian corpus overall.

One could discuss several other philosophers in addition to Yaḥyā b. ʿAdī, Miskawayh and al-Tawḥīdī. Al-ʿĀmirī[84] and the Brethren of Purity stand out as worthwhile possibilities among others, but a comprehensive analysis of philosophical approaches to friendship is not the intention here. These three suffice to show some primary themes of philosophical reflection about friendship during al-Sulamī's time and suffice to show that their direct influence upon al-Sulamī is not obvious. One should not overestimate differences in terminology and exaggerate the general absence of the term *ṣuḥba* in the writings of these philosophers. Such lexical differences exist among the philosophers themselves, despite the deep debt all three owe to the Greek philosophical tradition. Far more significant is the philosophers' strong claim about the political consequences of friendship, a claim that finds little overt expression in al-Sulamī. Especially in the case of Miskawayh and al-Tawḥīdī, one may attribute this concern to the sectarian divisions and social tensions diffused throughout the Būyid realm,[85] but all three make a rapid leap from their initial concern with friendship among virtuous people to an urgent concern for how the values of true friendship and the beneficial consequences of true friendship will manifest themselves among ruling elites. In this regard, while al-Tawḥīdī's account of *ṣadāqa* does involve an allergy to hierarchy, he nonetheless sees rulers as an essential intermediate link in this broader social transformation. Due to the powerful influence that courtiers exert over the well-being of the common people, one simply cannot envision the transformation that will yield broader social flourishing without the marks of authentic friendship upon them.

Al-Sulamī does not share al-Tawḥīdī's assumptions here, due to his fundamental disinclination to associate himself with worldly power. One might justly attribute to early Sufism on the whole a rejection, in principle, of the search for temporal power and the company of the powerful.[86] Over the broader sweep of history, Ṣūfīs adopt a variety of responses to the dilemma. A believer in a society racked with corruption, injustice and immorality can choose two basic options for involvement with politics: either engage with worldly powers to transform them or create an alternative society with marked distance from them. In modern Sufism, a strategy of 'engaged distance' emerges from centuries in which political authorities have used the spiritual authority of prominent Ṣūfīs to legitimate their claims to power.[87] 'Abbāsid caliphs attempted to bolster their own legitimacy through the *'ulamā'* more so than through Ṣūfīs, although the line between the Ṣūfīs and the *'ulamā'* was always porous and state-sponsored Sufism did arise in the final decades before the fall of Baghdad.[88] Al-Sulamī's Nishapur involved a different kind of symbiosis between political authorities and prominent figures associated with Sufism. Most Ṣūfī leaders, including al-Sulamī, were members of patrician families and, by virtue of their education and personal connections, had access to the corridors of local power. At the same time, al-Sulamī's writings show an unambiguous lack of interest in proximity to that power, especially by comparison with the courtly concerns that consistently preoccupy al-Tawḥīdī.

One should distinguish in these texts between the question of proximity to worldly power and the rhetoric of worldly power. Royal imagery was common in Ṣūfī discourse in the formative period, particularly in Persian-speaking lands. *Kitāb ādāb al-ṣuḥba* contains a biting jibe al-Junayd directed at Abū Ḥafṣ, a symbol of the school of Khurasan. 'You disciplined your companions in the ways of princes (*ādāb al-salāṭīn*).' Abū Ḥafṣ responded, 'No, Abū l-Qāsim [al-Junayd]. It is only that the good comportment of the outer (*ḥusn adab al-ẓāhir*) indicates the good comportment of the inner (*ḥusn adab al-bāṭin*).'[89] The passage illustrates al-Sulamī's preoccupation with an integrated spirituality, a matter that has already been discussed at length in this study but prompts questions about the meaning of *salāṭīn*. Abū Ḥafṣ does not deny that he taught his disciples the comportment of the court, but he shifts the context implied by al-Junayd's rebuke. Given the connection between Abū Ḥafṣ and the Path of Blame, Abū Ḥafṣ certainly did not encourage his followers to ingratiate themselves to courtiers and draw near to worldly power. Most likely, a more egalitarian pattern of relations marked the circle of al-Junayd, who saw in the masters of Khurasan the seeds of a Ṣūfī *adab* that mirrored the customs of the Sassanid court, setting up the masters of *taṣawwuf* as a kind of parallel royalty. The anonymous fourth/tenth century *Kitāb adab al-mulūk fī bayān al-ḥaqā'iq* (*The Way of Kings on the Exposition of Realities*) draws heavily upon this rhetoric,[90] but especially after the time of al-Sulamī's student Abū Sa'īd b. Abī l-Khayr, such courtly etiquette became ever more ensconced into Sufism.[91] Considering the key role Abū Sa'īd b. Abī l-Khayr played in institutionalising these patterns of sociability into intra-Ṣūfī relations, the relative lack of such royal imagery in al-Sulamī's literary corpus is surprising. His citation of the exchange between al-Junayd and Abū Ḥafṣ does, however, indicate his favour for the latter.[92]

The influence of the Path of Blame left al-Sulamī deeply hesitant about contact with riches and political control. He penned only one brief treatise that treats the matter of rulers and how believers should deal with them, *Fuṣūl fī naṣīḥat al-umarā' wa-l-wuzarā'*. That text focuses on the theme of justice, as do so many in the 'Mirrors for Princes' genre. Al-Sulamī restricts himself to anecdotes about prior rulers, first and foremost in the era of the *rāshidūn*, who made wise decisions in choosing a vizier. Al-Sulamī's authorial voice is nearly absent, the concepts of companionship or friendship are understated[93] and the number of Ṣūfī figures in the treatise is small.[94] The scarcity of Ṣūfī masters comes as no surprise; in other texts, al-Sulamī reports few stories of their involvement with worldly authorities unless that contact involved the Ṣūfīs' persecution.[95]

Al-Sulamī's assumption about the ego-self's inclination towards rebelliousness and disharmony guides his general silence about the ruling elites.[96] The *nafs* wants power and pleasure. When al-Sulamī discusses wealth and worldly power, he discourages the desire for them. While he possessed a privileged social status himself as a member of a patrician family, his approach towards the way *ṣuḥba* infuses the realm with spiritual values can be adequately described as a grassroots approach. In this regard, one can and should understand al-Sulamī's approach to companionship as unmistakably 'political'; al-Sulamī expects the bond of companionship to affect the life of the larger community, albeit in a different chronological progression than al-Tawḥīdī seems to anticipate. *Ṣuḥba* is thoroughly political in the sense of shared life in the *polis*: companionship reminds believers of their responsibility to remain conscious of their responsibilities to each other and that the rights of Muslims must be protected. The philosophers' approach to the moral reform of the realm might be characterized as trickle down: by cultivating a few virtuous people among the ruling class, benefits will redound and diffuse for all the people. Al-Sulamī's approach, by contrast, could considered 'trickle out'. He spreads wise maxims about companionship and fellowship through the populace, like throwing stones into a lake and watching the ripples. Al-Sulamī foresees the fruits of *ṣuḥba* reaching the marketplace before they reach the courtiers,[97] and the authorities he values most highly are not viziers and their entourage but the possessors of knowledge. Reverence and respect belong to those whom God has made the elite among God's servants, and it is to them that this discussion now must turn.

The elevation of shaykhs and the bond of brothers

Modern scholarly discussions of Ṣūfī *ṣuḥba* typically note two aspects of the phenomenon. First, *ṣuḥba* in its fullest sense resides in the relationship between master and disciple. Second, the term has never been restricted to the relationship between master and disciple; it has always been used more broadly. From the beginnings of *taṣawwuf*, adherents organized themselves informally into groups as well as into pairs of teacher and student.[98] By the sixth/twelfth and seventh/thirteenth centuries, Ṣūfīs had consecrated a hierarchy and inequality within their own brotherhood centred on the role of the shaykh and had developed a strict etiquette around the master-disciple relationship, which served as a privileged locus for ethical growth.[99] Arthur F. Buehler sums up the assumption undergirding many studies of Sufism: 'Sufi transformative practices are supposed to be performed in the context of the shaykh-seeker relationship.'[100] The etiquette for that relationship focused on obedience, submission and dependence,[101] but the historical evolution of that etiquette is hotly debated.[102] As the preceding chapter has shown, al-Sulamī's *Kitāb ādāb al-ṣuḥba* uses the term *ṣuḥba* loosely, speaking little about shaykhs and never about a *murīd*. At the same time, the bond between master and disciple holds a significant place in al-Sulamī's thought, though one that has been under-discussed because the most relevant treatise on the matter was edited and published only recently.[103] An examination of al-Sulamī's near contemporaries shows that both concerns remain active throughout, despite the increased attention to the role of the shaykh.

A 1971 article by Fritz Meier remains the point of departure for most scholarly discussion of the evolution of *ṣuḥba*.[104] Meier recalls Ibn 'Abbād of Ronda's (d. 792/1390) famous comment about the evolution of the role of the shaykh in a disciple's growth. Ibn 'Abbād claimed that a change from the model of a shaykh as teacher (*shaykh al-ta'līm*) to shaykh as director (*shaykh al-tarbiya*) occurred in the fifth/eleventh century. Meier attempts to pinpoint this transition more precisely; he locates it in Khurasan in the time of al-Qushayrī.[105] Meier charts a slow process of change in Nishapur from the third/ninth to fifth/eleventh centuries, with al-Qushayrī clearly marking the end of the era of the teaching shaykh and the beginning of the era of the directing shaykh.

In this schema, a teaching shaykh expects disciples to spend long periods of time with him, perhaps even in residence, while he imparts his knowledge. A directing shaykh takes a much more individualized approach towards each disciple, imparting discipline especially suited to the disciple's needs and developing remedies for the defects in the disciple's soul. If the former model is that of teacher/student, the latter functions as doctor/patient. For Meier, training/directing means 'the direct intervention of the shaykh in the student's behaviour by means of instructions, the application of which he supervises, and the eventual outcome of which he then awaits and criticizes'.[106] Teaching and directing are not mutually exclusive, but disciples generally did not expect this kind of personal, direct intervention in the earlier period. This relationship of training involved a binding pact in which the *murīd* promises unquestioning obedience to the shaykh, a more formal initiation into *ṣuḥba*.[107] The development of this style of *tarbiya* did not exclude other forms of *ṣuḥba*, but according to Meier, al-Qushayrī marks the moment when the ideal of the *shaykh al-tarbiya* had become ingrained. The exponential growth in the body of Ṣūfī knowledge was likely also an important factor here, along with the proliferation of distinctive Ṣūfī schools and methods. With so much to impart to a beginner on the path, former methods of instruction no longer could suffice.[108]

Meier's work set the parameters for subsequent discussion of how the shaykh's role shifted. Laury Silvers has offered a direct critique, primarily to fault Meier for failing to recognize spiritual direction in the earlier period. Meier and scholars who follow him carry an overly restrictive notion of what constitutes the *tarbiya* of a shaykh, and as a result, they don't seem to notice that early shaykhs' instruction amounted to far more than mere 'lecturing'.[109] Early Ṣūfīs made no distinction between *taʿlīm* and *tarbiya*, so rather than assume the absence of *tarbiya*, Silvers claims that the two activities were intertwined.[110] Indeed, she assumes that one could characterize Muḥammad's instruction to his companions as spiritual direction.[111] Silvers notes that in al-Sulamī's *Ṭabaqāt al-ṣūfiyya*, early Ṣūfīs entered into *ṣuḥba* with multiple companions, but neither this fact nor the less formal character of the bonds annuls the reality that shaykhs personally directed their companions on the path. Shaykhs required their companions to undertake certain practices and did not consider any aspect of their companion's life off-limits in principle.[112] A believer seeking spiritual growth would seek direction wherever available, as 'the early Sufis seem to have understood themselves to be members of one far-flung community allied towards a common goal'.[113]

This debate permits no simple resolution and interest in it – at least in the terms under which it has been discussed thus far – has waned somewhat.[114] Quandries about research methods have done as much to hinder as to assist the search for consensus. The general trend in the field towards attending to sources from material culture sheds little light on the matter. Ṣūfī buildings from the period have not yet produced evidence that would be helpful here.[115] Abū Saʿīd b. Abī l-Khayr is often credited with dictating the ten basic rules of life of the Ṣūfī *khānaqā*, none of which involve the shaykh.[116] While the rules attributed to him presume the presence of the shaykh in the lodge and implicitly exclude the shaykh's role as an autocratic governor of the community, they do not clarify whether the shaykh's role in the lives of disciples was one of teaching or individualized direction. Fortunately, the emic/etic dynamic hovering over Ṣūfī studies and the tendency to criticize the orientalist 'construction' or 'invention' of Sufism do not seem at present to impede advances on the question. A fundamental coherence exists between the 'insider' account of Ibn 'Abbād and the 'outsider' Ibn Khaldūn (d. 808/1406), a non-Ṣūfī contemporary to the former who provides detailed historical witness to the evolution. Ibn Khaldūn finds the instruction of a shaykh unnecessary for initial progress on the path but essential for one to reach the highest levels of spiritual achievement; the growth in the number of disciples seeking this lofty rank likely drove the evolution of the shaykhs' activities.[117]

Insofar as the distinction between *ta'līm* and *tarbiya* holds – and most scholars of Sufism today continue to operate as though it does[118] – the model of the directing shaykh expresses well MacIntyre's fundamental insights about how traditions function and the narrative nature of an individual's life. A person's status as a master of a given craft depends not only on his or her own capacity to excel in it but on the knowledge of how to direct others to excel in it. A master understands the history and flow of the tradition in which the master is enmeshed, and thus can link past and future, interpreting and reinterpreting that tradition so that its *telos* becomes apparent in new and unexpected ways as they creatively progress towards it.[119] Aristotle appreciated, as did many later philosophers who saw themselves as his followers, that initiation into the moral life almost always happens through a practical programme of education at the hands of a teacher.[120] The Ṣūfī model of the directing shaykh takes this assumption about the formation of children and insists upon it even more stringently for believers who desire to rise to the higher levels of the spiritual life. Alexander Knysh leans upon imagery from athletics to describe not only the striving of the seeker but the necessity of a shaykh's guidance to outperform the norm.

> All the texts we have just mentioned and numerous others from the same age depict Sufism not just as a special doctrine and practice within Islam but also as an exclusive sports club of sorts. Joining the club requires abilities that commoners can hardly hope to obtain. No wonder, therefore, that the commoners were many, while the high-achieving athletes were few. Like professional sportsmen, the 'spiritual athletes' of Sufism submitted themselves willingly and unconditionally to the rigorous discipline, dietary restrictions, and constant supervision by an experienced and decorated mentor. Unlike usual paths of righteousness, which pious individuals could enter and navigate on their own, travelers on the path of supersensory unveiling (*suluk kashfi*) could not do without an experienced guide.[121]

Believers cannot accomplish this ascent without a master to direct them, and this does not occur optimally in a group of believers receiving standardized instruction from a teacher. Rather, one climbs in the personal, intimate contact with a master who knows the disciple's story and appreciates the unique opportunities and pitfalls in that disciple's unique life.

In the context of the relationship between master and disciple, MacIntyre's emphasis on the narrative quality of the human life takes on added meaning.[122] The teleological character of the master-disciple bond is clear throughout – indeed, progress towards the *telos* is the raison d'être for the bond in the first place – and the disciple understands throughout and embraces the fact that his subjectivity is correlative.[123] The disciple is not the sole author of his own narrative. He walks the path as part of the master's story and the master is part, even a co-author, of the disciple's narrative quest. One could say here that the stories of Ṣūfī *murīd*s advancing in the stations at the hands of their shaykhs embodies an element of MacIntyre's account that MacIntyre himself left undeveloped. For all his emphasis on the continuity of a tradition, MacIntyre offers few details about the kinds of concrete communities conducive to promoting and sustaining the virtues.[124] Stories of the pedagogy of Ṣūfī masters with a keen apprehension of the currents of their tradition accomplish precisely this. A number of different shaykhs could be selected, but two giants of Ṣūfī literature provides a helpful pathway for comparison: al-Sulamī's predecessor al-Sarrāj and al-Sulamī's student al-Qushayrī. Here the continuity between master and disciple is clear, particularly in the role of the shaykh.

Al-Sarrāj: Companions to disturb and to serve

Al-Sarrāj's *Kitāb al-luma'* shows the author's capacity for systematization, especially in the book's glossary of the Ṣūfī lexicon. Al-Sarrāj does not display that capacity for precision in his section on *ṣuḥba*, a collection of disparate wisdom sayings and brief vignettes drawn from various spiritual masters. The section on companionship lies in the chapter devoted to *ādāb*, but unlike the sections that precede and succeed it, which meticulously examine key Ṣūfī terms, al-Sarrāj does not explore the meaning of *adab* or *ādāb* as concepts. Instead, he compiles a pastiche of materials from which one must surmise the principles that should guide companions. These sayings occur with no discernible organization, whether chronological, thematic, geographic or otherwise, and they lack the detailed instruction present in al-Sarrāj's *ādāb* for clothing, for fasting, for the proper mosques to visit on pilgrimage and the like. *Kitāb al-luma'* does not provide one sole vision of companionship, instead using *ṣuḥba* to indicate at least three styles of bond: a relationship of spiritual direction between a shaykh and his subordinate, a relationship between two believers of equal rank and the bond shared by all those on the Ṣūfī path.[125] Al-Sarrāj does not provide a set of regulations to constitute and maintain companionship among the Ṣūfīs. He instead provides snapshots of the mutual love and care that mark authentic companionship, images with a sense of immediate relevance. He moves fluidly between longer anecdotes and short didactic sayings, providing a collage of what companionship meant to the Ṣūfī masters whose wisdom he strove to preserve.

While al-Sulamī's corpus provides several examples of believers asking the question, 'with whom should I keep company?' (*man aṣḥab*?), stories of the poignant moment when two souls come together are infrequent in his texts. Al-Sarrāj, by comparison, shows less interest in sustaining companionship and more in the moment that companionship begins. Abū Ḥafṣ al-Naysābūrī, Dhū l-Nūn al-Miṣrī, al-Junayd, al-Bisṭāmī, al-Tustarī and others provide models from whom sincere believers can infer beneficial wisdom throughout this section. That wisdom comes from some poignant stories crafted to shock or surprise, dislodging a person from the ordinary social mores of fellowship and driving home the different nature – the blessed strangeness – of the more intimate, more intentional and more pedagogical relationship al-Sarrāj recounts here. A handful of selections illustrates the type of material at the forefront of al-Sarrāj's mind when he considers the beginning of *ṣuḥba*.[126]

> A man said to Sahl b. ʿAbdallāh [al-Tustarī], 'I want to be your companion.' Sahl said to him, 'If one of us were to die and the other were to keep company with someone else, let him keep company with that person now.'[127] … Abū ʿUthmān [al-Ḥīrī] said, 'I was a companion of Abū Ḥafṣ [al-Naysābūrī] when I was a servant boy. At first, he drove me away and said, "Don't sit in my presence." I did not return his words by turning my back on him. I walked away backwards, keeping my face turned towards him until I was absent from him. Then I decided to dig a well for myself next to his door. I went down into it and sat in it and I would not leave without his permission. When he saw this, he drew near to me and he kissed me and he made me one of the elite (*khawāṣṣ*) of his companions until his death.'[128] … When Ibrāhīm b. Adham kept company with a person, he laid down three conditions: that he [Ibrāhīm] would do all the service, that he would call out the summons to prayer and that he would receive the same portion of any worldly sustenance God provided them. A man from among his companions said to him, 'I cannot do that.' He said, 'I am amazed at your honesty!'[129] … Abū ʿAlī l-Ribāṭī said, 'I kept company with ʿAbdallāh al-Marwazī, and he entered the desert without provisions before I had become his companion. When I became his companion, he said to me, "What is more pleasing to you? That I be in charge (*amīr*)? Or you?" I said, "No! You are in charge!" He said, "Then you must obey." I said, "Yes." He took a sack and he placed provisions into it, and he put it on his back, and when I said to him, "Give it to me so that I can carry it," he said, "Am I not in charge and must you not obey me?" Then it rained on us during the night, and he stayed (from the night) until the morning. I was seated and he held a covering over my head, protecting me from the rain, and I said to myself, "Would that I had died and not said to him, 'You are in charge!' " Then he said to me, "When a man becomes your companion, keep company with him as you have seen me, the same way I have kept company with you." '[130]

Each of these anecdotes in different ways relate to the moment of mutual decision when two believers choose to become companions of each other, and the humour in them shows the unanticipated consequences that *ṣuḥba* can bring into a person's life. A seemingly small decision by Abū ʿAlī l-Ribāṭī to allow ʿAbdallāh al-Marwazī to take control of their journey leads him into intense regret before he understands ʿAbdallāh's pedagogical intention. The vignette about Ibrāhīm b. Adham (d. *c.* 165/782) functions similarly. The anonymous man admires Ibrāhīm and desires to learn from him, expecting to serve him; he quickly learns that *ṣuḥba* with Ibrāhīm entails accepting the difficult and counter-intuitive condition that Ibrāhīm will serve and not be served. Ibrāhīm insists on equality in provisions and on taking a role in their common prayer other than that of the prayer leader (*imām*). By claiming the role to proclaim the call to prayer, Ibrāhīm ensures that he will never serve as prayer leader.

Not all the characteristics of an authentic companion have this destabilizing effect. Some could better be considered extensions of Khurasan's ordinary social code rather than an eccentric rupture with it.

> A man said to Dhū l-Nūn al-Miṣrī, 'With whom should I keep company?' He said, 'With the person who, when you are sick, will visit you, and when you sin, will repent on your behalf.'[131] One of them said, 'Every companion to whom you say, "Come with us," and he responds, "Where?" is not a companion.'[132] … Aḥmad b. Yūsuf al-Zajjājī said, 'Two companions are like two lights. If they come together, they can see by means of their being together what they were not able to see before. … Al-Junayd said, 'A transgressor of good character (*rajul fāsiq ḥusn al-khuluq*) who keeps company with me is more beloved than a Qurʾān reciter of poor character.'[133] … Yūsuf b. al-Ḥusayn (al-Rāzī) said to Dhū l-Nūn, 'With whom should I keep company?' He said, 'With someone from whom you do not conceal anything about you that God knows.'[134]

These vignettes describe a level of intimacy and candour that surely was uncommon in society but encourages deeds widely seen as commendable. Visiting a sick believer and repenting on behalf of a sinful fellow believer are pious actions that occurred outside any context of formal *ṣuḥba*, and the honest counsel urged by Dhū l-Nūn falls well within the range of the *naṣīḥa* encouraged by many Prophetic traditions. When coupled with the earlier passages about the initiation of companionship, however, al-Sarrāj's *Kitāb al-lumaʿ* does not paint a picture of a Ṣūfī companion who is merely a more intense or more devoted version of an ordinary believer, one who differs in degree but not in kind from the other Muslims around him. The decision demands a conversion.[135] One chooses a new mode of relationship characterized by an altered mode of attentiveness, one that opens spiritual doors and pathways that were not possibilities before. The prominence of conversion for al-Sarrāj accounts for the fact that by comparison with al-Sulamī, al-Sarrāj presents a greater percentage of teachings that actively discourage companionship – or more precisely, that al-Sarrāj's teachings serve to present *ṣuḥba* as attractive through the dissonance and curiosity these stories create. Al-Sulamī's *Kitāb ādāb al-ṣuḥba* contains many counsels against companionship with the wrong sort of people, but al-Sarrāj gathers examples of famous Ṣūfī masters resisting the initial attempts of fellow believers to join them. In the context of their entire lives, Abū Ḥafṣ al-Naysābūrī and Sahl al-Tustarī welcomed companions and rejoiced in these relationships, but only after the potential companion had proven his resolve and seriousness.

The balance of al-Sarrāj's material in this section tilts towards the initial establishment of *ṣuḥba* between two believers, but he also compiles several sayings or anecdotes that extol perseverance in authentic companionship. These teachings are neither less comical nor less demanding than those that treat the initial decision.

> Ibrāhīm b. Shaybān ... said, 'We did not keep company with anyone who said, "my sandals" (and "my cup").'[136] ... Al-Junayd said, 'I saw a bald man with Abū Ḥafṣ al-Naysābūrī and he was always silent, not speaking. I said to his companions, "Who is this?" It was said to me, "This man keeps company with Abū Ḥafṣ and serves us and had spent one hundred thousand dirhams on him, then he borrowed one hundred thousand more and spent it on him. Abū Ḥafṣ does not permit him to speak one word."'[137] ... Ibn Sālim [said] 'I was a companion of Sahl b. 'Abdallāh for sixty years. I said to him one day, "I have served you for sixty years and not one day did you consider me among those who were imitating you, the substitutes (*budalā'*) and the saints (*awliyā'*)." He said (to me), "Were you not the one who was responsible for bringing them into my presence every day? Did you not see that the person bringing the napkin and the toothbrush who was speaking to you yesterday was among them?"' ... Sahl b. 'Abdallāh ... said to one of his companions one day, 'If you are afraid of wild beasts, do not remain my companion.'[138] ... Abū Bakr al-Kattānī said, 'A man kept company with me, and my heart disagreed with him. One day, I gave him something – a garment or a robe – so that this dislike weighing on my heart would cease, but it did not. So I took him one day to a house – or to some other place – and I said to him, "Place your foot on my cheek!" He refused, so I told him that he must do this and he did it. He ceased when the feeling on my heart was removed.'[139]

The spiritual masters described here go to extreme lengths to extricate any self-will from themselves and from others. The shaykhs are not portrayed as guiltless – al-Kattānī (d. 322/934) demands an instrument of discipline from his companion that his companion finds repulsive and bizarre but accomplishes its purpose. These shaykhs develop reputations for passing long years without allowing a companion to speak or without granting a companion any recognition at all, a reputation that garners respect because it demonstrates the shaykhs' correct assessment about the individual needs of these companions. Al-Sarrāj reports many examples of people speaking to Abū Ḥafṣ, for example, but his reaction to this believer demonstrates that man's need for silence as a means of discipline. A single word can speak volumes about a person's inner life, as in the person who says, 'my sandals'. That statement indicates an instinctive selfishness and desire for possessions, contradictory to the habits of generosity and shared ownership that mark the behaviour of true *ṣuḥba*.[140] Little of the material in al-Sarrāj's section on *ṣuḥba* involves precepts in the narrow sense, rules that a companion must obey.

Elsewhere, al-Sarrāj does offer such precepts, like his detailed instructions on whether, when and how Ṣūfīs can enter the *ḥammām* (bath).[141] In the section on *ṣuḥba*, aphorisms and anecdotes search out the attitudes of the heart, as well as mark the level of awareness among spiritual masters who can notice the minutiae that express a defect in a person's character and the means to refine it. Al-Sarrāj's discussion of companionship, then, belongs more to the realm of character than to custom, rule or behavioural norm. The maxim attributed to al-Junayd captures this best. Insofar as one can distinguish between outstanding religio-legal observance and excellence of character, al-Junayd prefers a companion marked by the latter.

The dicta and vignettes that al-Sarrāj narrates about these Ṣūfī masters recur again and again in the texts of later compilers, thus making a substantial contribution to historical knowledge of the period and the way Ṣūfīs revered the shaykhs who had come before them. Al-Sarrāj was not known as a Ṣūfī master himself, however, and this may account for some of the ambiguity in his text. He travelled widely to collect information about the Ṣūfīs and most likely lived as a Ṣūfī himself but was known as a scholar of them rather than a shaykh.[142] A more fully developed account of a shaykh's programme of instruction waited until the advent of al-Sulamī's student al-Qushayrī, who combined the breadth of his knowledge of the tradition with his personal experience training disciples.

Al-Qushayrī: Stability and exclusivity on the path

Al-Qushayrī's spiritual development primarily occurred through his companionship with and guidance under his father-in-law Abū ʿAlī l-Daqqāq. Al-Daqqāq provided an outstanding education for his daughter and founded the *madrasa* that al-Qushayrī would later lead and where they would be buried.[143] Al-Daqqāq and al-Sulamī knew each other well and had both studied under al-Naṣrābādhī,[144] so al-Qushayrī's decision to continue his training with al-Sulamī after al-Daqqāq's death does not surprise, though al-Qushayrī's time together with al-Sulamī before al-Sulamī's death was relatively short. Both masters offered a synthesis of Baghdad Sufism and the Path of Blame,[145] but al-Qushayrī's mature writings show that he primarily understood himself as a student of al-Daqqāq. One sees this in the notably different ways in which al-Qushayrī draws upon the authority of his teachers. The overwhelming majority of his references to al-Sulamī utilize al-Sulamī as a transmitter for the teachings of others, whether Baghdad Ṣūfīs or masters of the Path of Blame; by contrast, the majority of his references to al-Daqqāq present teachings of al-Daqqāq himself as an outstanding representative of Persian Sufism.[146] Al-Qushayrī became arguably the most influential intellectual in Nishapur in his time, both due to the strength of his mind and his prominent position in a network of patrician families after his father-in-law's death.[147]

Regarding spiritual companionship, al-Qushayrī's celebrated *Risāla* offers not only the best-known point of comparison but also the best focused.[148] Al-Qushayrī devotes a section to *ṣuḥba* in the third chapter of the *Risāla*, identifying companionship as a gift from God which bestows compassion.[149] He distinguishes between companionship and love, favouring love. One tradition says that the Prophet's passion for his beloved friends (*aḥbāb*) exceeds his passion for his companions (*aṣḥāb*), for his beloved friends trusted him without ever having seen him.[150] Al-Qushayrī's speech about love and companionship elsewhere shows the logic behind his decision to cite this Prophetic tradition. The section on love in the third chapter of the *Risāla* dwells on the mutual love between God and God's servant, not between one servant and another servant.[151] The Prophet lauds the ability of his beloved friends to trust him without having seen him, in parallel to the trust a believer places in the unseen God. In contrast, al-Qushayrī's writings on companionship deal almost entirely with relationships between persons. *Ṣuḥba* with God is possible and encouraged, but his discussion revolves around interpersonal companionship. Al-Qushayrī describes three ranks of companionship: *ṣuḥba* with one who is above you, which is service; with one who is below you, which requires compassion and kindness and making your companion's defects known to him; and with one who is equal to you, which demands spiritual chivalry (*futuwwa*) and giving preference to the companion. When one enters into companionship with a shaykh of a higher rank, the practice (*adab*) of the Ṣūfīs is to abandon all opposition to him and interpret his instructions in a positive light.[152] This tripartite division offers a general guide for behaviour in companionship but is not absolute. Al-Qushayrī's insistence on reverence for and veneration for one's master does not annul the assumption of the masters themselves that their role is one of service; al-Qushayrī's citation of the anecdote about Ibrāhīm b. Adham discussed in the previous section provides witness to this.[153] The section on *ṣuḥba* generally speaks about companions and not about shaykh/*ustādh* and *murīd*, although the context indicates that the person searching for a companion will be the person of a lower rank. Later Ṣūfīs might assume that when a seeker is ready, the shaykh will find him, but this suggests more about God's providential action than about a shaykh actively searching for disciples.[154] Al-Qushayrī assumes that the *murīd* is the one on the hunt, attentively seeking a master.

The striking element of al-Qushayrī's description of companionship relates not to the comparative ranks of two companions but to the necessity of maintaining only one companion. Al-Qushayrī tells a story of one man accompanying another; after a time, one of the two desires to separate and asks the other for permission. His companion replies, 'Only on the condition that your next companion be superior to us. And if this is the case, then you should still not be his companion, since you chose us as your first companion.'[155] This text deliberately excludes a reading in which a *murīd* could change companions to find a guide of a higher rank. Al-Qushayrī refers to each companion simply as *rajul* (a man) and does not specify who has a loftier status and who desires to leave the other. The permanence of the companionship between them is more important for al-Qushayrī than any impetus to find a more advanced companion and thus an abler guide.

In other places, al-Qushayrī's prohibition on severing companionship seems directed at the companion of lower rank, presumably because the inferior believer struggles to persevere in obedience to his master and becomes frustrated.

Al-Qushayrī exhibits extreme confidence in the forgiveness in shaykhs' hearts, so he worries more about a disciple ending a relationship than a master ending it. He offers in several places a developed exposition of the relationship between *ustādh* and *murīd*,[156] and in this he reveals a slight shift from al-Sulamī's approach to the matter. While al-Sulamī exhorts all believers to show reverence for shaykhs, al-Qushayrī treats the matter within a more narrowly Ṣūfī context, focusing on the honour that seekers owe to shaykhs.[157] Al-Qushayrī insists that God protects the hearts of Ṣūfī shaykhs and thus one should not oppose one's master in anything the master teaches or desires. The shaykh is not impeccable (*ʿiṣma*) but does possess the knowledge to discern right from wrong, and the disciple must trust the shaykh's guidance.[158] The separation between Moses and Khiḍr when Moses disagreed with him provides the Qurʾānic foundation for the Ṣūfī practice that when a disciple opposes the will of his master, the disciple breaks the bond of *ṣuḥba* between them. The two may continue to occupy the same space, but their companionship has ended.[159] Al-Qushayrī attributes a demand for unquestioning obedience to al-Sulamī's master al-Ṣuʿlūkī, providing more contextual detail for this matter of *adab* than does al-Sulamī himself.[160] Al-Qushayrī thus frames matters consistently with al-Sulamī's own writings and builds significantly upon them. The consistency lies in the authority of the master. The obligation to guard and protect the teachings of one's master recurs again and again in al-Sulamī's writings, including the demand for unquestioning obedience to a shaykh.[161] Al-Sulamī transmits the teaching that a disciple should never ask his master, 'why?', but should trust the words of his master, even unto the command to get married.[162] Passages about the abandonment of self-direction and self-will (*tadbīr al-maʿīsha*, *ikhtiyār*, *siyāsat al-nufūs* etc.) also arise in the context of entrusting oneself to a shaykh, not merely obedience to the *sharīʿa* or to God's will in a more general sense.[163] Al-Qushayrī's writings on these themes stand in continuity with al-Sulamī, as al-Qushayrī casts a rupture of *ṣuḥba* as a major taboo.[164] Whoever opposes his master violates the bond of *ṣuḥba* and must repent; al-Qushayrī reports that some Ṣūfī masters deny that any repentance can expiate this sin of disobedience.[165] Al-Qushayrī stresses more than al-Sulamī the requirement of unquestioning obedience, repeating the injunction against asking 'why?' and bolstering it with a series of anecdotes about shaykhs issuing incomprehensible commands to their disciples that subsequently result in unforeseeable benefits.[166]

The discontinuity between al-Sulamī and al-Qushayrī lies in the necessity of keeping a bond of companionship with one single master and the consequences this holds for one's other relationships. Al-Sulamī insists that one should honour, revere and obey shaykhs but does not explicitly suggest that a believer must restrict himself to a single shaykh. For a variety of reasons, including the frequency with which believers travelled in search of knowledge, al-Sulamī does not frown upon changing teachers or adding teachers. Al-Qushayrī conceives the relationship between master and disciple as more exclusive, to the point that a disciple's duties to his shaykh outweigh a disciple's duties to his parents; disobeying his shaykh counts as a more serious offense than disobeying his own father.[167] Al-Qushayrī's insistence in the superiority of the Ṣūfī path also discourages – if not excludes entirely – the possibility of seeking instruction from learned persons outside the Ṣūfī path. He repeats the distinction between two types of learning, that of received knowledge (*naql*, obtained by reports) and that of rational knowledge (*'aql*, obtained by proper use of one's mental faculties). The masters of the Ṣūfī *ṭā'ifa* transcend this division, seeing as manifest what remains unknown to others.[168] In al-Qushayrī's mind, the greatest teachers among the Ṣūfīs have always been superior in the Islamic sciences over the greatest teachers who did not follow the Ṣūfī path, and non-Ṣūfīs like Aḥmad b. Ḥanbal (d. 241/855) and al-Shāfi'ī (d. 204/820) came to acknowledge this.[169] If one has no immediate access to such a learned Ṣūfī master, he must travel until he finds one; if he is serious about the path, he has no reason to divide his loyalties among any other teachers, including other Ṣūfī masters. Al-Qushayrī considers it detrimental for an aspirant to find himself among an assembly of advanced Ṣūfī masters and their companions; this is not the place for a beginner. Al-Qushayrī attends particularly to this time of novitiate (*ibtidā'*), when one first places oneself in the hands of a single master. The attitude of a *murīd* attitude during this period provides an ample indication of how the remainder of his journey will go, so al-Qushayrī broaches no gradualism in a seeker's commitment to this path. The *murīd* must oppose nothing the master directs him to do, confess any disagreements to his master immediately and not dare to conceal even one breath from his master.[170]

Like al-Sulamī before him, al-Qushayrī does not restrict his use of the term *ṣuḥba* to a formal bond of spiritual companionship between master and disciple. This was evident earlier on in the tripartite division that allows a Ṣūfī to keep company with someone of equal rank, but even the section focused on advice for aspirants (*waṣiyya lil-murīdīn*) continues to speak of companionship in a more general sense. The specialized language of this section, including detailed etiquette for audition sessions (*samā'*) and how to behave in the company of shaykhs, does not preclude a broader consideration of companionship. In this case, al-Qushayrī uses that broader framework to forbid aspirants to seek the company of youth (*aḥdāth*), calling it one of the gravest afflictions on the path.[171] Citing a strong consensus of the Ṣūfī masters who preceded him, he prohibits mixing with youths using several different terms: *ṣuḥba*, *mu'āshara*, *mukhālaṭa*, *min mujālasat al-aḥdāth* and others. Al-Qushayrī recognizes only one objection to justify mixing with youth: the well-known fact that some famous Ṣūfīs have publicly behaved in ways that seemed sinful, ways that, in prudence, they might have concealed. A *murīd* should never dare to use such examples as an excuse to mingle with youths. In this, al-Qushayrī proves himself a faithful heir to al-Junayd's understanding of the propriety of keeping certain behaviours and teachings private. Such talk amounts to *shirk* and *kufr*. Al-Qushayrī leaves no doubt here about the degree of scandal that adheres to inappropriate relationships with youth. The matter is not simply a failure of humility, by which an aspirant desires to have disciples and aspirants under him before he has made the necessary progress. Al-Qushayrī condemns this longing for prominence.[172] His prohibition on keeping company with youths is categorical, however, and does not depend upon the motivation of the shaykh; he forbids companionship with *aḥdāth* in a section of the *Risāla* dedicated to his advice for aspirants. This shows the consistency of his teaching with that of his teacher al-Sulamī. In context, the passages in which al-Sulamī makes exceptions and allows a believer to keep company with a young *murīd* are not examples of formal *ṣuḥba*; they are more limited friendships that a believer must abandon if his attitude towards the youth changes. Many believers have falsely looked to youths as a reflection of divine beauty and considered association with youths a minor matter, not a grave sin.[173] Al-Qushayrī insists that Ṣūfī aspirants see the real danger in these relationships: they are a door to abandonment and rejection by God, a trial from which one must flee.

This prohibition on mixing with youths serves as a reminder that one should not exaggerate the differences between al-Sulamī and al-Qushayrī. In broad strokes, their understandings of companionship share many facets. They both discuss the possibility of companionship with God. Al-Qushayrī uses al-Sulamī as a resource for this teaching, concluding his section on *ṣuḥba* with a teaching of Abū Bakr al-Tamastānī (d. 340/951) that al-Sulamī transmitted to al-Qushayrī. 'Be God's companions, and if you are not able, then keep company with God's companions, so that the blessings of their companionship brings you to the companionship of God.'[174] However, while both al-Sulamī and al-Qushayrī recognize the possibility of companionship with God, they devote the lion's share of their discussions of companionship to a bond shared between fellow believers. On balance, al-Qushayrī's treatment of companionship deals more with the formal bond between *ustādh* and *murīd* than does al-Sulamī's, but their understandings of the bond cohere. Thibon has grounds for his insistence that the shift from the *shaykh al-taʿlīm* to the *shaykh al-tarbiya* finds expression in the mature al-Sulamī and did not wait until the writings of al-Qushayrī.[175] Al-Qushayrī certainly expresses this in a more systematic way, augmenting al-Sulamī's hortatory rhetoric about the honour and reverence due to shaykhs with a novel focus on the exclusivity of companionship. But finally, both men can and do speak about companionship in a more general sense, especially when concerned about the possibility of a Ṣūfī bringing public scandal to the brotherhood. Passages that urge Ṣūfīs to avoid the company of women or youths do not primarily forbid the bestowal of a *khirqa* or the other rites of initiation. They exist to discourage Ṣūfīs from bringing disrepute on the brotherhood by placing a brother in situations that could raise suspicion of scandal and could distract others from their progress on the path.

A number of other shaykhs could be added here. Al-Hujwīrī crafted his renowned *Kashf al-maḥjūb* at the same time as al-Qushayrī yet offers little evidence of the evolution into the model of the directing shaykh, thus bearing out Meier's thesis that this shift occurred first in Khurasan. Al-Hujwīrī also has a strong notion of spousal companionship despite his general preference for celibacy among the dervishes,[176] evidence that some lived in quasi-coenobitic communities,[177] and he prizes equality among the dervishes – horizontal companionship. Abū Ṭālib al-Makkī (d. 386/996), al-Kalābādhī and al-Kharkūshī (d. 407/1016) provide worthwhile material for comparison, and recent publications of the writings of Abū Khalaf al-Ṭabarī (d. *c.* 470/1077) and Abū l-Ḥasan ʿAlī l-Sīrjānī (d. *c.* 470/1077) also could add to the discussion. Al-Sīrjānī, for example, insists just as strenuously as al-Qushayrī on the necessity of a spiritual guide to make progress on the path, citing the famous dictum also preserved by al-Qushayrī, 'Whoever does not have a guide has Satan as his guide.'[178] However, the aim here is not a comprehensive survey, but to set al-Sulamī's spiritual pedagogy in its proper relief and allow his distinctive contribution to come forward.

Conclusion

Al-Sulamī's understanding of companionship neither emerged in a vacuum nor left behind a vacuum after his death. This survey of philosophical attitudes towards love and friendship in the period as well as approaches to companionship among some of al-Sulamī's near contemporaries in Sufism provides several instructive points of comparison and contrast in the evolution of *ṣuḥba* and *ṣadāqa*. First, philosophers reflecting on these themes tended to focus more on the political consequences of friendship, in the context of the ruling elites. They manifest an elitist – and often, classist – understanding of friendship in which only a few have acquired the virtue necessary to engage in friendship in the full sense. Their agenda for friendship involves the moral development of the rulers of the realm, anticipating that this ethical reform will effect a broader social transformation. Al-Tawḥīdī stands out for his acknowledgement that commoners can achieve this level of virtue, but even his reflections turn reflexively to the rulers of the realm and the political consequences of friendship, assuming that the healthy and moral friendship among righteous viziers and courtiers will effect a broader social transformation. Ṣūfīs in the period, and al-Sulamī in particular, do not share this instinctive shift in attention towards the court. The shaykhs' disinterest in wealth and power functions as a literary trope to some degree, but the many colourful vignettes about Ṣūfī companionship are largely bereft of references to persons of economic or political power, including the assumption that a foreseeable consequence of *ṣuḥba* will be the moral reform of the economic and cultural elites. Recognizing this disinterest in worldly power does not inject a false dichotomy between the temporal and the spiritual or between the political and the religious. One cannot say that these Ṣūfīs were 'apolitical' or 'anti-political'. Their companionship was political, in the sense that they expected it to yield benefits and blessings for the *polis*; it was apolitical only in the sense that they did not foresee that their *ṣuḥba* would affect the court. Al-Sulamī and al-Qushayrī wrote voluminously, including advice for worldly rulers. When they and their Ṣūfī colleagues considered the reality of companionship, that was not the segment of society to which their minds turned. In their vision, the rulers of the realm bequeath their status as the portal for social transformation to the Ṣūfī shaykhs, whose role gradually amplifies in the decades preceding and succeeding al-Sulamī.

Second, this period witnesses a significant amplification of the role of the Ṣūfī shaykh. Whether or not one considers the greater prominence that a shaykh holds in the life of the shaykh's companion a simple passage from *taʿlīm* to *tarbiya*, al-Sulamī begins a period in which the exaltation of the shaykh's role and the insistence on magnifying esteem and reverence for the shaykh become commonplace in Ṣūfī literature. The discussion of whether shaykhs engaged in 'spiritual direction' prior to al-Sulamī runs into the limitations of the evidence available. Hints of the later model are present in al-Sarrāj and find fuller expression later, but one cannot doubt that al-Sulamī asserts the indispensability of a shaykh for the achievement of the higher levels of spiritual progress. A mature disciple depends not only upon God but must come to realize as a fact his dependence on an earthly master. Al-Sulamī grounds his luscious praise for the wisdom and blessings of the shaykhs primarily upon this dependence, and that praise congeals in al-Qushayrī's *Risāla* into a mandate for unquestioning obedience to one's shaykh in the context of a permanent, solitary bond.

Third, Ṣūfī reflections on companionship in the period maintain a continuing concern for horizontal bonds, even in the more hierarchical and detailed training programme of al-Qushayrī. While modern scholars with an interest in *ṣuḥba* have tended to focus on the relationship between master and disciple – a bond which the texts of the period increasingly magnify – this should not eclipse the ongoing consciousness among Ṣūfīs that relationships among brothers of equal spiritual rank provide an opportunity for growth in the knowledge of God. Giants of the Ṣūfī tradition like al-Qushayrī retain a consciousness of the importance of horizontal bonds between believers of lower spiritual rank – bonds I have discussed as 'ordinary' companionship – but the role of the shaykh constantly increases and provides the logical extension of al-Sulamī's own assumptions. Al-Sulamī saw companionship as a natural and voluntary human act that helps a believer grow, and he exhorts believers to keep company with virtuous persons. It follows that one who seeks *ṣuḥba* would only do so as a bond of great intensity and would only do so with the most excellent of persons, the shaykhs. This is precisely the shift that occurs in many subsequent Ṣūfī texts. Here again, *Kitāb ādāb al-ṣuḥba* serves as a hinge. The treatise addresses believers at an early stage of the spiritual path, persons less zealously focused on *taṣawwuf* as a spiritual programme. Al-Sulamī assumes that companionship and fellowship are natural, human acts and then proceeds to exhort believers to only keep company with the best of persons. If one takes that advice to the extreme, developments in the subsequent generation follow logically. The bond becomes something very intense or it becomes nothing at all. If a believer chooses to enter it, that believer chooses the wisest of companions or chooses no one at all. Al-Sulamī subtly inscribes this distinctively Ṣūfī wisdom into the life of a city that knew and valued these relationships already, and he called them to embrace these bonds with greater intensity. Whether Ṣūfī literature spoke about horizontal *ṣuḥba* or *ṣuḥba* with a shaykh, one finds a bond that – as can be seen in al-Sarrāj and al-Qushayrī – can both shake a person and provide solace, and can admonish even as it assures security. A believer will need a shaykh to attain the higher stations, but the bond of companionship is a blessing al-Sulamī frames as available and desirable for all. Once a believer experiences the blessing of that bond, the believer's eyes instinctively turn to the higher spiritual stations that cannot be attained without the guidance of a master.

CONCLUSION

'A man follows the religion of his friend, so let each of you consider whom you treat as a friend.'[1] This prescient tradition sums up not only al-Sulamī's *Kitāb ādāb al-ṣuḥba* but his larger approach to spiritual growth and the role of one's coreligionists in it. A believer's religious life is inextricably connected to the bonds of friendship the believer chooses to form, so al-Sulamī offers practical wisdom to form and persevere in those bonds with intention and with commitment. Scholars have long credited al-Sulamī for his biographical dictionaries and his compilations of *tafsīr*, both of which preserve teachings of earlier masters that would have been lost without his diligence. This study has attempted to highlight another aspect of al-Sulamī's contribution, lest it be lost: his teaching on companionship.

This study examined two key features of al-Sulamī's spiritual pedagogy, *ādāb* and *akhlāq*, with an eye towards their meaning in the context of companionship. By comparison with his contemporaries, al-Sulamī stands out for his elevation of *adab/ādāb* to a central point in his discourse. He uses the term in the plural more frequently than do his near contemporaries, but not in the sense of rituals or customs, like the etiquette of a Ṣūfī lodge. Rather, he refers to patterns of behaviour of a more general order, including habits of the mind to sustain those patterns of behaviour. His counsels in *Kitāb ādāb al-ṣuḥba* thus fall somewhere between the Ṣūfī binary of *ẓāhir* and *bāṭin*. They necessarily involve an attitudinal orientation, but they also necessarily involve external expression. In sum, al-Sulamī continually returns to the integration between a believer's inner life and external comportment. These must progress together, and that progress enables the development of one's *akhlāq*. A believer is responsible for performing *ādāb* through the believer's own volition, but *akhlāq* often depend upon God's transformation of the believer. Through the believer's effort and God's favour, a believer receives dispositions that orient the believer towards proper action and sustain the believer in that behaviour. These are stable in the sense that they are constant and not momentary, but the believer must exert continual effort to persevere in them. *Akhlāq* are also manifest in a visible, public way. For this reason, I have argued that one can understand them as 'virtues'. The *akhlāq* are cultivated excellences that enable a believer to achieve the goods of Ṣūfī practice.

Believers manifest these *ādāb* and *akhlāq* in their companionship and fellowship with others. I have argued that al-Sulamī uses *ṣuḥba* and *ʿishra* to refer to two different types of relationships, the former being an intimate, intentional, mutual, voluntary bond between believers, and the latter being the normal social relations that characterize the life of a believer. Al-Sulamī's encouragement for one's fellowship with others include traditional Ṣūfī values like generosity, sincerity and forgiveness, but his larger interest is companionship. Believers should seek only the best of believers as their companions, for this bond involves a high-stakes choice with great consequences for one's standing before God and one's aspiration to draw near to God.

This study offers a corrective to some scholarship of Sufism in the period by noting two distinctive features of al-Sulamī's approach to companionship. First, al-Sulamī addresses believers at an earlier stage on their spiritual path. While some of his writings reflect the heights of mystical experience, other treatises – in particular *Kitāb ādāb al-ṣuḥba* – address a broader audience. Works like *Ṭabaqāt al-ṣūfiyya* and *Kitāb alfāẓ al-ṣūfiyya* show al-Sulamī's thorough fluency with the Ṣūfī lexicon, but works like *Kitāb ādāb al-ṣuḥba* and *Kitāb al-futuwwa* show his ability with a different rhetorical style that eschews the technical language of Sufism. He instead uses poetry, Prophetic traditions and other wise maxims carefully selected to subtly infuse the insights of the Ṣūfī tradition into the interpersonal relationships among believers in his city. I have called this al-Sulamī's project of 'sufization', the flip side to his project of 'uṣūlization' as other scholars have discussed it.[2] The Ṣūfī habits of the mind can grant access to the heights of mysticism if practiced in the long term, but texts like *Kitāb ādāb al-ṣuḥba* focus on a simpler, holistic process of character development that enables believers to learn from their friends and draw near to God at the same time. Second, al-Sulamī speaks about spiritual companionship in a much broader sense than the relationship between master and disciple. His writings manifest his reverence for the role of the shaykh, but his attention often returns to ordinary friendships – which one should still cultivate only among the best of believers. In this regard, one can see a consistent logic playing out in the transition from al-Sulamī to his student al-Qushayrī and other later Ṣūfī masters who intently emphasize the role of the shaykh in a Ṣūfī's spiritual development. The more that one insists upon a believer only keeping company with the best of believers, the more restricted the pool of candidates for companionship. Al-Sulamī witnesses a historical moment in which one should exercise great discernment in choosing one's companions but a moment in which a person would have several companions and would expect to come to greater knowledge of God through them.

MacIntyre, al-Sulamī and avenues for future research

Alasdair MacIntyre's *After Virtue* is, in many and various ways, a dark book. It is a hopeful book but a dark book. In the midst of widespread moral confusion, well-intended mortals grope around in obscurity for a path forward, waiting for a new St. Benedict of Nursia who can create and sustain forms of community to keep the virtues alive in the meantime.[3] Perhaps, if the virtuous can survive an era where people cannot tell right from wrong, truth from lie, the whole world will be different. One could easily imagine a spiritual master in al-Sulamī's Nishapur seeing himself in such a 'Benedict-ine' role, creating small circles of virtuous people to support each other through the increasingly ominous darkness, as the city descended further and further into factionalism. This study has shown that al-Sulamī did not see himself in any such way. He proposes a more optimistic vision, a vision in which companionship is real, fellowship is real and growth in them is possible. Al-Sulamī anticipates that Ṣūfī practice – *adab* – will contribute to social cohesion and draw the population more closely together. His project of sufization certainly did involve long hours spent with an intimate circle of disciples, but what he describes in treatises like *Kitāb ādāb al-ṣuḥba* is broader and bigger. He quietly saturates the discourse around him with elements of the Ṣūfī tradition and thus contributes to the health, stability and common good of the *polis*.

This study points to the relevance of the contemporary renewal in virtue ethics for the study of Sufism. I have drawn primarily upon MacIntyre not in a simple attempt to read al-Sulamī through a MacIntyrean lens, still less to prove that al-Sulamī was a latent MacIntyrean. The larger relevance of MacIntyre for this project is threefold. First, MacIntyre is a seminal thinker in the Anglophone philosophical academy whose voice has not wielded much influence among scholars of Islam and merits to do so. MacIntyre provokes worthwhile questions about the nature of human flourishing, human rationality and life well lived. The possibilities for bringing MacIntyre into conversation with Muslim philosophers indebted to the Greek tradition, like Miskawayh or al-Tawḥīdī, are obvious. But the running dialogue with al-Sulamī over the course of these chapters has demonstrated the value of virtue ethics to assist in understanding a figure with whom he shares little, prima facie, in the way of vocabulary or a philosophical framework.

Second, MacIntyre's framework of tradition-based rationality permits criticism without antagonism, scholarly rigor without hostility, as a methodological principle. His account of tradition allows traditions to challenge each other and gives a credible account for why one tradition might prevail over its rival.[4] Such an understanding of tradition allows outsiders to put questions to a tradition in a way that is constructive, to probe the resources within that tradition and see which avenues have been foreclosed and which avenues have not yet been adequately considered. This study has approached al-Sulamī in that key: as an outsider, seeking to understand a medieval figure in his proper historical context, but more to look for ideas that lay underappreciated and unexplored and have continuing relevance for perennial themes like friendship and virtue.

Third, several of MacIntyre's key notions interact well with aspects of al-Sulamī's thought. I have argued that MacIntyre's notion of practice provides a viable analogue for what al-Sulamī means by *adab* and thus have attempted to open up some new terms and categories by which the dynamics of *adab* might be considered. I have also argued that al-Sulamī's understanding of *taṣawwuf* functions as a good analogue for MacIntyre's understanding of a tradition, especially regarding the epistemic function of a tradition and its ongoing evolution. Finally, I have argued that *akhlāq* provide a valid analogue for virtues, *mutatis mutandis*.

Some of the fruits of this interaction are first, bringing the virtue of acknowledged dependence into dialogue with al-Sulamī, in the context of the vulnerabilities of one's companion. *Kitāb ādāb al-ṣuḥba* vexes readers because it constantly exhorts readers to associate with the best of people but then proceeds with the recognition that most believers are not constantly associating with the best of people. Further, even when a believer associates with the best of people, al-Sulamī's frequent pleas to forgive the brothers, to overlook their faults and to never allow long-term friendships to shatter demonstrate that relations between the 'best of people' were rife with tensions and conflict. These tensions and conflicts provide a vehicle for growth in the virtues, even when al-Sulamī does not frame the shortcomings of the brothers as benefits in themselves. Comparing al-Sulamī's vision to an understanding of companionship almost exclusively focused on the bond between master and disciple, one struggles to see how that master's shortcomings could play any positive role, as all or nearly all of a believer's potential spiritual growth resides in a relationship with that one wise master to whom that believer is singularly and irrevocably committed. On the other hand, in a model of companionship in which spiritual growth lies in successful navigation of mutual voluntary commitments to people who are weak, sinful and ignorant, other avenues open up. If the defects of a believer's companion come to have some value in themselves – that is, if they act as more than obstacles to be avoided or shortcomings to be tolerated – then this model enables a believer to find God present in them. For his part, al-Sulamī does not go this far. His limited acceptance of the companionship of a fool, for example, does not amount to a positive valuation for the shortcomings of another. I suggest this as a future avenue for research for other scholars of *taṣawwuf.* What would be the possibilities, for example, for a Ṣūfī version of a community in which intellectual or physical disabilities are celebrated positively as gifts? Could this be articulated in an Islamic, or specifically Ṣūfī, context? The recent growth in disability studies suggests the potential for this line of thinking. Al-Sulamī contains fleeting glimpses of such a possibility, but in the final analysis, his insistence that believers should keep company only with those who excel in virtue and learning seems to preclude the possibility of celebrating weaknesses.

Second, this study suggests that scholars of Sufism, if not Islam in general, would do well to become more conversant with contemporary virtue ethicists. In some circles of Anglophone moral philosophy, the language of virtue has come back with a vengeance, but elsewhere it often seems like a dusty remnant of a bygone age, discourse drawn from a quaint and curious volume of forgotten lore. If moral philosophers with an interest in virtue continue the present trend of an active and robust engagement with the social sciences,[5] the future of the study of Sufism lays wide open and scholars of Sufism will benefit from terms of discourse that scholars in related fields are increasingly using to grapple with how we can become better people.

Third, practice and tradition function well together to articulate the boundaries and the function of Ṣūfī *adab*. MacIntyre's notion of internal goods and the evolving standards of excellence for internal goods – particularly considering the more complex account of common goods developed in *Dependent Rational Animals* – captures well the elusive, slippery goals of Ṣūfī devotion. Towards what end does all this Ṣūfī *adab* tend? Especially given the lack of agreement about the sequence of stations along the way – the *maqāmāt* – among major Ṣūfī masters in the formative period, the constant evolution of this spiritual path stands in full display. MacIntyre's framework permits a robust debate among practitioners about whether they long for *'ilm*, for *ma'rifa*, for *dhawq*, for *'ishq*, for *qurba* or for any of the many other pregnant terms that circulate in Ṣūfī discourse. Practitioners could and will disagree about the systematic ordering of the goods they seek, and a MacIntyrean frame preserves one other truism regardless of what that ordering is: Ṣūfī practice will be the most effective, if not the only, way to reach those highest goods. An outsider can obtain a basic comprehension, sufficient to consider departing his own tradition, but can never achieve these goods fully without full commitment to the tradition and the cultivation of its virtues. Al-Sulamī would add that if one does commit oneself to this, one can hope to be among those to whom God will grant success.

And God knows better.

NOTES

Introduction: What does virtue ethics have to do with Sufism?

1 Among other recent bestsellers on this theme, see David Brooks, *The Road to Character* (New York: Random House, 2015).
2 The interdisciplinary initiative 'The Character Project' stands out, involving collaboration from several major university communities. www.thecharacterproject.com (8 December 2023). See also essays collected in Christian B. Miller, R. Michael Furr, Angela Knobel and William Fleeson, eds, *Character: New Directions from Philosophy, Psychology, and Theology* (New York: Oxford University Press, 2015), as well as other writings by Miller and his collaborators.
3 Both the Christian philosopher Yaḥyā b. ʿAdī (d. 363/974) and the Muslim philosopher Miskawayh (d. 421/1030) penned treatises with this title.
4 The title of a treatise by al-Ḥakīm al-Tirmidhī (d. 295–300/905–10), to be discussed in turn.
5 Some scholars draw a meaningful distinction between *taṣawwuf* and Sufism using the former to indicate an internal Islamic discursive domain and the latter to indicate an analytical horizon for modern scholars. I do not employ this distinction and will generally use 'Ṣūfī' and 'Sufism' as functionally synonymous with *mutaṣawwif* and *taṣawwuf*, respectively, to refer to persons who utilize(d) the spiritual practices associated with *taṣawwuf*. For discussion of these and similar terminological problems, see Sara Sviri, 'Sufism: Reconsidering Terms, Definitions and Processes in the Formative Period of Islamic Mysticism', in *Les maîtres soufis et leurs disciples: IIIe–Ve siècles de l'hégire (IXe–XIe s.)*, ed. Geneviève Gobillot and Jean-Jacques Thibon (Damascus: Institut français du Proche-Orient, 2012), 17–34; Paul L. Heck, 'Sufism – What Is It Exactly?' *RC* 1, no. 1 (2007): 148–64; Nathan C. Hofer, *The Popularisation of Sufism in Ayyubid and Mamluk Egypt, 1173–1325* (Edinburgh: Edinburgh University Press, 2015), 1–7.
6 Alexandre Papas, 'What Is a Ṣūfī Institution?', in *Handbook of Sufi Studies. Volume I: Sufi Institutions*, ed. Alexandre Papas (Leiden: Brill, 2021), 1–24.
7 Ėmile Durkheim, *The Elementary Forms of Religious Life*, trans. Karen E. Fields (New York: Free Press, 1995), 9.
8 Nathan C. Hofer's comment focuses on a slightly later period but can be justly applied here. Despite some other deficiencies, Durkheim's assumption does, as I shall argue in this thesis, capture an element at the heart of *taṣawwuf*. Hofer, *The Popularisation of Sufism*, 5.
9 Most scholars locate these manuals of etiquette first in the life of al-Sulamī's student Abū Saʿīd b. Abī l-Khayr (d. 440/1049). The fullest treatment of this master remains Fritz Meier, *Abū Saʿīd-i Abū l-Ḫayr (357–440/967–1049): Wirklichkeit und Legende* (Leiden: Brill, 1976). For some major studies of the development of the Ṣūfī orders – each belonging to the second trend indicated by Papas – see J. Spencer Trimingham, *The Sufi Orders in Islam* (Oxford: Clarendon, 1971); Alexandre Popovic and Gilles

Veinstein, eds, *Les ordres mystiques dans l'Islam: Cheminements et situation actuelle* (Paris: Editions de l'Ecole des hautes études en sciences sociales, 1986); Gilles Veinstein and Alexandre Popovic, eds, *Les voies d'Allah: Les ordres mystiques dans l'Islam des origines á aujourd'hui* (Paris: Fayard, 1996).

10 Paul L. Heck identifies this awareness as the central feature of Ṣūfī ethics. Paul L. Heck, 'Ethics, in Ṣūfism', *EI*³.

11 Al-Sulamī describes a Ṣūfī's *ṣuḥba* with the Prophet and with the Prophet's companions, clearly indicating that believers living centuries after the deaths of these persons can enter into a bond with them. Abū Bakr provides the example of authentic companionship par excellence, which later Ṣūfīs sought to emulate in their service. To be clear, Ṣūfī *ṣuḥba* with other (living) Ṣūfīs presumes a robust and intentional relationship, an emulation of the Prophet's bond to his closest companions, not those counted among the *ṣaḥāba* who had met him once or only occasionally. Some of al-Sulamī's important texts on this score include *KAṢ*, 80; *AMM*, §8.

12 Jamil M. Abun-Nasr, *Muslim Communities of Grace: The Sufi Brotherhoods in Islamic Religious Life* (New York: Columbia University Press, 2007), 60.

13 Variants on this dictum abound; al-Qushayrī's, attributed there to Abū Yazīd al-Bisṭāmī (d. 261/874–5), is one of the most frequently cited. Abū l-Qāsim al-Qushayrī, *al-Risāla al-qushayriyya fī 'ilm al-taṣawwuf* (Cairo: Dār al-Muqaṭṭam, 2009), al-Waṣiyya lil-murīdīn, 523; al-Qushayrī, *Al-Qushayri's Epistle on Sufism: Al-Risala al-qushayriyya fi 'ilm al-tasawwuf*, trans. Alexander Knysh (Reading: Garnet, 2007), 405–6.

14 For a survey of these developments that also witnesses these scholarly trends, see Arthur F. Buehler, *Sufi Heirs of the Prophet: The Indian Naqshbandiya and the Rise of the Mediating Sufi Shaykh* (Columbia: University of South Carolina Press, 1998), 1–54.

15 For an example, see John Renard, *Historical Dictionary of Sufism*, 2nd ed. (Lanham, MD: Rowman & Littlefield, 2016), 80, 294.

16 Cf. al-Sulamī, *Kitāb ṭabaqāt al-ṣūfiyya*, ed. Johannes Pedersen (Leiden: Brill, 1960), 29.

17 Mark Sedgwick, 'The Organisation of Mysticism', in Papas, *Handbook of Sufi Studies*, 335.

18 Among the many scholarly works dedicated to this topic, the volume *Les maîtres soufis et leurs disciples*, edited by Gobillot and Thibon, stands out for its quality and singular focus.

19 Robert Moore, 'Companionship', *EI*³.

20 I use this neologism to denote al-Sulamī's attempt to actively infuse society with the distinctive insights proper to *taṣawwuf* as al-Sulamī understood it. I do not employ 'sufization' to refer to the attempt to claim that persons, rituals or texts are or were 'Ṣūfī', as Jean-Jacques Thibon seems to with his use of *soufiser*, but to refer to the attempt to transform things that the agent considers 'not-Ṣūfī' or 'insufficiently Ṣūfī' into a more authentic expression of *taṣawwuf*. That is, I use it to refer to the process of making people Ṣūfī, not calling people 'Ṣūfī'. Mostafa Vaziri and others have faulted al-Sulamī for engaging in faulty labelling, identifying persons as Ṣūfīs who in fact were not. Al-Sulamī doubtlessly applied the moniker 'Ṣūfī' to persons who would not have identified themselves as such, but his liberality in the use of this label is not the aspect of al-Sulamī's work I indicate with the term 'sufization'. Mostafa Vaziri, *Rumi and Shams' Silent Rebellion: Parallels with Vedanta, Buddhism, and Shaivism* (New York: Palgrave Macmillan, 2015), 65; Jean-Jacques Thibon, *L'œuvre d'Abū 'Abd al-Raḥmān al-Sulamī (325/937–412/1021) et la formation du soufisme* (Damascus: Institut français du Proche-Orient, 2009), 339.

21 English translations of these treatises are forthcoming, apart from *Jawāmiʿ ādāb al-ṣūfiyya*, which was published in English more than a decade ago. Al-Sulamī, *A Collection of Sufi Rules of Conduct*, trans. Elena Biagi (Cambridge: Islamic Texts Society, 2010); al-Sulamī, *Treatises on the Sufi Path*, trans. Safaruk Z. Chowdhury and Jason Welle (Cambridge: Islamic Texts Society, forthcoming).

22 Jean-Jacques Thibon, who emphasizes pedagogy as a core element of al-Sulamī's literary personality, makes this point in particular about the treatise *Kitāb ādāb al-ṣuḥba*. Thibon, *L'œuvre*, 265.

23 A conference on virtue sponsored by the Research Center for Islamic Ethics and Legislation (CILE) at Hamid Bin Khalifa University in Doha is but one example. For its published proceedings, see *JIE* 4 (2020).

24 This comment does not exclude the fact that scholars like George F. Hourani a generation ago did extensive studies along meta-ethical lines, particularly regarding the reception of Aristotle. Cyrus Zargar, 'Virtue and Manliness in Islamic Ethics', *JIE* 4 (2020): 1; George F. Hourani, *Reason and Tradition in Islamic Ethics* (Cambridge: Cambridge University Press, 1985).

25 Ida Zilio-Grandi, *Le virtù del buon musulmano* (Turin: Einaudi, 2020), 8.

26 Al-Ṭabarānī, *al-Muʿjam al-awsaṭ* (Cairo: Dār al-Ḥaramayn, 1995), 7:74, Ḥ. 6895; al-Khaṭīb al-Tabrīzī, *Mishkāt al-maṣābīḥ* (Damascus: al-Maktab al-Islāmī, 1961), K. al-faḍā'il wa-l-shamā'il, B. sayyid al-mursalīn, Ḥ. 5770; cf. al-Bukhārī, *al-Adab al-mufrad* (Jubayl: Dār al-Ṣadīq, 2000), B. ḥusn al-khuluq (135), Ḥ. 273; Ibn Abī l-Dunyā, *Makārim al-akhlāq*, in *Mawsūʿat Ibn Abī l-Dunyā* (Riyadh: Dār Aṭlas al-Ḥaḍrā', 2012), 6:72, Ḥ. 13/11140, 14/11141; Aḥmad b. Ḥanbal, *al-Musnad* (Beirut: Mu'assasat al-Risāla, 1413–21/1993–2001), 14:512–13, Ḥ. 8952; see the editor's note to Ibn Ḥanbal's *Musnad* for the many instances of other variants.

27 Sophia Vasalou, *Virtues of Greatness in the Arabic Tradition* (Oxford: Oxford University Press, 2019).

28 Atif Khalil, 'Humility in Islamic Contemplative Ethics', *JIE* 4 (2020): 223–52.

29 Atif Khalil, 'On Cultivating Gratitude (*Shukr*) in Sufi Virtue Ethics', *JSS* 4 (2015): 1–26; Atif Khalil, 'The Embodiment of Gratitude (*Shukr*) in Sufi Ethics', *SI* 111 (2016): 159–78; cf. Zilio-Grandi, 'The Gratitude of Man and the Gratitude of God: Notes on *Šukr* in Traditional Islamic Thought', *ISCH* 38 (2012): 45–61.

30 For an exceptional discussion of the question, see Taneli Kukkonen, 'Al-Ghazālī on the Origins of Ethics', *Numen* 63, nos. 2–3 (2016): 271–98.

31 Taneli Kukkonen made this haunting comment in an online conference sponsored by CILE in December 2020.

32 Alasdair C. MacIntyre, *After Virtue: A Study in Moral Theory*, 3rd ed. (Notre Dame, IN: University of Notre Dame Press, 2007).

33 The fundamentally hostile approach of Hamid R. Ziaei's unpublished dissertation provided an initial foray. Hamid R. Ziaei, 'Relativism, MacIntyre, Religion: An Islamic Analysis' (PhD, University of Lancaster, 2006). More recently, David J. Brewer constructively utilizes MacIntyre's notion of tradition-based rationality as a resource for interreligious dialogue. David J. Brewer, *Faith Encounters of the Third Kind: Humility and Hospitality in Interfaith Dialogue* (Eugene, OR: Cascade Books, 2021). I will not engage Brewer's volume in depth in this study, because some of the presuppositions about deep religious pluralism would take the discussion too far afield; for my review, see Jason Welle, 'Review of *Faith Encounters of the Third Kind: Humility and Hospitality in Interfaith Dialogue*, by David J. Brewer', *Journal of*

Interreligious Studies 38 (2023): 118–20. For some other less-developed discussions of MacIntyre's relevance for Islamic studies, see Muhammad Qasim Zaman, *The Ulama in Contemporary Islam: Custodians of Change* (Princeton, NJ: Princeton University Press, 2002), 4–7; Brian Silverstein, *Islam and Modernity in Turkey* (New York: Palgrave Macmillan, 2011), esp. 133–54; Brian Silverstein, 'Disciplines of Presence in Modern Turkey: Discourse, Companionship, and the Mass Mediation of Islamic Practice', *Cultural Anthropology* 23, no. 1 (2008): 120; via Talal Asad's notion of tradition, see Katharina Anna Ivanyi, 'Virtue, Piety and the Law: A Study of Birgivi Meḥmed Efendi's "Al-Ṭarīqa al-Muḥammadiyya"' (PhD, Princeton University, 2012), 64.

34 Drawing on modern philosophers in this way has become increasingly common. For example, Faraz Sheikh's monograph on al-Ḥārith al-Muḥāsibī (d. 243/847) and Said Nursi (d. 1379/1960) construes their teachings in a Foucauldian register, using Foucault's technologies of the self as a tool to examine subjectivity and moral formation. I intend something similar here, although the differences in methodology will become clear in due course. Faraz Sheikh, *Forging Ideal Muslim Subjects: Discursive Practices, Subject Formation & Muslim Ethics* (London: Lexington Books, 2020), esp. 17–21.

35 Mohammad Rustom, 'The End of Islamic Philosophy', *Sacred Web* 40 (2017): 131.

36 Safaruk Z. Chowdhury, *A Ṣūfī Apologist of Nīshāpūr: The Life and Thought of Abū 'Abd al-Raḥmān al-Sulamī* (Sheffield: Equinox, 2019), 87.

37 For a more extensive biography of al-Sulamī, including specific discussion of the relevant entries in various biographical dictionaries and historical chronicles, see Thibon, *L'œuvre*, 23–33, 93–124. The most important sources are 'Abd al-Ghāfir al-Fārisī's (d. 529/1134–5) *Kitāb al-siyāq li-tārīkh Nīsābūr*, Shams al-Dīn al-Dhahabī's (d. 748/1325) *Siyar a'lām al-nubalā'*, al-Dhahabī's *Tārīkh al-islām*, al-Khaṭīb al-Baghdādī's (d. 463/1071) *Tārīkh Baghdād*, Ibn al-Jawzī's (d. 597/1201) *al-Muntaẓam*, Tāj al-Dīn al-Subkī's (d. 771/1369) *Ṭabaqāt al-shāfi'iyya* and al-Jāmī's (d. 898/1492) *Nafaḥāt al-uns*.

38 For discussion of his birthdate, see Thibon, *L'œuvre*, 97.

39 For more on this tribe, see Michael Lecker, *The Banū Sulaym: A Contribution to the Study of Early Islam* (Jerusalem: Hebrew University, 1989).

40 For a brief biography, see Jean-Jacques Thibon, 'Ibn Nujayd', *EI*[3]; see also Chowdhury, *A Ṣūfī Apologist*, 57–61.

41 Al-Qushayrī, *Risāla*, B. al-tawba, 113.

42 Al-Qushayrī, *Risāla*, B. ḥifẓ qulūb al-mashāyikh, 340.

43 Al-Sulamī, *JAṢ*, §55, 62; *AMM*, throughout.

44 Chowdhury devotes a chapter to the main intellectual influences on al-Sulamī, restricting himself to the figures I mention here in brief. Chowdhury, *A Ṣūfī Apologist*, 55–86.

45 Ahmet T. Karamustafa considers it unclear that al-Ṣu'lūkī trained disciples in Sufism, despite al-Qushayrī's apparent belief that al-Ṣu'lūkī had instructed disciples in this way. Al-Qushayrī reports that al-Sulamī referred to al-Ṣu'lūkī as both 'my shaykh' and as *ustādh*, in a context that clearly counts al-Ṣu'lūkī among the Ṣūfī masters. The use of *shaykh* and *ustādh* is not always technical in texts of the period. Al-Qushayrī frequently refers to Abū 'Alī l-Daqqāq (d. 405/1015) as his *ustādh* just as he describes al-Ṣu'lūkī as the *ustādh* of al-Sulamī, and al-Qushayrī clearly understood al-Daqqāq as his chief master in esoteric learning. The absence of al-Ṣu'lūkī in al-Sulamī's *Ṭabaqāt* continues to intrigue scholars; this void stands as the most serious challenge to al-Ṣu'lūkī's status as a guide in *taṣawwuf*, and in particular, as al-Sulamī's master.

Ahmet T. Karamustafa, *Sufism: The Formative Period* (Edinburgh: Edinburgh University Press, 2007), 62, 78; al-Qushayrī, *Risāla*, B. al-taṣawwuf, 292, B. ḥifẓ qulūb al-mashāyikh, 340; Thibon, *L'œuvre*, 107; Alexander Knysh, *Islamic Mysticism: A Short History* (Leiden: Brill, 2000), 125.

46 Al-Sulamī never mentions this cloak, and the entry for al-Naṣrābādhī in *Ṭabaqāt al-ṣūfiyya* offers no indication that al-Naṣrābādhī had been al-Sulamī's master. Al-Jāmī's biographical dictionary of Ṣūfīs is the first source to state that al-Naṣrābādhī bestowed the *khirqa* upon al-Sulamī and from that point many sources mention it. Al-Sulamī, *ṬṢ*, 484–8; Nūr al-Dīn 'Abd al-Raḥmān al-Jāmī, *Nafaḥāt al-uns min ḥaḍarāt al-quds* (Calcutta: Maṭba' Līssī, 1858), 352–3 (#371); Karamustafa, *Sufism: The Formative Period*, 62–3, 120–1; Thibon, *L'œuvre*, 100; Chowdhury, *A Ṣūfī Apologist*, 63–7; Gerhard Böwering, 'The Major Sources of Sulamī's Minor Qur'ān Commentary', *Oriens* 35 (1996): 36; Lutz Berger, '*Geschieden von allem ausser Gott*': *Sufik und Welt bei Abū 'Abd ar-Raḥmān as-Sulamī (936–1021)* (Hildesheim: Olms, 1998), 40–2.

47 Al-Khaṭīb al-Baghdādī, *Tārīkh Baghdād (Tārīkh madīnat al-salām)* (Beirut: Dār al-Gharb al-Islāmī, 2001), 3:43–4; al-Dhahabī, *Siyar a'lām al-nubalā'* (Beirut: Mu'assasat al-Risāla, 1996), 17:254–5; al-Qushayrī, *Risāla*, B. al-firāsa, 247; for discussion of the episode, see Thibon, *L'œuvre*, 100–2.

48 On the relationship between Abū Nu'aym and al-Sulamī, see Christopher Melchert, 'Abū Nu'aym's Sources for *Ḥilyat al-awliyā'*, Sufi and Traditionist', in Gobillot and Thibon, *Les maîtres soufis et leurs disciples*, 145–59; on the connection between *Ḥilyat al-awliyā'* and al-Sulamī's *Ṭabaqāt al-ṣūfiyya*, see Jawid A. Mojaddedi, *The Biographical Tradition in Sufism: The Ṭabaqāt Genre from al-Sulamī to Jāmī* (Richmond, UK: Curzon Press, 2001), 41–67.

49 Muḥammad b. al-Munavvar, *The Secrets of God's Mystical Oneness [Asrār Al-Towḥid]*, trans. John O'Kane (Costa Mesa, CA: Mazda Publishers, 1992).

50 The entries in Brockelmann and Sezgin remain a good starting point, but many other manuscripts have since been discovered. *GAL*, 1:201; S1:361; *GAS*, 1:671–4.

51 Alternative schemas include divisions according to purpose (Etan Kohlberg), audience (Kenneth L. Honerkamp) and theme. Kohlberg suggests a division according to the two distinct aims of al-Sulamī's works: 'to defend Sufism against its many critics, and to spread knowledge of Sufism both among the general public and among the Sufis'. Honerkamp drew upon Kohlberg and emphasized the different audiences al-Sulamī addressed: some of his writings for Ṣūfīs were intended for initiates (*murīdūn*) and others for elites. This gives rise to a distinction between 'applied Sufism', intended for initiates, and texts for elites. A genre-based schema predominates, however. Gerhard Böwering consistently uses the tripartite schema suggested here, as do Rkia E. Cornell and Elena Biagi. Nūr al-Dīn Shurayba also divides according to genre, noting that al-Sulamī wrote about *ḥadīth*, about *tafsīr* and about Sufism. Al-Sulamī, *Jawāmi' ādāb al-ṣūfiyya* and *'Uyūb al-nafs wa-mudāwātuhā*, ed. Etan Kohlberg (Jerusalem: Jerusalem Academic Press, 1976), 8–9; Kenneth L. Honerkamp, 'A Sufi Itinerary of Tenth Century Nishapur Based on a Treatise by Abū 'Abd al-Raḥmān al-Sulamī', *JIS* 17, no. 1 (2006): 48, 67; al-Sulamī and al-Ḥakīm al-Tirmidhī, *Three Early Sufi Texts*, trans. and ed. Nicholas Heer and Kenneth L. Honerkamp (Louisville: Fons Vitae, 2003), 87; al-Sulamī, *A Collection of Sufi Rules of Conduct*, xvii; al-Sulamī, *Ṭabaqāt al-ṣūfiyya*, ed. Nūr al-Dīn Shurayba (Cairo: Maktabat al-Khānjī, 1969), 29.

52 Al-Sulamī, *Kitāb ṭabaqāt al-ṣūfiyya*, ed. Pedersen; *Ṭabaqāt al-ṣūfiyya*, ed. Shurayba.

53 Al-Sulamī, *al-Malāmatiyya wa-l-ṣūfiyya wa-ahl al-futuwwa [Risālat al-malāmatiyya]*, ed. Abū l-ʻAlā ʻAfīfī (Cairo: ʻĪsā l-Bābī l-Ḥalabī 1945); al-Sulamī, *Kitab ādāb aṣ-ṣuḥba*, ed. M. J. Kister (Jerusalem: Israel Oriental Society, 1954); al-Sulamī, *Jawāmiʻ ādāb al-ṣūfiyya* and *ʻUyūb al-nafs wa-mudāwātuhā* [ed. Kohlberg, 1976]; al-Sulamī, '*Manāhij al-ʻārifīn*, a Treatise on Ṣūfism by Abū ʻAbd al-Raḥmān al-Sulamī', ed. Etan Kohlberg, *JSAI* 1 (1979): 19–39; al-Sulamī, *al-Muqaddima fī l-taṣawwuf wa-ḥaqīqatihi*, ed. Ḥusayn Amīn (Baghdad: Dār al-Qādisiyya lil-Ṭibāʻa, 1984).

54 Al-Sulamī, *Tisʻat kutub li-Abī ʻAbd al-Raḥmān Muḥammad b. al-Ḥusayn b. Mūsā l-Sulamī*, ed. Süleyman Ateş (Ankara: Üniversitesi Basımevi, 1981); citations follow a subsequent edition, *Tisʻat kutub fī uṣūl al-taṣawwuf wa-l-zuhd* (Beirut: al-Nāshir, 1993).

55 Described in Gerhard Böwering, 'Two Early Ṣūfī Manuscripts', *JSAI* 31 (2006): 209–31.

56 al-Sulamī, *Sufi Treatises of Abū ʻAbd al-Raḥmān al-Sulamī (Rasāʼil ṣūfiyya li-Abī ʻAbd al-Raḥmān al-Sulamī)*, ed. Gerhard Böwering and Bilal Orfali (Beirut: Dār al-Mashriq, 2009); al-Sulamī and Ibn Nujayd, *Sufi Inquiries and Interpretations of Abū ʻAbd al-Raḥmān al-Sulamī and A Treatise of Traditions by Ismāʻīl b. Nujayd al-Naysābūrī (Masāʼil wa-taʼwīlāt ṣūfiyya li-Abī ʻAbd al-Raḥmān al-Sulamī wa-yalīhi Juzʼ min aḥādīth Ismāʻīl b. Nujayd al-Naysābūrī)*, ed. Gerhard Böwering and Bilal Orfali (Beirut: Dār al-Mashriq, 2010).

57 Al-Sulamī, *Early Sufi Women: Dhikr an-niswa al-mutaʻabbidāt aṣ-ṣūfiyyāt*, ed. and trans. Rkia E. Cornell (Louisville: Fons Vitae, 1999).

58 Al-Sulamī, *Majmūʻa-i āthār Abū ʻAbd al-Raḥmān al-Sulamī (Collected Works on Early Sufism)*, ed. Nasrollah Pourjavady and Muḥammad Soori (Tehran: Markaz-i Nashr-i Dānishgāhī, 2009–10).

59 Al-Sulamī, *Ḥaqāʼiq al-tafsīr*, ed. Sayyid ʻUmrān (Beirut: Dār al-Kutub al-ʻIlmiyya, 2001); al-Sulamī, *Ziyādāt ḥaqāʼiq al-tafsīr (the Minor Qurʼān Commentary of Abū ʻAbd ar-Raḥmān Muḥammad b. al-Ḥusayn as-Sulamī [d. 412/1021])*, ed. Gerhard Böwering (Beirut: Dār al-Mashriq, 1995). ʻUmrān's edition of *Ḥaqāʼiq al-tafsīr* unfortunately draws upon only one manuscript and is riddled with errors. Orfali has planned to bring to completion Böwering's initial labours on a critical edition of this text.

60 Gerhard Böwering, 'The Qurʼān Commentary of al-Sulamī', in *Islamic Studies Presented to Charles J. Adams*, ed. Wael B. Hallaq and Donald P. Little (Leiden: Brill, 1991), 41–56; Gerhard Böwering, 'Sulamī's Treatise on the Science of the Letters (*ʻIlm al-ḥurūf*)', in *In the Shadow of Arabic: The Centrality of Language to Arabic Culture*, ed. Bilal Orfali (Leiden: Brill, 2011), 339–97; Gerhard Böwering, 'The Major Sources of Sulamī's Minor Qurʼān Commentary'; Kenneth L. Honerkamp, 'Abû ʻAbd Al-Rahmân Al-Sulamî (d. 412/1201) on Samâʻ, Ecstasy and Dance', *Journal of the History of Sufism* 4 (2004): 27–40; Kenneth L. Honerkamp, 'The Ethical-Mystical Foundations of the Master-Disciple Relationship in Formative Sufism in Ninth and Tenth Century Nīšābūr', in Gobillot and Thibon, *Les maîtres soufis et leurs disciples*, 79–97; Honerkamp, 'A Sufi Itinerary'; Frederick S. Colby, 'The Subtleties of the Ascension: Al-Sulamī on the Miʻrāj of the Prophet Muhammad', *SI* 94 (2002): 167–83.

61 Berger, '*Geschieden von allem ausser Gott.*'

62 Thibon, *L'œuvre.*

63 Al-Sulamī, *Les générations des Soufis:* Ṭabaqāt al-ṣūfiyya *de Abū ʻAbd al-Raḥmān, Muḥammad b. Ḥusayn al-Sulamī (325/937 – 412/1021)* (Leiden: Brill, 2019); shorter pieces will be cited and discussed in due course.

64 For a more detailed assessment, see Jason Welle, 'Review of *A Ṣūfī Apologist of Nīshāpūr: The Life and Thought of Abū 'Abd al-Raḥmān al-Sulamī* by S. Z. Chowdhury', *Arabica* 68 (2021): 437–42.
65 Arin Shawkat Salamah-Qudsi, *Sufism and Early Islamic Piety: Personal and Communal Dynamics* (Cambridge: Cambridge University Press, 2019).
66 Salamah-Qudsi, *Sufism and Early Islamic Piety*, 1.
67 MacIntyre, *After Virtue*, 263.

1 *The emergence of* ādāb *in al-Sulamī's spiritual method*

1 Fritz Meier, 'A Book of Etiquette for Sufis', in *Essays on Islamic Piety and Mysticism*, ed. Bernd Radtke (Leiden: Brill, 1999), 50.
2 Abū 'Uthmān 'Amr al-Jāḥiẓ, *Kitāb fī l-mu'allimīn*, in *Rasā'il al-Jāḥiẓ* (Cairo: Maktabat al-Khanjī, 1964), 3:34.
3 Antonella Ghersetti, *La letteratura d'*adab (Rome: Istituto per l'Oriente C. A. Nallino, 2021), 27, citing André Miquel, *La littérature arabe* (Paris: Presses universitaires de France, 1969), 66. The relationship between *adab* and *'ilm* remains under debate in the scholarly literature. Susanne Enderwitz argues that the existence of works of *adab* dedicated to the duties of particular professions negates any attempt to classify *adab* as general knowledge and *'ilm* (or any other term) as specific knowledge. *Adab* and *'ilm* neither subsume nor exclude each other; they complement each other. Susanne Enderwitz, 'Adab, b) and Islamic Scholarship in the 'Abbāsid Period', *EI*[3]; see also Franz Rosenthal, *Knowledge Triumphant: The Concept of Knowledge in Medieval Islam* (Leiden: Brill, 2007), 240–77.
4 Wolfhart Heinrichs, 'The Classification of the Sciences and the Consolidation of Philology in Classical Islam', in *Centres of Learning: Learning and Location in Pre-Modern Europe*, ed. J. W. Drijvers and A. A. MacDonald (Leiden: Brill, 1995), 119–20, cited in the introduction to Abū Manṣūr al-Tha'ālibī, *The Book of Noble Character*, ed. Bilal Orfali and Ramzi Baalbaki (Leiden: Brill, 2015), 1.
5 Ghersetti, *La letteratura d'*adab, 18–23.
6 Jaakko Hämeen-Anttila, '*Adab*, a) Early Arabic Developments', *EI*[3].
7 Charles Pellat, 'Adab, ii. Adab in Arabic Literature', *EIr*.
8 Hämeen-Anttila, '*Adab*, a) Early Arabic Developments'.
9 Jalal Khaleghi-Motlagh, 'Adab i. in Iran', *EIr*, citing al-Jāḥiẓ, *Rasā'il*, 2:191–2.
10 Ghersetti, *La letteratura d'*adab, 29.
11 Ghersetti, *La letteratura d'*adab, 31–3.
12 Peter Heath, 'Al-Jāḥiẓ, *Adab*, and the Art of the Essay', in *Al-Jāḥiẓ: A Muslim Humanist for Our Time*, ed. Arnim Heinemann, John L. Meloy, Tarif Khalidi and Manfred Kropp (Beirut: Ergon Verlag Würzburg, 2009), 143.
13 Luca Patrizi emphasizes the cross-cultural nature of the image of the divine banquet, discussing courtly *adab* in both Greek and Persian contexts, see Luca Patrizi, 'The Allegory of the Divine Banquet and the Origin of the Notion of *Adab*', *Knowledge and Education in Classical Islam: Religious Learning between Continuity and Change*, ed. Sebastian Günther (Leiden: Brill, 2020), 1:516–38.
14 Hämeen-Anttila, '*Adab*, a) Early Arabic Developments'.
15 Al-Hujwīrī, *The Kashf Al-Mahjub: A Persian Treatise on Sufism* (Leiden: Brill, 1911), 341.

16 Erik S. Ohlander, 'Adab, in Ṣūfism', *EI*[3].
17 Cf. Salamah-Qudsi, *Sufism and Early Islamic Piety*, 18.
18 Al-Sulamī, *Kitāb ādāb al-ṣuḥba*, 6–8.
19 Al-Sulamī, *Kitāb ādāb al-ṣuḥba*, 6.
20 Hämeen-Anttila, '*Adab*, a) Early Arabic Developments'.
21 Al-Thaʿālibī, *The Book of Noble Character*, 2; Bilal Orfali, *The Anthologist's Art: Abū Manṣūr al-Thaʿālibī and His* Yatīmat al-dahr (Leiden: Brill, 2016), 2.
22 The most obvious parallel is with *Kitāb al-futuwwa*; Thibon lays out the similarities between these two texts in detail. I suggest that *Kitāb ādāb al-ṣuḥba* may have served as a prototype because unlike *Kitāb al-futuwwa* it lacks a division into parts and its contents are even more jumbled than some of al-Sulamī's other treatises (few of which are systematically organized in any case). Al-Sulamī, *Kitāb al-futuwwa / Tasavvufta fütüvvet*, ed. and trans. Süleyman Ateş (Ankara: Ankara Üniversitesi İlāhiyat Fakültesi Yayınları, 1977); Thibon, *L'œuvre*, 267–8.
23 Ohlander, 'Adab, in Ṣūfism'.
24 For this reason, S. A. Bonebakker challenges the usefulness of the term, as if it indicated a literary genre. S. A. Bonebakker, '*Adab* and the Concept of *Belles-Lettres*', in *ʿAbbasid Belles-Lettres*, ed. Julia Ashtiany (New York: Cambridge University Press, 1990), 27, 30.
25 Al-Sulamī, *Kitāb ādāb al-ṣuḥba*, 8.
26 Thibon, *L'œuvre*, 262, 270.
27 See especially al-Sulamī, *Jawāmiʿ ādāb al-ṣūfiyya*, *Kitāb maḥāsin al-taṣawwuf* and *Kitāb bayān al-sharīʿa wa-l-ḥaqīqa*.
28 Al-Sulamī, *ṬṢ*, 119 (#19). Thibon casts some doubt upon the historical authenticity of this attribution, but, in any case, its succinct summary of the integral link between Sufism and good comportment explains why many modern scholars cite the maxim. Jean-Jacques Thibon, '*Adab* et éducation spirituelle (*tarbiya*) chez les maîtres de Nīshābūr aux IIIe/IXe et IVe/Xe siècles', in *Ethics and Spirituality in Islam: Sufi* Adab, ed. Francesco Chiabotti, Eve Feuillebois-Pierunek, Catherine Mayeur-Jaouen and Luca Patrizi (Leiden: Brill, 2016), 126.
29 For al-Sulamī as well as other masters, such aphorisms were not intended to provide historical data, lexical information or technical structure; they 'are not definitions in any sense of the word'. Rather, these maxims – particularly when they occur in proximity to complementary 'definitions' of the same term, as was common in Ṣūfī anthologies – evoke together the mass of beliefs, character traits and practices that a shaykh values. Tamar Frank, '"Taṣawwuf is …": On a Type of Mystical Aphorism', *JAOS* 104, no. 1 (1984): 73.
30 Al-Sulamī, *MA*, §16.
31 Al-Sulamī, *KMT*, §7. The soundness of Ṣūfī customs and moral behaviour acts as a lynchpin in this apologetic treatise. Critics of Sufism only desire to discuss the distinctive licenses of Ṣūfī practice, but al-Sulamī insists that no believer can question the customs and the moral behaviour of Ṣūfīs, as they are in accord with the Qurʾān and the *sunna*. Al-Sulamī uses this treatise to discuss these disputed *rukhaṣ*, saying he had already discussed Ṣūfī *ādāb*, *akhlāq* and *aḥwāl* in the now-lost *Sunan al-ṣūfiyya* (*The Customs of the Ṣūfīs*). The term *rukhṣa* (pl. *rukhaṣ*) literally means 'facilitation' or 'alleviation'; jurists typically use it to describe a special dispensation in which a mitigating circumstance permits a believer to not perform an obligatory

act or to perform an act that is otherwise prohibited. Al-Sulamī responds to a frequent criticism of the Ṣūfīs, namely that they practice unjustified flexibility in their adherence to all the commands and prohibitions of the divine law. Marion Holmes Katz, '*'Azima* and *rukhṣa*', *EI*[3].

32 Al-Sulamī, *BAṢ*, 366–7.

33 Al-Sulamī, *BAṢ*, 368.

34 Al-Sulamī, *AMM*, §2.

35 Al-Sulamī, *AMM*, §21.

36 Al-Sulamī, *MA*, §6–7.

37 Compare this to the progression anticipated in Abū Najīb al-Suhrawardī (d. 563/1168), whose book of conduct for novices, *Ādāb al-murīdīn*, focuses on correct behaviour (*ādāb*) and neglects stations (*maqāmāt*) and states (*aḥwāl*), precisely because the author deemed *ādāb* more relevant to those beginning on the path and discussion of stations and states less relevant until one has advanced further on the path. Ian Richard Netton, 'The Breath of Felicity: *Adab, Aḥwāl, Maqāmāt* and Abū Najīb al-Suhrawardī', in *Classical Persian Sufism from its Origins to Rumi*, ed. Leonard Lewisohn (London: Khaniqahi Nimatullahi Publications, 1993), 459; al-Suhrawardī, *A Sufi Rule for Novices*, trans. Menahem Milson (Cambridge: Harvard University Press, 1975), 16–17.

38 Kenneth L. Honerkamp thus describes *adab* and *akhlāq* as the 'active principles of the process of spiritual transformation'. Kenneth L. Honerkamp, 'The Ethical-Mystical Foundations of the Master-Disciple Relationship in Formative Sufism in Ninth and Tenth Century Nīšābūr', in Gobillot and Thibon, *Les maîtres soufis et leurs disciples*, 13.

39 Chowdhury, *A Ṣūfī Apologist*, 32.

40 Al-Sulamī, *RAK*.

41 Al-Sulamī, *MA*, §16; *BAṢ*, 368.

42 Chowdhury recognizes this when in his translation of *ādāb iktisāb*, he does not settle for 'acquired' but adds that these ways are 'acquired through effort'. Chowdhury, *A Ṣūfī Apologist*, 158, citing al-Sulamī, *MA*, §16. For a discussion of the origins of the concept of *kasb*, including the conclusion that al-Ash'arī himself (d. 324/935–6) both accepted a certain reality to the human person's willing and attached little importance to the notion of *iktisāb*, see W. Montgomery Watt, 'The Origin of the Islamic Doctrine of Acquisition', *JRAS* 75, nos. 3–4 (1943): 234–47; for further discussion, see Richard M. Frank, 'The Structure of Created Causality according to al-Aš'arî: An Analysis of the 'Kitâb Al-Luma'', §§ 82–164', *SI* 25 (1966): 13–75; Binyamin Abrahamov, 'A Re-Examination of Al-Ash'arī's Theory of 'Kasb' According to 'Kitāb Al-Luma'', *JRAS* 121, no. 2 (1989): 210–21; for a description of the growing divide between Ṣūfīs in Iraq in the period and Mu'tazilīs, see Florian Sobieroj, 'The Mu'tazila and Sufism', in *Islamic Mysticism Contested: Thirteen Centuries of Controversies and Polemics*, ed. Frederick de Jong and Bernd Radtke (Leiden: Brill, 1999), 68–92.

43 Thibon generally interprets al-Sulamī as eclectic regarding *madhhab*, seeing little evidence to claim that he adhered to Ash'arism but little evidence to argue otherwise, given the default association between Nishapur's Shāfi'ī families and the Ash'arī school. The point is a missed opportunity in Chowdhury's volume, which discusses Nishapur as an Ash'arī intellectual centre in the period but does not examine in detail al-Sulamī's engagement with this theological school. Thibon, *L'œuvre*, 167; Chowdhury, *A Ṣūfī Apologist*, 31–4, 61–2.

44 Al-Sulamī, *MA*, §2.

45 Rather than explain what *akhlāq* are, al-Sulamī provides a limited list: 'Regarding the virtues, they are good character, generosity, humility, forbearance, accepting judgments with contentment, and minimizing disharmony with the brothers.' Al-Sulamī, *BAṢ*, 368.
46 Al-Sulamī, *MA*, §2, 16.
47 Al-Sulamī, *KMT*, §8; *JAṢ*, §4.
48 Al-Sulamī, *AṢ*, §113.
49 The treatise where one might expect to find a fuller definition of what a spiritual state is in fact contains no such attempt. In *Bayān aḥwāl al-ṣūfiyya*, al-Sulamī simply provides a limited list of the phenomenon: 'Regarding the states, they are asceticism (*zuhd*), scrupulosity (*wara'*), dependence [upon God] (*tawakkul*), relegation [of power to God] (*tafwīḍ*), humility (*khushū'*), surrender [to God's will] (*taslīm*), sincerity (*ikhlāṣ*), certainty (*yaqīn*), fear (*khawf*), hope (*rajā'*), contentment [with God's decree] (*qanā'a*) and similar things.' Al-Sulamī, *BAṢ*, 369.
50 Thomas D'Andrea sees this diagnosis already present in 1966's *A Short History of Ethics*. Alasdair C. MacIntyre, *A Short History of Ethics: A History of Moral Philosophy from the Homeric Age to the Twentieth Century* (Notre Dame, IN: University of Notre Dame Press, 1998); Thomas D. D'Andrea, *Tradition, Rationality, and Virtue: The Thought of Alasdair MacIntyre* (Burlington, VT: Ashgate, 2006), 49.
51 MacIntyre, *After Virtue*, 22.
52 MacIntyre, *After Virtue*, 24.
53 For an outstanding summary, especially regarding the relationship between the crucial terms 'virtue', 'practice' and 'narrative', see Brad J. Kallenberg, 'The Master Argument of MacIntyre's *After Virtue*', in *Virtues and Practices in the Christian Tradition: Christian Ethics after MacIntyre*, ed. Nancey C. Murphy, Brad J. Kallenberg and Mark Nation (Notre Dame, IN: University of Notre Dame Press, 2003), 7–29.
54 Alasdair C. MacIntyre, *Whose Justice? Which Rationality?* (Notre Dame, IN: University of Notre Dame, 1988), 7.
55 MacIntyre, *Whose Justice? Which Rationality?*, 12.
56 Jean Porter, 'Tradition in the Recent Work of Alasdair MacIntyre', in *Alasdair MacIntyre*, ed. Mark C. Murphy (New York: Cambridge University Press, 2003), 43, citing MacIntyre, *Whose Justice? Which Rationality?*, 354.
57 John Horton and Susan Mendus, 'Alasdair MacIntyre: *After Virtue* and After', in *After MacIntyre: Critical Perspectives on the Work of Alasdair MacIntyre*, ed. John Horton and Susan Mendus (Notre Dame, IN: University of Notre Dame Press, 1994), 11.
58 MacIntyre, *After Virtue*, 187.
59 Christopher Stephen Lutz, *Tradition in the Ethics of Alasdair MacIntyre: Relativism, Thomism, and Philosophy* (Lanham, MD: Lexington Books, 2004), 41.
60 MacIntyre, *After Virtue*, 219.
61 D'Andrea, *Tradition, Rationality, and Virtue*, 269.
62 MacIntyre, *After Virtue*, xiv.
63 MacIntyre, *After Virtue*, 215.
64 MacIntyre, *After Virtue*, 52.
65 MacIntyre, *After Virtue*, 58.
66 Al-Sulamī, *KAṢ*, 86.
67 Most famously, MacIntyre frustrated many educators by denying that teaching is a practice. For discussion, see Alasdair Macintyre and Joseph Dunne, 'Alasdair MacIntyre on Education: In Dialogue with Joseph Dunne', *JPE* 36, no. 1 (2002): 1–19;

see also papers collected in a special edition as a follow-up to this interview, *JPE* 37, no. 2 (2003).

68 MacIntyre's example of architecture applies analogously here: for him, architecture is a practice but bricklaying is not. To be sure, *dhikr* and *samāʿ* are far more psychologically complex activities than bricklaying. Neither is merely a technical skill, but still, neither in itself serves as the organizing concept for a believer's participation in a coherent and complex form of human activity in the way that *adab* does. The strongest evidence against my resistance to classify *dhikr* and *samāʿ* as practices lies in the treatises *Mas'alat ṣifāt al-dhākirīn wa-l-mutafakkirīn* and *Kitāb al-samāʿ*, but even in those texts, these customs remain too circumspect about their role in the believer's journey. In the former, al-Sulamī's praise for *dhikr* rests on *dhikr*'s capacity to advance a believer in *maʿrifa* and *maḥabba*. *Maʿrifa* and *maḥabba* are certainly goods that Ṣūfīs strive to realize, suggesting that *dhikr* could be a practice to enable this, but al-Sulamī's other writings describe and promote the other customs that facilitate, in complementary ways, the realization of these same goals. In the latter treatise, al-Sulamī explores *samāʿ* in relation to Ṣūfī stations and states. Here again, he subsumes *samāʿ* under his larger goal of establishing the legitimacy of Ṣūfī *adab*; he stresses 'the integral nature of *samāʿ* within a Ṣūfī methodology'. That broader Ṣūfī methodology, *adab*, functions as the best analogue for MacIntyre's notion of practice, while customs like *dhikr* and *samāʿ* function more like bricklaying, hole digging, computer-aided drafting or the many other activities that together constitute the larger practice of architecture and transform the goals towards which practitioners of architecture strive. Interestingly, the situation begins to shift only one generation later. Francesco Chiabotti points out that while al-Sulamī gives *adab* a central role in a disciple's evolution, his student al-Qushayrī accords that place to *dhikr*, increasing the scope of *dhikr* in a Ṣūfī's process of spiritual realization. Al-Sulamī generally uses *dhikr* to describe discrete attempts to recall the presence of God, regardless of whether this takes the form of *dhikr* of the tongue, *dhikr* of the heart or other kinds of *dhikr*. Al-Qushayrī, by contrast turns *dhikr* into a totalizing concept for the seeker's remembrance of God in all moments of life. Al-Sulamī, *ṢDM*, §205–8; *KS*, §4–5, §13; MacIntyre, *After Virtue*, 187; Honerkamp, 'Abû 'Abd al-Rahmân al-Sulamî (d. 412/1201) on *Samâʿ*, Ecstasy and Dance', 8; Francesco Chiabotti, 'Entre soufisme et savoir islamique: L'œuvre de 'Abd al-Karīm al-Qushayrī (376–465/ 986–1072)' (PhD, Aix-Marseille Université, 2014), 626.

69 Brian Silverstein has suggested MacIntyre as a means to understand how *sohbet* (Ar. *ṣuḥba*) functions for modern Turkish Ṣūfīs, casting *sohbet* as a MacIntyrean practice. Silverstein, 'Disciplines of Presence in Modern Turkey', 120.

70 Al-Sulamī, *KAṢ*, 86.

71 Some critics reject the idea that the distinction between internal and external goods is as clean-cut as MacIntyre would have it; see Paul Hager, 'Refurbishing MacIntyre's Notion of Practice', *JPE* 45, no. 3 (2011): 552–6.

72 MacIntyre, *After Virtue*, 190–1.

73 Jean-Jacques Thibon, 'Malāmatiyya', *EI*[3].

74 MacIntyre, *After Virtue*, 198.

75 Annabel Keeler offers an outstanding and more detailed survey of some of the masters who follow and includes some omitted here. Annabel Keeler, 'The Concept of *adab* in Early Sufism with Particular Reference to the Teachings of Sahl b. 'Abdallāh al-Tustarī (d. 283/896)', in Chiabotti et al., *Ethics and Spirituality in Islam*, 63–101.

76 For a general discussion of the etymology of the term *adab* and its relationship to other Arabic terms denoting custom, etiquette or comportment, see Meier, 'A Book of Etiquette for Sufis', 49–54.

77 Ibn ʿArabī, for example, considers the primary heritage of *adab* to be qualitative, an attitude observed in respect of God in the relation between master and disciple that Ibn ʿArabī then elevates to the level of doctrine. Only a few decades later, Ṣūfī convents in India prized the same term, *adab*, to signify a practical norm of etiquette, conduct that is laudable and inherited from those who have come before. Denis Gril, '*Adab* and Revelation or One of the Foundations of the Hermeneutics of Ibn 'Arabi', in *Muhyiddin Ibn 'Arabi: A Commemorative Volume*, ed. Stephen Hirtenstein and Michael Tiernan (Shaftesbury: Element, 1993), 228; Denis Matringe, '*Ādāb al-ṣūfiya*: Les règles de vie dans les couvents soufis de l'Inde médiévale', *JA* 289, no. 1 (2001): 68.

78 Gerhard Böwering, 'The Adab Literature of Classical Sufism: Anṣārī's Code of Conduct', in *Moral Conduct and Authority: The Place of Adab in South Asian Islam*, ed. Barbara Daly Metcalf (Berkeley: University of California Press, 1984), 71.

79 The major *ḥadīth* collections do not contain a Prophetic *ḥadīth* cited by al-Sulamī and popular among Ṣūfīs, 'Truly, God trained me with the best way of conduct and perfected my conduct' (*inna Allāh addabanī fa-aḥsana adabī*). A variant, *addabanī rabbī fa-aḥsana taʾdībī*, is found in more *ḥadīth* collections and illustrates the synonymous usage of *adab* and *taʾdīb* for some Arabs in the period. The verbal form *addabanī* appears nine times in al-Majlisī's major work of Shīʿī traditions, *Biḥār al-anwār*. Azartash Azarnoosh and Suheyl Umar, 'Adab', *EI*[3]. On the former tradition, see al-Sulamī, *KAṢ*, 86; *JAṢ*, §7; *AMM*, §16; al-Sarrāj, *The Kitāb al-lumaʿ*, K. al-uswa wa-l-iqtidāʾ, B. mā ruwiya ʿan Rasūl Allāh fī akhlāqihi wa-afʿālihi wa-aḥwālihi; K. ādāb al-mutaṣawwifa, B. fī dhikr al-ādāb; see also Biagi's comment in al-Sulamī, *A Collection of Sufi Rules of Conduct*, 62en22. On the latter tradition, see Ibn Taymiyya, *Majmūʿat al-fatāwā* (al-Manṣūra: Dār al-Wafāʾ, 2005), 18:375; Ibn Taymiyya, *Aḥādīth al-quṣṣāṣ* (Cairo: al-Dār al-Miṣriyya al-Lubnāniyya, 1993), 27, Ḥ. 1; Ibn Taymiyya, *Shaykh al-Islām Ibn Taymiyya wa-juhūduhu fī l-ḥadīth wa-ʿulūmihi* (Riyadh: Dār al-ʿĀṣima, 2010), 2:465–7, Ḥ. 251; al-Suyūṭī, *Jāmiʿ al-aḥādīth* (Beirut: Dār al-Fikr, 1994), 1:133, Ḥ. 780; al-Suyūṭī, *al-Durar al-muntathira* (Riyadh: Jāmiʿat al-Malik Saʿūd, n.d.), 45, Ḥ. 8; al-Sakhāwī, *al-Ajwiba al-murḍiyya* (Riyadh: Dār al-Rāya, 1997), 1:245, Ḥ. 59; al-Albānī, *Silsilat al-aḥādīth al-ḍaʿīfa wa-l-mawḍūʿa wa-athrihā l-shayʾ fī l-umma* (Riyadh: Maktabat al-Maʿārif, 1992), 1:173, Ḥ. 72; see also al-Thaʿlabī, *al-Kashf wa-l-bayān fī tafsīr al-Qurʾān* (Beirut: Dār al-Kutub al-ʿIlmiyya, 2004), 6:250.

80 For a representative example from a rarely discussed treatise, see Gavin N. Picken, *Spiritual Purification in Islam: The Life and Works of Al-Muḥāsibī* (New York: Routledge, 2011), 190.

81 Al-Ḥārith al-Muḥāsibī, *Badʾ man anāba ilā Allāh wa-yalīhi ādāb al-nufūs* (Cairo: Dār al-Salām, 1991), 25.

82 Keeler, 'The Concept of *adab* in Early Sufism', 68.

83 Picken, *Spiritual Purification in Islam*, 69.

84 Annemarie Schimmel, *Mystical Dimensions of Islam* (Chapel Hill: University of North Carolina Press, 1975), 54. Tales about his early life suggest that he was both a knowledgeable and scrupulous child, characteristics that later marked his mature spirituality. Picken, *Spiritual Purification in Islam*, 47–50.

85 Roger Arnaldez, 'Al-Muḥāsibī', *EI*[2]. Some scholars have argued that al-Muḥāsibī should be considered neither a Ṣūfī nor a mystic, characterizing him instead as a

'moralizing pious theologian'. Knysh rightly argues that the boundaries between 'theology' and mystical themes in al-Muḥāsibī's writings are porous and Sheikh essentially argues the same regarding the false dichotomy between juridical discourse and mystical discourse. For the purposes of this study, whether al-Muḥāsibī (or al-Ḥakīm al-Tirmidhī) should be classified as 'Ṣūfīs' is less important than whether their writings express the attitude towards *adab* that characterized the intellectual currents influential on al-Sulamī, and that point is beyond doubt. Julian Baldick, *Mystical Islam: An Introduction to Sufism* (London: I.B. Tauris, 1989), 34; Knysh, *Islamic Mysticism*, 48.

86 Ohlander, 'Adab, in Ṣūfism'.

87 Sheikh, *Forging Ideal Muslim Subjects*, 33. One lacuna in Sheikh's study of al-Muḥāsibī is Sheikh's lack of attention to *adab* as a concept.

88 Picken, *Spiritual Purification in Islam*, 69; Schimmel, *Mystical Dimensions of Islam*, 86. Al-Muḥāsibī devoted an entire chapter of *al-Riʿāya* to the exploration and criticism of *riyā'* (ostentation). Al-Muḥāsibī, *al-Riʿāya li-ḥuqūq Allāh* (Beirut: Dār al-Kutub al-ʿIlmiyya, 2010), 153–306.

89 Picken, *Spiritual Purification in Islam*, 74.

90 Published editions create confusion about where al-Muḥāsibī used the term himself, where a later copyist inserted it and where a modern editor inserted it; in certain cases, editors take liberty to add *ādāb* into a heading or subheading when the text does not demand it.

91 Al-Muḥāsibī, *Ādāb al-nufūs wa-yalīhi Kitāb al-tawahhum* (Beirut: Mu'assasat al-Kutub al-Thaqāfiyya, 1991), 34ff. For example, al-Muḥāsibī offers one section on beneficial ways to ascribe praise (*madḥ*) or blame (*dhamm*), to help believers identify and overcome their instinctive desires to seek the approval of others and avoid their scorn. Ibid., 70–5. A later series of successive questions aimed at increasing and deepening one's level of self-scrutiny further fosters the achievement of sincerity of intention. Ibid., 96.

92 For an English translation, see Kermit A. Schoonover, '*Kitāb Al-Riʿāya Li Ḥuqūq Allāh* by Al-Muḥāsibī: A Translation with Introduction and Notes' (PhD, Harvard University, 1948); for a published summary of the author's primary conclusions, see Schoonover, 'Al-Muḥāsibī and His Al-Ri'āya', *MW* 39 (1949): 26–35.

93 The 'eight rules' implausibly attributed to al-Junayd undergo a similar development: an initial attitude of renunciation that focused more on moral qualities than on techniques gave way to techniques for the training of the *nafs*, which then gave way to the specific code of conduct governing the master-disciple relationship and the common practices of Ṣūfī brothers. Christopher Melchert, 'Khargūshī, *Tahdhīb al-asrār*', *BSOAS* 73, no. 1 (2010): 41–2; Bernd Radtke, 'The Eight Rules of Junayd: A General Overview of the Genesis and Development of Islamic Dervish Orders', in *Reason and Inspiration in Islam: Theology, Philosophy and Mysticism in Muslim Thought*, ed. Todd Lawson (London: I.B. Tauris, in association with the Institute of Ismaili Studies, 2005), 492.

94 The key passage in *Bad'* deals with fasting and the importance of experiencing true hunger. Al-Muḥāsibī, *Bad' man anāba ilā Allāh wa-yalīhi Ādāb al-nufūs*, 27.

95 Picken, *Spiritual Purification in Islam*, 77.

96 Keeler, 'The Concept of *adab* in Early Sufism', 68.

97 Al-Sulamī, *ṬṢ*, 56–60.

98 As an example, al-Junayd's *Adab al-muftaqir* (*The Comportment of the Mendicant*) argues that restraining the ego-self will bring about a proper inner orientation

free from dangerous temptations, but al-Junayd does not rely on *adab* as a central governing concept. The Syrian shaykh Abū ʿAbdallāh al-Rūdhbārī's (d. 369/979) *Adab al-faqīr* presents a helpful point of contrast, as al-Rūdhbārī insists that each state on the quest has its own proper *adab* through which the highest level of that state can be attained. Al-Rūdhbārī demands that believers know and master the principal requirements of that state in terms of outward comportment, including patterns of speech. Keeler, 'The Concept of *adab* in Early Sufism', 66; Ali Hassan Abdel-Kader, *The Life, Personality and Writings of al-Junayd: A Study of a Third/ Ninth Century Mystic with an Edition and Translation of his Writings* (London: Luzac, 1962), English 178–83, Arabic 58–62.

99 Keeler, 'The Concept of *adab* in Early Sufism', 75.

100 Al-Tustarī's approach is evident in his comment on a Qur'ānic verse frequently mentioned by al-Sulamī and other Ṣūfīs, 'Truly you have a magnificent character.' The Prophet was trained in the *adab* of the Qur'ān, showing the way for other believers. Al-Tustarī, *Tafsīr al-Qur'ān al-ʿaẓīm* (Cairo: Dār al-Ḥaram al-Turāth, 2004); *Tafsīr al-Tustarī*, trans. Annabel Keeler and Ali Keeler (Amman: Royal Aal al-Bayt Institute for Islamic Thought, 2011), Q. 68:4.

101 Al-Tustarī, *Tafsīr*, Q. 4:171.

102 In a passage that conforms to later adherents of the Path of Blame, al-Tustarī insists that true spiritual poverty resides in a person when no one knows of the person's hunger and the severity of the person's personal discipline. Al-Tustarī, *al-Muʿāraḍa wa-l-radd ʿalā ahl al-firaq wa-ahl al-daʿāwā fī l-aḥwāl* (Cairo: Dār al-Insān lil-Ta'līf wa-l-Tarjamah wa-l-Nashr, 1980), 124.

103 For examples, see al-Tustarī, *Tafsīr*, Q. 7:176, 8:1, 48:4 and 79:40.

104 Gerhard Böwering, *The Mystical Vision of Existence in Classical Islam: The Qur'ānic Hermeneutics of the Ṣūfī Sahl at-Tustarī (d. 283/896)* (Berlin: de Gruyter, 1980), 241–61, esp. 253–61.

105 Al-Tustarī, *Tafsīr*, Q. 22:52. Al-Tustarī at points describes those disciplines using the second form of the verb, *ta'dīb*, suggesting that while *adab* includes these ascetic exercises, *adab* cannot be reduced to them. Ibid., Q. 48:9.

106 Keeler, 'The Concept of *adab* in Early Sufism', 79, 97.

107 See the saying attributed to al-Tustarī in al-Sulamī, *ṬṢ*, 207 (#4); see also al-Tustarī, *Tafsīr*, Q. 16:90.

108 For one example, see al-Tustarī, *Tafsīr*, Q. 48:4.

109 Al-Tustarī, *Tafsīr*, Q. 74:56; Keeler, 'The Concept of *adab* in Early Sufism', 96–7 (emphasis Keeler's).

110 Keeler, 'The Concept of *adab* in Early Sufism', 75.

111 Al-Tustarī, *Tafsīr*, Q. 7:172. Translation Keeler's, with slight modifications.

112 Cf. Patrizi, 'The Allegory of the Divine Banquet.'

113 Al-Tustarī, *al-Muʿāraḍa*, 90.

114 Al-Tustarī, *Tafsīr*, Q. 13:43.

115 Aiyub Palmer, *Sainthood and Authority in Early Islam: Al-Ḥakīm al-Tirmidhī's Theory of* wilāya *and the Reenvisioning of the Sunnī Caliphate* (Leiden: Brill, 2020), 166–95.

116 On the meaning of *ḥakīm* in the context of Islamic mysticism in the period, see Palmer, *Sainthood and Authority in Early Islam*, 86–110; Bernd Radtke, 'Theologen und Mystiker in Ḫurāsān und Transoxanien', *ZDMG* 136, no. 3 (1986): 551–65.

117 Keeler, 'The Concept of *adab* in Early Sufism', 68.

118 Scholars diverge on whether certain writings traditionally ascribed to al-Ḥakīm al-Tirmidhī were written by him, although the ascription of these two texts is broadly accepted. For an illustration of how much hinges on this question, see Bernd Radtke's withering indictment of Geneviève Gobillot, 'Some Recent Research on al-Ḥakīm al-Tirmidhī', *Der Islam* 83, no. 1 (2006): 39–89.

119 The extent of al-Ḥakīm al-Tirmidhī's engagement with the Malāmatiyya remains uncertain, although he certainly met them due to his travels throughout the region. Al-Ḥakīm al-Tirmidhī, *The Concept of Sainthood in Early Islamic Mysticism*, trans. Bernd Radtke and John O'Kane (Richmond: Curzon, 1996), 1–2.

120 Sara Sviri, 'Ḥakīm Tirmidhī and the Malāmatī Movement in Early Sufism', in Lewisohn, *Classical Persian Sufism*, 611. For a passage that illustrates al-Ḥakīm al-Tirmidhī's thinking on this matter, see al-Ḥakīm al-Tirmidhī, *Bayān al-farq bayn al-ṣadr wa-l-qalb wa-l-fu'ād wa-l-lubb* (Cairo: Markaz al-Kitāb lil-Nashr, 1998), 64–7; al-Sulamī and al-Ḥakīm al-Tirmidhī, *Three Early Sufi Texts*, 40–2.

121 Al-Ḥakīm al-Tirmidhī, *Adab al-nafs* (Cairo: al-Dār al-Miṣriyya al-Lubnāniyya, 1993), 63.

122 Al-Ḥakīm al-Tirmidhī, *Drei Schriften des Theosophen von Tirmidh*, trans. and ed. Bernd Radtke (Stuttgart: Steiner, 1992), 1:74–5, 2:213.

123 Thibon, '*Adab* et éducation spirituelle', 104.

124 Sviri, 'Ḥakīm Tirmidhī and the Malāmatī Movement', 611.

125 Al-Ḥakīm al-Tirmidhī, *Riyāḍat al-Nafs* (Beirut: Dār al-Kutub al-'Ilmiyya, 2005), 38.

126 Al-Ḥakīm al-Tirmidhī, *Adab al-nafs*, 27.

127 Al-Ḥakīm al-Tirmidhī, *Riyāḍat al-nafs*, 75–6. Al-Ḥakīm al-Tirmidhī's use of *adab* to describe the training of an animal is neither novel nor particular to the Ṣūfīs; the use of *ta'dīb* to train a horse has precedent in *ḥadīth*. See Luca Patrizi, '*Adab al-mulūk:* L'utilisation de la terminologie du pouvoir dans le soufisme médiéval', in Chiabotti et al., *Ethics and Spirituality in Islam*, 200; Bonebakker, '*Adab* and the Concept of *Belles-Lettres*', 18; Azarnoosh and Umar, 'Adab.'

128 One cannot, of course, presume that any one shaykh provides an accurate summary of the spirituality of the city in which he lives, but scholars have found in *Ta'arruf* indications of the different local trends in Sufism there. Jacqueline Chabbi argues that al-Kalābādhī was not only less likely than others – especially al-Sulamī – to flatten the differences between Ṣūfīs, but that al-Kalābādhī's more prudently articulated version of Ḥallājism demonstrates the heterogeneity of primitive Sufism in the region. Jacqueline Chabbi, 'Réflexions sur le soufisme iranien primitif', *JA* 266, no. 1 (1978): 52.

129 Abū Bakr Muḥammad al-Kalābādhī, *Kitāb al-ta'arruf li-madhhab ahl al-taṣawwuf*, ed. A. J. Arberry (Cairo: Maktabat al-Khānjī, 1933), 12, 35; trans. A. J. Arberry as *The Doctrine of the Ṣūfīs* (New York: Cambridge University Press, 1977), 13–14, 44; Thibon, '*Adab* et éducation spirituelle', 106; A. J. Arberry, *Sufism: An Account of the Mystics of Islam* (Mineola, NY: Dover Publications, 2002), 69.

130 A. J. Arberry famously questioned whether al-Sulamī plagiarized al-Sarrāj in a section of *Risālat al-malāmatiyya* that contains material identical to al-Sarrāj's *Kitāb al-luma'*. Arberry recognized that al-Sulamī's reliance on al-Sarrāj was an abridgment, not a simple copying, claiming that Sulamī's 'précis is not even a particularly intelligent one'. The section in question is now recognized as a separate treatise, *Ghalaṭāt al-ṣūfiyya*. Thibon provides a full response to Arberry, concluding that al-Sulamī's text is not a vulgar plagiarism; due to al-Sulamī's abridgment and occasional modification, the later text is a 'discrete work of re-writing'. A similar

abridgment occurs in al-Sulamī's brief glossary of Sufi terminology, *Tafsīr alfāẓ al-ṣūfiyya*. Most of al-Sulamī's definitions are identical or nearly identical to those in the relevant section of al-Sarrāj and they occur in precisely the same sequence. In that case, Fuat Sezgin hypothesized that al-Sulamī and al-Sarrāj used a common source, a now-lost treatise by Abū ʿAlī al-Rūdhbārī. Sezgin's theory is plausible but cannot be proven. These two glossaries do vindicate al-Sulamī of Arberry's charge of unintelligence in abridgment. Al-Sulamī's contribution lies in the handiness of his treatise, a tightly woven glossary that omits al-Sarrāj's repetition and lacks citations to past Ṣūfī masters that al-Sulamī eagerly provides elsewhere but passes over here for the sake of elegant brevity. Al-Sulamī, *GṢ*, *AṢ*; al-Sarrāj, *The Kitāb al-Lumaʿ fī al-Taṣawwuf*, ed. Reynold A. Nicholson (Leiden: Brill, 1914), 333–74, 409–35; A. J. Arberry, 'Did Sulamī Plagiarize Sarrāj?' *JRAS* 69, no. 3 (1937): 461–5; *GAS*, 1:673fn5; Thibon, *L'œuvre*, 526; see also J. A. Qureshi, 'The Book of Errors: A Critical Edition and Study of *Kitāb al-Aghālit* by Abū ʿAbd al-Raḥmān al-Sulamī (d. 412/1021)' (M.A., University of Georgia, 2002), 11–13; Chowdhury, *A Ṣūfī Apologist*, 98–102.

131 Keeler, 'The Concept of *adab* in Early Sufism', 69.

132 Karamustafa, *Sufism: The Formative Period*, 67; Ohlander, 'Adab, in Ṣūfism.'

133 Keeler, 'The Concept of *adab* in Early Sufism', 95.

134 Al-Sarrāj, *Kitāb al-lumaʿ*, K. ādāb al-mutaṣawwifa, B. fī dhikr al-ādāb; see also a very similar saying attributed to Kulthūm al-ʿAtābī in al-Kharkūshī, *Kitāb tahdhīb al-asrār* (Abu Dhabi: al-Majmaʿ al-Thaqāfī, 1999), 214.

135 Al-Sarrāj, *Kitāb al-lumaʿ*, K. ādāb al-mutaṣawwifa, B. fī dhikr al-ādāb.

136 Near the end of his discussion of fasting, al-Sarrāj mentions this as the intention of the fast. Al-Sarrāj, *Kitāb al-lumaʿ*, K. ādāb al-mutaṣawwifa, B. fī dhikr al-ṣawm wa-ādābihim fīhi.

137 Likewise, Meier amplifies one aspect of *ādāb* in al-Sulamī's writings. While it is true that 'all of Sufism is subordinated to the concept of *ādāb*' for al-Sulamī, this statement only holds if one understands *ādāb* more broadly than the aspect of customary practice and good behaviour on which Meier focuses his inquiry. Meier, 'A Book of Etiquette for Sufis', 51–3.

138 Al-Sarrāj, *Kitāb al-lumaʿ*, K. ādāb al-mutaṣawwifa, B. dhikr ādābihim fī l-ṣuḥba.

139 Here, the connection Stefan Sperl posits between *ḥadīth* literature and classical Arabic *adab* shows its relevance. At precisely the moment in which al-Sarrāj abandons language of *ādāb*, al-Sarrāj slips into the type of open-ended anecdotes that lead Sperl to classify *ḥadīth* literature as postmodern. Al-Sarrāj has employed moral and aesthetic criteria to choose the anecdotes that best exemplify his understanding of authentic companionship and convey to the reader a collapse of the time between that sacred moment and the present moment. Stefan Sperl, 'Man's "Hollow Core": Ethics and Aesthetics in *Ḥadīth* Literature and Classical Arabic *Adab*', *BSOAS* 70, no. 3 (2007): 459–86.

140 These are the types of prescriptions that appear elsewhere under the mantle of *ādāb*. Al-Sarrāj, *Kitāb al-lumaʿ*, K. ādāb al-mutaṣawwifa, B. ādābihim fī l-wuḍūʾ wa-l-ṭahārāt.

141 Al-Sarrāj, *Kitāb al-lumaʿ*, K. ādāb al-mutaṣawwifa, B. dhikr ādābihim fī l-ṣuḥba.

142 Al-Sarrāj, *Kitāb al-lumaʿ*, K. ādāb al-mutaṣawwifa, B. dhikr ādābihim fī l-ṣuḥba.

143 Translation Knysh; the same passage occurs with only cosmetic changes in al-Kharkūshī's (d. 407/1016) *Tahdhīb al-asrār* and al-Qushayrī's *Risāla*, attributed

there also to al-Jalājilī. Al-Sarrāj, *Kitāb al-luma'*, K. ādāb al-mutaṣawwifa, B. fī dhikr al-ādāb; al-Kharkūshī, *Tahdhīb al-asrār*, 215; al-Qushayrī, *Risāla*, B. al-adab.

144 Al-Sarrāj, *Kitāb al-luma'*, K. ādāb al-mutaṣawwifa, Faṣl ākhar fī ādāb al-ṣalāt.

145 Keeler, 'The Concept of *adab* in Early Sufism', 95.

146 Thibon, '*Adab* et éducation spirituelle', 111.

147 Qamar-ul Huda, 'The Light Beyond the Shore in the Theology of Proper Sufi Moral Conduct (*Adab*)', *JAAR* 72, no. 2 (2004): 461.

148 Thibon, '*Adab* et éducation spirituelle', 126.

149 Among the treatises ascribed to al-Sulamī, *Dhikr ādāb al-ṣūfiyya* stands as an outlier. It lacks thematic unity, it lacks the style of introduction that characterizes his other writings and the internal references to al-Sulamī himself create doubt about how much of the work al-Sulamī prepared and how much shows the hand of later editing and redaction. Both Nadia Zeidan, who edited the treatise, and Thibon concur that the style and manner of treating the subject are certainly that of al-Sulamī. I am less confident than either of them. While the teachings are consistent with al-Sulamī's writings elsewhere – and for this reason I here discuss the treatise as representative of his approach to *ādāb* – differences in terminology, phrasing, Qur'ānic passages and traditions cited are striking. *Dhikr ādāb al-ṣūfiyya*, while adequately conveying the thought of al-Sulamī, has undergone heavy revision. Thibon, *L'œuvre*, 322.

150 Al-Sulamī, *AMM*, §3. Al-Sulamī's discussion elsewhere of these *rukhaṣ* is often vague, not identifying exactly which dispensations are under dispute. Here, it suffices to note that he couples his acknowledgement of certain *rukhaṣ* for the Ṣūfīs with the assumption that their particular path entails its own meritorious and weighty obligations and that the pseudo-Ṣūfī embraces the legal licenses without embracing the special obligations of this path. Marion Holmes Katz, '*'Azima* and *rukhṣa*', *EI*[3].

151 Al-Sulamī, *DAṢ*, 542.

152 Al-Sulamī, *DAṢ*, 542. This understanding of *rasm* is consistent with al-Sarrāj's definition of the term in *Kitāb al-luma'* and al-Sulamī's abridgement of that definition in *Tafsīr alfāẓ al-ṣūfiyya*. Both glossaries unite word and action as a component of an individual's *rasm*, connoting the type of total comportment al-Sulamī demands of a person prior to considering the question of legal concessions. Al-Sarrāj, *Kitāb al-luma'*, K. al-bayān 'an al-mushkilāt, B. bayān hādhihi l-alfāẓ; al-Sulamī, *AṢ*, §122.

153 *Samā'* is mentioned only briefly in *Dhikr ādāb al-ṣūfiyya* but treated at greater length in *Kitāb al-samā'* and some of al-Sulamī's other treatises. *Kitāb al-samā'* discusses the particulars of one's comportment with the shaykh during these sessions but only after driving home the fundamental principle that the *adab* of these sessions demands detachment from the ego-self. Al-Sulamī sees an eager attraction to *samā'* as a sign of a person's frivolity and spiritual immaturity. Likewise, the intense emotions and physical agitation that can occur during these sessions are acceptable for a believer truly on the path but can also spring from attachment to the *nafs* and may be a sign of this. Honerkamp, 'Abû 'Abd Al-Rahmân Al-Sulamî (d. 412/1201) on Samâ', Ecstasy and Dance', 1–14.

154 Jean-Jacques Thibon, 'La relation maître-disciple ou les éléments de l'alchimie spirituelle d'après trois manuscrits de Sulamī', in *Mystique musulmane: Parcours en compagnie d'un chercheur: Roger Deladrière: Actes du colloque du 9 Mars 2001, Universitè Jean-Moulin à Lyon*, ed. Geneviève Gobillot (Paris: Cariscript, 2002), 119.

Thibon comments here on *Kitāb maḥāsin al-taṣawwuf*, but his assessment applies to al-Sulamī's treatment of *rukhaṣ* in *Dhikr ādāb al-ṣūfiyya* as well.

155 Locating *adab/ʿamal* at the intermediate stage of the journey creates some tension with the schema of progress from *ādāb* to *akhlāq* to *aḥwāl* mentioned earlier. The primary reason al-Sulamī here considers *adab/ʿamal* intermediate is that it signifies a substantial degree of integration between the external requirements of the religious law and the inner realities signified. That is, this intermediate *adab* denotes conduct that apprehends the fuller meaning of Ṣūfī practice, what Damghani calls the 'practical Ṣūfism' (Persian *taṣawwuf-i ʿamali*) of many early Persian masters. Ahmad Mahdavi Damghani, 'Persian Contributions to Sufi Literature in Arabic', in Lewisohn, *Classical Persian Sufism*, 36.

156 Al-Sulamī, *DAṢ*, 551.

157 For my English translation of this treatise, see the forthcoming *Treatises on the Sufi Path*; for additional general introduction, see Böwering, 'Two Early Ṣūfī Manuscripts', 227; Chowdhury, *A Ṣūfī Apologist*, 116.

158 Al-Sulamī, *MFA*, §43.

159 From the time of Ibn Hishām (d. 213/828 or 218/833), the term *sīra* (pl. *siyar*) often indicated a literary genre, the biography of the Prophet. Al-Sulamī clearly does not use *siyar* in this sense; the genre of *Māʾiyyat al-faqr wa-ādābihi* differs in no significant respect from *Adab mujālasat al-mashāyikh wa-ḥifẓ ḥurumātihim*, *Jawāmiʿ ādāb al-ṣūfiyya* or *Kitāb ādāb al-ṣuḥba*.

160 Al-Sulamī, *MFA*, §56.

161 See, among other places, al-Sulamī, *QTM*, §6–11; *DM*, §10.

162 Al-Sulamī, *MFA*, §52.

163 Al-Sulamī, *MFA*, §58; cf. *AMM*, §16; *ṬṢ*, 122 (#33); *KAṢ*, 86.

164 Sezgin attributes *Ādāb al-faqr wa-sharāʾiṭuhu* to al-Sulamī but erroneously locates it in MS Fātiḥ 2650; it survives in MS Fātiḥ 2553 (fols. 60v–62v) and MS Göttingen 8° Cod. Arab. 312 (fols. 74v–79r). Nadia Zeidan edited it, and several modern scholars, including Keeler, mention it in their discussions of *ādāb*. Al-Sulamī, *SA*, §22–4; Nadia Zeidan, 'Six opuscules mystiques inédits' (PhD, EPHESS, 1974), 5–9; *GAS*, 1:673; *GAL*, 1:201; Keeler, 'The Concept of *adab* in Early Sufism', 70; Thibon, *L'œuvre*, 506–9, 570; Chowdhury, *A Ṣūfī Apologist*, 122.

165 Sviri, 'Ḥakīm Tirmidhī and the Malāmatī Movement', 601; for discussion, see Chowdhury, *A Ṣūfī Apologist*, 69.

166 Al-Sulamī, *SA*, §23.

167 The *faqīr* labours in constant striving, both externally and internally (*yaʿmal fī dawām al-mujāhada ẓāhiran wa-bāṭinan*). Al-Sulamī, *SA*, §23.

168 Al-Sulamī, *SA*, §24.

169 Al-Sulamī, *SA*, §25.

170 Al-Sulamī and al-Ḥakīm al-Tirmidhī, *Three Early Sufi Texts*, 87.

171 For my English translation of this treatise, see the forthcoming *Treatises on the Sufi Path*.

172 Thibon, *L'œuvre*, 282.

173 Thibon, '*Adab* et éducation spirituelle', 112.

174 Al-Sulamī's predilection for Abū Bakr as an example to be emulated, particularly regarding a believer's attitude, extends to several other areas of Ṣūfī practice; for an example, see the discussion of the effects of *samāʿ* in al-Sulamī, *KS*, §5.

175 Q. 31:15; al-Sulamī, *AMM*, §1.

176 Al-Sulamī, *AMM*, §9; see also *GṢ*, §3–4. Thibon rightly notes in context that for believers generally, such unquestioning adherence to a shaykh's teaching and example is not necessary for *ḥusn al-adab* but that this is necessary for formal *ṣuḥba*. Thibon, *L'œuvre*, 275fn62.

177 Al-Sulamī, *AMM*, §2.

178 Al-Sulamī, *AMM*, §3–4. His praise for the *'ulamā'* here does not contradict his criticism elsewhere for the pride that often infects scholars and eclipses the humility (*tawāḍu'*) with which God desires them to expound their knowledge. Al-Sulamī contrasts this pride and boasting with the attitude of the biblical prophets named in the Qur'ān, from Adam down to Jesus; then continues to give the example of Muḥammad, the great Ṣūfī masters, and finally the companions of the Prophet. See al-Sulamī, *DTU*, esp. §170.

179 Al-Sulamī, *AMM*, §9, 11.

180 *ḥusn adab al-ẓāhir 'unwān ḥusn adab al-bāṭin*. Al-Sulamī, *AMM*, §16; see also *ṬṢ*, 122 (#33); *KAṢ*, 86; *MFA*, §58.

181 Al-Hujwīrī distinguishes between good comportment in general and the etiquette proper to a *mujālasa* with one's master; al-Sulamī relies upon this distinction. Thibon, *L'œuvre*, 278.

182 Al-Sulamī, *AMM*, §11.

183 Al-Sulamī, *AMM*, §16; *JAṢ*, §7; *KAṢ*, 86; see also al-Tha'labī, *al-Kashf wa-l-bayān*, 6:250.

184 Al-Sulamī, *AMM*, §20. Thibon refers to al-Sulamī's understanding of the connection between the Ṣūfī shaykhs and the Prophet as a 'spiritual caliphate'. Thibon, *L'œuvre*, 274.

185 Lloyd V. J. Ridgeon, 'Reading Sufi History through *ādāb:* The Perspectives of Sufis, Jawānmardān and Qalandars', in Chiabotti et al., *Ethics and Spirituality in Islam*, 379–402.

186 Keeler makes this point even though *Jawāmi'* departs from earlier models like those of al-Muḥāsibī or al-Ḥakīm al-Tirmidhī in structure and organization. Keeler, 'The Concept of *adab* in Early Sufism', 70.

187 Al-Sulamī, *JAṢ*, §2.

188 Al-Sulamī, *Jawāmi' Ādāb al-Ṣūfiyya* and *'Uyūb al-Nafs wa-Mudāwātuhā*, 13.

189 Al-Sulamī, *JAṢ*, §170. I have modified Biagi's translation of this passage.

190 Also note that on this point, al-Sulamī cites statements by al-Tustarī and al-Ḥakīm al-Tirmidhī. Al-Sulamī, *JAṢ*, §7, 24, 55.

191 One of the most important paragraphs in *Jawāmi'* on this theme echoes the main argument of *Adab mujālasat al-mashāyikh:* 'Among their customs is keeping reverence for the one who trained them and for the training they received from him' (*wa-min ādābihim ḥifẓ ḥurumāt man addabahum wa-ta'addubihim bi-hi*), Al-Sulamī, *JAṢ*, §55.

192 Al-Sulamī's citation of al-Ḥakīm al-Tirmidhī is exemplary here,

> Truly, *adab* is for [the Ṣūfī] to be careful in his actions, so that his masters may not reproach him; to take nothing from this world, so that the ascetics may not reproach him; to never prefer this world to the next world, so that the men of wisdom may not reproach him; and to behave with his Lord during his spiritual retreat in such a way that the recording angels may not reproach him.

Al-Sulamī does not record this saying in *Ṭabaqāt al-ṣūfiyya*, and I have not noticed it in al-Ḥakīm al-Tirmidhī's writings to this point. The concern for the reproach of the other does, of course, mark a shift from a personal discipline that categorically shuns any interest in the opinions of others. Al-Sulamī, *JAṢ*, §26.

193 Kohlberg's introduction to *Jawāmiʿ* claims that the *ādāb* described could be divided into three categories: the Ṣūfī's attitude towards God, the Ṣūfī's attitude towards himself and the Ṣūfī's attitude towards his fellow Ṣūfīs. Al-Sulamī, *Jawāmiʿ Ādāb al-Ṣūfiyya* and *ʿUyūb al-Nafs wa-Mudāwātuhā*, 13.

194 Ridgeon, 'Reading Sufi History through *ādāb*', 382. Al-Sulamī once uses *adab* in the dual. Unlike al-Sarrāj, who cites a distinction between the *adab* of speech and the *adab* of action, al-Sulamī cites Abū ʿUthmān al-Ḥīrī's distinction between internal and external *adab*. The former involves the purity of heart from defects, and the latter the avoidance of sins and vices. He contrasts *adab al-sirr* with *adab al-ẓāhir*, using *sirr* as a synonym for *bāṭin*. This paragraph is out of keeping with al-Sulamī's approach throughout the treatise. While individual teachings tend to deal with either behavioural norms or interior attitudes, if he mentions both aspects, he emphasizes the twofold reality of *adab*, not to suggest that two different *adab*s (inner and outer) exist, as he does here. Al-Sulamī, *JAṢ*, §30.

195 Al-Sulamī, *JAṢ*, §82. Abū Ḥafṣ exhorts Ṣūfīs to respect shaykhs, to maintain good fellowship with the brothers, to give counsel to the young, to abstain from quarrels and to avoid accumulating wealth, among other counsels. Al-Sulamī, *JAṢ*, §119; compare to *KAṢ*, 24, among other places.

196 Al-Sulamī, *JAṢ*, §69.

197 See the instruction on the *siwāk*, al-Sulamī, *JAṢ*, §160.

198 Al-Sulamī, *JAṢ*, §106ff.

199 Al-Sulamī, *JAṢ*, §124.

200 Al-Sulamī, *Jawāmiʿ Ādāb al-Ṣūfiyya* and *ʿUyūb al-Nafs wa-Mudāwātuhā*, 13.

201 Al-Sulamī, *JAṢ*, §67.

202 Al-Sulamī, *JAṢ*, §170; see also *JAṢ*, §7. I depart from Biagi's preference for 'knowledge' as a translation for *maʿrifa* in this passage; *pace* Franz Rosenthal, this permits a consistent distinction between *maʿrifa* and *ʿilm*, highlighting the spiritual and elite nature of the knowledge indicated by the former. Any connotation of unorthodoxy evoked by the early Christian heresy of gnosticism is obviously not intended. For discussion, see Reza Shah-Kazemi, 'The Notion and Significance of *Maʿrifa* in Sufism', *JIS* 13, no. 2 (2002): 155–81; Mohammed Rustom, 'Forms of Gnosis in Sulamī's Sufi Exegesis of the Fātiḥa', *ICMR* 16, no. 4 (2005): 327–44; Rosenthal, *Knowledge Triumphant*, 97–142, esp. 138–42.

203 Al-Sulamī, *SA*, §28.

204 Keeler finds the nature of this relationship in *Jawāmiʿ* vexing, stating that al-Sulamī 'equates *ādāb* if not exactly with the commands that are given in the Qurʾān, those which come to embody the *sharīʿa*, then with the ethical principles that underlie them'. Keeler, 'The Concept of *adab* in Early Sufism', 79fn80.

205 Regarding the earliest Ṣūfīs, Louis Massignon understands *ḥaqīqa* as the '"closed" or finite reality (as opposed to the "open" or infinite Real; as "deity" is to God), which, through static bad usage, finally came to mean the ultimate (ideal) divine reality of the universe'. Louis Massignon, *Essay on the Origins of the Technical Language of Islamic Mysticism* (Notre Dame, IN: University of Notre Dame Press, 1998), 28.

206 Annemarie Schimmel, *Deciphering the Signs of God: A Phenomenological Approach to Islam* (Albany: SUNY Press, 1994), 77.

207 Al-Sulamī, *AṢ*, §113; al-Sarrāj, *Kitāb al-lumaʿ*, K. al-bayān ʿan al-mushkilāt, B. bayān hādhihi l-alfāẓ. In al-Sulamī's understanding of a person's spiritual centres (*laṭāʾif*),

the *qalb* has the power of perception and awareness of divine things, a point to be explored in the following chapter.

208 Al-Sulamī uses both terms in the introduction to *Ḥaqā'iq al-tafsīr*; for other examples, see al-Sulamī, *KS*, §1; *MT*, §4.

209 *'ilm al-sharī'a 'ilm al-ādāb wa-'ilm al-ḥaqīqa 'ilm al-aḥwāl.* Al-Sulamī, *SḤ*, §3. Al-Sulamī here attempts to distinguish the merits and fruits of the Ṣūfī path from those of the divine law in a general sense. Many Ṣūfīs attempted such a distinction via the juxtaposition of *sharī'a* and *ḥaqīqa*; others developed a tripartite division between *sharī'a*, *ṭarīqa* and *ḥaqīqa*; others favoured a distinction between *sharī'a* and *ṭarīqa*. For an example and discussion of the second approach, see the treatise *Ādāb al-murīdīn* attributed to Najm al-Dīn al-Kubrā (d. 618/1221), eponym of the Kubrawiyya order. Meier, 'A Book of Etiquette for Sufis', 66; Schimmel, *Mystical Dimensions of Islam*, 98–9. For the third approach, see Seyyed Hossein Nasr, 'The Sufi Master as Exemplified in Persian Sufi Literature', in *Sufi Essays* (Albany: SUNY Press, 1972), 57.

210 Al-Sulamī, *SḤ*, §16. Across his œuvre, al-Sulamī transmits many teachings of earlier masters that add nuance to the nature of the knowledge acquired in *ḥaqīqa*. *Ḥaqīqa* denotes the gift of a more experiential knowledge, a synthesis of what has been known and what has been lived. *Ḥaqīqa* signifies the fullness of knowledge, including but transcending cognitive content to attain the most complete apprehension of the way things actually are. Al-Sulamī sometimes uses physical senses, especially taste (*dhawq*), to describe this apprehension, but he does not restrict such descriptions to the heights of knowledge; ordinary believers have their own proper *dhawq*. Al-Sulamī, *DṬḤ*, §288; *ḤT*, 1:36 (Q. 1:3); Ja'far al-Ṣādiq, *Spiritual Gems: The Mystical Qur'ān Commentary Ascribed to Ja'far al-Ṣādiq as Contained in Sulamī's* Ḥaqā'iq al-Tafsīr *from the Text of Paul Nwyia* (Louisville: Fons Vitae, 2011), 8–9.

211 Al-Sulamī, *SḤ*, §2.

212 Al-Sulamī, *SḤ*, §12.

213 Al-Sulamī, *SḤ*, §11.

214 Al-Sulamī, *AṢ*, §122; see also *DAṢ*, 542; al-Sarrāj, *Kitāb al-luma'*, K. al-bayān 'an al-mushkilāt, B. bayān hādhihi l-alfāẓ.

215 Al-Sulamī, *SḤ*, §6. Whoever fulfils the canonical prayers is a wayfarer (*sālik*) in the externals of the divine law but may only receive a third or a quarter of the merit of the prayer. The wayfarer receives the full value of his prayer. Cf. Abū Dā'ūd al-Sijistānī, *English Translation of Sunan Abu Dawud* (Riyadh: Darussalam, 2008), K. al-ṣalāt (2), B. mā jā'a fī nuqṣān al-ṣalāt (123), Ḥ. 796.

216 On the awareness of the *qalb*, see al-Sulamī, *QTM*, §8, §10, §20; *BTF*, §36; Kenneth S. Avery, *A Psychology of Early Sufi Samā': Listening and Altered States* (New York: RoutledgeCurzon, 2004), 80.

217 Al-Sulamī, *SḤ*, §18.

218 Al-Sulamī, *SḤ*, §8, §16.

219 Biagi's English translation habitually omits this refrain to facilitate smooth reading.

220 The subject of the *ādāb* distinguishes these two treatises: in *Jawāmi'*, al-Sulamī describes the practices of a visible, distinct social group, the Ṣūfīs, whereas in *Kitāb ādāb al-ṣuḥba*, al-Sulamī describes the practices of two interconnected types of relationship. The believers involved in the *ṣuḥba* and *'ishra* of *Kitāb ādāb al-ṣuḥba* are less easy to define, a problem that will be addressed in Chapter 3. Suffice it for now to

note that the agents of *ādāb* in these two treatises are not the same; I shall argue that the agents of *Kitāb ādāb al-ṣuḥba* are a much broader group.

221 Curiously, despite the abundance of definitions of *futuwwa* in *Kitāb al-futuwwa*, this one does not appear there. It also does not appear in al-Fuḍayl's section of *Ṭabaqāt al-ṣūfiyya*, although al-Sulamī includes a similar teaching attributed to Ruwaym b. Aḥmad (d. 303/915–16). Al-Sulamī, *ṬṢ*, 183 (#12); *KF*, 53.

222 Al-Sulamī, *KAṢ*, 29–30.

223 Al-Sulamī, *Jawāmiʿ Ādāb al-Ṣūfiyya* and *'Uyūb al-Nafs wa-Mudāwātuhā*, 13.

224 Al-Sulamī, *KAṢ*, 52.

225 Al-Sulamī, *KAṢ*, 22.

226 Aḥmad al-Khaṭīb al-Baghdādī transmitted on al-Sulamī's authority despite acknowledging the accusation of Muḥammad b. Yūsuf al-Qaṭṭān (d. 405/1015) that al-Sulamī forged *ḥadīth*. Over the centuries, later scholars recycle this charge.

227 Chowdhury has analysed with care the chains of transmission in *Kitāb ādāb al-ṣuḥba* and concludes that 'although al-Sulamī does report fabricated traditions, *he did not himself fabricate them.*' Chowdhury further argues that when one compares the number of acceptable traditions to the number of unacceptable traditions collected in the treatise, al-Sulamī's standards meet those of other scholars of *ḥadīth*, *akhlāq* and *fiqh* in the period. Chowdhury, *A Ṣūfī Apologist*, 96; emphasis in original. Kister likewise absolves al-Sulamī of the charge of forging *ḥadīth*, though acknowledging that al-Sulamī transmitted on the authority of many unreliable narrators. While al-Sulamī's traditions may not have been sound by all standards, he did not invent them; all the traditions in *Kitāb ādāb al-ṣuḥba* were in circulation prior to his time. Al-Sulamī, *Kitāb ādāb as-ṣuḥba*, 4.

228 In his introduction to *Ṭabaqāt al-ṣūfiyya*, Pedersen argues that even though al-Sulamī never defines the precise differences between these terms for the mode by which a tradition was transmitted, his usage shows that he respects the care other traditionists have taken in their transmission and attempts to retain their terminology. The discovery of MS 2118 undercuts Pedersen's argument. That manuscript, which certainly would be the base manuscript for any future edition of *Kitāb ādāb al-ṣuḥba*, contains many variants in the chains of transmission – variants regarding the mode of transmission, not the identities of the transmitters. Most of the discrepancies between MS 2118 and Kister's edition lie in the chains of transmission; the rest of Kister's edition would remain nearly unchanged. Al-Sulamī, *Kitāb ṭabaqāt al-ṣūfiyya*, 61–2.

229 Laury Silvers uses the phrase '*ahl al-ḥadīth* culture' to describe the Baghdad of Abū Bakr al-Wāsiṭī (d. 320/932), but it applies equally well to al-Sulamī's Nishapur and to al-Sulamī himself. Laury Silvers, *A Soaring Minaret: Abu Bakr Al-Wasiti and the Rise of Baghdadi Sufism* (Albany: SUNY, 2010), 2.

230 Al-Sulamī, *KAṢ*, 24, citing a widespread *ḥadīth*, 'Truly, souls encounter each other in the air and they draw near to each other, and those who recognise each other become friendly and those who do not recognise each other differ.'

231 See the series of Prophetic traditions on this theme in al-Sulamī, *KAṢ*, 24.

232 Al-Sulamī, *KAṢ*, 23.

233 Thibon, *L'œuvre*, 262.

234 For example, *Kitāb ādāb al-ṣuḥba* contains this teaching, which unmistakably parallels a shorter version in *Jawāmiʿ*: 'Among its ways (*ādāb*) is to strive to hide the defects of one's brothers, to make manifest their strengths, to conceal their shameful deeds, and to walk hand-in-hand with them at all times.' In *Kitāb ādāb al-ṣuḥba*,

al-Sulamī supports this with a *ḥadīth* on the authority of Anas, including a full *isnād*, followed by two passages of poetry attributed to Aḥmad b. Yaḥyā Tha'lab (d. 291/904) and one by Abū Firās al-Ḥamdānī (d. 357/968). By contrast, *Jawāmi'* omits the Prophetic *ḥadīth*, citing two anecdotes about Ibrāhīm b. Adham (d. 161/777–8) and Ruwaym. Al-Sulamī, *KAṢ*, 61–2; *JAṢ*, §142.

235 Al-Sulamī, *RM*, 112.

236 'Among their ways is to minimize speech and to obligate action.' Al-Sulamī, *JAṢ*, §102.

237 Among these, one can note his raw contempt for the ego-self, and his passing references to stations and states, especially the habit of keeping them secret. Al-Sulamī, *JAṢ*, §77, 110, 113, 150, and in several other places.

238 Al-Sulamī, *AMM*, §14.

239 Al-Sulamī, *AMM*, §10.

240 Al-Sulamī, *AMM*, §11.

241 The categorical prohibition on minors speaking in the presence of elders stands as an exception to this. Al-Sulamī, *KAṢ*, 76.

242 Al-Sulamī, *KAṢ*, 42.

243 Al-Sulamī, *KAṢ*, 58.

244 Al-Sulamī, *KAṢ*, 34.

245 Al-Sulamī, *KAṢ*, 84.

246 Al-Sulamī, *KAṢ*, 37, 57; see also 70.

247 Al-Sulamī, *KAṢ*, 63.

248 MacIntyre, *After Virtue*, 193–4.

249 MacIntyre, *After Virtue*, 190.

250 MacIntyre, *After Virtue*, 157; D'Andrea, *Tradition, Rationality, and Virtue*, 258.

2 Virtue and character in al-Sulamī's thought

1 For an overview of the Persian contribution to Islamic philosophy in the fourth/tenth and fifth/eleventh centuries, see Seyyed Hossein Nasr, 'Philosophy and Cosmology', in *The Cambridge History of Iran*, ed. Richard N. Frye (Cambridge: Cambridge University Press, 1968), 4:419–41.

2 Traditions drawing on the notion of *makārim al-akhlāq* circulated even more widely in the fifth/eleventh century and following, but the collections of traditionists like al-Ṭabarānī (d. 360/971) and Tammām al-Rāzī (d. 414/1023) demonstrate that such traditions circulated during the time of al-Sulamī. Richard Walzer and Hamilton A. R. Gibb, 'Ak̲h̲lāḳ', *EI*², citing Bishr Farès, *Makārim al-aḫlāq: une formule prestigieuse de morale musulmane traditionnelle* (Rome: Rendiconti della Reale accademia dei Lincei, 1935), 417.

3 Paul L. Heck, 'The Crisis of Knowledge in Islam (I): The Case of Al-'Āmirī', *Philosophy East and West* 56, no. 1 (2006): 115.

4 Scholars remain uncertain precisely when *Nicomachean Ethics* was translated into Arabic, but this probably occurred in the third/ninth century and certainly no later than the fourth/tenth. Syriac versions existed before that point and scholars like Yaḥyā b. 'Adī and Miskawayh would have had access to them. For discussion, see the introduction to Aristotle, *The Arabic Version of the Nicomachean Ethics*, ed. Anna Akasoy et al. (Leiden: Brill, 2005).

5 Yaḥyā b. ʻAdī, *The Reformation of Morals: A Parallel Arabic-English Text*, ed. and trans. Sidney Harrison Griffith (Provo: Brigham Young University Press, 2002), xxxi–xxxii. Marie-Thérèse Urvoy's introduction to her translation of *Tahdhīb al-akhlāq* emphasized the influences from pre-Islamic Arabic culture and Persian philosophy that also shape Yaḥyā's text. The line between Greek and Persian currents of influence is not always easy to draw; any discussion of pre-Islamic or Persian influence upon *Tahdhīb al-akhlāq* aids an understanding of the text so long as it does not cause a reader to underestimate the overwhelming dominance of Greek thought – particularly Galen – in this work. Yaḥyā b. ʻAdī, *Traité d'éthique d'Abû Zakariyyâ' Yahyâ Ibn ʻAdî*, trans. Marie-Thérèse Urvoy (Paris: Cariscript, 1991), 13–26, esp. 13–14, 21–2; Ida Zilio-Grandi, 'Il 'kitāb tahḏīb al-aḫlāq' di Yaḥyā Ibn ʻAdi († 974/363): riflessioni sul tema dell'etica nel periodo abbaside', in *La letteratura arabo-cristiana e le scienze nel periodo abbaside (750–1250 d.C.)*, ed. Davide Righi (Turin: Silvio Zamorani Editore, 2008), 273–83.

6 Some medieval sources about this polymath identify him as Ibn Miskawayh, others simply as Miskawayh.

7 For discussion, see Richard Walzer, 'Some Aspects of Miskawaih's *Tahdhīb al-Akhlāq*', in *Greek into Arabic: Essays on Islamic Philosophy* (Cambridge: Harvard University Press, 1962), 220–35; Peter Adamson, 'Ethics in Philosophy', *EI*[3].

8 Aristotle, *The Arabic Version of the Nicomachean Ethics*, 146–7 (1102a).

9 Aristotle, *The Arabic Version of the Nicomachean Ethics*, 166–7 (1105b). These 'states' translate the Greek *hexis*, rendered in medieval Latin as *habitus* and occasionally in English translations of Aristotle as 'habit'.

10 Adamson, 'Ethics in Philosophy'.

11 Majid Fakhry, *Ethical Theories in Islam* (Leiden: Brill, 1991), 101.

12 Aristotle, *The Arabic Version of the Nicomachean Ethics*, 210–13 (1114b–15a).

13 Nuha A. Alshaar, *Ethics in Islam: Friendship in the Political Thought of al-Tawḥīdī and his Contemporaries* (New York: Routledge, 2015), 198.

14 Fakhry posits such a division, whereas Hourani distinguishes first between normative and analytical approaches to ethics, each of which could be approached in either a religious or a secular key, thus yielding four possible types of ethical writing. Fakhry, *Ethical Theories in Islam*, 151; Hourani, *Reason and Tradition in Islamic Ethics*, 15.

15 Heck, 'Ethics in Ṣūfism'.

16 Adapted from Christian B. Miller, *Character and Moral Psychology* (New York: Oxford University Press, 2014), 33.

17 Miller's precise formulation is this: 'The virtues are all and only those good traits of character which are such that, other things being equal, when they lead directly to action (whether mental or bodily), the action is (typically) a good action and is performed for the appropriate reasons.' *Character and Moral Psychology*, 34.

18 MacIntyre, *After Virtue*, 146.

19 For a fuller definition, see MacIntyre, *After Virtue*, 12.

20 Ovamir Anjum, 'Islam as a Discursive Tradition: Talal Asad and His Interlocutors', *Comparative Studies of South Asia, Africa and the Middle East* 27, no. 3 (2007): 656–72; Silverstein, *Islam and Modernity in Turkey*, 140; Silverstein, 'Sufism and Modernity in Turkey: From the Authenticity of Experience to the Practice of Discipline', in *Sufism and the 'Modern' in Islam*, ed. Martin Van Bruinessen and Julia Day Howell (New York: I.B. Tauris, 2007), 40; Marion Holmes Katz, 'Shame (Ḥayā') as an Affective

Disposition in Islamic Legal Thought', *Journal of Law, Religion and State* 3 (2014): 140; Zaman, *The Ulama in Contemporary Islam*, 5–7.

21 Nathan C. Hofer, 'The Origins and Development of the Office of the "Chief Sufi" in Egypt, 1173–1325', *JSS* 3, no. 1 (2014): 8.

22 Bernd Radtke, 'Anti-Ṣūfī Polemics', *EI*[3].

23 Such interpersonal conflicts are a focal point of Salamah-Qudsi's study; for her comments on some tensions among Baghdad Ṣūfis, particularly regarding Ruwaym, see *Sufism and Early Islamic Piety*, 191–8.

24 Particularly helpful summaries are Knysh, *Islamic Mysticism: A Short History*, 83–149; Karamustafa, *Sufism: The Formative Period*, 60–71.

25 Al-Sulamī, *SA*, §30–5.

26 MacIntyre, *After Virtue*, 219.

27 MacIntyre, *After Virtue*, 273–4.

28 Alshaar, *Ethics in Islam*, 198. For discussion of al-ʿĀmirī's peculiar approach to this matter, see Elvira Wakelnig, 'Philosophical Fragments of Al-ʿĀmirī Preserved Mainly in al-Tawḥīdī, Miskawayh, and in the Texts of the *Ṣiwān al-ḥikma* Tradition', in *In the Age of al-Fārābī: Arabic Philosophy in the Fourth/Tenth Century*, ed. Peter Adamson (London: Warburg Institute, 2008), 236.

29 Miskawayh identifies wisdom (*ḥikma*), temperance (*ʿiffa*), courage (*shajāʿa*) and justice (*ʿadāla*) as cardinal virtues; justice is the virtue uniting the first three when the three faculties of the soul act properly. Aḥmad b. Muḥammad Miskawayh, *Tahdhīb al-akhlāq*, ed. Constantine K. Zurayk (Beirut: American University of Beirut, 1966), 18; English trans. by Constantine K. Zurayk as *The Refinement of Character* (Beirut: American University of Beirut, 1968), 17. Subsequent citations of Miskawayh refer to Zurayk's critical edition of the Arabic text, as those page numbers are preserved in the marginal apparatus of Zurayk's English translation.

30 Among modern philosophers, MacIntyre's project in *Dependent Rational Animals* provides a case in point, attempting to move beyond the problems of Aristotelian biology and yet preserve a fundamentally Aristotelian approach to the virtue. Owen Flanagan's work on Mencius and Confucius provides another example; Flanagan speaks about the four cardinal virtues of Confucian thought despite the absence of faculties of the soul to regulate them, and about virtue in general as a stable disposition to believe, desire and act in certain ways. MacIntyre, *Dependent Rational Animals: Why Human Beings Need the Virtues* (London: Duckworth, 2009), x; Owen Flanagan, *Moral Sprouts and Natural Teleologies: 21st Century Moral Psychology Meets Classical Chinese Philosophy* (Milwaukee: Marquette University Press, 2014).

31 Louis Massignon, *The Passion of Al-Hallāj: Mystic and Martyr of Islam* (Princeton, NJ: Princeton University Press, 1980), 1:341ff.

32 Al-Sulamī, *DAṢ*, 554.

33 Berger, '*Geschieden von allem ausser Gott*', 80.

34 Al-Sulamī, *DṢT*, §4.

35 Al-Sulamī, *AṢ*, §114.

36 Al-Sulamī, *LM*, §81 (Colby #8); *LM*, §85 (Colby #16).

37 Al-Sulamī, *MA*, §1. This is the first line of the treatise in the two published versions, but Thibon's more recent translation includes manuscript evidence that was not available to Kohlberg or Ateş and situates the line in the third paragraph. In anticipation of Thibon's publication of a new edition of this treatise, it suffices to say

here that the additional material does not resolve the ambiguity regarding al-Sulamī's use of the term *maqām*.

38 Al-Sulamī, *MA*, §6.

39 Al-Sulamī, *MA*, §16.

40 Thibon, *L'œuvre*, 211–12, 436–40.

41 Atif Khalil, *Repentance and the Return to God:* Tawba *in Early Sufism* (Albany: SUNY Press, 2018).

42 Khalil, *Repentance and the Return to God*, 78–9.

43 'Amr b. 'Uthmān al-Makkī (d. 291/903–4), not to be confused with the author of *Qūt al-qulūb*, developed one of the first *laṭā'if* theories, though substantially different from al-Sulamī's. Shigeru Kamada, 'A Study of the Term *Sirr* (Secret) in Sufi *Laṭā'if* Theories', *Orient* (*Tokyo*) 19 (1983): 9.

44 Al-Sulamī does not rely upon the term *laṭīfa* (pl. *laṭā'if*) to refer to what Roger Deladrière calls these *niveaux de conscience* to the extent that some of his successors in Sufism would, but because al-Sulamī's ideas about these spiritual centres so closely parallel those of his confreres in Sufism, I shall apply the term to his thought. He does define the term at one point, saying that *laṭīfa* indicates a light emerging within one's understanding or a sparkling within one's mind, but this reproduces verbatim the definition of al-Sarrāj, who then says that the term is too elusive to define. Al-Sulamī, *AṢ*, §130; Al-Sulamī, *Lucidité implacable: Épître des hommes du blâme*, trans. Roger Deladrière (Paris: Arléa, 1991), 16; al-Sarrāj, *Kitāb al-luma'*, K. al-bayān 'an al-mushkilāt, B. bayān hādhihi l-alfāẓ.

45 Al-Sulamī, *RM*, 100; *MA*, §5.

46 Kamada's study treats only *Risālat al-malāmatiyya*, but al-Sulamī also discusses these four levels of *dhikr* in (*Mas'alat*) *ṣifāt al-dhākirīn wa-l-mutafakkirīn*. At one point in *Risālat al-malāmatiyya*, al-Sulamī does equate *dhikr al-lisān* with *dhikr al-nafs*. In *Ṣifāt al-dhākirīn wa-l-mutafakkirīn*, he never uses the term *dhikr al-nafs*. Al-Sulamī, *RM*, 104; *ṢDM*, §206; Kamada, 'A Study of the Term *Sirr*', 10.

47 Al-Sulamī, *QTM*, §8.

48 Al-Sulamī, *MFA*, §47.

49 Al-Ḥakīm al-Tirmidhī, *Bayān al-farq*, 17.

50 Berger, '*Geschieden von allem ausser Gott*', 51–8; al-Sulamī and Ḥakīm al-Tirmidhī, *Three Early Sufi Texts*, 96–7; Kamada, 'A Study of the Term *Sirr*', 9–11; al-Sulamī, *Lucidité implacable*, 16–17; Richard Hartmann, 'As-Sulamī's Risālat al-Malāmatīja', *Der Islam* 8 (1918): 164–5.

51 Cf. al-Sulamī, *MFA*, §54.

52 Al-Sulamī, *DṢT*, §13.

53 Al-Sulamī, *ḤW*, §72; *QTM*, §5.

54 Berger's decision to describe these spiritual centres using the German *Organen* or *Kräften* translates the idea more accurately than Bahram Jassemi's *Stufen*. The *laṭā'if* are not merely rungs on a ladder or steps on a staircase that one can surpass and leave behind; they are independent loci of perception. Berger, '*Geschieden von allem ausser Gott*', 51–8; Bahram Jassemi, *Kosmologie und Psychologie im Sufismus* (Neukirchen: Verlag Make a Book, 2007), 327–70.

55 Al-Qushayrī, *Risāla*, B. al-nafs (trans. Knysh, 109, with modifications).

56 Al-Sulamī, *UNM*, §3. In Kohlberg's edition of this treatise, he emphasizes that al-Sulamī speaks of three parts of the one soul, not of three separate *anfus*, but whether al-Sulamī saw this point as important is not clear. Al-Sulamī, *Jawāmi' Ādāb Al-Ṣūfiyya and 'Uyūb Al-Nafs Wa-Mudāwātuhā*, 14.

57 Q. 12:53.
58 Q. 75:1–2.
59 Q. 89:28. This verse does not use the phrase *nafs muṭma'inna* but speaks of the soul returning to its Lord, well pleased and well pleasing.
60 Thinkers drawing on the platonic tripartite conception of the soul were not themselves in agreement about how to articulate the soul's 'threeness'. Galen, whose *Peri Ēthōn* survives only in its Arabic abridgement, confesses his ambivalence about whether one should call these three 'things' (*ashyā'*) separate souls, parts of one soul or three faculties of the same essence. Yaḥyā b. 'Adī affirms that the soul has three faculties (*quwā*) but that each of these is still called a 'soul' (*nafs*). Miskawayh posits three *aqsām* in the soul, labelling each one a 'faculty' (*quwwa*), but says that sometimes these faculties are considered three souls and other times three faculties of one soul. Such reflections run in parallel to al-Ḥakīm al-Tirmidhī's discourse about the heart. At the outset of his treatise on the subject, he writes that *qalb* is a comprehensive term that includes all the interior stations of the human person (*ism al-qalb ism jāmi', yaqtaḍī maqāmāt al-bāṭin kullahā*) but that *qalb* also designates a specific station within the person. Galen, 'Kitāb al-Akhlāq li-Jālīnus', *Bulletin of the Faculty of Arts of the Egyptian University* (*Majallat Kulliyyat al-Ādāb bi-l-Jāmi'a al-Miṣriyya*) 5, no. 1 (1937): 36 (#193); Yaḥyā b. 'Adī, *The Reformation of Morals*, 14–15; Miskawayh, *Tahdhīb al-akhlāq*, 15; cf. J. N. Mattock, 'A Translation of the Arabic Epitome of Galen's Book ΠΕΡΙ ΗΘΩΝ', in *Islamic Philosophy and the Classical Tradition*, ed. S. M. Stern, Albert Hourani, and Vivian Brown (Oxford: Cassirer, 1972), 237; Galen, *Galen: Psychological Writings* (Cambridge: Cambridge University Press, 2013), 138; al-Ḥakīm al-Tirmidhī, *Bayān al-farq*, 17.
61 *Risālat al-malāmatiyya* does not invoke the *nafs lawwāma* as a significant part of its argument, despite the shared root *l-w-m*; rather, the *nafs ammāra* takes a more prominent place in the treatise. The Malāmatiyya were far from the only Muslims to focus on the *nafs ammāra*. Al-Muḥāsibī does so as well, even though his writings leave less of a visible mark on al-Sulamī's corpus. For discussion, see Picken, *Spiritual Purification in Islam*, 168–205.
62 Thibon, *L'œuvre*, 481.
63 Berger, '*Geschieden von allem ausser Gott*', 54.
64 Al-Sulamī, *JAṢ*, §170.
65 Al-Sulamī, *BTF*, §13, 31.
66 Al-Sulamī, *UNM*, §7, 13.
67 Al-Sulamī, *ṬṢ*, 455 (#8); *BAṢ*, 368; cf. Chowdhury, *A Ṣūfī Apologist*, 58.
68 Al-Sulamī, *BTF*, §7–8.
69 Al-Sulamī's contemporary al-Daqqāq shared this concern regarding *samā'*: common folk should not attend such audition sessions because they remain under the sway of their ego-self. Al-Qushayrī, *Risāla*, B. al-samā'; for discussion, see Avery, *A Psychology of Early Sufi Samā'*, 178.
70 Al-Sulamī, *UNM*, §18; *ṢDM*, §208. Al-Sulamī's discussion of the differences between *dhikr* and *tafakkur* suggests the same concern about self-referentiality. The Qur'ān encourages *tafakkur* (reflection), and thus al-Sulamī also praises it, but he lauds *dhikr* above *tafakkur* because *dhikr* involves only knowledge of the one remembered. Reflection contains a peril: one can become stuck thinking about oneself, one's past, one's future and never pass beyond these concerns.
71 Al-Sulamī, *MA*, §1.
72 Samuela Pagani, 'Heart, in Ṣūfism', *EI*[3].

73 Hussein Ali Akash, *Die sufische Koranauslegung: Semantik und Deutungsmechanismen der išārī-Exegese* (Berlin: Klaus Schwarz Verlag, 2006), 211.
74 Al-Ḥakīm al-Tirmidhī, *Bayān al-farq*, 17.
75 Q. 17:25.
76 Al-Sulamī, *ZḤT*, 82; al-Tustarī, *Tafsīr*, Q. 17:25. Al-Sulamī transmits a slightly different version of al-Tustarī's words, though the import is the same.
77 Al-Sulamī, *MA*, §1.
78 Al-Sulamī, *UNM*, §18.
79 Al-Sulamī, *QTM*, §8, 10, 20.
80 Al-Sulamī, *ḤT*, 2:269–71 (Q. 50:35–7).
81 Lutz Berger sees the *qalb* as the *Aufnahmeorgan*, the organ able to receive the divine light. By contrast, the *nafs* is the *Aufnahmeorgan* for the world and all that causes separation from God. Berger, '*Geschieden von allem ausser Gott*', 55–6.
82 Al-Sulamī and al-Ḥakīm al-Tirmidhī, *Three Early Sufi Texts*, 97; on the heart as a middle point, see also Akash, *Die sufische Koranauslegung*, 216.
83 Al-Sulamī, *MTḤ*, 29, 50–1.
84 Al-Sulamī, *MA*, §5; *ṢDM*, §211. It should be mentioned that *Mas'alat ṣifāt al-dhākirīn wa-l-mutafakkirīn*, the treatise which discusses *tafakkur* at the greatest length, does not frequently associate the practice with the heart; al-Sulamī relies less on these four spiritual centres in that treatise.
85 In this, al-Sulamī's understanding comports with his earlier predecessor al-Sarrāj, who saw the heart's knowledge extending beyond the intellectual to involve 'direct, intuitive and ecstatic apprehension'. Avery, *A Psychology of Early Sufi Samāʿ*, 80.
86 Al-Sulamī, *AT*, §36.
87 See the saying of Ruwaym, in al-Sulamī, *ṬṢ*, 182 (#9); *BTF*, §36.
88 Al-Sulamī, *MA*, §2.
89 Al-Sulamī, *UNM*, §19.
90 Al-Sulamī, *MA*, §3; *FT*, §46, 48; al-Bukhārī, *The Translation of the Meanings of Sahîh Al-Bukhâri* (Riyadh: Darussalam, 1997), K. al-īmān (2), B. faḍl man istabara'a li-dīnihi (39), Ḥ. 52; Muslim b. al-Ḥajjāj, *English Translation of Sahîh Muslim* (New York: Darussalam, 2007), K. al-musāqa (20), B. akhdh al-ḥalāl wa-tark al-shubuhāt (22), Ḥ. 1599; Ibn Māja al-Qazwīnī, *English Translation of Sunan Ibn Mâjah* (Riyadh: Darussalam, 2007), Abwāb al-fitan (36), B. al-wuqūf ʿind al-shubuhāt (14), Ḥ. 3984; Berger, '*Geschieden von allem ausser Gott*', 56. Each version of this tradition found in one of the major *ḥadīth* collections contains additional material which makes explicit that *muḍgha* refers to the heart; whether al-Sulamī knew these versions of the tradition or not, he clearly understood it this way and repeating the gloss would have caused needless redundancy.
91 Ibn Manẓūr, *Lisān al-ʿarab* (Cairo: Dār al-Maʿārif, 1900), 5:3713.
92 Al-Sulamī, *MF*, §127, 145. On the stillness of the heart (*sukūn al-qalb*), see *QTM*, §14; *MTḤ*, 30, among other places.
93 Al-Sulamī, *DM*, §25.
94 For examples, see al-Sulamī, *MF*, §100–10, and the *ḥadīth* about Sāriyya, *MF*, §116.
95 Al-Sulamī, *QTM*, §5, 38. Al-Sulamī's association of Q. 3:159, 'if you had been harsh and stern of heart, they would have scattered…' with the Prophet's good fellowship and nobility of companionship also evokes imagery of purity, from the opposite side. Al-Sulamī, *KAṢ*, 22.
96 Al-Sulamī, *MFA*, §47–9.
97 Al-Sulamī, *MFA*, §60.

98 Al-Sulamī, *MTḤ*, 28.
99 Al-Sulamī, *RM*, 95, 100, 104; *MFA*, §50; *ḤW*, §74; *MF*, §128; see especially *MF*, §133; Kamada, 'A Study of the Term *Sirr*', 10.
100 See, for example, al-Sulamī, *MF*, §133.
101 Al-Sulamī, *UNM*, §42.
102 With reference to the heart, not the secret, see al-Sulamī, *DM*, §25.
103 Al-Sulamī, *MF*, §115.
104 Al-Sulamī, *QTM*, §2; *MFA*, §47, 52, 58; *ḤW*, §67.
105 Al-Sulamī, *LM*, §93.
106 Al-Sulamī, *MFA*, §67.
107 Al-Sulamī, *MFA*, §61.
108 Berger, '*Geschieden von allem ausser Gott*', 58.
109 Al-Sulamī, *BTF*, §5, 45. This connection between the secret and spiritual poverty is another manifestation of the Malāmatī current in al-Sulamī's thought; see *RM*, 113.
110 Al-Sulamī, *RM*, 104; *ṢDM*, §206.
111 If one accepts the authenticity of the treatise *Kitāb nasīm al-arwāḥ*, one can sketch a more highly developed pneumatology for al-Sulamī. Thibon states that al-Sulamī is probably not the author; I am even more sceptical and consider the ascription of that text to al-Sulamī highly improbable. Fritz Meier also questioned the validity of this attribution. Because the frequent and slightly different usage of *qalb* and *rūḥ* in that treatise could colour a discussion of al-Sulamī's psychology, I have omitted the treatise from consideration here. Thibon, *L'œuvre*, 457–63; Fritz Meier, 'An Important Manuscript Find for Sufism', in *Essays on Islamic Piety and Mysticism*, 169.
112 Q. 15:29; al-Sulamī, *MF*, §128.
113 Al-Sulamī, *MTḤ*, 13.
114 Al-Sulamī, *MF*, §137.
115 In one example, al-Sulamī – in his own authorial voice – sets three types of gnosis (*ma'rifa*) into a hierarchy: the gnosis of the tongue, the gnosis of the heart and the gnosis of the spirit. Al-Sulamī, *MTḤ*, 22.
116 *Nafs* obviously functions this way in many places, but al-Sulamī also uses *qalb* in a way that ignores the subtler centres, saying that God looks not to appearances or deeds but into hearts and intentions of believers. The versions of this tradition in the canonical collections say that God looks into believers' hearts and at their deeds; al-Sulamī's version stands in concert with his emphasis elsewhere that intentions are better than deeds. The well-known tradition *innamā l-a'māl bi-l-niyya/niyyāt* does not fully reconcile this tension – al-Sulamī's concern does not lie with whether actions fulfil one's religious duties (the concern of the *ḥadīth*) but with spiritual progress. Al-Sulamī, *UNM*, §32; *KAṢ*, 30, 54; for the former tradition, see Muslim, *Ṣaḥīḥ*, K. al-birr wa-l-ṣila wa-l-ādāb (45), B. taḥrīm ẓulm al-muslim (10), Ḥ. 2564; cf. Ibn Māja, *Sunan*, K. al-zuhd (37), B. al-qanā'a (9), Ḥ. 4143; for one of the many instances of the latter tradition, see al-Bukhārī, *Ṣaḥīḥ*, K. bad' al-waḥy (1), B. kayfa bad' al-waḥy (1), Ḥ. 1.
117 Berger, '*Geschieden von allem ausser Gott*', 58. Thibon also shows great balance regarding the *laṭā'if*, invoking them frequently but not over-representing them in the overall context of al-Sulamī's spiritual pedagogy.
118 Al-Sulamī, *KMT*, §8.
119 Al-Sulamī, *JAṢ*, §4.

120 Al-Sulamī, *AṢ*, §113; al-Sarrāj, *Kitāb al-luma'*, K. al-bayān 'an al-mushkilāt, B. bayān hādhihi l-alfāẓ; Avery, *A Psychology of Early Sufi Samā'*, 69–70.
121 Yaḥyā draws this definition from Galen. Galen, 'Kitāb al-akhlāq li-Jālīnūs', 25 (#191), 28 (#197); Yaḥyā b. 'Adī, *The Reformation of Morals*, 9; Alshaar, *Ethics in Islam*, 198.
122 Miskawayh, *Tahdhīb al-akhlāq*, 3. For Miskawayh's account of human perfection, see *Tahdhīb al-akhlāq*, 38–46; see also Mohammed Nasir Omar, *Christian and Muslim Ethics: A Study of How to Attain Happiness as Reflected in the Works on Tahdhib al-Akhlaq by Yahya Ibn 'Adi (d. 974) and Miskawayh (d. 1030)* (Kuala Lumpur: Dewan Bahasa dan Pustaka, 2003), 161–4.
123 Al-Sulamī, *MA*, §2, 6; see also *MA*, §10.
124 Al-Sulamī, *MA*, §2; for similar usage see also *DAṢ*, 551, *KAṢ*, 47; *AMM*, §3.
125 Al-Sulamī, *KAṢ*, 22.
126 To be clear, the other elements of Galen's and Yaḥyā b. 'Adī's definition of a *khuluq* are specialized terms that al-Sulamī uses in very different ways. I do not suggest here a direct dependency of al-Sulamī on them but wish to explore a broader coherence. Galen, 'Kitāb al-akhlāq li-Jālīnūs', 25 (#191), 28 (#193).
127 Al-Sulamī, *BAṢ*, 368.
128 Al-Sulamī gives this death date; other chroniclers differ. See Thibon's comments in al-Sulamī, *Les générations des Soufis*, 66.
129 Al-Sulamī, *KAṢ*, 34.
130 Shurayba's edition truncates the list to four, omitting compassion. Al-Sulamī, *ṬṢ*, 51 (#9) (Shurayba), 44 (Pedersen).
131 Al-Sulamī, *KAṢ*, 47.
132 MacIntyre, *After Virtue*, 223.
133 Al-Tha'ālibī, *The Book of Noble Character*, 2; Orfali, *The Anthologist's Art*, 2.
134 While this typology for styles of Sufism became much more widespread after al-Hujwīrī penned *Kashf al-maḥjūb*, *sukr* and *ṣaḥw* were common terms in the Ṣūfī lexicon long before this. Al-Sulamī briefly defined them in his glossary of Ṣūfī terms. Al-Sulamī, *AṢ*, §117; Jawid A. Mojaddedi, 'Getting Drunk with Abū Yazīd or Staying Sober with Junayd: The Creation of a Popular Typology of Sufism', *BSOAS* 66, no. 1 (2003): 1–13. The willingness of some 'sober' Ṣūfīs to neglect or disavow al-Ḥallāj or al-Bisṭāmī for their ecstatic utterances does not call into question whether these very different figures belong to the same tradition. In MacIntyre's scheme, vibrant, even polemical, internal debate often facilitates the development of a tradition.
135 Thibon assumes that although the treatise in principle deals with all Muslims, it was destined first for aspirants (*murīd*s). This may be true insofar as practically speaking, aspirants might have been the most likely to study the treatise, but it does cause one to wonder why, among all his treatises, al-Sulamī chose such a highly inclusive style for a text destined for those who have already decided to embark on the Ṣūfī path. Thibon, *L'œuvre*, 263.
136 Al-Sulamī, *KAṢ*, 23.
137 Al-Sulamī, '*Manāhij al-'ārifīn*, a Treatise on Ṣūfism by Abū 'Abd al-Raḥmān al-Sulamī', ed. Etan Kohlberg, *JSAI* 1 (1979), 21.
138 Omar, *Christian and Muslim Ethics*, 163.
139 Al-Sulamī, *KF*, 88, 100.
140 The recent doctoral dissertation of Riccardo Paredi is a major step forward, as are forthcoming articles by Paul L. Heck. Riccardo Paredi, 'Early Islamic Emotions: Sadness (*ḥuzn*) from the Quran to Early Renunciant and Sufi Literature' (PhD, American University of Beirut, 2023).

141 Ibn Ḥazm, *Kitāb al-akhlāq wa-l-siyar, aw, Risāla fī mudāwāt al-nufūs wa-tahdhīb al-akhlāq wa-l-zuhd fī l-radhā'il* (Uppsala: [s.n.], 1980), 5; for discussion, see Fakhry, *Ethical Theories in Islam*, 169–71.
142 Gavin Picken's otherwise insightful account of *tazkiyyat al-nafs* in al-Muḥāsibī occasionally tracks in this direction. Picken, *Spiritual Purification in Islam*, 168–205.
143 Hourani, *Reason and Tradition in Islamic Ethics*, 171.
144 Kukkonen criticizes most of the available studies on al-Ghazālī for neglecting this point. Taneli Kukkonen, 'Al-Ghazālī on the Emotions', in *Islam and Rationality: The Impact of al-Ghazālī*, ed. George Tamer (Leiden: Brill, 2015), 137–8.
145 Rosalind Hursthouse, 'Virtue Ethics and the Emotions', in *Virtue Ethics: A Critical Reader*, ed. Daniel Statman (Edinburgh: Edinburgh University Press, 1997), 99–117.
146 Karen Bray and Stephen D. Moore, 'Introduction: Mappings and Crossings', in *Religion, Emotion, Sensation: Affect Theories and Theologies*, ed. Karen Bray and Stephen D. Moore (New York: Fordham University Press, 2020), 1.
147 Q. 22:9.
148 A. J. Wensinck, *Concordance et indices de la tradition musulmane* (Leiden: Brill, 1936–69), 4:261–2.
149 The absence of entries on subjects like 'emotion(s)', 'passion(s)', 'feeling(s)' and so on in major encyclopaedias in the field testifies to the point, as does the general inattentiveness in surveys of Islamic ethics by scholars like Fakhry and Hourani.
150 Kukkonen, 'Al-Ghazālī on the Emotions', 142.
151 Muslim, *Ṣaḥīḥ*, K. al-īmān (1), B. taḥrīm al-kibr (39), Ḥ. 91; Ibn Ḥanbal, *Musnad*, 28:437–40, Ḥ. 17206–7; 28:599, Ḥ. 17369.
152 Oliver Leaman, 'Poetry and the Emotions in Islamic Philosophy', in *Classic Issues in Islamic Philosophy Today*, ed. Anna-Teresa Tymieniecka and Nazif Muhtaroglu (New York: Springer, 2010), 139–50.
153 In decreasing order of importance, see al-Sulamī, *ḤW*; *FT*, §52; *DM*, §13; *KAṢ*, 48; *ṬṢ*, 162 (#27), 310 (#15), 468–9 (#7); *RRM*, §7.
154 *ra's makārim al-akhlāq al-ḥayā'*. Ibn Abī l-Dunyā, *Makārim al-akhlāq*, 6:86.
155 Katz, 'Shame (Ḥayā') as an Affective Disposition', 142.
156 Katz, 'Shame (Ḥayā') as an Affective Disposition', 142.
157 Al-Sulamī, *DM*, §13; cf. partial translation in Chowdhury, *A Ṣūfī Apologist*, 156.
158 He also calls it 'an oriented deportment with God that exhibits propriety'. Chowdhury, *A Ṣūfī Apologist*, 155.
159 Al-Sulamī, *ṬṢ*, 162 (#27), 310 (#15).
160 Chowdhury, *A Ṣūfī Apologist*, 156. Katz focuses on the anticipatory nature of shame, that *ḥayā'* causes discomfort when the believer imagines – in advance – transgressing the divine law. I do not see this anticipatory shame in al-Sulamī, who concentrates almost exclusively on past and present defects.
161 Silvers, *A Soaring Minaret*, 2.
162 Melchert, 'Khargūshī, *Tahdhīb al-asrār*', 442; al-Qushayrī, *Risāla*, B. al-ḥayā'; al-Qushayrī, *Kitāb al-Arba'īn fī taṣḥīḥ al-mu'āmala* (Amman: Dār al-Fatḥ, 2013), Ḥ. 3; cf. Abū Khalaf al-Ṭabarī, *Salwat al-'ārifīn wa-uns al-mushtāqīn [The Comfort of the Mystics]* (Leiden: Brill, 2013), §239; al-Ghazālī, *Iḥyā' 'ulūm al-dīn* (Beirut: Dār al-Qalam, 1990), K. al-faqr wa-l-zuhd (34), Bayān faḍīlat al-zuhd, 4:207; Eng. trans. by Anthony F. Shaker as *On Poverty and Abstinence: Kitāb al-faqr wa'l-zuhd (Book XXXIV of* The Revival of the Religious Sciences) (Cambridge: Islamic Texts Society, 2019), 92.

163 Al-Sulamī, *ḤW*, §68; Ibn Ḥanbal, *Musnad*, 6:187, Ḥ. 3671; al-Tirmidhī, *English Translation of Jāmiʿ at-Tirmidhī* (Riyadh: Darussalam, 2007), K. Ṣifat al-qiyāma (37), B. (24), Ḥ. 2458; cf. al-Khaṭīb al-Tabrīzī, *Mishkāt al-maṣābīḥ*, K. al-janā'iz (5), B. tamannī l-mawt wa-dhikrihi (2), H. 1608; Abū Yaʿlā l-Mawṣilī, *Musnad* (Damascus: Dār al-Ma'mūn, 1986), 8:461, Ḥ. 5047; al-Ḥākim al-Naysābūrī, *al-Mustadrak ʿalā l-ṣaḥīḥayn* (Beirut: Dār al-Kutub al-ʿIlmiyya, 2002), 4:359, Ḥ. 72/7915; al-Bayhaqī, *Shuʿab al-īmān* (Beirut: Dār al-Kutub al-ʿIlmiyya, 2000), 6:142, Ḥ. 7730; 7:354, Ḥ. 10561; al-Bayhaqī, *al-Ādāb* (Beirut: Dār al-Kutub al-ʿIlmiyya, 1986), 510–11, Ḥ. 1155; Abū Nuʿaym al-Iṣfahānī, *Ḥilyat al-awliyā' wa-ṭabaqāt al-aṣfiyā'* (Cairo: Maktabat al-Khānjī, Beirut: Dār al-Fikr, 1996), 4:209; al-Ṭabarānī, *al-Muʿjam al-kabīr* (Cairo: Maktabat Ibn Taymiyya, 1983), 10:188, Ḥ. 10290; al-Ṭabarānī, *al-Muʿjam al-ṣaghīr* (Beirut: Dār al-Kutub al-ʿIlmiyya, 1983), 1:177; al-Haythamī, *Majmaʿ al-zawā'id wa-manbaʿ al-fawā'id* (Beirut: Dār al-Kutub al-ʿIlmiyya, 2001), 10:366, Ḥ. 18042. Al-Albānī judged this tradition *ḥasan*. *Ṣaḥīḥ al-jāmiʿ al-ṣaghīr wa-ziyādatuhu* (*al-Fatḥ al-kabīr*) (Beirut: al-Maktab al-Islāmī, 1988), 222, Ḥ. 935.

164 Al-Bukhārī, *al-Adab al-mufrad*, B. al-jafā' (638), Ḥ. 1314; Ibn Māja, *Sunan*, K. al-zuhd (37), B. al-ḥayā' (17), Ḥ. 4184; al-Tirmidhī, *Jāmiʿ*, K. al-birr wa-l-ṣila (25), B. mā jā'a fī l-ḥayā' (65), Ḥ. 2009; al-Sulamī, *KAṢ*, 32; *ḤW*, §77–8; Melchert, 'Khargūshī, *Tahdhīb al-asrār*', 444; cf. Ibn Abī l-Dunyā, *Makārim al-akhlāq*, 6:86–7, Ḥ. 71/11198, 72/11199, 74/11201.

165 Al-Bukhārī, *Ṣaḥīḥ*, K. al-īmān (2), B. umūr al-īmān (3), Ḥ. 9; al-Bukhārī, *al-Adab al-mufrad*, B. al-ḥayā' (271), Ḥ. 598; Muslim, *Ṣaḥīḥ*, K. al-īmān (1), B. bayān ʿadad shuʿab al-īmān (12), Ḥ. 35; Ibn Māja, *Sunan*, K. al-muqaddima [Introduction] (0), B. fī l-īmān (9), Ḥ. 57–8; Abū Dā'ūd, *Sunan*, K. al-sunna (39), B. radd al-irjā' (14), Ḥ. 4676; see three traditions in al-Nasā'ī, *English Translation of Sunan an-Nasâ'i* (Riyadh: Darussalam, 2007), K. al-īmān wa-sharā'iʿihi (47), B. dhikr shuʿab al-īmān (16), Ḥ. 5007–9; cf. al-Tirmidhī, *Jāmiʿ*, K. al-birr wa-l-ṣila (25), B. mā jā'a fī l-ʿiyy (80), Ḥ. 2027; Ibn Ḥanbal, *Musnad*, 15:443, Ḥ. 9710; cf. 15:212–13, Ḥ. 9361; 36:649, Ḥ. 22312; al-Nawawī, *Riyāḍ al-ṣāliḥīn* (Beirut: Dār Ibn Kathīr, 2007), K. al-adab (1), B. al-ḥayā' (84), Ḥ. 682; al-Sulamī, *KAṢ*, 32; *ḤW*, §76; al-Makkī, *Qūt al-qulūb fī muʿāmalat al-maḥbūb* (Cairo: Maktabat Dār al-Turāth, 2001), 3:1298; Melchert, 'Khargūshī, *Tahdhīb al-asrār*', 440; cf. Ibn Abī l-Dunyā, *Makārim al-akhlāq*, 6:87, Ḥ. 73/11200.

166 Muslim, *Ṣaḥīḥ*, K. al-īmān (1), B. bayān ʿadad shuʿab al-īmān (12), Ḥ. 37; Abū Dā'ūd, *Sunan*, K. al-adab (40), B. al-ḥayā' (6), H. 4796; Ibn Ḥanbal, *Musnad*, 33:51, Ḥ. 19817; 33:137–8, Ḥ. 19905; 33:175, Ḥ. 19957; 33:187, Ḥ. 19976; 33:203, Ḥ. 19999; 33:210–11, Ḥ. 20008; Ibn Abī l-Dunyā, *Makārim al-akhlāq*, 6:87–90, Ḥ. 75/11202, 78/11205, 84/11211, 87/11214; al-Ṭabarānī, *al-Muʿjam al-kabīr*, 18:202, Ḥ. 493; 18:227, Ḥ. 565; al-Sulamī, *ḤW*, §74; Melchert, 'Khargūshī, *Tahdhīb al-asrār*', 445.

167 Al-Bukhārī, *Ṣaḥīḥ*, K. al-adab (78), B. al-ḥayā' (77), Ḥ. 6117; Muslim, *Ṣaḥīḥ*, K. al-īmān (1), B. bayān ʿadad shuʿab al-īmān (12), Ḥ. 37; Ibn Ḥanbal, *Musnad*, 33:64, Ḥ. 19830; Ibn Abī l-Dunyā, *Makārim al-akhlāq*, 6:93, Ḥ. 98/11225; al-Nawawī, *Riyāḍ al-ṣāliḥīn*, K. al-adab (1), B. al-ḥayā' (84), Ḥ. 681; al-Sulamī, *ḤW*, §75.

168 Sheikh, *Forging Ideal Muslim Subjects*, 79.

169 Sheikh, *Forging Ideal Muslim Subjects*, 80.

170 Cf. al-Ghazālī, *Iḥyā' ʿulūm al-dīn*, K. riyāḍat al-nafs (22), Bayān al-ṭarīq fī riyāḍat al-ṣibyān, 3:71; Eng. trans. by T. J. Winter as *On disciplining the soul: Kitāb Riyāḍat al-nafs* and *On Breaking the Two Desires: Kitāb Kasr al-shahwatayn*

(*Books XXII and XXIII of* The Revival of the Religious Sciences *Iḥyāʾ ʿulūm al-dīn*) (Cambridge: Islamic Texts Society, 1995), 76.

171 Any impetus to secrecy or concealment in this treatise always relates to the affairs of one's brothers. A believer should keep their sins, shortcomings and faults from the eyes of others.

172 One of the most frequently cited figures is Abū ʿUthmān al-Ḥīrī, arguably the most famous master of the Path of Blame. Thibon, *L'œuvre*, 260.

173 Al-Sulamī, *KAṢ*, 45. Interestingly, the psychological dynamics of borrowing and lending provide an outstanding illustration for *ḥayāʾ*; al-Ghazālī picks up and reworks a scenario crafted by al-Muḥāsibī to delineate valid and less valid reasons to lend someone money. Al-Ghazālī, *Iḥyāʾ ʿulūm al-dīn*, K. dhamm al-jāh wa-l-riyāʾ (28), Bayān al-rukhṣa fī kitmān al-dhunūb, 3:302; al-Muḥāsibī, *al-Riʿāya li-ḥuqūq Allāh*, B. mā yastaḥibb fīhi al-ḥayāʾ wa-mā yakrah fīhi, 281–2; for discussion, see Sheikh, *Forging Ideal Muslim Subjects*, 78–9.

174 *ādāb al-ẓawāhir ʿunwān ādāb al-sarāʾir*. Al-Sulamī, *KAṢ*, 86; cf. *AMM*, §16; *ṬṢ*, 122 (#33); *SA*, §11; *ṬṢ*, 58 (#3); *ḤMA*, §69.

175 *ḥusn adab al-ẓāhir ʿunwān ḥusn adab al-bāṭin*. Al-Sulamī, *KAṢ*, 86; *AMM*, §16; *ṬṢ*, 122 (#33).

176 Al-Sulamī, *KAṢ*, 86. This tradition does not appear in any of the major Sunnī collections. Al-Albānī judged it defective (*mawḍūʿ*). Al-Albānī, *Silsilat al-aḥādīth al-ḍaʿīfa*, 1:227–8, Ḥ. 110.

177 Al-Sulamī, *KAṢ*, 87.

178 For example, in one of al-Sulamī's discussions of Ṣūfī *rukhaṣ*, he bluntly states that no one can find fault with the Ṣūfīs' *ādāb*, *akhlāq* or *aḥwāl*, so he assumes that legal concessions must be the root of others' objections to *taṣawwuf*. Al-Sulamī, *KMT*, §9; see also *MFA*, §16; *BTF*, §15–16.

179 Some historians have seen a continuity between the scorn for worldly esteem that marks the Path of Blame and the systematic transgression of social norms practices by the Qalandars, but this thesis has been thoroughly debunked. Ahmet T. Karamustafa, *God's Unruly Friends: Dervish Groups in the Islamic Later Middle Period 1200–1550* (Oxford: Oneworld, 2006), 25–38.

180 Al-Sulamī, *KAṢ*, 28–9.

181 Al-Sulamī, *KAṢ*, 45.

182 Al-Sulamī, *KAṢ*, 87.

183 Al-Sulamī, *KAṢ*, 29. Here, the phrase *aḥkām al-bawāṭin* suggests that al-Sulamī recognizes a distinct set of precepts that should govern a person's *bāṭin* and that these precepts can be realized and voluntarily accepted. His discussion of *ādāb al-bāṭin* in several places could have an attitudinal sense, more so in other treatises than this one, but *aḥkām* carries a stronger sense of norms imposed from without that must be freely obeyed.

184 Another example of these two moving in tandem occurs regarding spiritual insight (*firāsa*); see al-Sulamī, *MF*, §124.

3 Al-Sulamī's vision of fellowship and spiritual companionship

1 Never was the strangeness of this lexicon better on display than when al-Nūrī returned after a few years outside of Baghdad and found himself unable to

participate in conversations with al-Junayd's circle, who had developed entirely new expressions for their spiritual discourse in the meantime. Karamustafa, *Sufism: The Formative Period*, 7–13.

2 Several of these may depend, directly or indirectly, on a lost treatise by Abū 'Alī l-Rūdhbārī. The most significant modern study of these early lexicons remains Massignon's classic investigation of al-Ḥallāj. Massignon, *Essay on the Origins of the Technical Language of Islamic Mysticism*.

3 Ibn Fāris' *Maqāyīs* posits two major meanings in the root *'-sh-r*, the first relating to the number ten and the second to the notion of mixture or mingling. Al-Jawharī's *al-Ṣiḥāḥ* also associates *'ishra* with this meaning of mixing, equating *'ishra* with *mukhālaṭa*; Ibn Manẓūr (d. 711/1312) later retained this in *Lisān al-'arab*. Aḥmad Ibn Fāris al-Qazwīnī, *Mu'jam maqāyīs al-lugha* (Cairo: 'Īsā l-Bābī l-Ḥalabī, 1946), 4:324–7; Ismā'īl b. Ḥammād al-Jawharī, *al-Ṣiḥāḥ: Tāj al-lugha wa-ṣiḥāḥ al-'arabiyya* (Beirut: Dār al-'Ilm lil-Milāyīn, 1984), 2:746–8.

4 *Lisān al-'arab* at one point equates *'ashīr* with *qarīb* and *ṣadīq*, but clearly in the context of familial relationships, not in the more general sense of friendship. Elsewhere, *Lisān al-'arab* complicates the matter by equating *ṣāḥib* with *mu'āshir* without any explanatory distinction, as well as equating the third form of these verbal roots (*ṣāḥaba* and *'āshara*) with each other without any explanatory distinction. Ibn Manẓūr witnesses the voluntary nature of *ṣuḥba* in his discussion of the tenth verbal form from that root, *istaṣḥaba*. This verb means to call someone to *ṣuḥba* and all that is obligatory in that relationship. Ibn Manẓūr, *Lisān al-'arab* (Cairo: Dār al-Ma'ārif, 1900), 4:2400–1, 2955.

5 Lloyd V. J. Ridgeon's comment that al-Sulamī's *Kitāb al-futuwwa* was the first 'systematic discussion' of spiritual chivalry among Ṣūfīs is overly generous, though it was the first Ṣūfī attempt to treat the topic in depth. Ridgeon, '*Futuwwa* (in Ṣūfism)', *EI*[3].

6 Kister offers no explanation of the treatise's organization. Thibon assumes that a logic to the organization of this treatise exists but admits that it eludes him. Thibon, *L'œuvre*, 259.

7 Al-Sulamī, *AMM*, §9. The absence of a teaching so relevant to the primary theme of *Kitāb ādāb al-ṣuḥba* suggests that al-Sulamī completed *Kitāb ādāb al-ṣuḥba* before he completed *Adab mujālasat al-mashāyikh*, although no established chronology exists for his shorter treatises. Nearly all the teachings found in *Kitāb ādāb al-ṣuḥba* that bear directly on the primary themes of *Adab mujālasat al-mashāyikh* appear there with very similar wording. Thibon's description of *Adab mujālasat al-mashāyikh* as the completion, in some sense, of *Kitāb ādāb al-ṣuḥba* holds true not just thematically but chronologically. Thibon, '*Adab* et éducation spirituelle', 112.

8 Thibon, *L'œuvre*, 259–62. In the section dealing with this treatise, Thibon suggests that *'ishra* is a more nebulous term, denoting life in society in a more general way than the more structured, codified relationships implied by *ṣuḥba*. However, he casts this difference as one of private/public rather than lasting/temporary.

9 Al-Sulamī, *KAṢ*, 23; cf. *DM*, §17. In the second part of this passage, al-Sulamī's choice of vocabulary is striking. Most of *Kitāb ādāb al-ṣuḥba* does not speak explicitly about Sufism and does not rely on the specialized terms of the Sufi lexicon, but here each of the terms al-Sulamī uses comes from al-Ḥakīm al-Tirmidhī's well-developed hierarchy of the saints. Elsewhere al-Sulamī uses these terms little; while al-Sulamī shows that he understands the usage of these terms by prior masters, *walāya* is an underdeveloped theme in his writings. His concern is more pedagogical than theoretical. Al-Sulamī,

KMT, §5; al-Ḥakīm al-Tirmidhī, *Khatm al-awliyā'* (Beirut: al-Maṭba'a al-Kāthūlīkiyya, 1965), 142–4, 451–2; for discussion of theories of sainthood in the period, see Palmer, *Sainthood and Authority in Early Islam*; Schimmel, *Mystical Dimensions of Islam*, 199–200; Richard McGregor, 'The Development of the Islamic Understanding of Sanctity', *Religious Studies and Theology* 20, no. 1 (2001): 52–6; with specific reference to al-Sulamī, see Thibon, *L'œuvre*, 249–52, 419; Berger, '*Geschieden*', 142–9.

10 Thibon, *L'œuvre*, 262.

11 Al-Sulamī, *KAṢ*, 79; see also *AMM*, §9.

12 Al-Sulamī, *KAṢ*, 24; cf. al-Bukhārī, *Ṣaḥīḥ*, K. al-adab (78), B. raḥmat al-nās wa-l-bahā'im (27), Ḥ. 6011; Muslim, *Ṣaḥīḥ*, K. al-birr wa-l-ṣila wa-l-adab (45), B. tarāḥūm al-mu'minīn wa-ta'āṭufuhum wa-ta'āḍuduhum (17), Ḥ. 2586; al-Tha'labī, *al-Kashf wa-l-bayān*, 2:124.

13 Al-Sulamī, *KAṢ*, 24; al-Bukhārī, *Ṣaḥīḥ*, K. al-ṣalāt (8), B. tashbīk al-aṣābi' fī l-masjid wa-ghayrihi (88), Ḥ. 481; K. al-maẓālim (46), B. naṣr al-maẓlūm (5), Ḥ. 2446; K. al-adab (78), B. ta'āwun al-mu'minīn ba'ḍihim ba'ḍ (36), Ḥ. 6026; Muslim, *Ṣaḥīḥ*, K. al-birr wa-l-ṣila wa-l-adab (45), B. tarāḥūm al-mu'minīn wa-ta'āṭufuhum wa-ta'āḍuduhum (17), Ḥ. 2585; al-Nasā'ī, *Sunan*, K. al-zakāt (23), B. ajr al-khāzin idhā taṣaddaqa bi-idhn mawlāhu (67), Ḥ. 2561; al-Tirmidhī, *Jāmi'*, K. al-birr wa-l-ṣila (25), B. mā jā'a fī shafaqat al-muslim 'alā l-muslim (18), Ḥ. 1928; al-Tha'labī, *al-Kashf wa-l-bayān*, 2:124.

14 Al-Sulamī, *KAṢ*, 61. This tradition does not appear in any of the major *ḥadīth* collections. Al-Tha'ālibī, *The Book of Noble Character*, 86; Kister notes that al-Makkī mentions it in *Qūt al-qulūb*, as do several other later Ṣūfī sources.

15 Al-Sulamī, *KAṢ*, 25; al-Bukhārī, *Ṣaḥīḥ*, K. aḥādīth al-anbiyā' (60), B. al-arwāḥ junūd mujannada (2), Ḥ. 3336; al-Bukhārī, *al-Adab al-mufrad*, B. al-arwāḥ junūd mujannada (401), Ḥ. 900–1; Muslim, *Ṣaḥīḥ*, K. al-birr wa-l-ṣila wa-l-adab (45), B. al-arwāḥ junūd mujannada (49), Ḥ. 2638; Abū Dā'ūd, *Sunan*, K. al-adab (40), B. man yu'mar an yujālis (16), Ḥ. 4834.

16 Al-Sulamī, *KAṢ*, 25; cf. Abū Dā'ūd, *Sunan*, K. al-adab (40), B. man yu'mar an yujālis (16), Ḥ. 4833; al-Tirmidhī, *Jāmi'*, K. al-zuhd (34), B. ḥadīth al-rajul 'alā dīn khalīlihi (45), Ḥ. 2378; Ibn Ḥanbal, *Musnad*, 13:398, Ḥ. 8028; al-Albānī, *Silsilat al-aḥādīth al-ṣaḥīḥa wa-shay' min fiqhihā wa-fawā'idihā* (Riyadh: Maktabat al-Ma'ārif, 1995–2002), 2:597–9, Ḥ. 927; cf. Sulamī, *DAṢ*, 550. Many Sufi texts draw on this *ḥadīth*; to the several that Kister reports in his footnote, one may add Abū l-Ḥasan al-Sīrjānī, *Sufism, Black and White: A Critical Edition of* Kitāb al-Bayāḍ wa-l-Sawād *by Abū l-Ḥasan al-Sīrjānī (d. ca. 470/1077)* (Leiden: Brill, 2012), §371. According to Ibn 'Asākir, this was the only tradition that Ṣūfī master Bundār b. al-Ḥusayn (d. 353/964) chose to transmit, though al-Sulamī neither mentions this in the entry for Bundār in *Ṭabaqāt al-ṣūfiyya* nor narrates the tradition through him. Ibn 'Asākir, *Tabyīn kadhib al-muftarī* (Damascus: al-Qudsī, 1928), 180.

17 Al-Sulamī, *KAṢ*, 26; Ṭarafa b. al-'Abd, *Dīwān* (Beirut: Dār Ṣādir, 1961), 44.

18 Al-Sulamī, *KAṢ*, 27. Many Ṣūfī texts cite these verses; see Kister's footnote for a sampling.

19 Al-Sulamī, *AMM*, §9.

20 Whether al-Sulamī takes this approach because he intends to transcend *madhhab* factionalism or merely because this treatise attempts to establish a foundation without which factionalism would not be relevant – likely the latter – he restricts himself to teachings that could garner broad acceptance in his society.

21 I have not found any *ḥadīth* collection that records al-Sulamī's variant of this tradition verbatim, but near variants abound, albeit not in the Six Books. Al-Albānī rates the tradition *ḥasan*. Al-Ṭayālisī, *Musnad Abī Dā'ūd al-Ṭayālisī* (Giza: Hajar, 1999), 3:313, Ḥ. 1862; Abū l-Shaykh al-Anṣārī, *Ṭabaqāt al-muḥaddithīn bi-Iṣbahān* (Beirut: Mu'assasat al-Risāla, 1992), 2:281–2, Ḥ. 244; al-Bayhaqī, *Shu'ab al-īmān*, 7:348–9, Ḥ. 10540–1; Abū Nu'aym, *Ḥilyat al-awliyā'*, 3:253; al-Ṭabarānī, *al-Mu'jam al-awsaṭ*, 4:306–7, Ḥ. 4258; al-Albānī, *Silsilat al-aḥādīth al-ṣaḥīḥa*, 2:483–5, Ḥ. 831; al-Albānī, *Ṣaḥīḥ al-jāmi'*, 1:76, Ḥ. 73, 2:803, Ḥ. 4355; al-Albānī, *Tamām al-minna* (Riyadh: Dār al-Rāya, 1988), Ḥ. 245–6.

22 Al-Sulamī, *UNM*, §38.

23 Al-Sulamī, *KAṢ*, 74–5.

24 Ibn Ḥazm, *Kitāb al-akhlāq wa-l-siyar*, 34.

25 Nuha Alshaar resists a caricature of al-Tawḥīdī as a socially alienated loner, but he famously struggled to suffer rulers who fell short of the high standards for learning and trustworthiness al-Tawḥīdī associated with governance. Whatever the reason for his pattern of broken relationships, Wadād al-Qāḍī rightly summarizes that al-Tawḥīdī's social life was 'by his own admission, a series of tragic failures'. Wadād al-Qāḍī, 'Abū Ḥayyān al-Tawḥīdī: A Sunnī Voice in the Shī'ī Century', in *Culture and Memory in Medieval Islam: Essays in Honour of Wilferd Madelung*, ed. Farhad Daftary and Josef W. Meri (London: I.B. Taurus, 2003), 129; Alshaar, *Ethics in Islam*, 59–118.

26 I accept the fundamental contours of Richard W. Bulliet's explanation for the development of this factionalism, sketched first in *The Patricians of Nishapur* in 1972 and continually revisited in subsequent publications. Deborah G. Tor has recently pushed back against Bulliet's theory that the true roots of this *madhhab* factionalism were more social and economic than religious; she faults Bulliet for minimizing the religious element of the conflict and points to the mutual *takfīr* between the Shāfi'īs and the Ḥanafīs, as well as the wholehearted involvement in the conflict of the greatest religious leaders of the day. Regarding al-Sulamī, the question of the origins of this *'aṣabiyya* is not of fundamental importance; it suffices to note that he lived at a time when the social fabric was coming apart. Richard W. Bulliet, *The Patricians of Nishapur: A Study in Medieval Islamic Social History* (Cambridge: Harvard, 1972); Richard W. Bulliet, 'Local Politics in Eastern Iran under the Ghaznavids and Seljuks', *IS* 11, no. 1/4 (1978): 35–56; Deborah G. Tor, 'Rayy and the Religious History of the Seljūq Period', *Der Islam* 93, no. 2 (2016): 386–7; Deborah G. Tor, 'The Religious History of the Seljuq Period', in *The Seljuqs and their Successors: Art, Culture and History*, ed. Sheila Canby, Deniz Beyazit and Martina Rugiadi (Edinburgh: Edinburgh University Press, 2020), 54–5, 69.

27 Al-Qushayrī's lament of Nishapur's *madhhab* factionalism is muted, considering the circumstances; except for his famous *Shikāyat ahl al-sunna* protesting the persecution of the Ash'arīs, one might accidentally overlook that after his brief imprisonment he spent the better part of a decade in exile. His literary corpus does not read like the continual lament of a long-suffering man.

28 Al-Sulamī and al-Ḥakīm al-Tirmidhī, *Three Early Sufi Texts*, 89.

29 'Alqama's advice to his son became better known through more widely diffused texts like al-Ghazālī's *Bidāyat al-hidāya* and *Iḥyā' 'ulūm al-dīn*. In both cases, al-Ghazālī uses the anecdote to describe either the characteristics one should look for in a companion or the behaviour one should expect from a companion. In the former case, al-Ghazālī omits the commentary; in the latter, he includes it. W. Montgomery Watt challenged the attribution of this section of *Bidāyat al-hidāya* to al-Ghazālī. The

anecdote also appears with the commentary in *The Book of Noble Character* attributed to Abū Manṣūr al-Thaʿālibī (d. 429/1039), thus providing additional evidence for al-Sulamī's interpretation of the advice as a discouragement for companionship. Abū Ḥāmid al-Ghazālī, *Bidāyat al-hidāya* (Aleppo: ʿAbd al-Ghanī Abū l-ʿAbbās, 1970), 129; W. Montgomery Watt and al-Ghazālī, *The Faith and Practice of Al-Ghazālī* (London: G. Allen and Unwin, 1953), 152; W. Montgomery Watt, 'The Authenticity of the Works Attributed to Al-Ghazālī', *JRAS* 84, no. 1–2 (1952): 40–2; al-Ghazālī, *Iḥyāʾ ʿulūm al-dīn*, K. al-ulfa wa-l-ukhuwwa wa-l-ṣuḥba wa-l-muʿāshara, B. al-ṣifāt al-mashrūṭa fīman takhtar ṣuḥbatuhu, 2:158; al-Thaʿālibī, *The Book of Noble Character*, 84.

30 Al-Sulamī, *KAṢ*, 33.

31 Cf. Q. 49:13.

32 Al-Sulamī, *KAṢ*, 30.

33 Al-Sulamī, *KAṢ*, 30, 35.

34 Thibon, *L'œuvre*, 267–8, see also 378–9.

35 Al-Sulamī often uses *fuqarāʾ* to refer to the spiritually poor, a functional synonym for Ṣūfīs, and Bayrak's translation assumes as much. Here, his comments about respect and value suggest as much, but the fact that he immediately follows this counsel with talk of the rich – in a clearly material sense – implies that if he intends the spiritually poor, he intended *fuqarāʾ* who were also poor materially.

36 Al-Sulamī, *KF*, 69.

37 Al-Sulamī, *ḤW*, §87; *FT*, §15, 32, 47, 48; *MA*, §4, 14; *ṢDM*, §213; *DM*, §18; *DṬḤ*, §285.

38 Al-Sulamī, *KAṢ*, 29, 80.

39 Q. 7:199; al-Sulamī elsewhere cites this verse in *KAṢ*, 23; *JAṢ*, §7; *DM*, §17.

40 Al-Sulamī, *KAṢ*, 43.

41 Frank, '"*Taṣawwuf* is...": On a Type of Mystical Aphorism', 73.

42 Al-Sulamī, *KAṢ*, 29.

43 Al-Sulamī, *KAṢ*, 80; cf. *QF*, §244.

44 Thibon, *L'œuvre*, 259.

45 Baldick, *Mystical Islam*, 57–8.

46 On the use of this method in Qurʾānic studies, see Michel Cuypers, *The Banquet: A Reading of the Fifth Sura of the Qur'an* (Miami: Convivium, 2009); George Archer, *A Place Between Two Places: The Qurʾānic Barzakh* (Piscataway, NJ: Gorgias Press, 2017), esp. 63–106.

47 MacIntyre, *Dependent Rational Animals*, x.

48 MacIntyre, *Dependent Rational Animals*, 5.

49 MacIntyre, *Dependent Rational Animals*, 81.

50 MacIntyre, *Dependent Rational Animals*, 94–5.

51 MacIntyre, *Dependent Rational Animals*, 109.

52 Mohammed Ghaly, 'Disability in the Islamic Tradition', *RC* 10, no. 2 (2016): 151. Because the Qurʾānic macro-narrative is primarily concerned with how the human person should relate to the Creator, any pre-modern attempts to speak about persons with disabilities occur as a subgroup within larger categories of that macro-narrative; for this reason, Ghaly prefers to speak about a 'disabilities-plus group'.

53 Ghaly, 'Disability in the Islamic Tradition', 156–7. Curiously, the scion of '*adab* literature' is primarily known by a name indicating such a blight: *al-Jāḥiẓ*, 'the bug-eyed.'

54 Ibn Manẓūr, *Lisān al-ʿarab*, 4:3181.

55 Kristina L. Richardson, *Difference and Disability in the Medieval Islamic World: Blighted Bodies* (Edinburgh: Edinburgh University Press, 2012), 13–14.

56 Farhang Mehrvash, Farzin Negahban and Sadeq Sajjadi, 'Brotherhood', *EI*[s].

57 For a fuller treatment of this question, see Jason Welle, 'Cristo e cristiani nell'opera letteraria del maestro ṣūfī al-Sulamī', *ISCH* 48 (2022): 229–44. In sum, references to post-Qur'ānic Christians in al-Sulamī's corpus are exceedingly rare and little distinguishes his image of 'Isā b. Maryam, whom al-Sulamī portrays as a master of esoteric wisdom from his childhood, from other Muslim mystics in the period.

58 Among the three monographs on al-Sulamī in European languages, only Thibon even mentions Jesus Christ, and there in a footnote to an article comparing the Path of Blame to the Sermon on the Mount. While Chowdhury indicates some ways in which al-Sulamī's spiritual method may parallel the threefold way of medieval Christian mysticism (*via purgativa – via illuminativa – via unitiva*), this insight emerges more from Chowdhury's intuition than from any explicit connection in al-Sulamī's writings. Thibon, *L'œuvre*, 472fn918; Morris S. Seale, 'The Ethics of Malāmatīya Sufism and the Sermon on the Mount', *MW* 58, no. 1 (1968): 12–23; Chowdhury, *A Ṣūfī Apologist*, 184–90; Jason Welle, 'Review of *A Ṣūfī Apologist of Nīshāpūr: The Life and Thought of Abū 'Abd al-Raḥmān al-Sulamī*, by S. Z. Chowdhury', *Arabica* 68 (2021): 440.

59 As an example, Clifford Edmund Bosworth's first book on the Ghaznavid empire dedicated only three pages to the question of all the *dhimmī* communities; his later work on the later Ghaznavids never once mentions Christians in the index. Clifford Edmund Bosworth, *The Ghaznavids: Their Empire in Afghanistan and Eastern Iran, 994–1040* (Edinburgh: University Press, 1963), 200–2; Clifford Edmund Bosworth, *The Later Ghaznavids: Splendour and Decay: The Dynasty in Afghanistan and Northern India 1040–1186* (New York: Columbia University Press, 1977).

60 The famous geographer al-Muqaddasī (d. 380/990) reports that there were Christians in Nishapur. One text reports that the zealous Karrāmī preacher Abū Ya'qūb Isḥāq b. Maḥmashād (d. 383/993) converted more than five thousand *ahl al-kitāb* in Nishapur, but this must be an exaggeration; the continued existence of a non-Muslim population of this size in the city at that time is highly unlikely. I accept Bulliet's estimate that at the birth of al-Sulamī, Islam likely enjoyed a majority of 95 per cent in Nishapur. Youshaa Patel's recent monograph provides a fascinating and insightful exploration of the ways Muslims have attempted to differentiate themselves from non-Muslims around them, but such impulses were hardly relevant to al-Sulamī's Nishapur, where the meaningful differences were intra-Islamic. Al-Muqaddasī, *Kitāb aḥsan al-taqāsīm fī ma'rifat al-aqālīm* (*Descriptio imperii moslemici*) (Leiden: Brill, 1906), 323; Richard W. Bulliet, *Islam: The View from the Edge* (New York: Columbia University Press, 1994), 39; Bosworth, *The Ghaznavids*, 186, 200–2; Bulliet, *The Patricians of Nishapur*, 15; cf. Andrew C. S. Peacock, *The Great Seljuk Empire* (Edinburgh: Edinburgh University Press, 2015), 281; A. Christian van Gorder, *Christianity in Persia and the Status of Non-Muslims in Iran* (Lanham, MD: Lexington Books, 2010), 53; Annibale Bugnini, *La chiesa in Iran* (Rome: Edizioni Vincenziane, 1981), part 1; Youshaa Patel, *The Muslim Difference: Defining the Line between Believers and Unbelievers from Early Islam to the Present* (New Haven: Yale University Press, 2022).

61 Tor, 'The Religious History of the Seljuq Period', 60–2; Tor, 'Rayy and the Religious History of the Seljūq Period', 395.

62 Al-Sulamī, *KAṢ*, 23.

63 Al-Sulamī, *KAṢ*, 23.

64 Chowdhury mentions this in the context of al-Sulamī's 'uṣūlization' project, a term coined by Cornell to express al-Sulamī's attempt to bring Sufism 'into agreement with the *sunna* of the Prophet Muḥammad' as defined by *uṣūl* methodology. Chowdhury, *A Ṣūfī Apologist*, 41; al-Sulamī, *Early Sufi Women*, 37–8; cf. Thibon, *L'œuvre*, 81–92.

65 Listing all examples of such usage of *ikhwān* would be ponderous in the extreme. For the behaviour mentioned here, see al-Sulamī, *KAṢ*, 42–3, and especially *KAṢ*, 35, for Abū Ṣāliḥ's counsel to preserve the pious orientation of the brothers.

66 Al-Sulamī, *KAṢ*, 41.

67 Al-Sulamī, *KAṢ*, 41–2.

68 Al-Sulamī, *KAṢ*, 42.

69 Ridgeon confirms Meier's caution about identifying either the *ikhwān* or the *fityān* as some sort of corporate association. Al-Sulamī's encouragement for work – as opposed to Karrāmī mendicancy – does not mean that the *fityān* he describes constituted a primitive version of the labour guilds that would develop later. Ridgeon thus describes al-Sulamī's *futuwwa* as 'sanitized', an ethical ideal that al-Qushayrī and others would spiritualize even more intensely. Lloyd V. J. Ridgeon, *Morals and Mysticism in Persian Sufism: A History of Sufi-Futuwwat in Iran* (New York: Routledge, 2010), 42–5.

70 Al-Sulamī, *UNM*, §56; see also the truncated version of the saying earlier, *KAṢ*, 14. Many versions of this tradition appear in the major Sunnī *ḥadīth* collections, some verbatim and some very close parallels. Mālik b. Anas, *al- Muwaṭṭa'* (Dubai: Majmū'at al-Furqān al-Tijāriyya, 2003), K. ḥusn al-khuluq (47), B. mā jā'a fī l-muhājara (4), Ḥ. 1795; al-Bukhārī, *Ṣaḥīḥ*, K. al-adab (78), B. mā yunhā 'an al-taḥāsud wa-l-tadābur (57), Ḥ. 6064–5, B. al-hijra (62), Ḥ. 6076; al-Bukhārī, *al-Adab al-mufrad*, B. hijrat al-muslim (189), Ḥ. 398; B. al-shaḥnā' (192), Ḥ. 408, 410; B. al-ẓann (622), Ḥ. 1287; Muslim, *Ṣaḥīḥ*, K. al-birr wa-l-ṣila wa-l-adab (45), B. taḥrīm al-taḥāsud wa-l-tabāghuḍ wa-l-tadābur (7), B. taḥrīm al-hajr fawq thalāthat ayyām (8), B. taḥrīm al-ẓann wa-l-tajassus (9), B. taḥrīm ẓulm al-muslim wa-khadhlihi (10), Ḥ. 2559–64; Ibn Maja, *Sunan*, Abwāb al-du'ā' (34), B. al-du'ā' bi-l-'afw wa-l-'āfiyya (5), Ḥ. 3849; Abū Dā'ūd, *Sunan*, K. al-adab (40), B. fī hijrat al-rajul akhāhu (47), Ḥ. 4910; al-Tirmidhī, *Jāmi'*, Abwāb al-birr wa-l-ṣila (25), B. mā jā'a fī l-ḥasad (24), Ḥ. 1935; see also Ibn Abī l-Dunyā, *al-Ghība wa-l-namīma*, in *Mawsū'at Ibn Abī l-Dunyā*, 2:44, Ḥ. 24; Ibn Abī l-Dunyā, *al-Ṣamt wa-ādāb al-lisān*, in *Mawsū'at Ibn Abī l-Dunyā*, 5:118–19, Ḥ. 163.

71 Al-Sulamī, *KAṢ*, 50–1.

72 Cf. Alexander Knysh, *Sufism: A New History of Islamic Mysticism* (Princeton, NJ: Princeton University Press, 2017), 155ff.

73 Thibon, '*Adab* et éducation spirituelle', 112. Due to some literary features that make it an outlier in his corpus, al-Sulamī's authorship of *Adab mujālasat al-mashāyikh* can only be considered probable and not entirely certain. The first line clearly attributes the treatise to al-Sulamī, and it bears important resemblances to *Manāhij al-'ārifīn* and *Darajāt al-ṣādiqīn fī l-taṣawwuf*. The treatise appears in the middle of the oldest manuscript containing texts attributed to al-Sulamī (MS 2118) as well as in two other manuscripts. Only one of these, however, directly ascribes authorship to him (Tehran MS 3989), and the work does not appear in the lists of al-Sulamī's writings. By comparison with al-Sulamī's other writings, the style of the introduction and conclusion are odd; the structure suggests that it would fit better as a chapter of a larger work, regardless of whether al-Sulamī wrote it. The author argues in his own voice throughout, which would not be unique in al-Sulamī's

corpus but is nonetheless irregular. The treatise contains a more intense and more consistent demand for the reverence that Ṣūfī aspirants owe their shaykhs than one sees elsewhere in al-Sulamī's writings, and the placement of Abū Bakr as the central model of true companionship is unique for al-Sulamī. Finally, some of the material the author cites in this treatise is unknown elsewhere in al-Sulamī's corpus. The third paragraph offers a list of sayings attributed to prominent Ṣūfī masters; none of these sayings are found, to my knowledge, in al-Sulamī's other writings. If al-Sulamī authored this treatise, this paragraph may show the hand of a later redactor. Böwering, 'Two Early Ṣūfī Manuscripts', 224, 227; Thibon, *L'œuvre*, 271–83.

74 In his French translation of *Kitāb ādāb al-ṣuḥba*, Tahar Gaïd regularly translates both *'ishra* and *mu'āshara* with *fréquentation.*
75 Al-Sulamī, *AMM*, §7; *KAṢ*, 57.
76 Al-Sulamī, *AMM*, §7.
77 Al-Sulamī, *AMM*, §3.
78 Al-Sulamī cites this Qur'ānic verse in several places, and in his *tafsīr*, transmits an interpretation of al-Tustarī that connects the Prophet's character to the concept of *adab*. 'You have taken on the *adab* of the Qur'ān and have not exceeded its bounds, according to [God's] words, "Truly, God enjoins justice and virtue"'. Al-Sulamī, *ḤT*, 1:343; *KAṢ*, 22; *KF*, 87; *JAṢ*, §4; *AMM*, §16; *DM*, §17; *MTḤ*, 49; see also Keeler, 'The Concept of *adab* in Early Sufism', 88–9.
79 *inna Allāh addabanī fa-aḥsana adabī*; for discussion of this tradition and a near variant, see note 79 in Chapter 1; see also al-Tha'labī, *al-Kashf wa-l-bayān*, 6:250.
80 Thibon, *L'œuvre*, 274.
81 Radtke, 'Anti-Ṣūfī Polemics', *EI*[3].
82 Al-Sulamī, *AMM*, §4.
83 Laury Silvers tallied the entries in *Ṭabaqāt al-ṣūfiyya*, finding that the most common number of shaykhs per companion is two. Only one-fifth of the entries report that a Ṣūfī had only one shaykh; one companion had more than eight. Laury Silvers, 'The Teaching Relationship in Early Sufism: A Reassessment of Fritz Meier's Definition of the *shaykh al-tarbiya* and the *shaykh al-ta'līm*', *MW* 93, no. 1 (2003): 80.
84 Al-Sulamī, *AMM*, §9.
85 Thibon, *L'œuvre*, 275fn62.
86 Thibon, *L'œuvre*, 277.
87 Al-Sulamī, *AMM*, §13.
88 Thibon, *L'œuvre*, 281.
89 Al-Sulamī, *AMM*, §16.
90 Al-Sulamī, *AMM*, §16; *ṬṢ*, 122 (#33); *KAṢ*, 86; see also *SA*, §11. Here, al-Sulamī cites a teaching of Abū Ḥafṣ, *ḥusn adab al-ẓāhir 'unwān ḥusn adab al-bāṭin*. The same maxim appears in *Ṭabaqāt al-ṣūfiyya* and *Kitāb ādāb al-ṣuḥba*, which add a reference to a Prophetic tradition that does not appear in any of the canonical Sunnī collections: 'If his heart had submitted, then his extremities also would have submitted' (*law khasha'a qalbuhu la-khasha'at jawāriḥuhu*). *Kitāb ādāb al-ṣuḥba* gives the context for Abū Ḥafṣ's statement, an interchange with al-Junayd, but this information is absent in the other places.
91 Al-Sulamī, *AMM*, §3.
92 Al-Sulamī, *AṢ*, §125; al-Sarrāj, *Kitāb al-luma'*, K. al-bayān 'an al-mushkilāt, B. bayān hādhihi l-alfāẓ. The English pair intermediaries/Originator does not carry the resonance of the Arabic *asbāb/musabbib*, words deriving from the same verbal root. Both al-Sulamī and al-Sarrāj treat the term *sabab* (pl. *asbāb*) in their glossaries of

the Sufi lexicon. Al-Sulamī hastily summarizes that the word means 'intermediary'; al-Sarrāj's fuller definition explains that the intermediaries lie between creation and God, and that someone who contemplates the intermediary that God has created will enter into the full contemplation of the Originator.

93 Al-Sulamī, *AMM*, §20.

94 Rosenthal, *Knowledge Triumphant*, 33.

95 Q. 7:199; al-Sulamī, *KAṢ*, 23, 43, 86; *JAṢ*, §7; *DM*, §17; *KF*, 71. Al-Sulamī cites this same passage near the beginning of *Jawāmiʿ ādāb al-ṣūfiyya*, uniting it there with two traditions widely in circulation among Ṣūfīs about the conduct (*adab*) and virtues (*akhlāq*) of the Prophet. In the first, the Prophet states that God has trained him with the best manner of conduct and perfected his training; in the second, God commands the Prophet to uphold noble virtues (*makārim al-akhlāq*), a command the Prophet sees in the Qurʾānic passage cited here. In *Kitāb ādāb al-ṣuḥba*, al-Sulamī severs these two traditions from this Qurʾānic passage, citing the former tradition near the end of the treatise. He does not cite the latter tradition but cites a similar one which says that the Prophet loved the highest character (*maʿālī l-akhlāq*). None of these traditions appear in any of the major Sunnī collections. Regarding the first, Ibn Taymiyya affirmed the soundness of its meaning despite the weakness of its chain of transmission, an assessment affirmed by al-Albānī. Ibn Taymiyya, *Shaykh al-Islām Ibn Taymiyya wa-juhūduhu fī l-ḥadīth wa-ʿulūmihi*, 2:466; al-Albānī, *Silsilat al-aḥādīth al-ḍaʿīfa*, 1:173, Ḥ. 72; see also al-Thaʿlabī, *al-Kashf wa-l-bayān*, 6:250. Regarding the tradition about the highest character, see al-Albānī, *Silsilat al-aḥādīth al-ṣaḥīḥa*, 3:366–7, Ḥ. 1378.

96 Al-Sulamī, *KAṢ*, 25, 26.

97 Al-Sulamī, *KAṢ*, 27; Alī b. Abī Ṭālib, al-Jāḥiẓ and al-Qāḍī Muḥammad b. Salāma al-Quḍāʿī, *A Treasury of Virtues and One Hundred Proverbs* (New York: New York University Press, 2013), 214–15. Translation Tahera Qutbuddin's.

98 See especially al-Sulamī, *KAṢ*, 79.

99 Al-Sulamī, *KAṢ*, 72.

100 Al-Sulamī, *KAṢ*, 72.

101 Al-Sulamī, *KAṢ*, 43.

102 MacIntyre, *Dependent Rational Animals*, 135.

103 See also al-Sulamī, *KAṢ*, 38.

104 Al-Sulamī, *KAṢ*, 35–6.

105 For a fuller treatment of this question, see Jason Welle, 'Mind the Gap: The Spiritual Progress of Early Ṣūfī Women', in *Les enjeux de l'écriture mystique*, ed. Nejmeddine Khalfallah and Abdelaziz El Aloui (Paris: Editions des archives contemporaines, 2020), 95–116. My comments here are largely a summary of that chapter, with some minor additions; two other significant studies of the question are Christopher Melchert, 'Before *Ṣūfiyyāt*: Female Renunciants in the 8th and 9th centuries CE', *JSS* 5 (2016): 115–39; Salamah-Qudsi, *Sufism and Early Islamic Piety*, 60–77.

106 Thibon, *L'œuvre*, 131–64.

107 Al-Sulamī mentions this about her but does not identify any traditions she transmitted. Al-Sulamī, *Early Sufi Women*, 230–1.

108 Al-Sulamī, *Early Sufi Women*, 46.

109 The scope of Cornell's claim about al-Sulamī's agenda vacillates; her assessment of al-Sulamī's assumptions about women generally is not clear. Cf. al-Sulamī, *Early Sufi Women*, 46, 50, 58, 70.

110 Al-Sulamī, *Early Sufi Women*, 48, 50, 70.

111 Al-Sulamī, *KAṢ*, 51; *BTF*, §44.
112 Q. 4:19; al-Sulamī, *KAṢ*, 51.
113 Al-Sulamī, *KAṢ*, 51; al-Majlisī, *Biḥār al-anwār* (Tehran: al-Maktaba al-Islāmiyya, 1969), 103:224, Ḥ. 3.
114 Al-Sulamī, *KAṢ*, 82; al-Bukhārī, *Ṣaḥīḥ*, K. al-nikāḥ (67), B. al-mudārā maʿa l-nisāʾ (79), Ḥ. 5184, 5186; al-Bukhārī, *al-Adab al-mufrad*, 259–60, Ḥ. 747; Muslim, *Ṣaḥīḥ*, K. al-riḍāʾ (17), B. al-waṣiyya bi-l-nisāʾ (17), Ḥ. 1466; K. al-riḍāʾ (17), B. al-waṣiyya bi-l-nisāʾ (20), Ḥ. 1470; al-Tirmidhī, *Jāmiʿ*, K. al-ṭalāq wa-l-liʿān (11), B. mā jāʾa fī mudārāt al-nisāʾ (12), Ḥ. 1188; Ibn Ḥanbal, *Musnad*, 2:428, Ḥ. 9524; 2:449, Ḥ. 9795; 2:530, Ḥ. 10856; 6:270, Ḥ. 26384; cf. 5:164, Ḥ. 21454; 5:151, Ḥ. 21339; see also Hūd b. Muḥakkam al-Huwwārī, *Tafsīr kitāb Allāh al-ʿazīz* (Beirut: Dār al-Gharb al-Islāmī, 1990), 1:345–6 (Q. 4:1); Karen Bauer, *Gender Hierarchy in the Qurʾān: Medieval Interpretations, Modern Responses* (New York: Cambridge University Press, 2015), 112–13.
115 Salamah-Qudsi, *Sufism and Early Islamic Piety*, 56.
116 Ruth Roded, *Women in Islamic Biographical Collections: From Ibn Saʿd to* Who's Who (London: Lynne Rienner, 1994), 109.
117 Laury Silvers, 'Early Pious, Mystic Sufi Women', in *The Cambridge Companion to Sufism*, ed. Lloyd Ridgeon (New York: Cambridge University Press, 2015), 27–8.
118 On the dating of the development of cross-gender companionship, see Melchert, 'Before *Ṣūfiyyāt*', 132.
119 Al-Sulamī, *BTF*, §44; *KAṢ*, 51; *ṬṢ*, 190 (#22), 396 (#6), 487 (#10); *SA*, §24; *KMT*, §7; *QTM*, §41; *MA*, §16.
120 Several sources record Dhū l-Nūn's comment, but several render the comment using the feminine *ustādha*. Al-Sulamī and Ibn al-Jawzī have *ustādh*, consistent with a grammatical convention by which extraordinary Ṣūfī women essentially become men. Al-Sulamī, *Early Sufi Women*, 142–5; Ibn al-Jawzī, *Ṣifat al-ṣafwa* (Beirut: Dār al-Maʿrifa, 1985), 4:124 (#688); Ibn al-Athīr, *al-Mukhtār min manāqib al-akhyār* (Al Ain, United Arab Emirates: Markaz Zāyid lil-Turāth wa-l-Tārīkh [Zayed Center for Heritage and History], 2002), 5:275 (#571); al-Munāwī, *al-Kawākib al-durriyya fī tarājim al-sāda al-ṣūfiyya* (Cairo: al-Maktaba al-Azhariyya lil-Turāth, 1994), 1:474 (#271); al-Shaʿrānī, *al-Ṭabaqāt al-kubrā* (Cairo: Maktabat al-Thaqāfa al-Dīniyya, 2005), 1:122 (#126); for discussion of such usage, see Silvers, 'Early Pious, Mystic Sufi Women', 47; Thibon, *L'œuvre*, 332fn287; al-Sulamī, *Early Sufi Women*, 45.
121 Roded rightly notes that in biographical dictionaries, Ṣūfī men asking women for advice often use the command, *ʿiẓinī*, meaning, 'provide [me] knowledge to induce correct behavior'. Roded, *Women in Islamic Biographical Collections*, 104. The evolution of the role of the shaykh will be discussed at greater length in the following chapter.
122 Salamah-Qudsi, *Sufism and Early Islamic Piety*, 67.
123 I have argued at length against Cornell's hypothesis that al-Sulamī uses *niswān* as a technical term for female practitioners of *futuwwa*. My claim does not annul the appreciation these women had for the virtues of *futuwwa*; on that, I fully agree with Cornell and Salamah-Qudsi. Welle, 'Mind the Gap', 106–9; cf. Salamah-Qudsi, *Sufism and Early Islamic Piety*, 66–9.
124 Nusiyya bt. Salmān (fl. late second/early ninth century) desired nothing other than service (*khidma*) to God but lamented the fact that God prevented this by busying her with a child. Al-Sulamī, *Early Sufi Women*, 92–3.
125 Welle, 'Mind the Gap', 112.

126 Al-Sulamī, *KAṢ*, 53.
127 Al-Sulamī, *KAṢ*, 53.
128 Q. 47:38, cf. 35:15; al-Sulamī, *MFA*, §44.
129 Al-Sulamī, *MFA*, §64.
130 Al-Sulamī, *MFA*, §65.
131 Al-Sulamī, *JAṢ*, §35.
132 Al-Sulamī, *JAṢ*, §20.
133 Süleyman Ateş, *Sülemî ve Tasavvufî Tefsîrı* (Istanbul: Sönmez, 1969), 186.
134 Al-Sulamī, *JAṢ*, §13, 39; Wilferd Madelung, *Religious Trends in Early Islamic Iran* (Albany: Persian Heritage Foundation, 1988), 44.
135 Al-Sulamī, *KAṢ*, 54. The phrase 'sweetness of faith' (*ḥalāwat al-īmān*) appears several times in the Sunnī canonical *ḥadīth* collections, but the context always differs from al-Sulamī's usage here. Those traditions are consistent with each other, emphasizing that sweetness of faith resides in loving God and God's Messenger above all else, in loving others for God's sake and in preferring the fires of hell to reversion to unbelief. None of these traditions frames the love of neighbour with al-Sulamī's characteristic emphasis that a believer should desire for one's neighbour what one desires for oneself. Most of the major *ḥadīth* collections contain traditions that mention the sweetness of faith but say that a servant tastes this under three conditions. One of these is loving another person for God's sake; none of the traditions conclude the way al-Sulamī's does. The final clause in al-Sulamī's version, 'until he loves for his brother what he wants for himself', parallels a tradition of al-Ṭabarānī verbatim, although al-Ṭabarānī's does not connect it to the sweetness of faith. That tradition simply reads, 'A man does not believe until he loves for his brother what he wants for himself.' Al-Sulamī, *KAṢ*, 24; al-Ṭabarānī, *al-Mu'jam al-awsaṭ*, 8:356, Ḥ. 8861.
136 Salamah-Qudsi spells out many faces of the intra-Ṣūfī conflicts in al-Sulamī's day.
137 Al-Sulamī, *KAṢ*, 30, 54. This *ḥadīth* does not exist in any of the major Sunnī collections, and al-Sulamī fails to provide a chain of transmission both times that he refers to it in *Kitāb ādāb al-ṣuḥba*, a treatise in which he often furnishes the *isnād*. Different versions of the tradition circulated, most of which share the phrase cited by al-Sulamī (*niyyat al-mu'min khayr min 'amalihi*) verbatim but diverge in the additional phrases that follow. Depending on the chain of transmission, Al-Albānī judged it either defective (*mawḍū'*) or weak. Al-Albānī, *Silsilat al-aḥādīth al-ḍa'īfa*, 5:244–5, Ḥ. 2216; 6:303–5, Ḥ. 2789; 13:121–6, Ḥ. 6045–6. See Kister's footnote for other sources.

4 Ṣuḥba *in comparison: al-Sulamī's near contemporaries*

1 Lenn E. Goodman, *Islamic Humanism* (New York: Oxford University Press, 2003), 105.
2 Miskawayh, *Tahdhīb al-akhlāq*, 29; *Traité d'éthique*, trans. Mohammed Arkoun (Damascus: Institut français de Damas, 1969), 22. Zurayk here translates 'civic being' for *madanī*; Arkoun translates *politique par nature*. Miskawayh follows this citation of Aristotle with a reference to the *madīna*, saying that human beings need to live in a city with a large population to find true happiness. This statement seems to commend Zurayk's translation, but here, Miskwayh's emphasis falls on the aggregate number of people rather than on the distinctive expression of a large population,

a city. That is, *madanī* means that individuals cannot achieve authentic happiness without social connections broader than a household or a small village; these smaller groupings are not sufficiently 'social' to facilitate the fullness of happiness (Gk. *eudaimonia*, Ar. *sa'āda*). Confusion about the necessity of a city-state (or lack thereof) arises from ambiguity in the texts of Aristotle himself. Aristotle uses the phrase *zoon politikon* in three different senses in his writings: to refer to a human person's need for the city-state, to refer to a person's need for sociability inclusive of all social institutions (including the city-state) and to refer to a person's need to share in collective activity with other members of the same species (a need also observed in some non-human animals that do not participate in the human institution of the city-state). For discussion, see R. G. Mulgan, 'Aristotle's Doctrine that Man is a Political Animal', *Hermes* 102, no. 3 (1974), 438–45; for Miskawayh's approach towards the mutual affinity of animals, see *Tahdhīb al-akhlāq*, 136–7. Some Muslim philosophers in the period drew upon Arabic translations of Aristotle's key phrase here as *ḥayawān insī* rather than *madanī*; the closest passage in the predominant translation of the *Nicomachean Ethics* reads *madanī*. Al-Fārābī, '*Kitāb taḥṣīl al-sa'āda*', in *Rasā'il al-Fārābī* (Hyderabad: Maṭba'at Majlis Dā'irat al-Ma'ārif al-'Uthmāniyya, 1926), 14, cited in Louise Marlow, *Hierarchy and Egalitarianism in Islamic Thought* (Cambridge: Cambridge University Press, 1997), 51; Aristotle, *The Arabic Version of the Nicomachean Ethics*, 132–3, 516–17 (1097b, 1169b).

3 Miskawayh, *Tahdhīb al-akhlāq*, 11, 135; Yaḥyā b. 'Adī, *The Reformation of Morals*, 106–7; Omar, *Christian and Muslim Ethics*, 221; Alshaar, *Ethics in Islam*, 47.

4 Miskawayh, *Tahdhīb al-akhlāq*, 29–30, 155, 168; for discussion, see Omar, *Christian and Muslim Ethics*, 222–3.

5 Alshaar, *Ethics in Islam*, 214.

6 MacIntyre's notion of practices in *After Virtue* depended upon the distinction between internal goods and external goods; *Dependent Rational Animals* contains his attempt to explore the notion of common goods in greater detail. MacIntyre, *After Virtue*, 187–203; *Dependent Rational Animals*, 63–80, 99–118.

7 MacIntyre, *Whose Justice? Which Rationality?*, 141.

8 MacIntyre, *Dependent Rational Animals*, 129–46.

9 *Jawāmi' ādāb al-ṣūfiyya* contains vignettes that both encourage and criticize extremes of asceticism. To illustrate this contrast, see al-Sulamī, *JAṢ*, §8, 39.

10 For example, al-Sulamī, *JAṢ*, §165.

11 Al-Sulamī, *JAṢ*, §27, 67, 106, 108.

12 Al-Sulamī, *JAṢ*, §113, 167–8.

13 For discussion, see Vasalou, *Virtues of Greatness*, 13–64.

14 Aristotle, *The Arabic Version of the Nicomachean Ethics*, 210–13 (1123b).

15 Miskawayh, *Tahdhīb al-akhlāq*, 21; Vasalou, *Virtues of Greatness*, 22–3. Vasalou emphasizes that Miskawayh also includes *'iẓam al-himma*, 'greatness of spirit', as a virtue; this latter virtue constitutes a key contribution of her study.

16 A prominent example lies in an anecdote al-Sulamī transmits in *Ṭabaqāt al-ṣūfiyya*. 'Al-Junayd said, '*Futuwwa* is letting go of [one's own] opinion and abandoning [one's] connections.' Abū Ḥafṣ [al-Naysābūrī] said, 'What you have said is beautiful. But according to me, *futuwwa* is not justice (*adā' al-inṣāf*), but abandoning [one's] claim to justice (*tark muṭālabat al-inṣāf*).' Al-Junayd said, 'Arise, dear companions, for Abū Ḥafṣ is greater than Adam and his progeny.' Al-Sulamī, *TṢ*, 107–8, trans. Ridgeon, with slight modifications. For discussion, see Ridgeon, *Morals and Mysticism in Persian Sufism*, 32.

17 Yaḥyā b. 'Adī, *The Reformation of Morals*, 34–5. Translation Griffith's.
18 Yaḥyā b. 'Adī, *The Reformation of Morals*, 72–5. Translation Griffith's.
19 Yaḥyā b. 'Adī, *The Reformation of Morals*, 116–17.
20 Miskawayh, *Tahdhīb al-akhlāq*, 155.
21 See the discussion of Cicero in Julian Haseldine, 'Friendship, Equality and Universal Harmony: The Universal and the Particular in Aelred of Rievaulx's *De Spiritali Amicitia*,' in *Friendship East and West*, ed. Oliver Leaman (Surrey: Curzon, 1995), 192–214.
22 Miskawayh, *Tahdhīb al-akhlāq*, 155. Because Miskawayh typically urges moderation, his failure to criticize love in excess is striking. Miskawayh restricts his comment to the reason for the excess involved; if the passionate lover loves due to a desire for pleasure, the love is blameworthy, but if the lover loves due to a love for the good, the love is praiseworthy.
23 Fakhry, *Ethical Theories in Islam*, 104.
24 In the period, Muslims studying texts interacted intensively with a competent instructor. This model cannot be presumed as universal for all Christians, but it remained the most common form of pedagogy for all living in Yaḥyā b. 'Adī's Baghdad; Yaḥyā seems to presume it, or at the bare minimum, presumes a study circle composed of persons with some level of competence in the matter at hand. Jonathan Porter Berkey, *The Transmission of Knowledge in Medieval Cairo: A Social History of Islamic Education* (Princeton, NJ: Princeton University Press, 1992), 21.
25 Makdisi assumes that 'Abd al-Laṭīf thus tacitly recognizes that several people in fact were attempting to study in an autodidactic way. Al-Jāḥiẓ encouraged such self-study, arguing that the writing of books promotes social cohesion precisely because when one studies them in isolation, one is free of the prideful inclination to triumph in the debates that occur when one studies with others. Books by their nature encourage solitary study and diminish the causes of factionalism. However, the possibility of self-study does not annul the fact that in the period books were not often studied in isolation, but at the hand of a master. George Makdisi, *The Rise of Humanism in Classical Islam and the Christian West: With Special Reference to Scholasticism* (Edinburgh: Edinburgh University Press, 1990), 217–29, esp. 223; cf. Shawkat M. Toorawa, *Ibn Abī Ṭāhir Ṭayfūr and Arabic Writerly Culture: A Ninth-Century Bookman in Baghdad* (New York: RoutledgeCurzon, 2005), 1, 13–15; James E. Montgomery, *Al-Jāḥiẓ: In Praise of Books* (Edinburgh: Edinburgh University Press, 2013), 166; for a longer translation of the relevant passage from 'Abd al-Laṭīf, see George Makdisi, *The Rise of Colleges: Institutions of Learning in Islam and the West* (Edinburgh: University Press, 1981), 89.
26 See Miskawayh, *Tahdhīb al-akhlāq*, 135–73; Alshaar, *Ethics in Islam*, 163–4.
27 Aristotle, *Aristotle's Ethics: Writings from the Complete Works*, ed. Jonathan Barnes and Anthony Kenny (Princeton, NJ: Princeton University Press, 2014), 305–6 (1156a).
28 Miskawayh, *Tahdhīb al-akhlāq*, 137; Fakhry, *Ethical Theories in Islam*, 116.
29 Hélène Raymond, 'Sadāqa: l'amitié dans la tradition philosophique arabe', in *Encyclopédie de l'humanisme méditerranéen*, ed. Houari Touati, http://www.encyclopedie-humanisme.com/?Amitie-en-contexte-islamique.
30 Alshaar, *Ethics in Islam*, 185.
31 Alshaar, *Ethics in Islam*, 167.
32 Both philosophers identify *mawadda* with this affective component of sociability; Miskawayh's definition of *ṣadāqa* leaves the difference between *ṣadāqa* and *mawadda*

difficult to discern. Raymond, 'Sadāqa: l'amitié dans la tradition philosophique arabe'; Miskawayh, *Tahdhīb al-akhlāq*, 137–8.

33 Alshaar, *Ethics in Islam*, 47.

34 For a defence of Aristotle against the charge of egoism, see Lenn E. Goodman, 'Friendship in Aristotle, Miskawayh and Al-Ghazali', in Leaman, *Friendship East and West*, 165. Frederic M. Schroeder offers a more robust defence, claiming that the social character of goods annuls the contradiction between self-love and altruism; for Schroeder, calling Aristotle an egoist poses a false dilemma. Frederic M. Schroeder, 'Friendship in Aristotle and Some Peripatetic Philosophers', in *Greco-Roman Perspectives on Friendship*, ed. John T. Fitzgerald (Atlanta: Scholars Press, 1997), 41. For further discussion, including an argument that even pleasure-based friendships and utility-based friendships are not as entirely self-serving as one might initially assume, see John M. Cooper, 'Aristotle on the Forms of Friendship', *The Review of Metaphysics* 30, no. 4 (1977): 640–3.

35 MacIntyre, *Dependent Rational Animals*, 119.

36 MacIntyre, *Dependent Rational Animals*, 161.

37 Three well-known examples are Arkoun's monograph on Miskawayh and monographs by Kraemer and Makdisi on the period; each has also written shorter pieces in response to debates prompted by their work. Kraemer argues that the Būyid era shows signs of the 'discovery of the individual' or the 'strong sense of self-awareness' often attributed to developments in Italy in the fourteenth century. Mohammed Arkoun, *L'humanisme arabe au IVᵉ–Xᵉ siècle: Miskawayh, philosophe et historien*, 2nd ed. (Paris: Vrin, 1982); Makdisi, *The Rise of Humanism*; Joel L. Kraemer, *Humanism in the Renaissance of Islam: The Cultural Revival During the Buyid Age* (Leiden: Brill, 1986), 11–13.

38 Paul L. Heck, 'Friendship in the Service of Governance: *Makārim al-Akhlāq* in 'Abbāsid Political Culture', in *The Heritage of Arabo-Islamic Learning: Studies Presented to Wadad Kadi*, ed. Maurice A. Pomerantz and Aram A. Shahin (Leiden: Brill, 2015), 74–5.

39 Marc Bergé argues this point in his seminal monograph on al-Tawḥīdī. Marc Bergé, *Pour un humanisme vécu: Abū Ḥayyān al-Tawḥīdī* (Damascus: Institut français de Damas, 1979), 318.

40 Alshaar, *Ethics in Islam*, 159.

41 Alshaar argues this point at length. Alshaar, *Ethics in Islam*, 207, 225. One can recall here too Alexander Key's observation about the malleability of concepts like 'individualism' and 'humanism': they can be cast to mean almost anything, in which case they lack analytical force, or they can be used with their strict meaning in the context of European political history, in which case their application to a foreign culture like medieval Islam is anachronistic. Alexander Key, 'The Applicability of the Term "Humanism" to Abū Ḥayyān al-Tawḥīdī', *SI* 100 (2005): 75.

42 Alshaar, *Ethics in Islam*, 159–60.

43 Alshaar argues for a more hopeful reading of al-Tawḥīdī but perhaps overstates the difference between herself and Bergé on this point. While Bergé acknowledges the numerous obstacles to friendship catalogued by al-Tawḥīdī, he also emphasizes that in the end authentic friendship does exist. Alshaar, *Ethics in Islam*, 129–33; Marc Bergé, 'Une anthologie sur l'amitié d'Abū Ḥayyān at-Tawḥīdī', *BEO* 16 (1958): 40–5, 51ff.

44 Alshaar, *Ethics in Islam*, 45–6.

45 For further discussion, see Paul L. Heck, *Skepticism in Classical Islam: Moments of Confusion* (New York: Routledge, 2014), 66–107, esp. 75–80. For a passage in which al-Tawḥīdī justifies the existence of disputational theology (*'ilm al-kalām*), albeit with clear apprehension about its pitfalls and dangers, see Abū Ḥayyān 'Alī b. Muḥammad al-Tawḥīdī, *Risāla fī l-'ulūm*, in *Risālatān*, ed. al-Tawḥīdī (Constantinople: Maṭba'at al-Jawā'ib, 1883), 203. Al-Tawḥīdī himself was proficient in multiple fields of knowledge and generally attempted to rise above this kind of intellectual tribalism. He leaned more towards *fiqh, ḥadīth* and philosophy than to *kalām* or grammar but was fundamentally moderate, taking an intermediary stance between different groups. Alshaar, *Ethics in Islam*, 63.

46 Alshaar, *Ethics in Islam*, 162.

47 Alshaar, *Ethics in Islam*, 72, 175.

48 Bergé, 'Une anthologie sur l'amitié', 40.

49 Bergé, *Pour un humanisme vécu*, 408–9.

50 Bergé, *Pour un humanisme vécu*, 320–2.

51 Joel L. Kraemer expresses concern that much of our knowledge about al-Sijistānī's thought survives in the work of al-Tawḥīdī, a man with a reputation for forgery. Kraemer concludes, however, that although al-Tawḥīdī likely reformulated several of al-Sijistānī's arguments, al-Tawḥīdī did not simply use al-Sijistānī as a mouthpiece for al-Tawḥīdī's own ideas or as a foil against which to formulate his own superior position. Joel L. Kraemer, *Philosophy in the Renaissance of Islam: Abū Sulaymān al-Sijistānī and his Circle* (Leiden: Brill, 1986), 44.

52 Alshaar, *Ethics in Islam*, 164.

53 Al-Tawḥīdī, *al-Ṣadāqa wa-l-ṣadīq*, in *Risālatān*, 27; Kāmil Muṣṭafā l-Shaybī, *Sharḥ Dīwān al-Ḥallāj Abī l-Mughīth al-Ḥusayn b. Manṣūr b. Maḥmā l-Bayḍāwī* (Cologne: Al-Kamel Verlag, 2007), 290–1 (#52); Louis Massignon, *Le Dîwân d'al-Ḥallâj* (Paris: Paul Geuthner, 1931 = *Journal asiatique* 218 [Janvier – Mars 1931]), 68–9 (M.N. 32).

54 Massignon's translation shows that he clearly understood them in this way.

55 Al-Tawḥīdī, *al-Ṣadāqa wa-l-ṣadīq*, 67; Aristotle, *The Arabic Version of the Nicomachean Ethics*, 494–5 (1166a), 514–17 (1169b); Bergé, *Pour un humanisme vécu*, 324. Al-Tawḥīdī also manifests the influence of the Brethren of Purity. If Alshaar is correct that Ḥallājian notions of *ḥulūl* work their way into al-Tawḥīdī's understanding of *ṣadāqa*, this would clearly differentiate al-Sulamī from al-Tawḥīdī. While al-Sulamī does include an entry for al-Ḥallāj in *Ṭabaqāt al-ṣūfiyya*, he does not attempt to rehabilitate some of al-Ḥallāj's more provocative and controversial ideas. Al-Sulamī names the assertion of *ḥulūl* as an error some Ṣūfīs commit, and he explicitly rejects it. The possibility that Alshaar sees here does, however, permit for another innocent though perhaps unlikely explanation: seeing that al-Tawḥīdī only cites the final line of al-Ḥallāj's poem, al-Tawḥīdī might not have known its source or its original context. Alshaar, *Ethics in Islam*, 164–5, 223; al-Sulamī, *ṬṢ*, 307–11; *GṢ*, §28, 33, 38; Bergé, *Pour un humanisme vécu*, 15–19; Mojaddedi, *The Biographical Tradition in Sufism*, 42.

56 Alshaar, *Ethics in Islam*, 167.

57 Al-Sulamī, *KAṢ*, 53–5.

58 While Bulliet's pioneering research has spurred many scholars to discuss the factionalism in Nishapur, the troubled life of al-Tawḥīdī in several locales shows that a concern about toxic *'aṣabiyya* was far from limited to that city and continued well into the Seljuq period. For discussion, see Deborah G. Tor, 'Rayy and the Religious History of the Seljūq Period', 388–92.

59 Roy Mottahedeh famously divided these into 'acquired loyalties' of oath and benefit and 'loyalties of category' that rested upon family ties, similarity of occupation, geographic origin, or other categories. Roy Mottahedeh, *Loyalty and Leadership in an Early Islamic Society* (London: I.B. Tauris, 2001), 6.
60 Alshaar, *Ethics in Islam*, 166, 173.
61 Al-Sulamī, *KAṢ*, 23.
62 This point emerges strikingly in al-Tawḥīdī's citation of several sayings attributed to Jesus, some of which are consistent with the canonical gospels and others not. One of the non-canonical sayings restricts the universal thrust of neighbour love found in the other sayings cited, casting Jesus as a proponent of intimate friendship à la al-Tawḥīdī. al-Tawḥīdī, *Al-Ṣadāqa wa-l-ṣadīq*, 64; Bergé, *Pour un humanisme vécu*, 326–9.
63 Alshaar, *Ethics in Islam*, 168.
64 Al-Tawḥīdī's resentment of hierarchy rubs against the approach of many of his contemporaries among the literary elites. The Brethren of Purity, for example, craft an elaborate description of the divinely ordained social hierarchy; they saw a coherence in the universe that only intellectuals were able to perceive. *Mirrors for Princes* works likewise reinforced established social structures. For discussion, see Marlow, *Hierarchy and Egalitarianism in Islamic Thought*, esp. 117–55. Al-Sulamī did not prepare an influential work in this genre, though he did write a very brief collection of counsels for princes and viziers that has not yet received discussion in the scholarly literature. Al-Sulamī, *FNU.*
65 Alshaar, *Ethics in Islam*, 172.
66 Alshaar, *Ethics in Islam*, 203.
67 Wadād al-Qāḍī summarizes that al-Tawḥīdī 'took to the ascetic way of Sufi groups early in life' and that he died 'as a poor, lonely Sufi in exile', assumptions accepted by Lidia Bettini in her translation of *al-Hawāmil wa-l-shawāmil*. Many modern scholars, including Brockelmann, likewise accept Yāqūt's description of al-Tawḥīdī as a Ṣūfī shaykh, even though Ṣūfī biographical dictionaries do not include him and other works of *ṭabaqāt* either do not identify him with Ṣūfī practice or refer to it in only oblique ways. Unfortunately, some works attributed to al-Tawḥīdī that could clarify his relationship to *taṣawwuf* do not survive, but Watt's simple assessment that al-Tawḥīdī's intellectual formation involved 'at least a smattering of Sufism' is probably not far off the mark. For extended discussion of al-Tawḥīdī's engagement with Sufism, see Bergé, Key and Alshaar. Al-Qāḍī, 'Abū Ḥayyān al-Tawḥīdī: A Sunnī Voice in the Shī'ī Century', 128; al-Tawḥīdī and Miskawayh, *Il libro dei cammelli errabondi e di quelli che li radunano*, trans. Lidia Bettini (Venice: Edizioni Ca' Foscari, 2017), 29; Yāqūt al-Ḥamawī, *Mu'jam al-udabā'* (Beirut: Dār al-Gharb al-Islāmī, 1993), 2:1925 (#820); Bergé, *Pour un humanisme vécu*, 15–19; Key, 'The Applicability of the Term "Humanism" to Abū Ḥayyān al-Tawḥīdī', 73–8; Alshaar, *Ethics in Islam*, 61–2; W. Montgomery Watt, 'Abū Ḥayyān Tawḥīdī,' *EI*[2].
68 *Al-Ṣadāqa wa-l-ṣadīq* contains at least three references to al-Junayd, as well as isolated references to al-Fuḍayl b. 'Iyāḍ, al-Shiblī, Ruwaym, Abū 'Uthmān al-Ḥīrī and other Ṣūfī masters. Most notably, al-Tawḥīdī recalls an exchange in which al-Junayd was asked with whom he keeps company. Al-Junayd responded, 'With the person who forgets the amount of his wealth and makes judgments according to what he is obliged to do.' Al-Tawḥīdī, *al-Ṣadāqa wa-l-ṣadīq*, 142; al-Sulamī, *TṢ*, 161 (#25).
69 Al-Tawḥīdī, *al-Ṣadāqa wa-l-ṣadīq*, 38.

70 Bergé, *Pour un humanisme vécu*, 330, 337. For al-Tawḥīdī's attempts to parse the nuances in key terms like *ṣadāqa*, *ʿalāqa*, *maḥabba*, *ʿishq*, *ḥanīn* and others, see *al-Ṣadāqa wa-l-ṣadīq*, 44, 67.
71 Miskawayh, *Tahdhīb al-akhlāq*, 148–9.
72 MacIntyre, *Dependent Rational Animals*, 119–28.
73 Al-Sulamī rejects, for example, pseudo-Ṣūfīs who prefer freedom (*ḥurriyya*) to servanthood (*ʿubūdiyya*), but this rhetoric responds to a very different set of claims than does MacIntyre. Al-Sulamī, *GṢ*, §24.
74 MacIntyre, *Dependent Rational Animals*, 164.
75 Alshaar, *Ethics in Islam*, 173.
76 Cf. Marlow, *Hierarchy and Egalitarianism in Islamic Thought*, 45.
77 I have argued that al-Sulamī attempts a 'sufization' of his society, in the sense that he desires to transform that society by infusing it with the virtues of *taṣawwuf*. One could credibly argue that he intends instead a 'futuwwization' of his society, so central are the principal elements of *futuwwa* to his spiritual pedagogy. On balance, his literary corpus leans much more heavily on the rhetoric of *taṣawwuf* than that of *futuwwa*, but his integration of *futuwwa* under the umbrella of *taṣawwuf* shows that he sees a near-perfect alignment between the values associated with each.
78 Deborah G. Tor's research exemplifies the dichotomy associated with *futuwwa*, as she attempts to rehabilitate the reputation of the *ʿayyār*s as violent rogues. She locates the initial connection between Sufism, *futuwwa* and the *ʿayyār*s in the third/ninth century, a much earlier period than many scholars presuppose. The chivalric ideals connoted by these terms were never unambiguous because they always carried an element of violent power. The use of force can maintain social order or threaten it; al-Tawḥīdī's reticence about *futuwwa* suggests his preoccupation with the latter. Deborah G. Tor, *Violent Order: Religious Warfare, Chivalry, and the* ʿAyyār *Phenomenon in the Medieval Islamic World* (Würzburg: Ergon, 2007), 195–218, 231–87.
79 Sedgwick, 'The Organisation of Mysticism', 342.
80 Chowdhury, *A Ṣūfī Apologist*, 41.
81 The parallels between al-Sulamī's *Kitāb al-futuwwa* and *Kitāb ādāb al-ṣuḥba* are numerous. Both involve the attempt to infuse society with spiritual-moral ideals often associated with Sufism or the Path of Blame. Thibon, *L'œuvre*, 266–8.
82 For a discussion of al-Tawḥīdī's approach to the general social relations signified by *ʿishra* and the more specific bond of *ṣadāqa*, see Bergé, *Pour un humanisme vécu*, 317.
83 Al-Tawḥīdī, *al-Ṣadāqa wa-l-ṣadīq*, 24; Alshaar, *Ethics in Islam*, 171.
84 One might assume that al-ʿĀmirī, 'the Philosopher of Nishapur', would make the best point of comparison to al-Sulamī, as he was immensely popular in his day. Unfortunately, the most relevant work attributed to him, *Kitāb al-saʿāda wa-l-isʿād*, was most likely composed by someone else and possibly postdates al-Sulamī. Al-ʿĀmirī, Abū l-Ḥasan Muḥammad b. Yūsuf and Elvira Wakelnig, *Feder, Tafel, Mensch: Al-ʿĀmirīs Kitāb al-fuṣūl fī l-maʿālim al-ilāhīya und die arabische Proklos-Rezeption im 10. Jh.* (Leiden: Brill, 2006), 35–9; Everett K. Rowson, 'The Philosopher as Littérateur: Al-Tawḥīdī and His Predecessors', *Zeitschrift für Geschichte der arabisch-islamischen Wissenschaften* 6 (1990): 88; see also Wakelnig, 'Philosophical Fragments of Al-ʿĀmirī', 235–6.
85 Alshaar, *Ethics in Islam*, 213.
86 Luca Patrizi, 'Ṣūfī Terminology of Power', in Alexandre Papas, *Handbook of Sufi Studies* (Leiden: Brill, 2021), 294.

87 I borrow this term from Heck, who describes modern Ṣūfīs 'engaged with society but in principle distant from worldly power'. Paul L. Heck, 'The Politics of Sufism: Is there One?', in *Sufism Today: Heritage and Tradition in the Global Community*, ed. Catharina Raudvere and Leif Stenberg (New York: I.B. Tauris, 2009), 14.
88 For an outstanding recent study of the attempts by Saladin and subsequent leaders to utilize Ṣūfīs to legitimate their rule as well as accumulate blessings and merit for themselves, see Hofer, *The Popularisation of Sufism in Ayyubid and Mamluk Egypt*, 35–104, esp. 35–60.
89 Al-Mustamlī al-Bukhārī records a variant version of the exchange that involves al-Shiblī and Abū Ḥafṣ. Al-Sulamī, *KAṢ*, 86; al-Kharkūshī, *Tahdhīb al-asrār*, 214; al-Qushayrī, *Risāla*, B. al-adab; al-Mustamlī al-Bukhārī, *Sharḥ Kitāb al-ta'arruf li-madhhab al-taṣawwuf* (Tehran: Chāpkhānih-yi Dānishgāh-i Tehrān, 1346 H.), 1:192–3; cf. al-Sulamī, *ṬṢ*, 122 (#33); for discussion, see Patrizi, 'Ṣūfī Terminology of Power', 294–5; Salamah-Qudsi, *Sufism and Early Islamic Piety*, 159–60.
90 *Kitāb adab al-mulūk fī bayān ḥaqā'iq al-taṣawwuf [Ein Handbuch zur islamischen Mystik aus dem 4./10. Jahrhundert]*, ed. Bernd Radtke (Beirut: Franz Steiner Verlag, 1991).
91 Patrizi, 'Ṣūfī Terminology of Power,' 300.
92 He includes in *Ṭabaqāt al-ṣūfiyya* the same maxim of Abū Ḥafṣ, shorn of the crack by al-Junayd that prompted it. al-Sulamī, *ṬṢ*, 122 (#33).
93 The most significant passage in this regard is a statement al-Sulamī attributes to the Umayyad caliph 'Umar b. 'Abd al-'Azīz (d. 101/720) instructing anyone who wants to accompany him to do so in five ways, then detailing the type of advice he will require. Al-Sulamī, *FNU*, §204.
94 Al-Fuḍayl b. 'Iyāḍ and Yaḥyā b. Mu'ādh (d. 258/871–2) are the most notable exceptions to this rule; figures like Dhū l-Nūn or al-Junayd whom al-Sulamī cites most frequently elsewhere are absent entirely. Al-Sulamī, *FNU*, §211.
95 Even al-Sulamī's short compilation *Dhikr miḥan al-mashāyikh al-ṣūfiyya* records the struggles of famous Ṣūfī masters with other members of the *'ulamā'*, not solely with caliphs, viziers or others acting at their command.
96 Al-Sulamī, *FNU*, §198.
97 Al-Sulamī, *KAṢ*, 53–5.
98 Sedgwick, 'The Organisation of Mysticism', 337.
99 Honerkamp, 'The Ethical-Mystical Foundations of the Master-Disciple Relationship'.
100 Arthur F. Buehler, *Recognizing Sufism: Contemplation in the Islamic Tradition* (London: I. B. Tauris, 2016), 141.
101 Margaret Malamud, 'Gender and Spiritual Self-Fashioning: The Master-Disciple Relationship in Classical Sufism', *JAAR* 64, no. 1 (1996): 90. Malamud lays great emphasis on the gendered language for this relationship, including spiritual paternity and eroticism; Denis Gril roots this spiritual paternity in the Prophet's relationship with his companions. By the time of Abū Ḥafṣ 'Umar al-Suhrawardī's (d. 632/1234) *'Awārif al-ma'ārif*, these themes are important in Ṣūfī literature, but I find them almost entirely absent in al-Sulamī and rare in al-Qushayrī; Malamud falls into an overgeneralization about the formative period here. To take one example, al-Sulamī's compilation of Ṣūfī *tafsīr* on the early verses of *Sūrat al-Aḥzāb*, the verses Gril paints as the fount for this understanding of the Prophet as spiritual father, contains no comments along the lines of the approach to gender Malamud emphasizes. Al-Sulamī, *ḤT*, 2:140–2 (Q. 33:1–8); *ZḤT*, 129–30 (Q. 33:1–8); Denis Gril, 'Le modèle prophétique du maître spirituel en Islam,' in *Maestro e discepolo: Temi e*

problemi della direzione spirituale tra VI secolo a.C. e VII secolo d.C., ed. Giovanni Filoramo (Brescia: Morcelliana, 2002), 345–6, 351.

102 For a historical survey, see Karamustafa, *Sufism: The Formative Period*, 114–42.

103 al-Sulamī, *AMM*.

104 Fritz Meier, Ḫurāsān und das Ende der klassischen Ṣūfik', in *Atti del Convegno internazionale sul Tema: La Persia nel Medioevo* (Rome: Accademia Nazionale dei Lincei, 1971), 131–56; Eng. trans. 'Khurāsān and the End of Classical Sufism', in *Essays on Islamic Piety and Mysticism*, 189–219.

105 Meier, 'Khurāsān and the End of Classical Sufism', 217.

106 Meier, 'Khurāsān and the End of Classical Sufism', 195–6.

107 Meier, 'Khurāsān and the End of Classical Sufism', 200.

108 Knysh, *Sufism: A New History of Islamic Mysticism*, 153.

109 Silvers, 'The Teaching Relationship in Early Sufism', 69–97.

110 Along similar lines, Malamud describes al-Sulamī as a combination of the *shaykh al-taʿlīm* and *shaykh al-tarbiya*. She sees a parallel between the evolution of Ṣūfī structures of authority and the formation of the legal schools. 'The history of Sufism and the legal schools is intertwined.' Margaret Malamud, 'Sufi Organizations and Structures of Authority in Medieval Nishapur', *IJMES* 26, no. 3 (1994): 437.

111 Silvers, 'The Teaching Relationship in Early Sufism', 77.

112 Silvers, 'The Teaching Relationship in Early Sufism', 85–6.

113 Silvers, 'The Teaching Relationship in Early Sufism', 92.

114 Jamil M. Abun-Nasr's response to the data is tempting: he finds in the available information 'no basis for a comparison between the Sufi *shaykhs*' relationship with their disciples in the eleventh century and in former times'. Without doubt, Ṣūfī shaykhs had begun to emerge as authoritative guides of distinct Ṣūfī groups by the second half of the fourth/tenth century, and this identity was clear and coherent by the second half of the fifth/eleventh century, but Abun-Nasr insists that a supposed distinction between *taʿlīm* and *tarbiya* prior to this cannot be sustained. Denis Gril has favoured the terms 'spiritual education' and 'spiritual guidance' over 'spiritual direction', but not in an explicit attempt to stake a position vis-à-vis Meier and Silvers on the matter of *taʿlīm/tarbiya*. Gril's methodological approach can be helpful: rather than trying to isolate the comportment of the Prophet with his companions in terms of discrete, repeatable customs, he attends to the holistic manner in which the Prophet formed his companions and the way that they later transmitted the Prophet's teaching. He suggests that Muḥammad taught his closest companions different rituals than those used by ordinary believers, and Gril considers it incontestable that the Prophet did not treat all his companions equally. Instead, the Prophet transmitted certain specific teachings to some and not to others. Gril's insistence that this type of individualized teaching existed both in the time of the Prophet and in the example of Ibrāhīm b. Adham, suggests Gril's fundamental agreement with Silvers. Buehler's earlier work utilizes the distinction between teaching and directing and then extends it to delineate the role of the mediating shaykh, but his chapter on 'The Relationship between the Shaykh and the Seeker' in *Recognizing Sufism* never invokes the distinction. Abun-Nasr, *Muslim Communities of Grace*, 59; Denis Gril, 'Compagnons ou disciples? La *ṣuḥba* et ses exigences: l'exemple d'Ibrāhīm b. Adham d'après la *Ḥilyat al-awliyāʾ*', in Gobillot and Thibon, *Les maîtres soufis et leurs disciples*, 36; Gril, 'Le modèle prophétique du maître spirituel en Islam', 356; Buehler, *Recognizing Sufism*, 141–60.

115 Ridgeon finds no evidence that Ṣūfī lodges had developed by this period, but this does not exclude the possibility that they existed; other corporate organizations like the Karrāmiyya had such spaces. Ridgeon, *Morals and Mysticism in Persian Sufism*, 45.

116 Trimingham lays emphasis on this point, but the authenticity of these rules is uncertain. Paul Ballanfat, accepting the attribution of these rules, insists that Abū Sa'īd's spiritual method involved an exclusive intimacy between master and disciple and that Abū Sa'īd certainly engaged in this type of spiritual direction. Gerhard Böwering and Matthew Melvin-Koushki, 'Ḵānaqāh', *EIr*; Trimingham, *The Sufi Orders in Islam*, 166–7; Paul Ballanfat, 'La direction spirituelle chez Abū Sa'īd b. Abī l-Ḫayr (357–440/967–1049)', in Gobillot and Thibon, *Les maîtres soufis et leurs disciples*, 263, 269–74.

117 Knysh, *Sufism: A New History of Islamic Mysticism*, 154–6.

118 Thibon employs the distinction in many of his writings, insisting that al-Sulamī functioned as a *shaykh al-tarbiya*; for other scholars continuing to find value in this distinction, see Christopher Melchert, 'Review of *Sufism, Black and White: A Critical Edition of* Kitāb al-Bayāḍ wa-l-Sawād *by Abū l-Ḥasan al-Sīrjānī (d. ca. 470/1077)*, ed. Bilal Orfali and Nada Saab', *JIS* 24, no. 2 (2013): 205; Malamud, 'Sufism in Twelfth-Century Baghdad: The Sufi Practices and Ribâṭ of Abû Najîb Al-Suhrawardî', *The Bulletin of the Henry Martyn Institute of Islamic Studies* 13 (1994): 6; Chiabotti, "Abd al-Karīm al-Qushayrī (d. 465/1072): Family Ties and Transmission in Nishapur's Sufi Milieu during the Tenth and Eleventh Centuries,' in *Family Portraits with Saints: Hagiography, Sanctity, and Family in the Muslim World*, ed. Catherine Mayeur-Jaouen and Alexandre Papas (Berlin: Klaus Schwarz Verlag, 2014), 299; Harith bin Ramli, 'The Sālimiyya and Abū Ṭālib al-Makkī: The Transmission of Theological Teachings in a Basran Circle of Mystics', in Gobillot and Thibon, *Les maîtres soufis et leurs disciples*, 101; Qureshi, 'The Book of Errors: A Critical Edition and Study of *Kitāb al-Aghālit*', 69.

119 MacIntyre, *Three Rival Versions*, 65.

120 MacIntyre, *Three Rival Versions*, 129.

121 Knysh, *Sufism: A New History of Islamic Mysticism*, 156–7.

122 MacIntyre, *After Virtue*, 207.

123 MacIntyre, *After Virtue*, 214–19.

124 MacIntyre's famous invocation of St. Benedict of Nursia in the final lines of *After Virtue* illustrates this lacuna: Benedict did not wait out the dark ages in solitude, but founded an alternative community to embody the narrative of the Christian life and grow in the virtues. MacIntyre, *After Virtue*, 263; L. Gregory Jones, 'Alasdair MacIntyre on Narrative, Community, and the Moral Life', *Modern Theology* 4, no. 1 (1987): 60–6.

125 Silvers, 'The Teaching Relationship in Early Sufism,' 78.

126 Al-Sarrāj, *Kitāb al-luma'*, B. dhikr ādābihim fī l-ṣuḥba. Some of the material in this section appears in various writings of al-Sulamī or in al-Kharkūshī's *Tahdhīb al-asrār*, and much was reproduced, either verbatim or with minor alterations, by al-Qushayrī, al-Sīrjānī, Abū Khalaf al-Ṭabarī and other later compilers. Notes within these passages of al-Sarrāj indicate some of the places where this material appears but do not attempt to be comprehensive. Where these various sources depend upon each other textually, al-Sarrāj can be presumed to be the source on which the others rely.

127 Al-Kharkūshī, *Tahdhīb al-asrār*, 265; al-Qushayrī, *Risāla*, B. al-ṣuḥba; Abū Khalaf al-Ṭabarī, *Salwat al-ʿārifīn*, §646. Al-Qushayrī's and al-Ṭabarī's versions of this exchange explicitly state that the companion of the remaining person would be God; they banish doubt about whether Sahl urges the anonymous man to look to God for *ṣuḥba* or merely to find a different earthly companion.
128 Al-Qushayrī, *Risāla*, wa-minhum Abū 'Uthmān Saʿīd Ismāʿīl al-Ḥīrī.
129 Al-Kharkūshī, *Tahdhīb al-asrār*, 266; al-Qushayrī, *Risāla*, B. al-ṣuḥba; Abū Khalaf al-Ṭabarī, *Salwat al-ʿārifīn*, §650.
130 Al-Qushayrī, *Risāla*, B. aḥkāmihim fī l-safar; Abū Khalaf al-Ṭabarī, *Salwat al-ʿārifīn*, §652.
131 Al-Kharkūshī, *Tahdhīb al-asrār*, 266; al-Qushayrī, *Risāla*, B. al-ṣuḥba; al-Sīrjānī, *Kitāb al-bayāḍ wa-l-sawād*, §376, §379; cf. al-Sulamī, *SA*, §24.
132 Al-Sulamī, *KF*, 32; *DAṢ*, 552; al-Qushayrī, *Risāla*, B. aḥkāmihim fī l-safar; al-Sīrjānī, *Kitāb al-bayāḍ wa-l-sawād*, §374; Abū Khalaf al-Ṭabarī, *Salwat al-ʿārifīn*, §655; cf. the saying attributed to Bundār b. al-Ḥusayn, who considers such a question poor *adab*. Al-Sulamī, *ṬṢ*, 468 (#5).
133 Al-Kharkūshī, *Tahdhīb al-asrār*, 266; al-Sīrjānī, *Kitāb al-bayāḍ wa l-sawād*, §374; cf. al-Qushayrī, *Risāla*, B. al-irāda; and a near parallel followed by Burhān's commentary in al-Tawḥīdī, *al-Ṣadāqa wa-l-ṣadīq*, 29.
134 Al-Kharkūshī, *Tahdhīb al-asrār*, 266; al-Qushayrī, *Risāla*, B. al-ṣuḥba. Compare to the sayings attributed to al-Junayd, to Abū Yazīd al-Bisṭāmī and to the saying on which Abū 'Abdallāh b. Khafīf (d. 371/982) comments. Al-Sulamī, *ṬṢ*, 161 (#25); al-Sīrjānī, *Kitāb al-bayāḍ wa l-sawād*, §371, §377.
135 The prominence of conversion stories in Islamic hagiographical literature is well known. While not all of the shaykhs mentioned by al-Sarrāj have a conversion story of their own, their behaviour towards their potential companions manifests their presupposition of the significant change and spiritual awakening which occurs at the moment this bond is formed. For a full discussion of *tawba* in texts of the period, see Khalil, *Repentance and the Return to God*, 61–122; John Renard, *Friends of God: Islamic Images of Piety, Commitment, and Servanthood* (Berkeley: University of California Press, 2008), 43–65.
136 Al-Sulamī, *MTḤ*, 9–10; al-Qushayrī, *Risāla*, B. al-ṣuḥba; al-Sīrjānī, *Kitāb al-bayāḍ wa-l-sawād*, §374; cf. al-Sulamī, *DAṢ*, 551; *GṢ*, §27; *JAṢ*, §87.
137 Al-Qushayrī, *Risāla*, B. al-ṣuḥba; Abū Khalaf al-Ṭabarī, *Salwat al-ʿārifīn*, §647.
138 Al-Kharkūshī, *Tahdhīb al-asrār*, 265; al-Qushayrī, *Risāla*, B. al-ṣuḥba; al-Sīrjānī, *Kitāb al-bayāḍ wa-l-sawād*, §374.
139 Al-Qushayrī, *Risāla*, B. al-ṣuḥba; Abū Khalaf al-Ṭabarī, *Salwat al-ʿārifīn*, §646.
140 See also al-Sulamī, *JAṢ*, §87.
141 These are the types of prescriptions that appear elsewhere under the mantle of *ādāb*. Al-Sarrāj, *Kitāb al-lumaʿ*, B. ādābihim fī l-wuḍūʾ wa-l-ṭahārāt.
142 Neither al-Sulamī nor al-Qushayrī preserve an entry for him in their biographical dictionaries despite their clear reliance on *Kitāb al-lumaʿ*. Karamustafa, *Sufism: The Formative Period*, 68.
143 Martin Nguyen, 'Al-Daqqāq, Abū 'Alī,' *EI*[3].
144 Thibon, *L'œuvre*, 100–2.
145 Francesco Chiabotti, 'Entre soufisme et savoir islamique: L'œuvre de 'Abd al-Karīm al-Qushayrī (376–465/ 986–1072)' (PhD, Aix-Marseille Université, 2014), 612; Karamustafa, *Sufism: The Formative Period*, 65–7.

146 Chiabotti, 'Entre soufisme et savoir islamique', 173; cf. Martin Nguyen, *Sufi Master and Qur'an Scholar: Abū'l-Qāsim al-Qushayrī and the* Laṭā'if al-ishārāt (London: Oxford University Press, 2012), 57–8. Al-Qushayrī's close identification with al-Daqqāq shows especially in the initiatory *isnād*, which al-Qushayrī traces through al-Daqqāq. While these chains of spiritual lineage would become ubiquitous in later centuries as the *silsila*, al-Qushayrī's *Risāla* offers the second-earliest example of such a chain.

147 For discussion of this genealogy, see Bulliet, *The Patricians of Nishapur*, 150–9; Chiabotti, 'Family Ties and Transmission', esp. 260.

148 The prominence of al-Qushayrī's *Risāla*, often called the 'Bible of Sufism', led to him eclipsing his teacher al-Sulamī in the consciousness of many later masters. The *Risāla* is 'dual generic', incorporating elements of a biographical dictionary and of a Ṣūfī manual. Where the influence of al-Sulamī's *Ṭabaqāt al-ṣūfiyya* survived, it often did so by means of its presence in al-Qushayrī's *Risāla*. Arthur J. Arberry, *Sufism: An Account of the Mystics of Islam* (Mineola, NY: Dover Publications, 2002), 71; Francesco Chiabotti and Martin Nguyen, 'The Textual Legacy of Abū l-Qāsim al-Qušayrī: A Bibliographic Record', *Arabica* 61 (2014): 379; Mojaddedi, *The Biographical Tradition in Sufism*, 100.

149 Al-Qushayrī, *Risāla*, B. al-ṣuḥba.

150 This tradition as al-Qushayrī transmits does not appear in any of the major Sunnī collections, but a tradition of a similar theme occurs in *Ṣaḥīḥ Muslim*. There, the Prophet visits a graveyard and refers to the deceased believers buried there as his brothers. Those who were with him ask whether they too are not his brothers, and the Prophet replies that they are his companions. Muslim, *Ṣaḥīḥ*, K. al-ṭahāra (2), B. istaḥbāb iṭāla al-ghurra (12), Ḥ. 249. Arberry offers a sceptical assessment of al-Qushayrī's status as a traditionist, saying that he 'did not hesitate to use Traditions concerning whose authenticity, as judged by the chains of transmission on which they depend, we are bound to feel considerable reserve'. The *Risāla* bears out Martin Nguyen's description of al-Qushayrī's intellectual milieu: al-Qushayrī made use of an array of material attributed to the Prophet, for he 'was enmeshed in a number of hadith networks' representing a 'wide and fluid range of prophetic reports'. Arberry, 'Al-Qushairī as Traditionist', in *Studia Orientalia Ioanni Pedersen Septuagenario A.D. VII Id. Nov. Anno MCMLIII* (Copenhagen [Hauniae]: E. Munksgaard, 1953), 20; Nguyen, *Sufi Master and Qur'an Scholar*, 162.

151 Al-Qushayrī, *Risāla*, B. al-maḥabba. Reuven Snir's analysis of this chapter exhibits al-Qushayrī's primary concern clearly; his lengthy investigation of al-Qushayrī's rhetoric never once touches on love between persons. Reuven Snir, '*Bāb al-maḥabba* (The Chapter on Love) in *Al-Risāla al-qušayriyya*: Rhetorical and Thematic Structure', *IOS* 19 (1999): 131–59.

152 Knysh's translation suggests that this abandonment of opposition occurs when one accompanies a shaykh of an equal rank, but the Arabic text indicates that the shaykh is above (*fawq*) the companion. Al-Qushayrī does insist that one should treat a companion of equal rank with deference, but *tark al-i'tirāḍ* belongs to the service one owes a higher shaykh. Al-Qushayrī, *Risāla*, B. al-ṣuḥba.

153 Al-Qushayrī, *Risāla*, B. al-ṣuḥba.

154 Whether or not a shaykh should seek disciples was debated among Ṣūfīs; al-Sulamī approved of such a search, seeing it as a natural consequence of preaching to the people. Caesar E. Farah, 'Rules Governing the Šayḫ-Muršid's Conduct', *Numen* 21, no. 2 (1974): 87; Buehler, *Recognizing Sufism*, 160.

155 Al-Qushayrī, *Risāla*, B. al-ṣuḥba.
156 In discussions of these matters, al-Qushayrī moves back and forth between the terms *shaykh* and *ustādh* with some freedom; any difference in meaning between the two is difficult to discern. He employs the greatest consistency regarding his own teachers, al-Daqqāq and al-Sulamī, to whom he consistently refers as *shaykh*.
157 Chiabotti, 'Entre soufisme et savoir islamique', 622. Chiabotti also identifies the different types of evidence mustered to support this reverence; al-Sulamī grounds reverence for shaykhs in Qur'ānic texts and Prophetic traditions, while al-Qushayrī more commonly draws upon anecdotes of Ṣūfī masters themselves – including al-Sulamī! – regarding the way that shaykhs should be treated.
158 Al-Qushayrī, *Risāla*, B. waṣiyya lil-murīdīn.
159 Al-Qushayrī, *Risāla*, B. ḥifẓ qulūb al-mashāyikh.
160 Al-Sulamī, *JAṢ*, §62; al-Qushayrī, *Risāla*, B. ḥifẓ qulūb al-mashāyikh.
161 Al-Sulamī, *JAṢ*, §55; *AMM* throughout.
162 Al-Sulamī, *JAṢ*, §62.
163 Al-Sulamī, *JAṢ*, §36.
164 Meier, 'Khurāsān and the End of Classical Sufism', 208.
165 Al-Qushayrī, *Risāla*, B. ḥifẓ qulūb al-mashāyikh.
166 Al-Qushayrī, *Risāla*, B. ḥifẓ qulūb al-mashāyikh.
167 For Miskawayh, the claim that a student owes greater honour to his teacher than to his parents has less traction than it does in the case of institutional Sufism. This exclusive relationship with a directing shaykh, to the point of preference in honour over one's father, develops as the institution of the *khānaqā* increasingly spread across the Middle East and the phenomenon of learned Ṣūfī families began to grow. Al-Qushayrī's personal story illustrates this tension. Al-Qushayrī studied with his father-in-law, although he probably did not wed al-Daqqāq's daughter until after al-Daqqāq's death. For him, this tension between obligations to one's parents and to one's master had daily consequences. Chiabotti, 'Family Ties and Transmission', 299.
168 Al-Qushayrī, *Risāla*, B. waṣiyya lil-murīdīn.
169 Al-Qushayrī, *Risāla*, B. waṣiyya lil-murīdīn.
170 Al-Qushayrī, *Risāla*, B. waṣiyya lil-murīdīn.
171 *Risāla*, B. waṣiyya lil-murīdīn. Al-Sulamī likewise prohibits companionship with youth in several places, often accompanying his disparagement of women. al-Sulamī, *BTF*, §44; *ṬṢ*, 189 (#14), 190 (#22), 232 (#11), 396 (#5); *SA*, §24; *KMT*, §7; *QTM*, §41; *MA*, §16; *DAṢ*, 550; cf. *ṬṢ*, 204–5 (#19); *KAṢ*, 76; for discussion, see Salamah-Qudsi, *Sufism and Early Islamic Piety*, 215–61.
172 Al-Qushayrī, *Risāla*, B. waṣiyya lil-murīdīn.
173 Al-Qushayrī cites Q. 24:15, which contrasts a sin that people considered *hayyin* but God considers *'aẓīm*.
174 This saying does not appear in the entry in *Ṭabaqāt al-ṣūfiyya* for Abū Bakr al-Tamastānī, nor have I noticed it elsewhere in al-Sulamī's writings. Al-Qushayrī, *Risāla*, B. al-ṣuḥba.
175 Thibon makes this claim in several of his writings about al-Sulamī; for the fullest discussion, see *L'œuvre*, 238–44.
176 Al-Hujwīrī, *Kashf al-maḥjūb*, 472–6 (Eng., 361–4).
177 Al-Hujwīrī, *Kashf al-maḥjūb*, 454–5 (Eng., 349).
178 Al-Sīrjānī attributes the saying to al-Junayd, al-Qushayrī to Abū Yazīd al-Bisṭāmī. Al-Sīrjānī, *Kitāb al-bayāḍ wa-l-sawād*, §216; al-Qushayrī, *Risāla*, B. waṣiyya lil-murīdīn.

Conclusion

1 Al-Sulamī, *KAṢ*, 25–6; cf. Abū Dā'ūd, *Sunan*, K. al-adab (40), B. man yu'mar an yujālis (16), Ḥ. 4833; al-Tirmidhī, *Jāmi'*, K. al-zuhd (34), B. ḥadīth al-rajul 'alā dīn khalīlihi (45), Ḥ. 2378; Ibn Ḥanbal, *Musnad*, 13:398, Ḥ. 8028; al-Albānī, *Silsilat al-aḥādīth al-ṣaḥīḥa*, 2:597–9, Ḥ. 927; cf. al-Sulamī, *DAṢ*, 550; al-Sīrjānī, *Kitāb al-bayāḍ wa-l-sawād*, §371.

2 Al-Sulamī, *Early Sufi Women*, 37–8; Chowdhury, *A Ṣūfī Apologist*, 41, 193; see note 63 to Chapter 3.

3 MacIntyre, *After Virtue*, 263; see also the affirmative comment in Recep Alpyağıl, *Fark ve yorum: Kur'an'ı anlama yolunda felsefi denemeler II* (Istanbul: īz Yayıncılık, 2009), 152.

4 This feature of MacIntyre's thought drives Brewer's interest in MacIntyre as a resource for interreligious dialogue.

5 In addition to the work of Christian B. Miller mentioned earlier, I think here of projects like Angela Duckworth's recent work on the virtue of grit, or similar psychological studies, geared towards themes of virtue and character. Angela Duckworth, *Grit: The Power of Passion and Perseverance* (New York: Simon and Schuster, 2016).

BIBLIOGRAPHY

Sources composed in Arabic, Persian, or Turkish (with translations, where available)

Abū Dā'ūd, Sulaymān b. al-Ash'ath al-Sijistānī. *English Translation of Sunan Abu Dawud*. Translated by Nasiruddin al-Khattab and Yaser Qadhi, 5 vols. Riyadh: Darussalam, 2008.

Abū Ḥayyān al-Tawḥīdī, 'Alī b. Muḥammad. *See al-Tawḥīdī, Abū Ḥayyān 'Alī b. Muḥammad.*

Abū l-Shaykh al-Anṣārī (al-Iṣfahānī), 'Abdallāh b. Muḥammad b. Ja'far b. Ḥayyān. *Ṭabaqāt al-muḥaddithīn bi-Iṣfahān wa-l-wāridīn 'alayhā*. Edited by 'Abd al-Ghafūr 'Abd al-Ḥaqq Ḥusayn al-Balūshī, 4 vols. Beirut: Mu'assasat al-Risāla, 1992.

Abū Nu'aym al-Iṣfahānī, Aḥmad b. 'Abdallāh. *Ḥilyat al-awliyā' wa-ṭabaqāt al-aṣfiyā'*, 11 vols. Cairo: Maktabat al-Khānjī, Beirut: Dār al-Fikr, 1996.

Abū Ya'lā l-Mawṣilī. *Musnad Abī Ya'lā l-Mawṣilī*, 14 vols. Damascus: Dār al-Ma'mūn, 1986.

Aḥmad b. Ḥanbal. *See Ibn Ḥanbal, Aḥmad.*

Al-Albānī, Muḥammad Nāṣir al-Dīn. *Ṣaḥīḥ al-jāmi' al-ṣaghīr wa-ziyādatuhu (al-Fatḥ al-kabīr)*, 3rd ed. Beirut: al-Maktab al-Islāmī, 1988.

Al-Albānī, Muḥammad Nāṣir al-Dīn. *Silsilat al-aḥādīth al-ḍa'īfa wa-l-mawḍū'a wa-athrihā l-shay' fī l-umma*, 14 vols. Riyadh: Maktabat al-Ma'ārif, 1992–2004.

Al-Albānī, Muḥammad Nāṣir al-Dīn. *Silsilat al-aḥādīth al-ṣaḥīḥa wa-shay' min fiqhihā wa-fawā'idihā*, 9 vols. Riyadh: Maktabat al-Ma'ārif, 1995–2002.

Al-Albānī, Muḥammad Nāṣir al-Dīn. *Tamām al-minna fī l-ta'līq 'alā fiqh al-sunna*. Riyadh: Dār al-Rāya, 1988.

Alī b. Abī Ṭālib, al-Jāḥiẓ, and al-Qāḍī Muḥammad b. Salāma al-Quḍā'ī. *A Treasury of Virtues and One Hundred Proverbs*. Translated and edited by Tahera Qutbuddin. New York: New York University Press, 2013.

Alpyağıl, Recep. *Fark ve yorum: Kur'an'ı anlama yolunda felsefi denemeler II*. İstanbul: İz Yayıncılık, 2009.

Al-Anṣārī, Abū l-Shaykh. *See Abū l-Shaykh al-Anṣārī.*

Ateş, Süleyman. *İşârî Tefsîr Okulu*. Ankara: Ankara Üniversitesi Basımevi, 1974.

Ateş, Süleyman. *Sülemî ve Tasavvufî Tefsîrı*. Istanbul: Sönmez, 1969.

Ateş, Süleyman. *Tasavvufun Ana İlkeleri: Sülemî'nin Risaleleri*. Ankara: Ankara Üniversitesi Basımevi, 1981.

Al-Bayhaqī, Abū Bakr Aḥmad b. al-Ḥusayn b. 'Alī. *Al-Ādāb*. Beirut: Dār al-Kutub al-'Ilmiyya, 1986.

Al-Bayhaqī, Abū Bakr Aḥmad b. al-Ḥusayn b. 'Alī. *Shu'ab al-īmān*, 9 vols. Beirut: Dār al-Kutub al-'Ilmiyya, 2000.

Al-Bukhārī, Muḥammad b. Ismā'īl. *Ṣaḥīḥ al-adab al-mufrad lil-imām al-Bukhārī*. Edited by Muḥammad Nāṣir al-Dīn al-Albānī, 2nd ed. Jubayl: Dār al-Ṣadīq, 2000.

Al-Bukhārī, Muḥammad b. Ismāʿīl. *The Translation of the Meanings of Sahîh Al-Bukhâri: Arabic-English*. Translated by Muhammad Muhsin Khan, 9 vols. Riyadh: Darussalam, 1997.
Al-Dhahabī, Shams al-Dīn Muḥammad b. Aḥmad. *Siyar aʿlām al-nubalā'*. Edited by Shuʿayb al-Arnaʾūṭ, 25 vols. Beirut: Muʾassasat al-Risāla, 1996.
Al-Dhahabī, Shams al-Dīn Muḥammad b. Aḥmad. *Tārīkh al-islām wa-wafayāt al-mashāhīr wa-l-aʿlām*. Edited by ʿUmar ʿAbd al-Salām Tadmurī, 52 vols. Beirut: Dār al-Kitāb al-ʿArabī, 1990.
Al-Fārābī, Abū Naṣr Muḥammad b. Muḥammad. *Rasāʾil al-Fārābī*. Hyderabad: Maṭbaʿat Majlis Dāʾirat al-Maʿārif al-ʿUthmāniyya, 1926.
Al-Fārisī, ʿAbd al-Ghāfir b. Ismāʿīl. *Al-Mukhtaṣar min kitāb al-siyāq li-tārīkh Naysābūr*. Edited by Muḥammad Kāẓim al-Maḥmūdī. Tehran: Markaz-i Nashr-i Mīrāsh-i Maktūb, 2005.
Al-Ghazālī, Abū Ḥāmid Muḥammad. *Bidāyat al-hidāya*. Edited by Muḥammad al-Ḥajjār. Aleppo: ʿAbd al-Ghanī Abū l-ʿAbbās, 1970.
Al-Ghazālī, Abū Ḥāmid Muḥammad. *Iḥyāʾ ʿulūm al-dīn*. Edited by ʿAbd al-ʿAzīz ʿIzz al-Dīn al-Sīrwānī, 3rd ed. 5 vols. Beirut: Dār al-Qalam, 1990. Translated by Fazl-ul-Karim as *Revival of Religious Learnings: Imam Ghazzali's* Ihya Ulum-Id-Din, 4 vols. Karachi: Darul-Ishaat, 1993.
Al-Ghazālī, Abū Ḥāmid Muḥammad. *On Disciplining the Soul: Kitāb Riyāḍat al-nafs* and *On Breaking the Two Desires: Kitāb Kasr al-shahwatayn (Books XXII and XXIII of* The Revival of the Religious Sciences *Iḥyāʾ ʿulūm al-dīn*). Translated by T. J. Winter. Cambridge: Islamic Texts Society, 1995.
Al-Ghazālī, Abū Ḥāmid Muḥammad. *On Poverty and Abstinence: Kitāb al-faqr waʾl-zuhd (Book XXXIV of* The Revival of the Religious Sciences). Translated by Anthony F. Shaker. Cambridge: Islamic Texts Society, 2019.
Al-Ḥakīm al-Tirmidhī, Muḥammad b. ʿAlī. *Adab al-nafs*. Edited by Aḥmad ʿAbd al-Raḥīm al-Sāyiḥ. Cairo: al-Dār al-Miṣriyya al-Lubnāniyya, 1993.
Al-Ḥakīm al-Tirmidhī, Muḥammad b. ʿAli. *Bayān al-farq bayn al-ṣadr wa-l-qalb wa-l-fuʾād wa-l-lubb*. Edited by Aḥmad ʿAbd al-Raḥīm al-Sāyiḥ. Cairo: Markaz al-Kitāb lil-Nashr, 1998. Translated by Nicholas Heer as 'A Treatise on the Heart'. In al-Sulamī and al-Ḥakīm al-Tirmidhī, *Three Early Sufi Texts*, 11–55.
Al-Ḥakīm al-Tirmidhī, Muḥammad b. ʿAli. *The Concept of Sainthood in Early Islamic Mysticism* [Badʾ shaʾn Abī ʿAbdallāh Muḥammad al-Ḥakīm al-Tirmidhī, Kitāb sīrat al-awliyāʾ]. Translated by Bernd Radtke and John O'Kane. Richmond: Curzon, 1996.
Al-Ḥakīm al-Tirmidhī, Muḥammad b. ʿAli. *Drei Schriften des Theosophen von Tirmidh*. Translated and edited by Bernd Radtke. Stuttgart: Steiner, 1992.
Al-Ḥakīm al-Tirmidhī, Muḥammad b. ʿAli. *Khatm al-awliyāʾ*. Beirut: al-Maṭbaʿa al-Kāthūlīkiyya, 1965.
Al-Ḥakīm al-Tirmidhī, Muḥammad b. ʿAli. *Riyāḍat al-Nafs*. Edited by Shams al-Dīn Ibrāhīm. Beirut: Dār al-Kutub al-ʿIlmiyya, 2005.
Al-Ḥallāj, Ḥusayn b. Manṣūr. *See Kāmil Muṣṭafā l-Shaybī and Louis Massignon.*
Al-Haythamī, ʿAlī b. Abī Bakr. *Majmaʿ al-zawāʾid wa-manbaʿ al-fawāʾid*, 12 vols. Beirut: Dār al-Kutub al-ʿIlmiyya, 2001.
Al-Ḥākim al-Naysābūrī, Abū ʿAbdallāh. *Al-Mustadrak ʿalā al-ṣaḥīḥayn*, 5 vols. 2nd ed. Beirut: Dār al-Kutub al-ʿIlmiyya, 2002.
Al-Hujwīrī, ʿAlī b. ʿUthmān. *Kashf al-maḥjūb*. Edited by Valentin Alekseyevich Zhukovskiĭ. Tehran: Amīr-i Kabīr, 1957. Translated by Reynold A. Nicholson as *The Kashf Al-Mahjub: A Persian Treatise on Sufism*. Leiden: Brill, 1911. Translated into

Arabic by Amīn ʿAbd al-Majīd al-Barwī as *Kashf al-maḥjūb*. Edited by Isʿād ʿAbd al-Hādī Qandīl, 2 vols. Cairo: Jamhūriyyat Miṣr al-ʿArabiyya, 1974.
Al-Huwwārī, Hūd b. Muḥakkam, *Tafsīr kitāb Allāh al-ʿazīz*. Edited by Bālḥājj b. Saʿīd al-Sharīfī, 4 vols. Beirut: Dār al-Gharb al-Islāmī, 1990.
Ibn Abī l-Dunyā. *Mawsūʿat Ibn Abī l-Dunyā*, 7 vols. Riyadh: Dār Aṭlas al-Ḥaḍrāʾ, 2012.
Ibn ʿAsākir, ʿAlī b. al-Ḥasan. *Tabyīn kadhib al-muftarī fī mā nusiba ilā l-imām Abī l-Ḥasan al-Ashʿarī*. Damascus: al-Qudsī, 1928.
Ibn ʿAsākir, ʿAlī b. al-Ḥasan. *Tārīkh madīnat Dimashq*. Edited by ʿUmar Gharāma al-ʿAmrawī, 80 vols. Beirut: Dār al-Fikr, 1995–2000.
Ibn al-Athīr, Majd al-Dīn Abū l-Saʿādāt al-Mubārak. *Al-Mukhtār min manāqib al-akhyār*, 6 vols. Al Ain, United Arab Emirates: Markaz Zāyid lil-Turāth wa-l-Tārīkh (Zayed Center for Heritage and History), 2002.
Ibn Fāris al-Qazwīnī, Aḥmad. *Muʿjam maqāyīs al-lugha*, 6 vols. Cairo: ʿĪsā l-Bābī l-Ḥalabī, 1946.
Ibn Ḥanbal, Aḥmad. *Al-Musnad*. Edited by Shuʿayb al-Arnaʾūṭ et al., 50 vols. Beirut: Muʾassasat al-Risāla, 1413–21/1993–2001.
Ibn Ḥazm, ʿAlī b. Aḥmad, and Eva Riad. *Kitāb al-akhlāq wa-l-siyar, aw, Risāla fī mudāwāt al-nufūs wa-tahdhīb al-akhlāq wa-l-zuhd fī l-radhāʾil*. Uppsala: [s.n.], 1980. Translated by Muhammad Abu Laylah as *In Pursuit of Virtue: The Moral Theology and Psychology of Ibn Hazm Al-Andalusi (384–456 AH 994–1064 AD); with a Translation of His Book Al-Akhlaq Waʾl-Siyar*. London: TaHa, 1990.
Ibn al-Jawzī, Abū l-Faraj ʿAbd al-Raḥmān b. ʿAlī. *Ṣifat al-ṣafwa*, 4 vols. Beirut: Dār al-Maʿrifa, 1985.
Ibn Kathīr, ʿImād al-Dīn Abū l-Fidāʾ Ismāʿīl. *Al-Bidāya wa-l-nihāya*, 20 vols. Beirut: Dār Ibn Kathīr, 2010.
Ibn Khaldūn, ʿAbd al-Raḥmān b. Muḥammad. *Al-Muqaddima*. Edited by ʿAbd al-Salām al-Shaddādī, 5 vols. Al-Dār al-Bayḍāʾ (Casablanca): Khizānat Ibn Khaldūn, Bayt al-Funūn wa-l-ʿUlūm wa-l-Ādāb, 2005. Abridged translation by Franz Rosenthal as *The Muqaddimah: An Introduction to History*. Princeton, NJ: Princeton University Press, 2005.
Ibn Manẓūr, Muḥammad b. Mukarram. *Lisān al-ʿarab*, 7 vols. Cairo: Dār al-Maʿārif, 1900.
Ibn Miskawayh, Abū ʿAlī Aḥmad b. Muḥammad. *See Miskawayh, Abū ʿAlī Aḥmad b. Muḥammad.*
Ibn Māja al-Qazwīnī, Muḥammad b. Yazīd. *English Translation of Sunan Ibn Mâjah*. Translated by Nasiruddin al-Khattab, 5 vols. Riyadh: Darussalam, 2007.
Ibn Taymiyya, Taqī l-Dīn Aḥmad. *Aḥādīth al-quṣṣāṣ*. Cairo: al-Dār al-Miṣriyya al-Lubnāniyya, 1993.
Ibn Taymiyya, Taqī l-Dīn Aḥmad. *Majmūʿ al-fatāwā*, 3rd ed. 37 vols. Al-Manṣūra: Dār al-Wafāʾ, 2005.
Ibn Taymiyya, Taqī l-Dīn Aḥmad. *Shaykh al-Islām Ibn Taymiyya wa-juhūduhu fī l-ḥadīth wa-ʿulūmihi*. Edited by ʿAbd al-Raḥmān b. ʿAbd al-Jabbār al-Faryawāʾī, 4 vols. Riyadh: Dār al-ʿĀṣima, 2010.
Jaʿfar al-Ṣādiq. *Spiritual Gems: The Mystical Qurʾān Commentary Ascribed to Jaʿfar al-Ṣādiq as Contained in Sulamī's* Ḥaqāʾiq al-Tafsīr *from the Text of Paul Nwyia*. Translated by Farhana Mayer. Louisville: Fons Vitae, 2011.
Al-Jawharī, Ismāʿīl b. Ḥammād. *Al-Ṣiḥāḥ: Tāj al-lugha wa-ṣiḥāḥ al-ʿarabiyya*, 6 vols. Beirut: Dār al-ʿIlm lil-Milāyīn, 1984.
Al-Jāḥiẓ, Abū ʿUthmān ʿAmr. *Rasāʾil al-Jāḥiẓ*. Edited by ʿAbd al-Salām Muḥammad Hārūn, 4 vols. Cairo: Maktabat al-Khanjī, 1964.

Al-Jāmī, Nūr al-Dīn 'Abd al-Rahmān. *Nafaḥāt al-uns min ḥaḍarāt al-quds*. Edited by William Nassau Lees. Calcutta: Maṭba' Līssī, 1858. Portions translated by Silvestre de Sacy as *Vie des soufis: ou, Les haleines de la familiarité*. Paris: Éditions orientales, 1977.

Al-Kalābādhī, Abū Bakr Muḥammad b. Isḥāq. *Kitab al-ta'arruf li-madhhab ahl al-taṣawwuf*. Edited by A. J. Arberry. Cairo: Maktabat al-Khānjī, 1933. Translated by A. J. Arberry as *The Doctrine of the Ṣūfīs*. New York: Cambridge University Press, 1977.

Al-Khalīfa al-Nīsābūrī, Aḥmad Muḥammad b. Ḥasan Aḥmad, 'Abd al-Ghāfir b. Ismā'īl al-Fārisī, Ibrāhīm b. Muḥammad al-Ṣarīfīnī and Richard N. Frye. *The Histories of Nishapur*. Cambridge: Harvard University Press, 1965.

Al-Kharkūshī, 'Abd al-Malik b. Muḥammad. *Kitāb tahdhīb al-asrār*. Edited by Bassām Muḥammad Bārūd. Abu Dhabi: al-Majma' al-Thaqāfī, 1999.

Al-Khaṭīb al-Baghdādī, Abū Bakr Aḥmad b. 'Alī. *Tārīkh Baghdād (Tārīkh madīnat al-salām)*. Edited by Bashshār 'Awwād Ma'rūf, 17 vols. Beirut: Dār al-Gharb al-Islāmī, 2001.

Al-Khaṭīb al-Tabrīzī, Abū Zakariyyā' Yaḥyā. *Mishkāt al-maṣābīḥ*, 3 vols. Damascus: al-Maktab al-Islāmī, 1961.

Kitāb adab al-mulūk fī bayān ḥaqā'iq al-taṣawwuf [Ein Handbuch zur islamischen Mystik aus dem 4./10. Jahrhundert]. Edited by Bernd Radtke. Beirut: Franz Steiner Verlag, 1991.

Kitāb 'ilm al-taṣawwuf. Edited by Nasrollah Pourjavady and Mohammed Soori. Tehran: Iranian Institute of Philosophy and Research Unit Intellectual History of the Islamicate World of Freie Universität Berlin, 2011.

Al-Majlisī, Muḥammad Bāqir. *Biḥār al-anwār*, 110 vols. Tehran: al-Maktaba al-Islāmiyya, 1969.

Al-Makkī, Abū Ṭālib Muḥammad b. 'Alī. *Qūt al-qulūb fī mu'āmalat al-maḥbūb wa-waṣf ṭarīq al-murīd ilā maqām al-tawḥīd*. Edited by Maḥmūd Ibrāhīm Raḍwāni, 3 vols. Cairo: Maktabat Dār al-Turāth, 2001.

Mālik b. Anas. *Al-Muwaṭṭa'*. Edited by Salīm al-Hilāli, 5 vols. Dubai: Majmū'at al-Furqān al-Tijāriyya, 2003. Translated by 'A'isha 'Abdarahman at-Tarjumana and Ya'qub Johnson as *al-Muwatta*. Norwich, UK: Diwan Press, 1982.

Al-Maqdisī, Muḥammad b. Aḥmad. *See Al-Muqaddasī, Muḥammad b. Aḥmad.*

Al-Māwardī, Abū l-Ḥasan 'Alī b. Muḥammad. *Adab al-dunyā wa-l-dīn*. Beirut: Dār al-Kutub al-'Ilmiyya, 1987. Translated by Thoreya Mahdi Allam as *The Discipline of Religious and Worldly Matters*. Rabat: Publications of the Islamic Educational, Scientific and Cultural Organization (ISESCO), 1995.

Miskawayh, Abū 'Alī Aḥmad b. Muḥammad. *Tahdhīb al-akhlāq*. Edited by Constantine K. Zurayk. Beirut: American University of Beirut, 1966. Translated by Constantine K. Zurayk as *The Refinement of Character*. Beirut: American University of Beirut, 1968. Translated by Mohammed Arkoun as *Traité d'éthique*. Damascus: Institut français de Damas, 1969.

Muḥammad b. al-Munavvar. *The Secrets of God's Mystical Oneness [Asrār Al-Towḥid]*. Translated by John O'Kane. Costa Mesa, CA: Mazda Publishers, 1992.

Al-Muḥāsibī, al-Ḥārith b. Asad. *Ādāb al-nufūs wa-yalīhi Kitāb al-tawahhum*, 2nd ed. Beirut: Mu'assasat al-Kutub al-Thaqāfiyya, 1991.

Al-Muḥāsibī, al-Ḥārith b. Asad. *Bad' man anāba ilā Allāh wa-yalīhi ādāb al-nufūs*. Edited by Majdī Fatḥī Sayyid. Cairo: Dār al-Salām, 1991.

Al-Muḥāsibī, al-Ḥārith b. Asad. *Al-Ri'āya li-ḥuqūq Allāh*. Edited by 'Abd al-Qādir Aḥmad 'Aṭā'. Beirut: Dār al-Kutub al-'Ilmiyya, 2010.

Al-Munāwī, Muḥammad. *Al-Kawākib al-durriyya fī tarājim al-sāda al-ṣūfiyya*, 4 vols. Cairo: al-Maktaba al-Azhariyya lil-Turāth, 1994.

Al-Muqaddasī (al-Maqdisī), Muḥammad b. Aḥmad. *Kitāb aḥsan al-taqāsīm fī ma'rifat al-aqālīm (Descriptio imperii moslemici)*. Edited by M. J. de Goeje, 2nd ed. Leiden: Brill, 1906.

Muslim b. al-Ḥajjāj al-Qushayrī. *English Translation of Sahîh Muslim*. Translated by Nasiruddin al-Khattab. Edited by Huda Khattab, 7 vols. New York: Darussalam, 2007.

Al-Mustamlī l-Bukhārī, Abū Ibrāhīm Ismā'īl. *Sharḥ Kitāb al-ta'arruf li-madhhab al-taṣawwuf*. Tehran: Chāpkhānih-yi Dānishgāh-i Tehrān, 1346 H.

Al-Nasā'ī, Aḥmad b. Shu'ayb. *English Translation of Sunan an-Nasâ'i*. Translated by Nasiruddin al-Khattab, 6 vols. Riyadh: Darussalam, 2007.

Al-Nawawī, Abū Zakariyyā'. *Riyāḍ al-ṣāliḥīn*. Beirut: Dār Ibn Kathir, 2007.

Al-Qushayrī, Abū l-Qāsim 'Abd al-Karīm b. Hawāzin. *Arba' rasā'il fī l-taṣawwuf*. Edited by Qāsim al-Sāmarrā'ī. Baghdad: al-Majma' al-'Ilmī al-'Irāqī, 1969.

Al-Qushayrī, Abū l-Qāsim 'Abd al-Karīm b. Hawāzin. *Kitāb al-Arba'īn fī taṣḥīḥ al-mu'āmala*. Amman: Dār al-Fatḥ, 2013.

Al-Qushayrī, Abū l-Qāsim 'Abd al-Karīm b. Hawāzin. *Laṭā'if al-ishārāt*. Edited by 'Abd al-Laṭīf Ḥasan 'Abd al-Raḥmān, 3 vols. Beirut: Dār al-Kutub al-'Ilmiyya, 2007.

Al-Qushayrī, Abū l-Qāsim 'Abd al-Karīm b. Hawāzin. *al-Rasā'il al-qushayriyya*. Edited by Muḥammad Ḥasan. Pakistan: al-Ma'had al-Markazī lil-Abḥāth al-Islāmiyya, 1964.

Al-Qushayrī, Abū l-Qāsim 'Abd al-Karīm b. Hawāzin. *Al-Risāla al-qushayriyya fī 'ilm al-taṣawwuf*. Edited by Abū Sahl Najāḥ 'Awaḍ Ṣiyām. Cairo: Dār al-Muqaṭṭam, 2009. Translated by Alexander Knysh as *Al-Qushayri's Epistle on Sufism: Al-Risala al-Qushayriyya fi 'Ilm al-Tasawwuf*. Reading: Garnet, 2007. Translated by B. R. von Schlegell as *Principles of Sufism*. Berkeley: Mizan Press, 1992. Translated by Rabia Harris as *Sufi Book of Spiritual Ascent*. Chicago: ABC Group International, 1997.

Al-Sakhāwī, Muḥammad b. 'Abd al-Raḥmān. *Al-Ajwiba al-murḍiyya*, 3 vols. Riyadh: Dār al-Rāya, 1997.

Al-Sarrāj, Abū Naṣr 'Abdallāh b. 'Alī. *The Kitāb al-Luma' fī al-Taṣawwuf*. Edited by Reynold A. Nicholson. Leiden: Brill, 1914. Translated by Richard Gramlich as *Schlaglichter über das Sufitum*. Stuttgart: Franz Steiner Verlag, 1990.

Al-Sha'rānī, 'Abd al-Wahhāb. *Al-Ṭabaqāt al-kubrā*, 2 vols. Cairo: Maktabat al-Thaqāfa al-Dīniyya, 2005.

Al-Shaybī, Kāmil Muṣṭafā. *Sharḥ Dīwān al-Ḥallāj Abī l-Mughīth al-Ḥusayn b. Manṣūr b. Maḥmā l-Bayḍāwī*. Cologne: Al-Kamel Verlag, 2007.

Al-Sīrjānī, Abū l-Ḥasan 'Alī b. al-Ḥasan. *Al-Bayāḍ wa-l-sawād (All about the Wisdom of the Sufis)*. Edited by Mohsen Pourmokhtar. Tehran: Iranian Institute of Philosophy, 2011.

Al-Sīrjānī, Abū l-Ḥasan 'Alī b. al-Ḥasan. *Sufism, Black and White: A Critical Edition of* Kitāb al-Bayāḍ wa-l-Sawād *by Abū l-Ḥasan al-Sīrjānī (d. ca. 470/1077)*. Edited by Bilal Orfali and Nada Saab. Leiden: Brill, 2012.

Al-Subkī, Tāj al-Dīn 'Abd al-Wahhāb b. 'Alī. *Ṭabaqāt al-shāfi'iyya al-kubrā*. Edited by Maḥmūd Muḥammad al-Ṭanāḥī and 'Abd al-Fattāḥ Muḥammad Ḥulw, 10 vols. Cairo: Dār Iḥyā' al-Kutub al-'Arabiyya, 1976.

Al-Suhrawardī, 'Abd al-Qāhir Abū Najīb and Menahem Milson. *A Sufi Rule for Novices = Kitāb Ādāb al-Murīdīn of Abū al-Najīb al-Suhrawardī*. Cambridge: Harvard University Press, 1975.

Al-Sulamī, Abū 'Abd al-Raḥmān Muḥammad b. al-Ḥusayn al-Naysābūrī. *Kitab ādāb aṣ-ṣuḥba*. Edited by M. J. Kister. Jerusalem: Israel Oriental Society, 1954. Translated by

Taher Gaïd as *La courtoisie en Islam*. Paris: Éd. Iqra, 2001. Translated by Jason Welle as 'The Ways of Companionship and Good Fellowship'. In al-Sulamī, *Treatises on the Sufi Path.*

Al-Sulamī, Abū 'Abd al-Raḥmān Muḥammad b. al-Ḥusayn al-Naysābūrī. *Early Sufi Women: Dhikr an-niswa al-muta'abbidāt aṣ-ṣūfiyyāt*. Translated and edited by Rkia E. Cornell. Louisville: Fons Vitae, 1999. Translated by 'Abd al-Raḥmān Andreucci as *Femmes soufies / La sainteté féminine dans l'hagiographie islamique*. Paris: Entrelacs, 2011. Translated by Giancarlo Rizzo as *Donne sûfi: La santità islamica al femminile*. Turin: Il leone verde, 2011. Selections translated by Ḥasan Bize and Ibrāhīm Estomba as *Anécdotas y enseñanzas santas sufís*. Buenos Aires: La Tablada, 2011.

Al-Sulamī, Abū 'Abd al-Raḥmān Muḥammad b. al-Ḥusayn al-Naysābūrī. *Ḥaqā'iq al-tafsīr*. Edited by Sayyid 'Umrān, 2 vols. Beirut: Dār al-Kutub al-'Ilmiyya, 2001.

Al-Sulamī, Abū 'Abd al-Raḥmān Muḥammad b. al-Ḥusayn al-Naysābūrī. *I Ṣūfī e i Medievali Peccati [Bayān zalal al-fuqarā']*. Translated by Giancarlo Rizzo. Aosta: Keltia Edizioni, 2010.

Al-Sulamī, Abū 'Abd al-Raḥmān Muḥammad b. al-Ḥusayn al-Naysābūrī. *Jawāmi' Ādāb al-Ṣūfiyya and 'Uyūb al-Nafs wa-Mudāwātuhā*. Edited by Etan Kohlberg. Jerusalem: Jerusalem Academic Press, 1976. *Jawāmi'* translated by Elena Biagi as *A Collection of Sufi Rules of Conduct*. Cambridge: Islamic Texts Society, 2010. *'Uyūb al-nafs* translated by Musa Furber as *Infamies of the Soul & Their Treatments*. Kuala Lampur: Islamosaic, 2018. Translated by Rachel Keane as *The Maladies of the Nafs and their Remedies*. Unpublished. Translated by Abdul Karim Zein as *Les maladies de l'âme et leurs remèdes: traité de psychologie soufie*. Milan: Archè, 1990. Translated by Italo Ponzato as *Le malattie dell'anima e i loro rimedi*. San Donato: Edizioni PiZeta, 1999. Translated by Francesc Gutierrez as *Las enfermedades del alma y sus remedios*. Palma de Mallorca: Olañeta, 2001. Translated as *La guérison de l'âme: Les maladies de l'âme, nafs-ego et leurs remèdes*. Paris: la Ruche, diff. Al-Ghazali, 2006.

Al-Sulamī, Abū 'Abd al-Raḥmān Muḥammad b. al-Ḥusayn al-Naysābūrī. *Kitāb al-futuwwa / Tasavvufta fütüvvet*. Edited and translated by Süleyman Ateş. Ankara: Ankara Üniversitesi İlâhiyat Fakültesi Yayınları, 1977. Translated by Tosun Bayrak as *The Book of Sufi Chivalry: Lessons to a Son of the Moment: Futuwwah*. New York: Inner Traditions, 1983. Translated by Franz Langmayr as *Der Sufi-Weg zur Vollkommenheit*. Freiburg im Breisgau: Bauer, 1985. Translated by Faouzi Skali as *Futuwah: Traité de chevalerie soufie*. Paris: Albin Michel, 1989. Translated by Giuditta Sassi as *La cavalleria spirituale*. Milan: Luni, 1998. Translated by Antonio López Ruiz as *Futuwah: Tratado de caballería sufí* . Barcelona: Paidós, 1991. Translated by Paolo Imperio as *Il libro della cavalleria: Kitab af-futuwah*. Rome: Atanor, 1990.

Al-Sulamī, Abū 'Abd al-Raḥmān Muḥammad b. al-Ḥusayn al-Naysābūrī. *Kitāb ṭabaqāt al-ṣūfiyya*. Edited by Johannes Pedersen. Leiden: Brill, 1960.

Al-Sulamī, Abū 'Abd al-Raḥmān Muḥammad b. al-Ḥusayn al-Naysābūrī. *Majmū'a-i āthār Abū 'Abd al-Raḥmān al-Sulamī (Collected Works on Early Sufism)*. Edited by Nasrollah Pourjavady and Muḥammad Soori [Sūrī], 3 vols. Tehran: Markaz-i Nashr-i Dānishgāhī, 2009–10.

Al-Sulamī, Abū 'Abd al-Raḥmān Muḥammad b. al-Ḥusayn al-Naysābūrī. *Al-Malāmatiyya wa-l-ṣūfiyya wa-ahl al-futuwwa [Risālat al-malāmatiyya]*. Edited by Abū l-'Alā 'Afīfī. Cairo: 'Īsā l-Bābī l-Ḥalabī, 1945. Translated by Roger Deladrière as *Lucidité implacable: Épître des hommes du blâme*. Paris: Arléa, 1991. Translated by Giuditta Sassi as *I custodi del segreto*. Milan: Luni, 1997. Translated as *La lucidez implacable: Epístola de los hombres de la reprobación*. Barcelona: Ediciones Obelisco, 2003.

Al-Sulamī, Abū ʿAbd al-Raḥmān Muḥammad b. al-Ḥusayn al-Naysābūrī. ʻ*Manāhij al-ʿārifīn*, a Treatise on Ṣūfism by Abū ʿAbd al-Raḥmān al-Sulamī'. Edited by Etan Kohlberg. *JSAI* 1 (1979): 19–39.

Al-Sulamī, Abū ʿAbd al-Raḥmān Muḥammad b. al-Ḥusayn al-Naysābūrī. *Al-Muqaddima fī l-taṣawwuf wa-ḥaqīqatihi*. Edited by Ḥusayn Amīn. Baghdad: Dār al-Qādisiyya lil-Ṭibāʿa, 1984. Also edited by Yūsuf Zaydān. Beirut: Dār al-Jīl, 1999. Translated by Demetrio Giordani as *Introduzione al sufismo*. Turin: Il leone verde, 2002.

Al-Sulamī, Abū ʿAbd al-Raḥmān Muḥammad b. al-Ḥusayn al-Naysābūrī. *Quarante hadiths sur le soufisme*. Translated by Jean Abd-al-Wadoud Gouraud. Beirut: Dar Albouraq, 2021.

Al-Sulamī, Abū ʿAbd al-Raḥmān Muḥammad b. al-Ḥusayn al-Naysābūrī. *La scala di luce: Tre antichi testi di scuola malâmatî*. Translated by Demetrio Giordani. Turin: Il leone verde, 2006.

Al-Sulamī, Abū ʿAbd al-Raḥmān Muḥammad b. al-Ḥusayn al-Naysābūrī. *The Subtleties of the Ascension: Early Mystical Sayings on Muḥammad's Heavenly Journey*. Edited and translated by Frederick S. Colby. Louisville: Fons Vitae, 2006.

Al-Sulamī, Abū ʿAbd al-Raḥmān Muḥammad b. al-Ḥusayn al-Naysābūrī. *Sufi Treatises of Abū ʿAbd al-Raḥmān al-Sulamī (Rasāʾil ṣūfiyya li-Abī ʿAbd al-Raḥmān al-Sulamī)*. Edited by Gerhard Böwering and Bilal Orfali. Beirut: Dār al-Mashriq, 2009.

Al-Sulamī, Abū ʿAbd al-Raḥmān Muḥammad b. al-Ḥusayn al-Naysābūrī. *Ṭabaqāt al-ṣūfiyya*. Edited by Nūr al-Dīn Shurayba. Cairo: Maktabat al-Khānjī, 1969. Translated by Jean-Jacques Thibon as *Les générations des Soufis:* Ṭabaqāt al-ṣūfiyya *de Abū ʿAbd al-Raḥmān, Muḥammad b. Ḥusayn al-Sulamī (325/937 – 412/1021)*. Leiden: Brill, 2019.

Al-Sulamī, Abū ʿAbd al-Raḥmān Muḥammad b. al-Ḥusayn al-Naysābūrī. *Tārīkh al-ṣūfiyya*. Edited by Muḥammad Adīb al-Jādir. Damascus: Dār Nīnawā, 2015.

Al-Sulamī, Abū ʿAbd al-Raḥmān Muḥammad b. al-Ḥusayn al-Naysābūrī. *Tisʿat kutub li-Abī ʿAbd al-Raḥmān Muḥammad b. al-Ḥusayn b. Mūsā l-Sulamī (Tasavvufun Ana İlkeleri: Sülemî'nin Risaleleri)*. Edited by Süleyman Ateş. Ankara: Üniversitesi Basımevi, 1981. Subsequent edition replacing Turkish introduction with Arabic introduction: *Tisʿat kutub fī uṣūl al-taṣawwuf wa-l-zuhd*. Beirut: al-Nāshir, 1993.

Al-Sulamī, Abū ʿAbd al-Raḥmān Muḥammad b. al-Ḥusayn al-Naysābūrī. *Treatises on the Sufi Path*. Translated by Safaruk Z. Chowdhury and Jason Welle. Cambridge: Islamic Texts Society, forthcoming.

Al-Sulamī, Abū ʿAbd al-Raḥmān Muḥammad b. al-Ḥusayn al-Naysābūrī. *ʿUyūb al-nafs*. Edited by Majdī Fatḥī l-Sayyid. Ṭanṭā: Dār al-Ṣaḥāba lil-Turāth, 1993.

Al-Sulamī, Abū ʿAbd al-Raḥmān Muḥammad b. al-Ḥusayn al-Naysābūrī. *ʿUyūb al-nafs wa-mudāwātuhā*. Edited by Muḥammad ʿAbd al-Munʿim Khafājī and ʿAbd al-ʿAzīz Sharaf. Cairo: Dār al-Shurūq, 1981.

Al-Sulamī, Abū ʿAbd al-Raḥmān Muḥammad b. al-Ḥusayn al-Naysābūrī. 'La voie des hommes sincères parmi les soufis'. *La Règle d'Abraham* 34 (2012): 27–64.

Al-Sulamī, Abū ʿAbd al-Raḥmān Muḥammad b. al-Ḥusayn al-Naysābūrī. *Ziyādāt ḥaqāʾiq al-tafsīr (the Minor Qurʾān Commentary of Abū ʿAbd ar-Raḥmān Muḥammad b. al-Ḥusayn as-Sulamī [d. 412/1021])*. Edited by Gerhard Böwering. Beirut: Dār al-Mashriq, 1995.

Al-Sulamī, Abū ʿAbd al-Raḥmān Muḥammad b. al-Ḥusayn al-Naysābūrī, and Abū l-Faḍl al-Muqrī. *Aḥādīth fī dhamm al-kalām wa-ahlihi*. Edited by Nāṣir b. ʿAbd al-Raḥmān b. Muḥammad al-Judayʾ. Riyadh: Dār Aṭlas, 1996.

Al-Sulamī, Abū ʿAbd al-Raḥmān Muḥammad b. al-Ḥusayn al-Naysābūrī, and Fakhruddin Owaisi. 'A Translation and Commentary of *Kitāb al-arbaʿīn fī 't-taṣawwuf* [the Forty Ḥadīth on Sufism] by Shaykh Abū-ʿAbd-Al-Raḥmān Al-Sulamī (d. 412/1021)'. *IPSA Journal of Islamic Studies (Cape Town, South Africa)* 7 (2008): 16–71.

Al-Sulamī, Abū ʿAbd al-Raḥmān Muḥammad b. al-Ḥusayn al-Naysābūrī, and Muḥammad b. ʿAlī al-Ḥakīm al-Tirmidhī. *Three Early Sufi Texts*. Translated and edited by Nicholas Heer and Kenneth Lee Honerkamp. Louisville: Fons Vitae, 2003.

Al-Sulamī, Abū ʿAbd al-Raḥmān Muḥammad b. al-Ḥusayn al-Naysābūrī, and Ibn Nujayd. *Sufi Inquiries and Interpretations of Abū ʿAbd al-Raḥmān al-Sulamī and A Treatise of Traditions by Ismāʿīl b. Nujayd al-Naysābūrī (Masāʾil wa-taʾwīlāt ṣūfiyya li-Abī ʿAbd al-Raḥmān al-Sulamī wa-yalīhi Juzʾ min aḥādīth Ismāʿīl b. Nujayd al-Naysābūrī)*. Edited by Gerhard Böwering and Bilal Orfali. Beirut: Dār al-Mashriq, 2010.

Al-Suyūṭī, Jalāl al-Dīn ʿAbd al-Raḥmān. *Al-Durar al-muntathira fī aḥādīth al-mushtahira*. Edited by Muḥammad b. Luṭfī l-Sabbāgh. Riyadh: Jāmiʿat al-Malik Saʿūd, n.d.

Al-Suyūṭī, Jalāl al-Dīn ʿAbd al-Raḥmān. *Jāmiʿ al-aḥādīth*, 21 vols. Beirut: Dār al-Fikr, 1994.

Al-Ṭabarānī, Abū l-Qāsim Sulaymān b. Aḥmad. *Al-Muʿjam al-awsaṭ*. Edited by Abū Muʿādh Ṭāriq b. ʿAwaḍ Allāh b. Muḥammad and Abū Faḍl ʿAbd al-Muḥsin b. Ibrāhīm al-Ḥusaynī, 10 vols. Cairo: Dār al-Ḥaramayn, 1995.

Al-Ṭabarānī, Abū l-Qāsim Sulaymān b. Aḥmad. *Al-Muʿjam al-kabīr*, 2nd ed. Cairo: Maktabat Ibn Taymiyya, 1983.

Al-Ṭabarānī, Abū l-Qāsim Sulaymān b. Aḥmad. *Al-Muʿjam al-ṣaghīr*, 2 vols. Beirut: Dār al-Kutub al-ʿIlmiyya, 1983.

Al-Ṭabarī, Abū Khalaf. *Salwat al-ʿārifīn wa-uns al-mushtāqīn [The Comfort of the Mystics: A Manual and Anthology of Early Sufism]*. Edited by Gerhard Böwering and Bilal Orfali. Leiden: Brill, 2013. Also published with an introduction by Hānī Ramaḍān. Beirut: Dār al-Mashriq, 2021.

Ṭarafa b. al-ʿAbd. *Dīwān Ṭarafa Ibn al-ʿAbd*. Beirut: Dār Ṣādir, 1961.

Al-Tawḥīdī, Abū Ḥayyān ʿAlī b. Muḥammad. *Risālatān (R. fī l-ṣadāqa wa-l-ṣadīq, R. fī l-ʿulūm)*. Constantinople: Maṭbaʿat al-Jawāʾib, 1883.

Al-Tawḥīdī, Abū Ḥayyān ʿAlī b. Muḥammad, and Abū ʿAlī Aḥmad b. Muḥammad Miskawayh. *Kitāb al-hawāmil wa-l-shawāmil*. Edited by Aḥmad Amīn and Aḥmad Ṣaqr. Cairo: Maṭbaʿat Lajnat al-Taʾlīf wa-l-Tarjama wa-l-Nashr, 1951. Translated by Sophia Vasalou and James E. Montgomery as *The Philosopher Responds*. New York: New York University Press, 2021. Translated by Lidia Bettini as *Il libro dei cammelli errabondi e di quelli che li radunano*. Venice: Edizioni Ca' Foscari, 2017.

Al-Ṭayālisī, Abū Dāʾūd. *Musnad Abī Dāʾūd al-Ṭayālisī*. Edited by Muḥammad b. ʿAbd al-Muḥsin al-Turkī, 4 vols. Giza: Hajar, 1999.

Al-Thaʿālibī, Abū Manṣūr. *The Book of Noble Character: Critical Edition of Makārim al-akhlāq wa-maḥāsin al-ādāb wa-badāʾiʿ al-awṣāf wa-gharāʾib al-tashbīhāt*. Edited by Bilal Orfali and Ramzi Baalbaki. Leiden: Brill, 2015.

Al-Thaʿlabī, Aḥmad b. Muḥammad. *Al-Kashf wa-l-bayān fī tafsīr al-Qurʾān (Tafsīr al-Thaʿlabī)*, 6 vols. Beirut: Dār al-Kutub al-ʿIlmiyya, 2004.

Al-Tirmidhī, Abū ʿĪsā. *English Translation of Jāmiʿ at-Tirmidhī*. Translated by Abu Khaliyi, 6 vols. Riyadh: Darussalam, 2007.

Al-Tustarī, Sahl b. ʿAbdallāh. *Al-Muʿāraḍa wa-l-radd ʿalā ahl al-firaq wa-ahl al-daʿāwā fī l-aḥwāl*. Edited by Muḥammad Kamāl Ibrāhīm Jaʿfar. Cairo: Dār al-Insān lil-Taʾlīf wa-l-Tarjama wa-l-Nashr, 1980.

Al-Tustarī, Sahl b. ʿAbdallāh. *Tafsīr al-Qurʾān al-ʿaẓīm*. Edited by Ṭāʾ Hāʾ ʿAbd al-Raʾūf Saʿd and Ḥasan Muḥammad ʿAlī Saʿd. Cairo: Dār al-Ḥaram al-Turāth, 2004. Translated by Annabel Keeler and Ali Keeler as *Tafsīr al-Tustarī*. Amman: Royal Aal al-Bayt Institute for Islamic Thought, 2011. See also www.altafsir.com (accessed 8 December 2023).

Yaḥyā b. ʿAdī. *The Reformation of Morals: A Parallel Arabic-English Text*. Translated and edited by Sidney Harrison Griffith. Provo: Brigham Young University Press, 2002.

Yaḥyā b. ʿAdī. *Traité d'éthique d'Abû Zakariyyâ' Yahyâ Ibn 'Adî*. Translated by Marie-Thérèse Urvoy. Paris: Cariscript, 1991.

Yāqūt b. ʿAbdallāh al-Ḥamawī. *Muʿjam al-udabāʾ*, 6 vols. Beirut: Dār al-Gharb al-Islāmī, 1993.

Sources composed in European languages

Abdel-Kader, Ali Hassan, and Abū l-Qāsim b. Muḥammad al-Junayd. *The Life, Personality and Writings of Al-Junayd: A Study of a Third/Ninth Century Mystic with an Edition and Translation of His Writings*. London: Luzac & Company, 1962.

Abdel-Latif, Sara. 'Mystical Qur'anic Exegesis and the Canonization of Early Sufis in Sulamī's "Ḥaqā'iq al-Tafsīr"'. *The International Journal of Religion and Spirituality in Society* 23, no. 4 (2016): 13–23.

Abrahamov, Binyamin. 'A Re-Examination of Al-Ash'arī's Theory of "Kasb" according to "Kitāb Al-Luma'"'. *JRAS* 121, no. 2 (1989): 210–21.

Abun-Nasr, Jamil M. *Muslim Communities of Grace: The Sufi Brotherhoods in Islamic Religious Life*. New York: Columbia University Press, 2007.

Adamson, Peter. 'Ethics in Philosophy'. *EI*³.

Adamson, Peter. *Studies on Early Arabic Philosophy*. Burlington, VT: Ashgate/Variorum, 2015.

Ajmal, Muhammad. 'A Note on *Adab* in the *Murshid-Murīd* Relationship'. In Metcalf, *Moral Conduct and Authority*, 241–51.

Akash, Hussein Ali. *Die sufische Koranauslegung: Semantik und Deutungsmechanismen der išārī-Exegese*. Berlin: Klaus Schwarz Verlag, 2006.

Allard, Michel. 'Un philosophe théologien: Muḥammad b. Yūsuf al-ʿÂmirī'. *Revue de l'histoire des religions* 187, no. 1 (1975): 57–69.

Alshaar, Nuha A. *Ethics in Islam: Friendship in the Political Thought of al-Tawḥīdī and his Contemporaries*. New York: Routledge, 2015.

Alwishah, Ahmed, and Josh Hayes, eds. *Aristotle and the Arabic Tradition*. Cambridge: Cambridge University Press, 2015.

Angier, Tom. 'Alasdair MacIntyre's Analysis of Tradition'. *European Journal of Philosophy* 22, no. 4 (2014): 540–72.

Anjum, Ovamir. 'Islam as a Discursive Tradition: Talal Asad and His Interlocutors'. *Comparative Studies of South Asia, Africa and the Middle East* 27, no. 3 (2007): 656–72.

Ansari, Hassan, and Sabine Schmidtke. 'Abū Sa'd al-Ḫargūšī and his *Kitāb Al-Lawāmiʿ*, A Ṣūfī Guide Book for Preachers from 4th/10th Century Nīšābūr'. *Arabica* 58, no. 6 (2011): 503–18.

Ansari, M. Abdul Haq. *The Ethical Philosophy of Miskawaih*. Aligarh, India: University Press, 1961.

Arberry, A. J. 'Did Sulamī Plagiarize Sarrāj?' *JRAS* 69, no. 3 (1937): 461–5.

Arberry, A. J. 'Al-Qushairī as Traditionist'. In *Studia Orientalia Ioanni Pedersen*, 12–20.

Arberry, A. J. *Sufism: An Account of the Mystics of Islam*. Mineola, NY: Dover Publications, 2002.
Archer, George. *A Place between Two Places: The Qur'ānic Barzakh*. Piscataway, NJ: Gorgias Press, 2017.
Aristotle. *The Arabic Version of the Nicomachean Ethics*. Edited by Anna Akasoy, Alexander Fidora and D. M. Dunlop. Leiden: Brill, 2005.
Aristotle. *Aristotle's Ethics: Writings from the Complete Works*. Edited by Jonathan Barnes and Anthony Kenny. Princeton, NJ: Princeton University Press, 2014.
Arkoun, Mohammed. 'La conquête du bonheur selon Abû-l-Ḥasan al-'Âmirî'. *SI* 22 (1965): 55–90.
Arkoun, Mohammed. 'L'humanisme arabe au IVe/Xe Siècle, d'après le *Kitâb al-Hawâmil wal-Šawâmil*'. *SI* 14 (1961): 73–108.
Arkoun, Mohammed. *L'humanisme arabe au IVe–Xe siècle: Miskawayh, philosophe et historien*, 2nd ed. Paris: Vrin, 1982.
Arkoun, Mohammed. 'Peut-on parler d'humanisme en contexte islamique?' *IOS* 19 (1999): 11–22.
Asad, Talal. *Genealogies of Religion: Discipline and Reasons of Power in Christianity and Islam*. Baltimore: Johns Hopkins University Press, 1993.
Asad, Talal. *The Idea of an Anthropology of Islam*. Washington, DC: Center for Contemporary Arab Studies, Georgetown University, 1986.
Avery, Kenneth S. *A Psychology of Early Sufi Samā': Listening and Altered States*. New York: RoutledgeCurzon, 2004.
Awn, Peter J. 'The Ethical Concerns of Classical Sufism'. *JRE* 11, no. 2 (1983): 240–63.
Azarnoosh, Azartash, and Suheyl Umar. 'Adab'. *EI*[3].
Al-'Āmirī, Abū l-Ḥasan Muḥammad b. Yūsuf, and Elvira Wakelnig. *Feder, Tafel, Mensch: Al-'Āmirīs Kitāb al-fuṣūl fī l-ma'ālim al-ilāhīya und die arabische Proklos-Rezeption im 10. Jh*. Leiden: Brill, 2006.
Baldick, Julian. *Mystical Islam: An Introduction to Sufism*. London: I.B. Tauris, 1989.
Ballanfat, Paul. 'La direction spirituelle chez Abū Sa'īd b. Abī l-Ḫayr (357–440/967–1049)'. In Gobillot and Thibon, *Les maîtres soufis et leurs disciples*, 245–89.
Başan, Aziz. *The Great Seljuqs: A History*. New York: Routledge, 2010.
Bauer, Karen. *Gender Hierarchy in the Qur'ān: Medieval Interpretations, Modern Responses*. New York: Cambridge University Press, 2015.
Bergé, Marc. *Pour un humanisme vécu: Abū Ḥayyān al-Tawḥīdī*. Damascus: Institut français de Damas, 1979.
Bergé, Marc. 'Tawḥīdī, un humaniste arabe du IVe/Xe siècle'. *Travaux et jours* 23 (1967): 43–61.
Bergé, Marc. 'Une anthologie sur l'amitié d'Abū Ḥayyān at-Tawḥīdī'. *BEO* 16 (1958): 15–60.
Berger, Lutz. '*Geschieden von allem ausser Gott': Sufik und Welt bei Abū 'Abd ar-Raḥmān as-Sulamī (936–1021)*. Hildesheim: Olms, 1998.
Berger, Lutz. 'Review of Jean-Jacques Thibon, *L'œuvre d'Abū Abd al-Raḥmān al-Sulamī (325/937–412/1021) et la formation du Soufisme*'. *BSOAS* 73 (2010): 545–6.
Berkey, Jonathan Porter. *The Transmission of Knowledge in Medieval Cairo: A Social History of Islamic Education*. Princeton, NJ: Princeton University Press, 1992.
Besser-Jones, Lorraine, and Michael Slote, eds. *The Routledge Companion to Virtue Ethics*. New York: Routledge, 2015.
Bhat, Badruddin. 'Miskawayh on Social Justice, Education and Friendship'. *IS* 25, no. 2 (1986): 197–210.

Blackledge, Paul, and Kelvin Knight, eds. *Virtue and Politics: Alasdair MacIntyre's Revolutionary Aristotelianism*. Notre Dame, IN: University of Notre Dame Press, 2011.
Bonebakker, S. A. '*Adab* and the Concept of *Belles-Lettres*'. In *'Abbasid Belles-Lettres*. Edited by Julia Ashtiany, 16–30. New York: Cambridge University Press, 1990.
Bosworth, C. Edmund. *The Ghaznavids: Their Empire in Afghanistan and Eastern Iran, 994–1040*. Edinburgh: University Press, 1963.
Bosworth, C. Edmund. *The Later Ghaznavids: Splendour and Decay: The Dynasty in Afghanistan and Northern India 1040–1186*. New York: Columbia University Press, 1977.
Bosworth, C. Edmund. 'Nishapur. i. Historical Geography and History to the Beginning of the 20th Century'. *EIr*.
Bosworth, C. Edmund. 'The Rise of the Karāmiyyah in Khurasan'. *MW* 50, no. 1 (1960): 5–14.
Böwering, Gerhard. 'The Adab Literature of Classical Sufism: Anṣārī's Code of Conduct'. In Metcalf, *Moral Conduct and Authority*, 62–87.
Böwering, Gerhard. 'The Major Sources of Sulamī's Minor Qur'ān Commentary'. *Oriens* 35 (1996): 35–56.
Böwering, Gerhard. *The Mystical Vision of Existence in Classical Islam: The Qur'ānic Hermeneutics of the Ṣūfī Sahl at-Tustarī (d. 283/896)*. Berlin: De Gruyter, 1980.
Böwering, Gerhard. 'The Qur'ān Commentary of al-Sulamī'. In *Islamic Studies Presented to Charles J. Adams*. Edited by Wael B. Hallaq and Donald P. Little, 41–56. Leiden: Brill, 1991.
Böwering, Gerhard. 'Sufi Hermeneutics in Medieval Islam'. *REI* 55–7 (1987): 255–70.
Böwering, Gerhard. 'Al-Sulamī'. *EI*[2].
Böwering, Gerhard. 'Sulamī's Treatise on the Science of the Letters (*'Ilm al-ḥurūf*)'. In *In the Shadow of Arabic: The Centrality of Language to Arabic Culture*. Edited by Bilal Orfali, 339–97. Leiden: Brill, 2011.
Böwering, Gerhard. 'Two Early Ṣūfī Manuscripts'. *JSAI* 31 (2006): 209–31.
Böwering, Gerhard, and Matthew Melvin-Koushki. 'Ḵānaqāh'. *EIr*.
Bray, Karen, and Stephen D. Moore, eds. *Religion, Emotion, Sensation: Affect Theories and Theologies*. New York: Fordham University Press, 2020.
Brewer, David J. *Faith Encounters of the Third Kind: Humility and Hospitality in Interfaith Dialogue*. Eugene, OR: Cascade Books, 2021.
Brockelmann, Carl. *Geschichte der arabischen Litteratur* (*GAL*), 5 vols. Leiden: Brill, 1898–1942. Translated by Joep Lameer as *History of the Arabic Written Tradition*. Leiden: Brill, 2016.
Brooks, David. *The Road to Character*. New York: Random House, 2015.
Buehler, Arthur F. *Recognizing Sufism: Contemplation in the Islamic Tradition*. London: I. B. Tauris, 2016.
Buehler, Arthur F. *Sufi Heirs of the Prophet: The Indian Naqshbandiyya and the Rise of the Mediating Sufi Shaykh*. Columbia: University of South Carolina Press, 1998.
Bugnini, Annibale. *La chiesa in Iran*. Rome: Edizioni Vincenziane, 1981.
Bulliet, Richard W. 'Conversion-Based Patronage and Onomastic Evidence in Early Islam'. In *Patronate and Patronage in Early and Classical Islam*. Edited by Monique Bernards and John Nawas, 246–62. Leiden: Brill, 2005.
Bulliet, Richard W. 'Conversion Stories in Early Islam'. In *Conversion and Continuity: Indigenous Christian Communities in Islamic Lands, Eighth to Eighteenth Centuries*. Edited by Michael Gervers and Ramzi Jibran Bikhazi, 123–33. Toronto: Pontifical Institute of Mediaeval Studies, 1990.

Bulliet, Richard W. *Conversion to Islam in the Medieval Period: An Essay in Quantitative History*. Cambridge: Harvard University Press, 1979.
Bulliet, Richard W. *Islam: The View from the Edge*. New York: Columbia University Press, 1994.
Bulliet, Richard W. 'Local Politics in Eastern Iran under the Ghaznavids and Seljuks'. *I'S* 11, no. 1/4 (1978): 35–56.
Bulliet, Richard W. 'Medieval Nishapur: A Topographic and Demographic Reconstruction'. *Studia Iranica* 5 (1976): 67–89.
Bulliet, Richard W. *The Patricians of Nishapur: A Study in Medieval Islamic Social History*. Cambridge: Harvard, 1972.
Bulliet, Richard W. 'The Political-Religious History of Nishapur in the Eleventh Century'. In Richards, *Islamic Civilisation, 950–1150*, 71–91.
Bulliet, Richard W. 'Why Nishapur?' *Eurasian Studies* 16 (2018): 100–23. Reprinted in David Durand-Guédy, Roy Mottahedeh and Jürgen Paul (eds), *Cities of Medieval Iran*, 100–23. Leiden: Brill, 2020.
Butterworth, Charles E. 'Ethics in Medieval Islamic Philosophy'. *JRE* 11, no. 2 (1983): 224–39.
Cahen, Claude, and Franz Taeschner. 'Futuwwa'. *EI*[2].
Carney, Frederick S. 'Some Aspects of Islamic Ethics'. *The Journal of Religion* 63, no. 2 (1983): 159–74.
Carr, David. 'Character and Moral Choice in the Cultivation of Virtue'. *Philosophy* 78, no. 2 (2003): 219–32.
Carr, David. 'Rival Conceptions of Practice in Education and Teaching'. *JPE* 37, no. 2 (2003): 253–66.
Carr, David, James Arthur and Kristján Kristjánsson, eds. *Varieties of Virtue Ethics*. New York: Palgrave Macmillan, 2017.
Carson, Nathan P. 'Getting into the Game of Tradition-Constituted Moral Inquiry: Does MacIntyre's Particularism Offer a Rational Way In?' *International Philosophical Quarterly* 54, no. 1 (2014): 25–42.
Casewit, Yousef. 'Al-Ghazālī's Virtue Ethical Theory of the Divine Names: The Theological Underpinnings of the Doctrine of *Takhalluq* in *al-Maqṣad al-Asnā*'. *JIE* 4 (2020): 155–200.
Chabbi, Jacqueline. 'Réflexions sur le soufisme iranien primitif'. *JA* 266, no. 1 (1978): 37–55.
Chabbi, Jacqueline. 'Remarques sur le développement historique des mouvements ascétiques et mystiques au Khurasan IIIe/IXe siècle – IVe/Xe siècle'. *SI* 46 (1977): 5–72.
Chabbi, Jacqueline. 'Zuhd et soufisme au Khorasan au IVe/Xe siècle'. In *La signification du bas moyen âge dans l'histoire et la culture du monde musulman. Actes du 8me congrès de l'Union Européenne des Arabisants et Islamisants [Aix-en-Provence ... 1976]*, 53–61. Aix-en-Provence: Edisud, 1978.
Chiabotti, Francesco. "Abd al-Karīm al-Qushayrī (d. 465/1072): Family Ties and Transmission in Nishapur's Sufi Milieu during the Tenth and Eleventh Centuries'. In *Family Portraits with Saints: Hagiography, Sanctity, and Family in the Muslim World*. Edited by Catherine Mayeur-Jaouen and Alexandre Papas, 255–307. Berlin: Klaus Schwarz Verlag, 2014.
Chiabotti, Francesco. 'Entre soufisme et savoir islamique: L'œuvre de 'Abd al-Karīm al-Qushayrī (376–465/ 986–1072)'. PhD, Aix-Marseille Université, 2014.

Chiabotti, Francesco. 'The Spiritual and Physical Progeny of 'Abd al-Karīm al-Qushayrī: A Preliminary Study in Abū Naṣr al-Qushayrī's (d. 514/1120) *Kitāb al-Shawāhid wa-l-Amthāl*'. *JSS* 2 (2013): 46–77.
Chiabotti, Francesco, Eve Feuillebois-Pierunek, Catherine Mayeur-Jaouen and Luca Patrizi, eds. *Ethics and Spirituality in Islam: Sufi* Adab. Leiden: Brill, 2016.
Chiabotti, Francesco, and Martin Nguyen. 'The Textual Legacy of Abū l-Qāsim al-Qušayrī: A Bibliographic Record'. *Arabica* 61 (2014): 339–95.
Chowdhury, Safaruk Z. *A Ṣūfī Apologist of Nīshāpūr: The Life and Thought of Abū 'Abd al-Raḥmān al-Sulamī*. Sheffield: Equinox, 2019.
Colby, Frederick S. 'The Subtleties of the Ascension: Al-Sulamī on the Mi'rāj of the Prophet Muhammad'. *SI* 94 (2002): 167–83.
Cooper, John M. 'Aristotle on the Forms of Friendship'. *The Review of Metaphysics* 30, no. 4 (1977): 619–48.
Cornell, Rkia E. 'Introduction: As-Sulami and His Sufi Women'. In Ridgeon, *Sufism: Critical Concepts in Islamic Studies*, 1:94–130.
Cornell, Rkia E. *Rabi'a from Narrative to Myth: The Many Faces of Islam's Most Famous Woman Saint Rabi'a al-'Adawiyya*. London: Oneworld Academic, 2019.
Cornell, Rkia E. 'Sufi Women's Spirituality: A Theology of Servitude'. In Vincent J. Cornell, *Voices of Islam*, 2:167–74.
Cornell, Vincent J., ed. *Voices of Islam*, 5 vols. Westport, CT: Praeger Publishers, 2007.
Crisp, Roger, and Michael Slote, eds. *Virtue Ethics*. Oxford: Oxford University Press, 1997.
Cuypers, Michel. *The Banquet: A Reading of the Fifth Sura of the Qur'an*. Miami: Convivium, 2009.
Damghani, Ahmad Mahdavi. 'Persian Contributions to Sufi Literature in Arabic'. In Lewisohn, *Classical Persian Sufism from its Origins to Rumi*, 33–57.
D'Andrea, Thomas D. *Tradition, Rationality, and Virtue: The Thought of Alasdair MacIntyre*. Burlington, VT: Ashgate, 2006.
Duckworth, Angela. *Grit: The Power of Passion and Perseverance*. New York: Simon and Schuster, 2016.
Durkheim, Émile. *The Elementary Forms of Religious Life*. Translated by Karen E. Fields. New York: Free Press, 1995.
Elias, Jamal J. 'Ṣūfī Tafsīr Reconsidered: Exploring the Development of a Genre'. *JQS* 12, no. 1 (2010): 41–55.
Encyclopaedia Iranica (*EIr*). Edited by Ehsan Yarshater. Boston: Routledge & Kegan Paul, 1982–.
Encyclopaedia Islamica (*EIs*). Edited by Farhad Daftary and Wilferd Madelung. Leiden: Brill, 2015–.
Encyclopaedia of Islam. First Edition (*EI*). Edited by M. Th. Houtsma et al. Leiden: Brill, 1913–36.
Encyclopaedia of Islam. Second Edition (*EI²*). Edited by Peri J. Bearman et al. Leiden: Brill, 1960–2009.
Encyclopaedia of Islam. Third Edition (*EI³*). Edited by Kate Fleet et al. Leiden: Brill, 2007–.
Encyclopaedia of the Qur'ān (*EQ*). Edited by Jane Dammen McAuliffe. Leiden: Brill, 2001–.
Enderwitz, Susanne. 'Adab b) in Islamic Scholarship in the 'Abbāsid Period'. *EI³*.
Fakhry, Majid. *Ethical Theories in Islam*. Leiden: Brill, 1991.
Farah, Caesar E. 'Rules Governing the Šayḫ-Muršid's Conduct'. *Numen* 21, no. 2 (1974): 81–96.

Farah, Caesar E. 'Social Implications of a Sufi Disciple's Etiquette'. In *Proceedings of the VI*[th] *Congress of Arabic and Islamic Studies: Visby 13–16 August, Stockholm 17–19 August 1972*, 45–57. Leiden: Brill, 1975.

Farès, Bishr. *Makārim al-aḫlāq: Une formule prestigieuse de morale musulmane traditionnelle*. Rome: Rendiconti della Reale accademia dei Lincei, 1935.

Fitzgerald, John T., ed. *Greco-Roman Perspectives on Friendship*. Atlanta: Scholars Press, 1997.

Flanagan, Owen. *Moral Sprouts and Natural Teleologies: 21st Century Moral Psychology Meets Classical Chinese Philosophy*. Milwaukee: Marquette University Press, 2014.

Frank, Richard M. 'The Structure of Created Causality according to al-Aš'arî: An Analysis of the 'Kitâb Al-Luma'', §§ 82–164'. *SI* 25 (1966): 13–75.

Frank, Tamar. '"Taṣawwuf Is…": On a Type of Mystical Aphorism'. *JAOS* 104, no. 1 (1984): 73–80.

Frye, Richard N., ed. *The Cambridge History of Iran. Vol. 4: The Period from the Arab Invasion to the Saljuqs*. Cambridge: Cambridge University Press, 1968.

Galen. *Galen: Psychological Writings*. Edited by Peter N. Singer. Cambridge: Cambridge University Press, 2013.

Galen. 'Kitāb al-Akhlāq li-Jālīnūs'. *Bulletin of the Faculty of Arts of the Egyptian University (Majallat Kulliyyat al-Ādāb bi-l-Jāmi'a al-Miṣriyya)* 5, no. 1 (1937): 1–51. Reprinted in *Galen in the Arabic Philosophical Tradition: Texts and Studies*, edited by Fuat Sezgin et al., 83–133. Frankfurt: Institute for the History of Arabic-Islamic Science, Johann Wolfgang Goethe University, 2000.

Ghaly, Mohammed. 'Disability in the Islamic Tradition'. *RC* 10, no. 2 (2016): 149–62.

Ghersetti, Antonella. *La letteratura d'*adab. Rome: Istituto per l'Oriente C. A. Nallino, 2021.

Gilliot, Claude. 'In Consilium Tuum Deduces Me: Le genre du "conseil," *naṣīḥa*, *waṣiyya* dans la littérature arabo-musulmane'. *Arabica* 54, no. 4 (2007): 466–99.

Gobillot, Geneviève, ed. *Mystique musulmane: Parcours en compagnie d'un chercheur: Roger Deladrière: Actes du colloque du 9 Mars 2001, Université Jean-Moulin à Lyon*. Paris: Cariscript, 2002.

Gobillot, Geneviève, and Jean-Jacques Thibon, eds. *Les maîtres soufis et leurs disciples: III*[e]*–V*[e] *siècles de l'hégire (IX*[e]*–XI*[e] *s.)*. Damascus: Institut français du Proche-Orient, 2012.

Goitein, Shelomo D. 'Formal Friendship in the Medieval Near East'. *PAPS* 115, no. 6 (1971): 484–9.

Goodman, Lenn E. 'Friendship in Aristotle, Miskawayh and Al-Ghazali'. In Leaman, *Friendship East and West*, 164–91.

Goodman, Lenn E. *Islamic Humanism*. New York: Oxford University Press, 2003.

Gorder, A. Christian van. *Christianity in Persia and the Status of Non-Muslims in Iran*. Lanham, MD: Lexington Books, 2010.

Green, Nile. *Sufism: A Global History*. Malden, MA: Wiley-Blackwell, 2012.

Gril, Denis. '*Adab* and Revelation or One of the Foundations of the Hermeneutics of Ibn 'Arabi'. In *Muhyiddin Ibn 'Arabi: A Commemorative Volume*. Edited by Stephen Hirtenstein and Michael Tiernan, 228–63. Shaftesbury: Element, 1993.

Gril, Denis. '*Adab* et éthique dans le soufisme: Quelques constats et interrogations'. In Chiabotti et al., *Ethics and Spirituality in Islam: Sufi* Adab, 45–62.

Gril, Denis. 'Compagnons ou disciples? La *ṣuḥba* et ses exigences: l'exemple d'Ibrāhīm b. Adham d'après la *Ḥilyat al-awliyā'*. In Gobillot and Thibon, *Les maîtres soufis et leurs disciples*, 35–53.

Gril, Denis. 'Le modèle prophétique du maître spirituel en Islam'. In *Maestro e discepolo: Temi e problemi della direzione spirituale tra VI secolo a.C. e VII secolo d.C.* Edited by Giovanni Filoramo, 345–60. Brescia: Morcelliana, 2002.
Günther, Sebastian, ed. *Knowledge and Education in Classical Islam: Religious Learning between Continuity and Change*, 2 vols. Leiden: Brill, 2020.
Hager, Paul. 'Refurbishing MacIntyre's Account of Practice'. *JPE* 45, no. 3 (2011): 545–61.
Hartmann, Martin. 'Sulamī oder Sullamī?' *Orientalistische Literaturzeitung* 15, no. 3 (1912): 127–9.
Hartmann, Richard. 'As-Sulamī's Risālat Al-Malāmatīja'. *Der Islam* 8 (1918): 157–203.
Hartmann, Richard. 'Futuwwa und Malāma'. *ZMDG* 72 (1918): 193–8.
Hartmann, Richard. 'Zur Frage nach der Herkunft und den Anfängen des Ṣûfîtums'. *Der Islam* 6 (1916): 31–70.
Haseldine, Julian. 'Friendship, Equality and Universal Harmony: The Universal and the Particular in Aelred of Rievaulx's *De Spiritali Amicitia*'. In Leaman, *Friendship East and West*, 192–214.
Hämeen-Anttila, Jaakko. '*Adab*, a) Early Arabic Developments'. *EI*³.
Heath, Peter. 'Al-Jāḥiẓ, *Adab*, and the Art of the Essay'. In *Al-Jāḥiẓ: A Muslim Humanist for Our Time*. Edited by Arnim Heinemann, John L. Meloy, Tarif Khalidi and Manfred Kropp, 133–72. Beirut: Ergon Verlag Würzburg, 2009.
Heck, Paul L. '*Adab* in the Thought of Ghazālī (d. 505/1111): In the Service of Mystical Insight'. In Chiabotti et al., *Ethics and Spirituality in Islam: Sufi* Adab, 298–324.
Heck, Paul L. 'The Crisis of Knowledge in Islam (I): The Case of Al-ʿĀmirī'. *Philosophy East and West* 56, no. 1 (2006): 106–35.
Heck, Paul L. 'Ethics in Ṣūfism'. *EI*³.
Heck, Paul L. 'Friendship in the Service of Governance: *Makārim al-Akhlāq* in ʿAbbāsid Political Culture'. In *The Heritage of Arabo-Islamic Learning: Studies Presented to Wadad Kadi*. Edited by Maurice A. Pomerantz and Aram A. Shahin, 73–90. Leiden: Brill, 2015.
Heck, Paul L. 'The Mystery of Friendship: The View from Islam'. *Oberlin Friendship Initiative*. https://new.oberlin.edu/dotAsset/2348084.pdf (accessed 8 December 2015).
Heck, Paul L. 'Mysticism as Morality'. *JRE* 34, no. 2 (2006): 253–86.
Heck, Paul L. 'The Politics of Sufism: Is There One?' In *Sufism Today: Heritage and Tradition in the Global Community*. Edited by Catharina Raudvere and Leif Stenberg, 13–29. New York: I.B. Tauris, 2009.
Heck, Paul L. *Skepticism in Classical Islam: Moments of Confusion*. New York: Routledge, 2014.
Heck, Paul L. 'Sufism – What Is It Exactly?' *RC* 1, no. 1 (2007): 148–64.
Heinrichs, Wolfhart. 'The Classification of the Sciences and the Consolidation of Philology in Classical Islam'. In *Centres of Learning: Learning and Location in Pre-Modern Europe*. Edited by J. W. Drijvers and A. A. MacDonald, 119–39. Leiden: Brill, 1995.
Hodgson, Marshall G. S. *The Venture of Islam: Conscience and History in a World Civilization*, 3 vols. Chicago: University of Chicago Press, 1974.
Hofer, Nathan C. *The Popularisation of Sufism in Ayyubid and Mamluk Egypt, 1173–1325*. Edinburgh: University Press, 2015.
Honerkamp, Kenneth Lee. 'Abû ʿAbd Al-Rahmân Al-Sulamî (d.412/1201) on Samâʿ, Ecstasy and Dance'. *Journal of the History of Sufism* 4 (2004): 27–40.
Honerkamp, Kenneth Lee. 'The Ethical-Mystical Foundations of the Master-Disciple Relationship in Formative Sufism in Ninth and Tenth Century Nīšābūr'. In Gobillot and Thibon, *Les maîtres soufis et leurs disciples*, 79–97.

Honerkamp, Kenneth Lee. 'A Sufi Itinerary of Tenth Century Nishapur Based on a Treatise by Abū 'Abd al-Raḥmān al-Sulamī'. *JIS* 17, no. 1 (2006): 43–67.
Honingmann, Ernest, and C. Edmund Bosworth. 'Nīs̲h̲āpūr'. *EI*².
Hooft, Stan van. *Understanding Virtue Ethics*. Chesham, England: Acumen, 2006.
Horton, John, and Susan Mendus, eds. *After MacIntyre: Critical Perspectives on the Work of Alasdair MacIntyre*. Notre Dame, IN: University of Notre Dame Press, 1994.
Horton, John, and Susan Mendus. 'Alasdair MacIntyre: *After Virtue* and After'. In Horton and Mendus, *After MacIntyre*, 1–16.
Hourani, George F. *Reason and Tradition in Islamic Ethics*. Cambridge: Cambridge University Press, 1985.
Howe, Nicholas, ed. *Visions of Community in the Pre-Modern World*. Notre Dame, IN: University of Notre Dame Press, 2002.
Huda, Qamar-ul. 'The Light Beyond the Shore in the Theology of Proper Sufi Moral Conduct (*Adab*)'. *JAAR* 72, no. 2 (2004): 461–84.
Hursthouse, Rosalind. 'Virtue Ethics and the Emotions'. In *Virtue Ethics: A Critical Reader*, Edited by Daniel Statman, 99–117. Edinburgh: Edinburgh University Press, 1997.
Hussaini, S. Sh. Kh. 'Abū 'Abd-al-Raḥmān Solamī'. *EIr*.
Ivanyi, Katharina Anna. 'Virtue, Piety and the Law: A Study of Birgivi Meḥmed Efendi's "Al-Ṭarīqa al-Muḥammadiyya"'. PhD, Princeton University, 2012.
Jassemi, Bahram. *Kosmologie und Psychologie im Sufismus*. Neukirchen: Verlag Make a Book, 2007.
Jones, L. Gregory. 'Alasdair MacIntyre on Narrative, Community, and the Moral Life'. *Modern Theology* 4, no. 1 (1987): 53–69.
Kallenberg, Brad J. 'The Master Argument of MacIntyre's *After Virtue*'. In Murphy, Kallenberg and Nation, *Virtues and Practices in the Christian Tradition*, 7–29.
Kamada, Shigeru. 'A Study of the Term *Sirr* (Secret) in Sufi *Laṭā'if* Theories'. *Orient (Tokyo)* 19 (1983): 7–28.
Karamustafa, Ahmet T. *God's Unruly Friends: Dervish Groups in the Islamic Later Middle Period, 1200–1550*. Oxford: Oneworld, 2006.
Karamustafa, Ahmet T. *Sufism: The Formative Period*. Edinburgh: Edinburgh University Press, 2007.
Katz, Jonathan G. 'Disciple in Ṣūfism'. *EI*³.
Katz, Marion Holmes. ''*Azima* and *rukhṣa*'. *EI*³.
Katz, Marion Holmes. 'Shame (Ḥayā') as an Affective Disposition in Islamic Legal Thought'. *Journal of Law, Religion and State* 3 (2014): 139–69.
Keeler, Annabel. 'The Concept of *adab* in Early Sufism with Particular Reference to the Teachings of Sahl b. 'Abdallāh al-Tustarī (d. 283/896)'. In Chiabotti et al., *Ethics and Spirituality in Islam: Sufi* Adab, 63–101.
Key, Alexander. 'The Applicability of the Term "Humanism" to Abū Ḥayyān al-Tawḥīdī'. *SI* 100 (2005): 71–112.
Khaleghi-Motlagh, Jalal. 'Adab i. in Iran'. *EIr*.
Khalidi, Tarif. *Arabic Historical Thought in the Classical Period*. Cambridge: Cambridge University Press, 1994.
Khalil, Atif. 'The Embodiment of Gratitude (*Shukr*) in Sufi Ethics'. *SI* 111 (2016): 159–78.
Khalil, Atif. 'Humility in Islamic Contemplative Ethics'. *JIE* 4 (2020): 223–52.
Khalil, Atif. 'On Cultivating Gratitude (*Shukr*) in Sufi Virtue Ethics'. *JSS* 4 (2015): 1–26.
Khalil, Atif. *Repentance and the Return to God:* Tawba *in Early Sufism*. Albany: SUNY Press, 2018.

Khalil, Atif. 'When Does a Virtue Become a Vice? Gratitude as Panacea and Poison in Sufi Ethics'. In *A Theology of Gratitude*. Edited by Mona Siddiqui and Nathanael Vette, 52–66. Cambridge: Cambridge University Press, 2023.
Kinberg, Leah. 'What Is Meant by *Zuhd*'. *SI* 61 (1985): 27–44.
Knysh, Alexander. '*Geschieden von allem ausser Gott: Sufik und Welt bei Abū Abd al-Rahmān as-Sulamī*. By Lutz Berger'. *JRAS* 12, no. 1 (2002): 95–7.
Knysh, Alexander. *Islamic Mysticism: A Short History*. Leiden: Brill, 2000.
Knysh, Alexander. *Sufism: A New History of Islamic Mysticism*. Princeton, NJ: Princeton University Press, 2017.
Kraemer, Joel L. *Humanism in the Renaissance of Islam: The Cultural Revival During the Buyid Age*. Leiden: Brill, 1986.
Kraemer, Joel L. *Philosophy in the Renaissance of Islam: Abū Sulaymān al-Sijistānī and his Circle*. Leiden: Brill, 1986.
Kukkonen, Taneli. 'Al-Ghazālī on the Emotions'. In *Islam and Rationality: The Impact of al-Ghazālī*. Edited by George Tamer, 138–64. Leiden: Brill, 2015.
Kukkonen, Taneli. 'Al-Ghazālī on the Origins of Ethics'. *Numen* 63, nos. 2–3 (2016): 271–98.
Lane, Edward William, and Stanley Lane-Poole. *An Arabic-English Lexicon*. New York: F. Ungar Publishing Company, 1955.
Lapidus, Ira M. *A History of Islamic Societies*. New York: Cambridge University Press, 1988.
Lapidus, Ira M. *Muslim Cities in the Later Middle Ages*. New York: Cambridge University Press, 1984.
Leaman, Oliver, ed. *Friendship East and West: Philosophical Perspectives*. Richmond: Curzon, 1995.
Leaman, Oliver. 'Poetry and the Emotions in Islamic Philosophy'. In *Classic Issues in Islamic Philosophy Today*. Edited by Anna-Teresa Tymieniecka and Nazif Muhtaroglu, 139–50. New York: Springer, 2010.
Lecker, Michael. *The Banū Sulaym: A Contribution to the Study of Early Islam*. Jerusalem: Hebrew University, 1989.
Lewisohn, Leonard, ed. *Classical Persian Sufism from Its Origins to Rumi*. London: Khaniqahi Nimatullahi Publications, 1993.
Lobel, Diana. 'On the Lookout: A Sufi Riddle in al-Sulamī, al-Qušayrī, and Baḥyā Ibn Paqūda'. In *Studies in Arabic and Islamic Culture*. Edited by Binyamin Abrahamov, 2:87–120. Ramat Gan: Bar Ilan University, 2006.
Lutz, Christopher Stephen. *Tradition in the Ethics of Alasdair MacIntyre: Relativism, Thomism, and Philosophy*. Lanham, MD: Lexington Books, 2004.
MacIntyre, Alasdair C. *After Virtue: A Study in Moral Theory*, 3rd ed. Notre Dame, IN: University of Notre Dame Press, 2007.
MacIntyre, Alasdair C. *Dependent Rational Animals: Why Human Beings Need the Virtues*. London: Duckworth, 2009.
MacIntyre, Alasdair C. *A Short History of Ethics: A History of Moral Philosophy from the Homeric Age to the Twentieth Century*. Notre Dame, IN: University of Notre Dame Press, 1998.
MacIntyre, Alasdair C. *Three Rival Versions of Moral Enquiry: Encyclopaedia, Genealogy, and Tradition*. Notre Dame, IN: University of Notre Dame Press, 1990.
MacIntyre, Alasdair C. 'Where We Were, Where We Are, Where We Need to Be'. In *Virtue and Politics: Alasdair MacIntyre's Revolutionary Aristotelianism*. Edited by Paul

Blackledge and Kelvin Knight, 307–34. Notre Dame, IN: University of Notre Dame Press, 2011.
MacIntyre, Alasdair C. *Whose Justice? Which Rationality?* Notre Dame, IN: University of Notre Dame Press, 1988.
MacIntyre, Alasdair C., and Joseph Dunne. 'Alasdair MacIntyre on Education: In Dialogue with Joseph Dunne'. *JPE* 36, no. 1 (2002): 1–19.
Madelung, Wilferd. *Religious Trends in Early Islamic Iran*. Albany: Persian Heritage Foundation, 1988. 'Sufism and the Karrāmiyya' reprinted in Ridgeon, *Sufism: Critical Concepts in Islamic Studies*, 1:131–44.
Makdisi, George. *The Rise of Colleges: Institutions of Learning in Islam and the West*. Edinburgh: University Press, 1981.
Makdisi, George. *The Rise of Humanism in Classical Islam and the Christian West: With Special Reference to Scholasticism*. Edinburgh: Edinburgh University Press, 1990.
Makdisi, George. '*Ṣuḥba* et *riyāsa* dans l'enseignement médiéval'. In *Recherches d'Islamologie: Recueil d'articles offert à Georges C. Anawati et Louis Gardet par leurs collègues et amis*, 207–21. Louvain: Peeters, 1977.
Malamud, Margaret. 'Gender and Spiritual Self-Fashioning: The Master-Disciple Relationship in Classical Sufism'. *JAAR* 64, no. 1 (1996): 89–117. Reprinted in Ridgeon, *Sufism: Critical Concepts in Islamic Studies*, 2:316–42.
Malamud, Margaret. 'The Politics of Heresy in Medieval Khurasan: The Karramiyya in Nishapur'. *I'S* 27, no. 1/4 (1994): 37–51.
Malamud, Margaret. 'Sufi Organizations and Structures of Authority in Medieval Nishapur'. *IJMES* 26, no. 3 (1994): 427–42. Reprinted in Ridgeon, *Sufism: Critical Concepts in Islamic Studies*, 1:212–30.
Malamud, Margaret. 'Sufism in Twelfth-Century Baghdad: The Sufi Practices and Ribâṭ of Abû Najîb Al-Suhrawardî'. *The Bulletin of the Henry Martyn Institute of Islamic Studies* 13 (1994): 6–18.
Marlow, Louise. *Hierarchy and Egalitarianism in Islamic Thought*. Cambridge: Cambridge University Press, 1997.
Martin, David L. 'An Account of Ruwaym b. Aḥmad from Al-Sulamī's *Ṭabaqāt Al-Ṣūfiyya*'. *Al-'Arabiyya* 16, no. 1–2 (1983): 27–55.
Martin, David L. 'An Account of Sumnūn b. Ḥamza from Al-Sulamī's *Ṭabaqāt Al-Ṣūfiyya*'. *Al-'Arabiyya* 17, no. 1–2 (1984): 25–46.
Massignon, Louis. *Le Dîwân d'al-Ḥallâj*. Paris: Paul Geuthner, 1931 = *Journal asiatique* 218 [Janvier – Mars 1931].
Massignon, Louis. *Essay on the Origins of the Technical Language of Islamic Mysticism*. Translated by Benjamin Clark. Notre Dame, IN: University of Notre Dame Press, 1998. Originally published as *Essai sur les origines du lexique technique de la mystique musulmane*, 2nd ed. Paris: J. Vrin, 1954.
Massignon, Louis. *La Passion d'al-Hosayn-Ibn-Mansour al-Hallaj*, 2nd ed. 4 vols. Paris: Gallimard, 1975. Translated by Herbert Mason as *The Passion of Al-Hallāj: Mystic and Martyr of Islam*, 4 vols. Princeton, NJ: Princeton University Press, 1980.
Matringe, Denis. '*Ādāb al-ṣūfiya*: Les règles de vie dans les couvents soufis de l'Inde médiévale'. *JA* 289, no. 1 (2001): 67–86.
Mattock, J. N. 'A Translation of the Arabic Epitome of Galen's Book ΠΕΡΙ ΗΘΩΝ'. In *Islamic Philosophy and the Classical Tradition*. Edited by S. M. Stern, Albert Hourani and Vivian Brown, 235–60. Oxford: Cassirer, 1972.
McGregor, Richard. 'The Development of the Islamic Understanding of Sanctity'. *Religious Studies and Theology* 20, no. 1 (2001): 51–79.

Mehrvash, Farhang, Farzin Negahban and Sadeq Sajjadi. 'Brotherhood'. *EI*[s].
Meier, Fritz. *Abū Saʿīd-i Abū l-Ḫayr (357–440/967–1049): Wirklichkeit und Legende.* Leiden: Brill, 1976.
Meier, Fritz. *Essays on Islamic Piety and Mysticism.* Translated by John O'Kane. Edited by Bernd Radtke. Leiden: Brill, 1999.
Meier, Fritz. 'Ḫurāsān und das Ende der klassischen Ṣūfik'. In *Atti del Convegno internazionale sul Tema: La Persia nel Medioevo*, 131–56. Rome: Accademia Nazionale dei Lincei, 1971.
Melchert, Christopher. 'Abū Nuʿaym's Sources for *Ḥilyat al-awliyā'*, Sufi and Traditionist'. In Gobillot and Thibon, *Les maîtres soufis et leurs disciples*, 145–59.
Melchert, Christopher. 'Before *Ṣūfiyyāt*: Female Renunciants in the 8th and 9th centuries CE'. *JSS* 5 (2016): 115–39.
Melchert, Christopher. 'The Etiquette of Learning in the Early Islamic Study Circle'. In *Education and Learning in the Early Islamic World.* Edited by Claude Gilliot, 1–12. Burlington, VT: Ashgate, 2012.
Melchert, Christopher. *Hadith, Piety, and Law: Selected Studies.* Atlanta: Lockwood, 2015.
Melchert, Christopher. 'Khargūshī, *Tahdhīb al-asrār*'. *BSOAS* 73, no. 1 (2010): 29–44.
Melchert, Christopher. 'Review of *Sufism, Black and White: A Critical Edition of* Kitāb al-Bayāḍ wa-l-Sawād *by Abū l-Ḥasan al-Sīrjānī (d. ca. 470/1077)*, ed. Bilal Orfali and Nada Saab'. *JIS* 24, no. 2 (2013): 204–6.
Melchert, Christopher. 'Sufis and Competing Movements in Nishapur'. *Iran* 39 (2001): 237–47.
Melchert, Christopher. 'The Transition from Asceticism to Mysticism at the Middle of the Ninth Century C.E'. *SI* 83 (1996): 51–70. Reprinted in Ridgeon, *Sufism: Critical Concepts in Islamic Studies*, 1:44–63. Reprinted in Melchert, *Hadith, Piety, and Law*, 119–38.
Metcalf, Barbara Daly, ed. *Moral Conduct and Authority: The Place of Adab in South Asian Islam.* Berkeley: University of California Press, 1984.
Miller, Christian B. *Character and Moral Psychology.* New York: Oxford University Press, 2014.
Miller, Christian B. *Moral Character: An Empirical Theory.* New York: Oxford University Press, 2013.
Miller, Christian B., R. Michael Furr, Angela Knobel and William Fleeson, eds. *Character: New Directions from Philosophy, Psychology, and Theology.* New York: Oxford University Press, 2015.
Miquel, André. *La littérature arabe.* Paris: Presses universitaires de France, 1969.
Mojaddedi, Jawid A. *The Biographical Tradition in Sufism: The Ṭabaqāt Genre from al-Sulamī to Jāmī.* Richmond: Curzon Press, 2001.
Mojaddedi, Jawid A. 'Getting Drunk with Abū Yazīd or Staying Sober with Junayd: The Creation of a Popular Typology of Sufism'. *BSOAS* 66, no. 1 (2003): 1–13. Reprinted in Ridgeon, *Sufism: Critical Concepts in Islamic Studies*, 1:171–87.
Mojaddedi, Jawid A. 'Legitimizing Sufism in Al-Qushayri's *Risala*'. *SI* 90 (2000): 37–50.
Montgomery, James E. *Al-Jāḥiẓ: In Praise of Books.* Edinburgh: Edinburgh University Press, 2013.
Moore, Robert. 'Companionship'. *EI*[3].
Morin, Olivier. *How Traditions Live and Die.* New York: Oxford University Press, 2016.
Mottahedeh, Roy P. *Loyalty and Leadership in an Early Islamic Society.* London: I.B. Tauris, 2001.

Mulgan, R. G. 'Aristotle's Doctrine that Man Is a Political Animal'. *Hermes* 102, no. 3 (1974): 438–45.

Murphy, Mark C., ed. *Alasdair MacIntyre*. New York: Cambridge, 2003.

Murphy, Nancey C., Brad J. Kallenberg and Mark Nation, eds. *Virtues and Practices in the Christian Tradition: Christian Ethics After MacIntyre*. Notre Dame, IN: University of Notre Dame Press, 2003.

Nasr, Seyyed Hossein, ed. *Islamic Spirituality: Foundations*. New York: Crossroad, 1997.

Nasr, Seyyed Hossein, ed. *Islamic Spirituality: Manifestations*. New York: Crossroad, 1991.

Nasr, Seyyed Hossein. *Knowledge and the Sacred*. Albany: State University of New York Press, 1989.

Nasr, Seyyed Hossein. 'Philosophy and Cosmology'. In Frye, *The Cambridge History of Iran*, 4:419–41.

Nasr, Seyyed Hossein. *Sufi Essays*. Albany: SUNY Press, 1972.

Nehamas, Alexander. *On Friendship*. New York: Basic Books, 2016.

Nguyen, Martin. 'Al-Daqqāq, Abū 'Alī'. *EI*[3].

Nguyen, Martin. *Sufi Master and Qur'an Scholar: Abū'l-Qāsim al-Qushayrī and the* Laṭā'if al-ishārāt. London: Oxford University Press, 2012.

Ohlander, Erik S. 'Adab, in Ṣūfism'. *EI*[3].

Ohlander, Erik S. *Sufism in an Age of Transition: 'Umar al-Suhrawardī and the Rise of the Islamic Mystical Brotherhoods*. Leiden: Brill, 2008.

Omar, Mohammed Nasir. *Christian and Muslim Ethics: A Study of How to Attain Happiness as Reflected in the Works on Tahdhib al-Akhlaq by Yahya Ibn 'Adi (d. 974) and Miskawayh (d. 1030)*. Kuala Lumpur: Dewan Bahasa dan Pustaka, 2003.

Orfali, Bilal. *The Anthologist's Art: Abū Manṣūr al-Thaʿālibī and His* Yatīmat al-dahr. Leiden: Brill, 2016.

Pagani, Samuela. 'Heart, in Ṣūfism'. *EI*[3].

Pakaluk, Michael, ed. *Other Selves: Philosophers on Friendship*. Indianapolis: Hackett, 1991.

Palmer, Aiyub. *Sainthood and Authority in Early Islam: Al-Ḥakīm al-Tirmidhī's Theory of* wilāya *and the Reenvisioning of the Sunnī Caliphate*. Leiden: Brill, 2020.

Papas, Alexandre, ed. *Handbook of Sufi Studies. Volume I: Sufi Institutions*. Leiden: Brill, 2021.

Paredi, Riccardo. 'Early Islamic Emotions: Sadness (*ḥuzn*) from the Quran to Early Renunciant and Sufi Literature'. PhD, American University of Beirut, 2023.

Patel, Youshaa. *The Muslim Difference: Defining the Line between Believers and Unbelievers from Early Islam to the Present*. New Haven: Yale University Press, 2022.

Patrizi, Luca. '*Adab al-mulūk:* L'utilisation de la terminologie du pouvoir dans le soufisme médiéval'. In Chiabotti et al., *Ethics and Spirituality in Islam: Sufi* Adab, 198–219.

Patrizi, Luca. 'The Allegory of the Divine Banquet and the Origin of the Notion of *Adab*'. In *Knowledge and Education in Classical Islam: Religious Learning between Continuity and Change*, edited by Sebastian Günther, 1:516–38. Leiden: Brill, 2020.

Patrizi, Luca. 'A proposito di alcune recenti traduzioni di opere di Sulamī sugli *Ādāb al-ṣūfiyya*'. *Kervan: Rivista internazionale di studii afroasiatici* 6 (2007): 109–12.

Patrizi, Luca. 'Ṣūfī Terminology of Power'. In Papas, *Handbook of Sufi Studies*, 292–302.

Paul, Jürgen. 'The Seljuq Conquest(s) of Nishapur: A Reappraisal'. *I'S* 38, no. 4 (2005): 575–85.

Peacock, Andrew C. S. *Early Seljūq History: A New Interpretation*. New York: Routledge, 2010.

Peacock, Andrew C. S. *The Great Seljuk Empire*. Edinburgh: Edinburgh University Press, 2015.

Pellat, Charles. 'Adab, ii. Adab in Arabic Literature'. *EI*².
Peters, F. E. *Aristotle and the Arabs: The Aristotelian Tradition in Islam*. New York: New York University Press, 1968.
Picken, Gavin N. *Spiritual Purification in Islam: The Life and Works of Al-Muḥāsibī*. New York: Routledge, 2011.
Popovic, Alexandre, and Gilles Veinstein, eds. *Les ordres mystiques dans l'Islam: Cheminements et situation actuelle*. Paris: Editions de l'Ecole des hautes études en sciences sociales, 1986.
Porter, Jean. 'Tradition in the Recent Work of Alasdair MacIntyre'. In *Alasdair MacIntyre*. Edited by Mark C. Murphy, 38–69. New York: Cambridge University Press, 2003.
(al-)Qāḍī, Wadād. 'Abū Ḥayyān al-Tawḥīdī: A Sunnī Voice in the Shī'ī Century'. In *Culture and Memory in Medieval Islam: Essays in Honour of Wilferd Madelung*. Edited by Farhad Daftary and Josef W. Meri, 128–59. London: I.B. Tauris, 2003.
Qureshi, J. A. 'The Book of Errors: A Critical Edition and Study of *Kitāb al-Aghālit* by Abū 'Abd al-Raḥmān al-Sulamī (d. 412/1021)'. M.A., University of Georgia, 2002.
Radtke, Bernd. 'Anti-Ṣūfī Polemics'. *EI*³.
Radtke, Bernd. 'The Eight Rules of Junayd: A General Overview of the Genesis and Development of Islamic Dervish Orders'. In *Reason and Inspiration in Islam: Theology, Philosophy and Mysticism in Muslim Thought*. Edited by Todd Lawson, 490–502. London: I.B. Tauris, 2005.
Radtke, Bernd. *Materialien zur alten islamischen Frömmigkeit*. Leiden: Brill, 2009.
Radtke, Bernd. 'Some Recent Research on al-Ḥakīm al-Tirmidhī'. *Der Islam* 83, no. 1 (2006): 39–89.
Radtke, Bernd. 'Theologen und Mystiker in Ḫurāsān und Transoxanien'. *ZDMG* 136, no. 3 (1986): 536–69.
Ramli, Harith bin. 'The Sālimiyya and Abū Ṭālib al-Makkī: The Transmission of Theological Teachings in a Basran Circle of Mystics'. In Gobillot and Thibon, *Les maîtres soufis et leurs disciples*, 101–29.
Raymond, Hélène. 'Sadāqa: l'amitié dans la tradition philosophique arabe'. In *Encyclopédie de l'humanisme méditerranéen*. Edited by Houari Touati. http://www.encyclopedie-humanisme.com/?sadaqa (accessed 8 December 2023).
Reinhart, A. Kevin. 'Islamic Law as Islamic Ethics'. *JRE* 11, no. 2 (1983): 186–203.
Renard, John. *Friends of God: Islamic Images of Piety, Commitment, and Servanthood*. Berkeley: University of California Press, 2008.
Renard, John. *Historical Dictionary of Sufism*, 2nd ed. Lanham, MD: Rowman & Littlefield, 2016.
Richards, D. S., ed. *Islamic Civilisation, 950–1150*. Oxford: Cassirer, 1973.
Richardson Kristina L. *Difference and Disability in the Medieval Islamic World: Blighted Bodies*. Edinburgh: Edinburgh University Press, 2012.
Ridgeon, Lloyd V. J., ed. *The Cambridge Companion to Sufism*. New York: Cambridge University Press, 2015.
Ridgeon, Lloyd V. J. '*Futuwwa* (in Ṣūfism)'. *EI*³.
Ridgeon, Lloyd V. J. *Morals and Mysticism in Persian Sufism: A History of Sufi-Futuwwat in Iran*. New York: Routledge, 2010.
Ridgeon, Lloyd V. J. 'Reading Sufi History through *ādāb*: The Perspectives of Sufis, Jawānmardān and Qalandars'. In Chiabotti et al., *Ethics and Spirituality in Islam: Sufi* Adab, 379–402.
Ridgeon, Lloyd V. J., ed. *Sufism: Critical Concepts in Islamic Studies*, 4 vols. New York: Routledge, 2008.

Roded, Ruth. *Women in Islamic Biographical Collections: From Ibn Sa'd to Who's Who*. London: Lynne Rienner, 1994.
Rosenthal, Franz. '"I Am You" – Individual Piety and Society in Islam'. In *Individualism and Conformity in Classical Islam*. Edited by Amin Banani and Speros Vryonis, 33–60. Wiesbaden: Harrassowitz, 1977.
Rosenthal, Franz. *Knowledge Triumphant: The Concept of Knowledge in Medieval Islam*. Leiden: Brill, 2007.
Rosenthal, Franz. *Muslim Intellectual and Social History a Collection of Essays*. Hampshire, UK: Variorum, 1990.
Rowson, Everett K. 'The Philosopher as Littérateur: Al-Tawḥīdī and His Predecessors'. *Zeitschrift für Geschichte der arabisch-islamischen Wissenschaften* 6 (1990): 50–92.
Rustom, Mohammed. 'The End of Islamic Philosophy'. *Sacred Web* 40 (2017): 131–67.
Rustom, Mohammed. 'Forms of Gnosis in Sulamī's Sufi Exegesis of the Fātiḥa'. *ICMR* 16, no. 4 (2005): 327–44.
Safi, Omid. *The Politics of Knowledge in Premodern Islam: Negotiating Ideology and Religious Inquiry*. Chapel Hill: University of North Carolina Press, 2006.
Salamah-Qudsi, Arin Shawkat. 'Abū al-Qāsim al-Qushayrī's *Waṣiyya* to Sufi Novices: A Testimony to Eleventh Century Sufism'. *Le Muséon* 132, nos. 3–4 (2019): 509–34.
Salamah-Qudsi, Arin Shawkat. *Sufism and Early Islamic Piety: Personal and Communal Dynamics*. Cambridge: Cambridge University Press, 2019.
Saleh, Walid A. *The Formation of the Classical Tafsīr Tradition: The Qur'ān Commentary of al-Tha'labī (d. 427/1035)*. Leiden: Brill, 2004.
Saleh, Walid A. 'The Last of the Nishapuri School of Tafsīr: Al-Wāḥidī (d. 468/1076) and His Significance in the History of Qur'anic Exegesis'. *JAOS* 126, no. 2 (2006): 223–43.
Salinger, Gerard. 'Was the Futūwa an Oriental Form of Chivalry?' *PAPS* 94, no. 5 (1950): 481–93.
Sands, Kristin Zahra. 'On the Subtleties of Method and Style in the *Laṭā'if al-ishārāt* of al-Qushayrī'. *JSS* 2 (2013): 7–16.
Sands, Kristin Zahra. *Ṣūfī Commentaries on the Qur'ān in Classical Islam*. London: Routledge, 2006.
Savant, Sarah Bowen. *The New Muslims of Post-Conquest Iran: Tradition, Memory and Conversion*. New York: Cambridge, 2013.
Schimmel, Annemarie. *Deciphering the Signs of God: A Phenomenological Approach to Islam*. Albany: State University of New York Press, 1994.
Schimmel, Annemarie. *Mystical Dimensions of Islam*. Chapel Hill: University of North Carolina Press, 1975.
Schoonover, Kermit A. '*Kitāb Al-Ri'āya Li Ḥuqūq Allāh* by Al-Muḥāsibī: A Translation with Introduction and Notes'. PhD, Harvard University, 1948.
Schoonover, Kermit A. 'Al-Muḥāsibī and His Al-Ri'āya'. *MW* 39 (1949): 26–35.
Schroeder, Frederic M. 'Friendship in Aristotle and some Peripatetic Philosophers'. In *Greco-Roman Perspectives on Friendship*. Edited by John T. Fitzgerald, 35–57. Atlanta: Scholars Press, 1997.
Seale, Morris S. 'The Ethics of Malāmatīya Sufism and the Sermon on the Mount'. *MW* 58, no. 1 (1968): 12–23.
Sedgwick, Mark. 'The Organisation of Mysticism'. In Papas, *Handbook of Sufi Studies*, 335–61.
Sezgin, Fuat, in collaboration with Mazen Amawi, Carl Ehrig-Eggert and Eckhard Neubauer. *Galen in the Arabic Philosophical Tradition: Texts and Studies*.

Frankfurt: Institute for the History of Arabic-Islamic Science, Johann Wolfgang Goethe University, 2000.
Sezgin, Fuat. *Geschichte des arabischen Schrifttums* (*GAS*). Leiden: Frankfurt am Main, 1967–2007.
Al-Shaar, Nuha. *See Alshaar, Nuha.*
Shah-Kazemi, Reza. 'The Notion and Significance of *Ma'rifa* in Sufism'. *JIS* 13, no. 2 (2002): 155–81.
Sheikh, Faraz. *Forging Ideal Muslim Subjects: Discursive Practices, Subject Formation and Muslim Ethics*. London: Lexington Books, 2020.
Sherman, Nancy. *Making a Necessity of Virtue: Aristotle and Kant on Virtue*. New York: Cambridge University Press, 1997.
Shils, Edward. *Tradition*. Chicago: University of Chicago Press, 1981.
Shulman, David, and Guy G. Stroumsa. *Self and Self-Transformation in the History of Religions*. New York: Oxford University Press, 2002.
Silvers, Laury. 'Early Pious, Mystic Sufi Women'. In *The Cambridge Companion to Sufism*. Edited by Lloyd Ridgeon, 24–52. New York: Cambridge University Press, 2015.
Silvers, Laury. '"God Loves Me": The Theological Content and Context of Early Pious and Sufi Women's Sayings on Love'. *Journal for Islamic Studies* 30 (2010): 33–59.
Silvers, Laury. *A Soaring Minaret: Abu Bakr Al-Wasiti and the Rise of Baghdadi Sufism*. Albany: SUNY, 2010.
Silvers, Laury. 'The Teaching Relationship in Early Sufism: A Reassessment of Fritz Meier's Definition of the *shaykh al-tarbiya* and the *shaykh al-ta'līm*'. *MW* 93, no. 1 (2003): 69–97.
Silverstein, Brian. 'Disciplines of Presence in Modern Turkey: Discourse, Companionship, and the Mass Mediation of Islamic Practice'. *Cultural Anthropology* 23, no. 1 (2008): 118–53.
Silverstein, Brian. *Islam and Modernity in Turkey*. New York: Palgrave Macmillan, 2011.
Silverstein, Brian. 'Sufism and Modernity in Turkey: From the Authenticity of Experience to the Practice of Discipline'. In *Sufism and the 'Modern' in Islam*. Edited by Martin Van Bruinessen and Julia Day Howell, 39–60. New York: I.B. Tauris, 2007.
Sirry, Mun'im. 'Pious Muslims in the Making: A Closer Look at Narratives of Ascetic Conversion', *Arabica* 57 (2010): 437–54.
Snir, Reuven. '*Bāb al-maḥabba* (The Chapter on Love) in *Al-Risāla al-qušayriyya*: Rhetorical and Thematic Structure'. *IOS* 19 (1999): 131–59.
Sobieroj, Florian. 'Literary Perspectives in Qushayrī's Meditations on Sufi Ethics: The *'Uyūn al-ajwiba fī funūn al-as'ila*'. In Chiabotti et al., *Ethics and Spirituality in Islam: Sufi* Adab, 142–64.
Sobieroj, Florian. 'The Mu'tazila and Sufism'. In *Islamic Mysticism Contested: Thirteen Centuries of Controversies and Polemics*. Edited by Frederick de Jong and Bernd Radtke, 68–92. Leiden: Brill, 1999.
Sperl, Stefan. 'Man's "Hollow Core": Ethics and Aesthetics in *Ḥadīth* Literature and Classical Arabic *Adab*'. *BSOAS* 70, no. 3 (2007): 459–86.
Statman, Daniel, ed. *Virtue Ethics: A Critical Reader*. Washington, DC: Georgetown University Press, 1997.
Stern-Gillet, Suzanne. *Aristotle's Philosophy of Friendship*. Albany: SUNY Press, 1995.
Studia Orientalia Ioanni Pedersen Septuagenario A.D. VII Id. Nov. Anno MCMLIII. Hauniae [Copenhagen]: E. Munksgaard, 1953.
Sviri, Sara. 'Between Fear and Hope: On the Coincidence of Opposites in Islamic Mysticism'. *JSAI* 9 (1987): 316–49.

Sviri, Sara. 'Ḥakīm Tirmidhī and the Malāmatī Movement in Early Sufism'. In Lewisohn, *Classical Persian Sufism from its Origins to Rumi*, 583–613. Reprinted in Ridgeon, *Sufism: Critical Concepts in Islamic Studies*, 1:145–70.

Sviri, Sara. *Perspectives on Early Islamic Mysticism: The World of al-Ḥakīm al-Tirmidhī and His Contemporaries*. New York: Routledge, 2020.

Sviri, Sara. 'The Self and Its Transformation in Ṣūfism'. In Shulman and Stroumsa, *Self and Self-Transformation in the History of Religions*, 195–215.

Sviri, Sara. 'Sufism: Reconsidering Terms, Definitions and Processes in the Formative Period of Islamic Mysticism'. In Gobillot and Thibon, *Les maîtres soufis et leurs disciples*, 17–34.

Sviri, Sara. 'Words of Power and the Power of Words: Mystical Linguistics in the Works of al-Ḥakīm al-Tirmidhī'. *JSAI* 27 (2002): 204–44.

Taeschner, Franz. 'As-Sulamī's Kitāb Al-Futuwwa'. In *Studia Orientalia Ioanni Pedersen*, 340–51.

Taeschner, Franz. 'Die islamischen Futuwwabünde. Das Problem ihrer Entestehung und die Grundlinien ihrer Geschichte'. *ZDMG* 12 (1934): 6–49.

Taeschner, Franz. *Zünfte und Bruderschaften im Islam: Texte zur Geschichte der Futuwwa*. Zürich: Artemis-Verlag, 1979.

Taeschner, Franz, and Claude Cahen. 'Futuwwa'. *EI*[2].

Thibon, Jean-Jacques. 'Abū 'Uthmān al-Ḥīrī et la synthèse de la spiritualité khurāsānienne'. In Gobillot and Thibon, *Les maîtres soufis et leurs disciples*, 55–77.

Thibon, Jean-Jacques. '*Adab* et éducation spirituelle (*tarbiya*) chez les maîtres de Nīshābūr aux IIIe/IXe et IVe/Xe siècles'. In Chiabotti et al., *Ethics and Spirituality in Islam: Sufi* Adab, 102–30.

Thibon, Jean-Jacques. 'L'amour mystique (*maḥabba*) dans la voie spirituelle chez les premiers soufis'. *Ishrāq (Moscow/Tehran)* 2 (2011): 647–66.

Thibon, Jean-Jacques. 'Hiérarchie spirituelle, fonctions du saint et hagiographie dans l'œuvre d'Sulamī'. In *Le saint et son milieu ou comment lire les sources hagiographiques*. Edited by Rachida Chih and Denis Gril, 13–31. Cairo: Institut français d'archéologie orientale, 2000.

Thibon, Jean-Jacques. 'Ibn Nujayd'. *EI*[3].

Thibon, Jean-Jacques. 'Malāmatiyya'. *EI*[3].

Thibon, Jean-Jacques. *L'œuvre d'Abū 'Abd al-Raḥmān al-Sulamī (325/937–412/1021) et la formation du soufisme*. Damascus: Institut français du Proche-Orient, 2009.

Thibon, Jean-Jacques. 'La relation maître-disciple ou les éléments de l'alchimie spirituelle d'après trois manuscrits de Sulamī'. In Gobillot, *Mystique musulmane*, 93–124.

Toorawa, Shawkat M. *Ibn Abī Ṭāhir Ṭayfūr and Arabic Writerly Culture: A Ninth-Century Bookman in Baghdad*. New York: RoutledgeCurzon, 2005.

Tor, Deborah Gerber. 'Rayy and the Religious History of the Seljūq Period'. *Der Islam* 93, no. 2 (2016): 377–405.

Tor, Deborah Gerber. 'The Religious History of the Seljuq Period'. In *The Seljuqs and their Successors: Art, Culture and History*. Edited by Sheila Canby, Deniz Beyazit and Martina Rugiadi, 53–71. Edinburgh: Edinburgh University Press, 2020.

Tor, Deborah Gerber. *Violent Order: Religious Warfare, Chivalry, and the* 'Ayyār *Phenomenon in the Medieval Islamic World*. Würzburg: Ergon, 2007.

Trimingham, J. Spencer. *The Sufi Orders in Islam*. Oxford: Clarendon, 1971.

Vadet, Jean-Claude. 'La futuwwa, morale professionelle ou morale mystique'. *REI* 46 (1978): 57–90.

Vadet, Jean-Claude. *Les idées morales dans l'Islam*. Paris: Presses universitaires de France, 1995.
Vasalou, Sophia. *Virtues of Greatness in the Arabic Tradition*. Oxford: Oxford University Press, 2019.
Vaziri, Mostafa. *Rumi and Shams' Silent Rebellion: Parallels with Vedanta, Buddhism, and Shaivism*. New York: Palgrave Macmillan, 2015.
Veinstein, Gilles, and Alexandre Popovic, eds. *Les voies d'Allah: Les ordres mystiques dans l'Islam des origines à aujourd'hui*. Paris: Fayard, 1996.
Wakelnig, Elvira. 'Philosophical Fragments of Al-ʿĀmirī Preserved Mainly in al-Tawḥīdī, Miskawayh, and in the Texts of the *Ṣiwān al-ḥikma* Tradition'. In *In the Age of al-Fārābī: Arabic Philosophy in the Fourth/Tenth Century*. Edited by Peter Adamson, 215–38. London: Warburg Institute, 2008.
Walzer, Richard. *Greek into Arabic: Essays on Islamic Philosophy*. Cambridge: Harvard University Press, 1962.
Walzer, Richard, and Hamilton A. R. Gibb. 'Akhlāḳ'. *EI*².
Watt, W. Montgomery. 'Abū Ḥayyān Tawḥīdī'. *EI*ʳ.
Watt, W. Montgomery. 'The Authenticity of the Works Attributed to Al-Ghazālī'. *JRAS* 84, no. 1–2 (1952): 24–45.
Watt, W. Montgomery. 'The Origin of the Islamic Doctrine of Acquisition'. *JRAS* 75, no. 3–4 (1943): 234–47.
Watt, W. Montgomery, and Abū Ḥāmid Muḥammad al-Ghazālī. *The Faith and Practice of Al-Ghazālī*. London: G. Allen and Unwin, 1953.
Welle, Jason. 'Cristo e cristiani nell'opera letteraria del maestro ṣūfī al-Sulamī'. *ISCH* 48 (2022): 229–44.
Welle, Jason. 'Mind the Gap: The Spiritual Progress of Early Ṣūfī Women'. In *Les enjeux de l'écriture mystique*. Edited by Nejmeddine Khalfallah and Abdelaziz El Aloui, 95–116. Paris: Editions des archives contemporaines, 2020. doi.org/10.17184/eac.3801
Welle, Jason. 'Review of *A Ṣūfī Apologist of Nīshāpūr: The Life and Thought of Abū ʿAbd al-Raḥmān al-Sulamī*, by S. Z. Chowdhury', *Arabica* 68 (2021): 437–42. doi: 10.1163/15700585-12341614.
Welle, Jason. 'Review of *Faith Encounters of the Third Kind: Humility and Hospitality in Interfaith Dialogue*, by David J. Brewer'. *Journal of Interreligious Studies* 38 (2023): 118–20.
Welle, Jason. '*Samāʿ* and the Senses: Listening along the Ṣūfī Path'. In *Le vie della mistica: tra ricerca di senso ed esperienza religiosa*. Edited by Donatella Scaiola, 199–216. Rome: Urbaniana University Press, 2020.
Wensinck, A. J. *Concordance et indices de la tradition musulmane*, 7 vols. Leiden: Brill, 1936–69.
Zadeh, Travis E. *The Vernacular Qur'an: Translation and the Rise of Persian Exegesis*. New York: Oxford University Press, 2012.
Zaman, Muhammad Qasim. *The Ulama in Contemporary Islam: Custodians of Change*. Princeton, NJ: Princeton University Press, 2002.
Zargar, Cyrus A. *The Polished Mirror: Storytelling and the Pursuit of Virtue in Islamic Philosophy and Sufism*. London: Oneworld, 2017.
Zargar, Cyrus A. 'Virtue and Manliness in Islamic Ethics'. *JIE* 4 (2020): 1–7.
Zeidan, Nadia. 'Six opuscules mystiques inédits'. PhD, EPHESS, 1974.
Ziaei, Hamid R. 'Relativism, MacIntyre, Religion: an Islamic analysis'. PhD, University of Lancaster, 2006.

Zilio-Grandi, Ida. 'The Gratitude of Man and the Gratitude of God: Notes on *Šukr* in Traditional Islamic Thought'. *ISCH* 38 (2012): 45–61.
Zilio-Grandi, Ida. 'Il «kitāb tahḏīb al-aḫlāq» di Yaḥyā Ibn 'Adi († 974/363): riflessioni sul tema dell'etica nel periodo abbaside'. In *La letteratura arabo-cristiana e le scienze nel periodo abbaside (750–1250 d.C.)*. Edited by Davide Righi, 273–83. Turin: Silvio Zamorani Editore, 2008.
Zilio-Grandi, Ida. *Le virtù del buon musulmano*. Turin: Einaudi, 2020.
Zysow, Aron. 'Karrāmiya'. *EI*ʳ.
Zysow, Aron. 'Two Unrecognized Karrāmī Texts'. *JAOS* 108, no. 4 (1988): 577–87.

INDEX OF PROPER NAMES AND PLACES

'Abbāsid (dynasty) 16, 111
Abū Ḥafṣ al-Naysābūrī 18, 29, 35, 37, 41, 67, 111–12, 117–19
Abū Sa'īd b. Abī l-Khayr 6, 112, 114
Aḥmad b. Ḥanbal, *see Ibn Ḥanbal, Aḥmad*
'Alī b. Abī Ṭālib 75, 90, 94
al-'Āmirī, Abū l-Ḥasan 46, 102, 110
Aristotle 4, 46–8, 64, 68, 102–6, 109, 115
Asad, Talal 49
al-Ash'arī, Abū l-Ḥasan 142 n.42
Ash'arī (school) 6, 8, 19, 28, 110, 168 n.27

Baghdad 24, 26–7, 41, 46, 50, 105, 109, 111, 120
Basra 24, 91
al-Bisṭāmī, Abū Yazīd 91, 117, 134 n.13, 162 n.134, 188 n.178
Bukhārā 28
Būyid (dynasty) 105, 111, 178 n.37

Chowdhury, Safaruk Z. 8, 17, 66, 154 n.227, 170 n.58, 171 n.64

al-Daqqāq, Abū 'Alī 120, 136 n.45, 159 n.69
Dhū l-Nūn al-Miṣrī 9, 52, 95, 117, 118
Durkheim, Émile 2

al-Fārābī 46
al-Fuḍayl b. 'Iyāḍ 39–40, 180 n.68, 182 n.94

Galen 46, 60, 159 n.60, 162 n.121
al-Ghazālī, Abū Ḥāmid 1, 4, 64, 66–7, 168 n.29

al-Ḥakīm al-Tirmidhī 27–8, 54, 57, 68, 145 n.85, 151
Ḥanafī (school) 110, 168 n.26
al-Ḥīrī, Abū 'Uthmān 6, 79, 152 n.194, 165 n.172, 180 n.68
al-Hujwīrī 73, 124, 151 n.181, 162 n.134

Ibn 'Abbād of Ronda 113, 115
Ibn Ḥanbal, Aḥmad 123
Ibn Ḥazm 64, 77
Ibn Nujayd 6, 56
Ibn Sayyār 106
Ibn Sīnā (Avicenna) 46
Ibrāhīm b. Adham 117–18, 121

al-Jāḥiẓ 9, 14–15, 17, 169 n.53, 177 n.25
al-Jalājilī l-Baṣrī 29
al-Junayd 29, 31, 39, 52, 57, 58, 67, 109, 111–12, 117, 118, 119, 120, 123, 145 n.93, 145 n.98, 166 n.1, 172 n.90, 176 n.16, 180 n.68, 182 n.92, 185 n.134, 188 n.178

al-Kalābādhī, Abū Bakr 28, 124
Karrāmiyya 18, 34, 97, 170 n.60, 171 n.69, 184 n.115
al-Kharkūshī 124
Khurasan 4, 7, 13, 17, 26–8, 34, 42, 46, 50–1, 83, 95, 112, 113, 118, 124

Llull, Ramon 106

MacIntyre, Alasdair 5, 10, 12, 44, 69, 105, 116, 128–31
  acknowledged dependence 72, 81–2, 87, 91, 110
  good(s) 92, 102
  practice 10, 13, 20–4, 43, 63
  tradition 45, 48–51, 115
  virtue 61–2, 68, 72, 81–2, 92, 116, 128
al-Makkī, Abū Ṭālib 124
Malāmatiyya (Path of Blame) 15, 18, 23, 25, 27, 34, 41, 51, 55–6, 62, 67–8
Mecca 6, 19
Miskawayh, Aḥmad b. Muḥammad 46–7, 52, 60–1, 102–5, 109–11, 129

al-Muḥāsibī, al-Ḥārith 13, 24–7, 39, 66–8, 165 n.173
Muḥammad b. Karrām 34
Muḥammad (Prophet) 4, 15, 58, 75, 107, 171 n.64
  brotherhood 82
  character of 87
  companionship with 35, 114

al-Naṣrābādhī, Abū l-Qāsim 6, 120
Nishapur 5–8, 19, 40, 84, 90, 120, 129
  diversity in 83
  factionalism in 77, 107, 110
  philosophy in 46
  Sufism in 110–11, 113
al-Nūrī, Abū l-Ḥusayn 58, 165 n.1

al-Qushayrī, Abū l-Qāsim 1, 6, 11, 49, 55, 66, 77, 101, 113–16, 120–6, 128

al-Rāghib al-Iṣfahānī 4

al-Sarrāj 11, 13, 28–30, 38, 65, 73, 116–20, 126, 158 n.44, 160 n.85, 172 n.92
al-Shāfiʿī, Muḥammad 123
Shāfiʿī (school) 6, 19, 83, 110, 168 n.26
al-Sijistānī, Abū Sulaymān 106–7
al-Sīrjānī, Abū l-Ḥasan ʿAlī 124
al-Sulamī
  and *adab/ādāb* 13, 17–20, 30–42, 49
  as apologist 17, 36
  and Ashʿarī school, 8, 19, 141 n.43
  biography of 5–6
  and companionship 1–2, 32, 35–6, 39–42, 61, 71–81, 89–91
  and divine law 37–9
  and *ḥadīth* science 40, 66, 82, 93–6, 154 n.227
  as historian 49
  and integration 10, 16, 33, 34, 38, 43, 50–3, 56, 59, 62, 65, 80, 84, 96, 112, 127
  literary influences on 28–9
  and Path of Blame 8, 15, 18, 23, 25, 41, 55–6, 62, 67–8, 91, 103
  and philosophy 4, 11, 46
  recent scholarship on 7–9
  and spiritual pedagogy 1–3, 10, 12
  and terminology 22, 40, 53, 65, 73, 79, 83 ,88
  and virtues 10, 17–20, 59–64

al-Ṭabarānī 4, 175 n.135
al-Ṭabarī, Abū Khalaf 124, 185 n.127
al-Tamastānī, Abū Bakr 124
Ṭarafa b. al-ʿAbd 75
Thibon, Jean-Jacques 8, 30, 35, 53, 86–7, 93, 124, 134 n.20, 141 n.43, 147 n.130, 149 n.149, 151 n.176, 157 n.37 161 n.111, 166 n.6–8, 170 n.58, 184 n.118
Transoxania 27
al-Tustarī, Sahl 9, 13, 26–7, 57, 68, 117, 118, 172 n.78

Vasalou, Sophia 4, 103

Yaḥyā b. ʿAdī 46–7, 52, 60–1, 102–3, 106, 134 n.3

Zilio-Grandi, Ida 4

Index of Qur'ān Citations

1 (*al-Fātiḥa*)
3: 153 n.210
3 (*Āl ʿImrān*)
159: 160 n.95
4 (*al-Nisāʾ*)
1: 174 n.114
19: 174 n.112
171: 146 n.101
7 (*al-Aʿrāf*)
199: 91, 169 n.39, 173 n.95
172: 146 n.111
176: 146 n.103
8 (*al-Anfāl*)
1: 146 n.103
12 (*Yūsuf*)
53: 159 n.57
13 (*al-Raʿd*)
42: 146 n.114
15 (*al-Ḥijr*)
29: 161 n.112
16 (*al-Naḥl*)
90: 146 n.107
17 (*al-Isrāʾ*)
25: 160 n.75–76
22 (*al-Ḥajj*)
9: 163 n.147
52: 146 n.105
24 (*al-Nūr*)
15: 187 n.173
31 (*Luqmān*)
15: 150 n.175
33 (*al-Aḥzāb*)
1–8: 182 n.101
47 (*Muḥammad*)
38: 175 n.128
48 (*al-Aḥqāf*)
4: 146 n.103, 146 n.108
9: 146 n.105
49 (*al-Ḥujurāt*)
13: 169 n.31
50 (*Qāf*)
35–7: 160 n.80
68 (*al-Qalam*)
4: 87, 146 n.100
74 (*al-Muddaththir*)
56: 146 n.109
75 (*al-Qiyāma*)
1–2: 159 n.58
89 (*al-Fajr*)
28: 159 n.59

Index of Themes and Terminology

adab (pl. *ādāb*, way/custom/practice) 3, 9–10, 14, 18, 22, 30, 39, 42, 51, 82, 139 n.3, 143 n.63, 144 n.77, 148 n.137, 150 n.155, 152 n.194
  as discipline 25, 34
  literature 14–17
  as MacIntyrean practice 20–4
aesthetics 65, 82
ʿāhāt (defects/blights) 81, 82, 91, 130, 169 n.52
aḥwāl (sg. *ḥāl*, mystical state/s) 18, 52
akhlāq (sg. *khuluq*, 'virtues', 'morals', 'character [traits]') 3, 10, 19, 28, 45, 51, 60, 142 n.45, 173 n.95
apologetics 17, 28, 36
ʿaql (mind/reason) 59, 94, 123
ʿaṣabiyya (factionalism) 77, 83, 107, 168 n.26, 179 n.58
awliyāʾ (saints) 19, 78, 86

begging 97

character 3, 20, 29, 46, 60, 68, 87, 120
Christians 83, 102, 170 n.57, 170 n.60
community 8, 19, 22, 71, 75, 86, 92, 114, 184 n.124

darajāt (stages) 53, 171 n.73
dependence 12, 45, 58, 71, 81, 86, 91, 126, 142 n.49
  acknowledged, MacIntyre and 72, 81–2, 87, 91, 110
dhikr (remembrance) 22, 54, 56, 143 n.68
disability, *see ʿāhāt*
duty (*farḍ*, *wājib*, *mawājib*) 18, 44, 102

emotion 52, 57, 64, 105, 149 n.153
ethics
  applied 4
  and *futuwwa* 110
  meta- 4
  Ṣūfī 47, 113
  theological/religious 47
  virtue 4, 10, 21–2, 45, 48, 61, 67, 71, 81, 129

faqr/*faqīr* ([spiritual] poverty) 33, 34, 54, 58, 97, 150 n.167
fiqh (jurisprudence) 19, 49, 65, 81–2
firāsa (spiritual insight) 57, 58, 165 n.184
friendship 9, 11, 40, 81, 84, 99, 103, 125, 128, 166 n.4
futuwwa (spiritual chivalry) 39, 55, 62, 96, 110, 121, 171 n.69, 174 n.123, 181 n.77

gnostic (*ʿārif*) 34, 152 n.202

ḥadīth (tradition/report) 24, 40, 49, 57, 66, 75, 82, 93, 109, 144 n.79, 148 n.139
happiness (*saʿāda*, *eudaimonia*) 26, 46–7, 102, 104, 108–9
ḥaqīqa (reality) 31, 32, 37–9, 43, 53, 59, 75, 88, 125
ḥayāʾ (shame/modesty) 63, 65–7
hermit 71, 102–3

ikhwān (brotherhood) 82–4, 96
iktisāb (acquisition) 19
ʿilm (knowledge) 13, 14, 26, 32, 38, 79, 90, 131, 139 n.3
the inner life 69, 79
ʿishra (fellowship) 72–4, 78, 85, 95, 99, 107, 127, 153 n.220, 166 n.8

jāhiliyya (age of ignorance) 90

kalām (dialectic theology) 19, 179 n.45
kasb (acquisition), *see iktisāb*
khidma (service) 88, 96

laṭāʾif (spiritual centres) 54, 59, 152 n.207

love (*ḥubb, maḥabba, ṣadāqa, wudd, philia*) 11, 40, 52, 58, 65, 75–6, 78, 98, 102–5, 121, 125, 177 n.32

maqām(āt) (station) 18, 31, 52–4, 61, 64, 131
ma'rifa (gnosis) 13, 18, 24, 31, 37–8, 62–3, 131
market 96–8
muḥāḍara (presentation/selectivity) 16, 62
murīd (seeker) 3, 9, 12, 25, 32, 34, 36, 79, 80, 85–9, 95, 113–14, 121–4
mystic(ism) 2–3, 8, 18, 20, 33, 50–2, 60, 73, 84, 91, 108, 128

nafs (soul/self/ego-self) 1, 76, 91, 112
  ammāra bi-l-sū' (soul that incites to evil) 55
  appetitive 55
  blame/disparagement of 27, 67–8
  ego-self 25–6, 54–7
  governance/discipline of 25, 28, 69
  greatness of 103
  irascible 55
  lawwāma (blaming soul) 55
  muṭma'inna (soul at peace) 55
  as spiritual centre 55–8
naql (received knowledge) 123

philosophy
  and friendship 102–13
  Greek (*falsafa*) 4, 10–11, 45–7, 55, 60–1, 64, 65, 81, 103–5, 106
  medieval 45–7, 52, 54–5, 59–61, 102–13
  moral, modern 4–5, 10–11, 20–2, 45, 81
polis 102, 112, 125, 129
'practice' 10, 13, 20–4, 43, 63
pride (*megalopsychia, kibr al-nafs*) 4, 42, 56, 97, 103

qalb (heart) 26, 54–9, 65

rasm (pl. *rusūm*, form/appearance) 31, 38
ritual 10, 18, 22, 29, 37, 41–3, 54
rūḥ (spirit) 54, 58–9
rukhaṣ (legal dispensations) 31–2, 35, 89

Satan(ic) 2, 66, 125
ṣadāqa (friendship) 11, 85, 102–11, 125
samā' (audition session) 22, 31, 123, 143 n.68, 149 n.153, 159 n.69
sharī'a (divine law) 26, 29–30, 31, 37–9, 43–4, 49–50, 68, 79, 122
shaykh 2–3, 9, 11–12, 19, 22, 35–6, 41–2, 71–2, 75–6, 85–9, 101, 113–16, 119–26
  and cross-sexual companionship 95
  directing (*tarbiya*) 9, 95, 113–15, 124
  Malāmatiyya 41–2
  teaching (*ta'līm*) 9, 95, 113–15, 124
sirr (secret) 54, 58–9, 75, 88
soul, *see nafs*
ṣuḥba (companionship) 3, 29, 32–4, 39–42, 61, 71–81, 89–91, 99, 121
  beginning of 116–20
  etymology 73, 109
  with God 36, 79, 80, 124
  as natural human phenomenon 101, 107, 126
  permanence of 120–2
  and politics 112
  with the Prophet 36, 106, 109
  with a shaykh 11–12, 35, 88, 95, 113–16, 121
  with women 93–6
sufization 3, 42, 63, 128–9
sunna 14–15, 18, 30, 34, 41, 43, 46, 49, 63, 69, 75, 79, 87–8, 89, 90, 95

ṭabaqāt (biographical dictionaries) 7–8, 93–5
taṣawwuf (Sufism)
  in Baghdad/Iraq 26–7, 34, 41, 50, 109, 120, 165 n.1
  in Khurasan 4, 13, 17, 26–8, 34, 42, 46, 50–1, 95, 112–13, 118, 124
  pseudo-Sufism 43, 62, 149 n.150, 181 n.73
  studies 2
ṭarīqa (order/path) 2–3, 153 n.209
telos (end) 22, 115–16
tradition 46, 61, 115–16
  ḥadīth 13, 16, 31, 39–41, 65, 66, 75, 80, 86, 87, 93, 94, 98, 121, 127
  MacIntyrean 5, 10, 20–4, 45, 48–52, 61–3, 69, 71, 115–16, 129
  Ṣūfī 54, 61–3, 69, 86, 109, 128
transmission
  of *ḥadīth* 8, 24, 40–1, 49, 66, 73, 93–6
  of knowledge 3, 57, 82, 123

ukhuwwa (brotherhood) 82–5
umma (nation) 84, 106
ustādh (teacher) 95, 121–2, 124, 136 n.45, 174 n.120, 187 n.156
uṣūlization 128, 171 n.64

virtue 3–5
  aesthetic 48
  and *akhlāq* 3, 18–19, 29, 45–7, 59–64, 69, 127, 130
  Aristotelian 44, 46–7, 103
  cardinal 52, 60
  as divine gift 20, 60
  and elitism 77, 125
  and emotions 64–7
  epistemic 48
  and *faḍīla* 46, 60–1
  growth in 67–9, 104
  and human agency 60
  and MacIntyre 61–2, 68, 72, 81–2, 92, 116, 128
  and *maqāmāt* 53
  and Muḥammad 66, 87
  and practices 21–2, 51–2
  stability of 69
  Ṣūfī 31, 65, 69, 71
  taxonomy/categorization of 52, 60–1
  visibility of 102

wealth/riches 76, 85, 97, 112, 125
women 7, 71–2, 93–5, 124

ẓāhir/bāṭin (exoteric/esoteric, exterior/interior) 10, 23, 31–4, 37, 42–3, 63, 67–9, 86, 88, 112, 127
zuhd (asceticism) 13, 18, 94

www.ingramcontent.com/pod-product-compliance
Ingram Content Group UK Ltd.
Pitfield, Milton Keynes, MK11 3LW, UK
UKHW021919180725
460950UK00006B/111

9 780755 652310